1987

Contents

Preface

Amid the general rejoicing in the United States Constitution's bicentennial, one frequently hears the criticism that the American founders, unlike their famous counterparts in the ancient world—e.g., Solon in Athens, Lycurgus in Sparta—failed to provide for the education of future generations of citizens in the principles and habits of republican government. According to this view, the neglect of education and character formation in our founding was not inadvertent or unavoidable, but a deliberate consequence of the founders' political theory. The Constitution was supposed to harness the ambitions of national office-holders and the self-interest of citizens in general to produce stability, peace, and prosperity—without Americans having to worry about what kind of a people they ought to be. The right kind of government would do away with politics, so to speak, and hence with the need for civic education.

Today, some prominent conservatives accept this view of the founders' intentions, but question whether the moral quality of the citizenry, and of government, has not declined as a result of America's turning its back on "soulcraft." What the country needs to do, in their opinion, is to adopt the principles of less democratic ages and wiser heads—Edmund Burke, in particular. Oddly enough, an influential group of liberals shares this squinting view of the founding, but draws the opposite conclusion: that the people are (by definition?) good and so do not need moral instruction, but that their evolving desires are being frustrated by the antidemocratic, eighteenth-century mechanisms of the Constitution—which produce not separated but deadlocked powers. With the President and the Congress at loggerheads, the country's social and economic problems multiply apace. To escape this stalemate, the people must be awakened to the progressive possibilities of direct or radical democracy and to the measures necessary to harmonize the Constitution with the spirit of the age.

Regardless of their differences, these liberals and conservatives share a deep-rooted critique of the founding that denies that the Constitution encourages healthy republican politics in America—or even that it was meant to; and so they turn for inspiration and instruction to other sources. This might be reasonable, if the political thought of America's founding were as thin or timebound as they believe. But surely their first obligation—*our* first obligation, as thoughtful citizens—ought to be to inquire more minutely into the principles of the American political tradition before abandoning it as inarticulate or indefensible.

This book is an effort to recapture a part of that tradition. The publication of *The Federalist*, first in the newspapers of the day and then in book form, marked a great chapter in the education of a free people, in the shaping of their future statesmen, and in the nation's contribution to the classics of political science. While the most famous defense of the U.S. Constitution is hardly in danger of being forgotten—in fact, it is certainly more widely read and perhaps more effusively praised than ever before—it *is* in danger of being misunderstood, and therefore misprized. *The Federalist*'s lesson in constitutionalism—the need for a permanent form of government anchored in a written constitution to protect man's unalienable rights, and to serve the public good; and the inculcation of man's duties under but also *to* the Constitution—is emphasized in the chapters that follow. But the connection between *The Federalist*'s political theory and America's political practice is not overlooked. The spectacle of a people really choosing their government aided by the sober, candid, public-spirited reflections of "Publius"—and his allies and opponents—is an unforgettable part of the drama of the American founding. And, as in the best dramas, form and substance are inseparable. The principles of the American Revolution that *The Federalist* and the Constitution did so much to save—these required a form of public discussion or deliberation, as much as they did a form of government. *The Federalist*'s civility was the indispensable complement of its constitutionalism: both helped to shape the American way of life, and both serve to connect *The Federalist* with the other great educational legacy of the Founding Fathers—the example of their own lives.

The chapters in this book were originally presented as essays at a 1985 conference on *The Federalist* sponsored by The Henry Salvatori Center at Claremont McKenna College. I have served as Associate Director of the Center and Assistant Professor of Government at the College since 1983, and I owe both institutions many thanks. I owe a special debt of gratitude to George C. S. Benson, who as Director of the Center allowed me many impertinences, including the freedom to organize this conference; and to his successor Ralph A. Rossum, who has been a generous friend and collaborator in this and many other projects.

The Earhart Foundation supported the conference with a liberal grant, for which I am very grateful. I could not have managed either the running of the conference or the editing of this book without the good-humored assistance of my unflappable secretary, Rosemary Shuker. And I am indebted to my editor at the Free Press, Grant Ujifusa, for his many acts of kindness.

Claremont was the natural place to hold the conference that began this book, since it was home for many years to the country's foremost scholars of *The Federalist*, Douglass Adair and Martin Diamond, both now deceased. All of the contributors to this book are indebted, in one way or another, to these men. Even those of us who disagree rather more than we agree with them gladly acknowledge their writings as a stimulus to our own thinking about *The Federalist*, and hence about America.

Charles R. Kesler
Claremont, California

SAVING THE
REVOLUTION

Introduction

CHARLES R. KESLER

"Saving the Revolution" has perhaps a melodramatic or even vaguely European air, as if it were necessary to rush off to the barricades in defense of a second or third republic, or even worse, in defense of a tyranny calling itself a republic. Americans like to think of their Revolution as successful from the very start, and can with pride affirm that they have never had to number their republics, or disguise their hatred of tyranny. We live under the same Constitution (leaving aside the subsequent amendments and Court decisions) that our forefathers established 200 years ago. As undertaken by the contributors to this volume, the study of the most famous defense of our republican form of government—*The Federalist Papers*, or more properly, *The Federalist*, which also turns 200 in 1987—is both an appreciation of this impressive success and an attempt, through new as well as familiar paths, to perpetuate it.

Yet the drafting and ratification of the Constitution, although essential to the security and happiness of the American people, cannot simply be regarded as the consummation of our politics. Even in the bicentennial year of the Constitution, when our duty to celebrate its achievements is proudly and pleasantly compelling, it would be a dereliction of duty to forget that in 1860, less than seventy-five years after its ratification, the Constitution teetered on the verge of collapse; and this not as the result of an external threat, but as the acute symptom of an internal disorder that had grown more serious as the country had grown more extensive and powerful.

This was not the first crisis, after all. Many times before, particularly in 1812 and 1832, the United States had experienced awful premonitions of what was to come, as the fabric of nationhood had been stretched almost to the breaking point. It would thus be presumptuous to attempt to celebrate the Constitution without remembering the men who saved both the Constitution and the Union in those perilous times—above all, without honoring

1

the statesman who could transubstantiate the bitterness and death of the Civil War into a new birth of freedom.

Abraham Lincoln was, and is, the quintessential American, but even (or rather, especially) he would be inconceivable apart from the essence of Americanism contained in the Declaration of Independence and the Constitution. The relation between these two great documents has always defined the country's highest aspirations, and sparked its gravest crises. This was as true in 1860, when the moral and political status of slavery in a regime of freedom had become the all-consuming question, as it was in 1787, when the American people faced the challenge of whether or not they could be governed as one nation under a republican form of government, the product of their own "reflection and choice," to use the exalted language of the first *Federalist*, rather than of "accident and force."

After the Revolutionary War had been brought to a successful conclusion, the new nation's first crisis occurred in the 1780s, when the federal government established by the Articles of Confederation began to deadlock, becoming a potent source of frustration, brinkmanship, and danger. Jealous of the liberty they had won in the war against Britain, the states clung tenaciously to their rights under the Articles, and neglected their duties under the Declaration of Independence—their duties to one another, to the Union, and to the cause of republican freedom. In the view of the ablest statesmen of the time, the spirit of the Revolution was by 1787, only eleven years after the signing of the Declaration and six years after the ratification of the Articles of Confederation, on the verge of succumbing to the spirit of faction and disunion. The Revolution, so gloriously begun, threatened to end in a great spectacle of national humiliation, as its enemies at home and abroad had predicted it would.

The Constitution that emerged from the Philadelphia Convention in September 1787 was an attempt to reground the Union in the principles of 1776. Its object was nothing less than to save the Revolution by constitutionalizing it: by providing the national government with power and authority sufficient to meet the exigencies of Union; by securing a separation of powers that would foster and protect the true principles of republican government against both the ambition of the few and the folly of the many; by confirming the equality of man in the rule of law. But as important as the specific provisions of the Constitution were—and as famous as its "auxiliary precautions" were to be made by later interpreters of *The Federalist*—the new Constitution would stand or fall by its effect on public opinion: immediately, insofar as its ratification depended on rallying support in at least nine and preferably all thirteen states; and ultimately, inasmuch as its perpetuation required the formation of a national public opinion that would be enlightened, moderate, just, yet also courageously loyal to the preservation and good name of the American republic.

But the first step was to secure the Constitution's ratification. The objections to it were numerous and in some respects contradictory, but the most radical (and therefore revealing, though not for that reason typical) was that it represented a betrayal of the Revolution—a repudiation of the Declaration of Independence. Facing the proponents of the Constitution, therefore, was the urgent task of persuading its critics, the so-called Anti-Federalists—as well as those Americans who still were undecided—of the necessity and justice of the new form of government. Simply to win by force of numbers was not enough. If the opponents of the Constitution were not made part of the new regime—if they were not eventually reconciled to the republicanism of the Constitution, and thus converted from estranged countrymen to fellow citizens—then America's attempt to show that "societies of men are really capable . . . of establishing good government from reflection and choice" would already have begun to fail. The Revolution would have begun to devour its own.

This education in self-government was the goal of *The Federalist*, and to recover it ought to be our goal in studying it today. For the bicentennial of the Constitution will be reduced to a mere pastime if we fail to understand not only why the Constitution was adopted but why it is *good*, and therefore worthy of attention and devotion today.

THE CONSTITUTIONALISM OF *THE FEDERALIST*

To anyone familiar with the syndicated columnists on today's editorial pages, *The Federalist* will appear in the first place as a journalistic tour de force. Written by Alexander Hamilton, James Madison, and John Jay under the pen name of "Publius," *The Federalist* began appearing in New York newspapers in late October 1787, about a month after the end of the Federal Convention in Philadelphia, and continued until early April 1788. Hamilton oversaw the publication of the eighty-five papers in two hardcover volumes in March and May 1788. At the height of the series, Hamilton and Madison were turning out the essays at the rate of three or four a week, triggering occasional protests from weary readers (stop "cramming us with the voluminous Publius," demanded "twenty-seven subscribers" to the *New York Journal*) and dismay on the part of their less prolific, and less gifted, political adversaries. But their accomplishment was not simply polemical, their object not merely to persuade the voters of New York to ratify the new Constitution. "The great wish," Hamilton wrote in the Preface to the first volume of the collected papers, "is that it may promote the cause of truth and lead to a right judgment of the true interests of the community." Promoting "the cause of truth" is not a goal whose beneficiaries are limited to the citizens of New York in 1787: it is a theoretical undertaking whose benefits may extend to the most distant posterity, indeed to anyone, any time, who has the necessary diligence and intelligence to devote to Publius's handiwork.

Those benefits were recognized at the time by the country's foremost statesmen. Washington complimented Hamilton on a work that "will merit the notice of posterity because in it are discussed the principles of freedom and the topics of government which will always be interesting to mankind, so long as they shall be connected with civil society."[1] Jefferson proclaimed the work to be "the best commentary on the principles of government, which ever was written,"[2] and many years later, in 1825, recommended it as an authority on the "distinctive principles" of the governments of Virginia and the United States, second in importance only to the Declaration of Independence. In a resolution he presented to the Board of Visitors of the University of Virginia, he endorsed *The Federalist* as "an authority to which appeal is habitually made by all, and rarely declined or denied by any as evidence of the general opinion of those who framed, and of those who accepted the Constitution of the United States, on questions as to its genuine meaning."[3]

The significance of these testimonials should not be blinked, particularly in view of the fact that Jefferson recommended *The Federalist* as a guide to the Constitution without bothering to recommend the Constitution itself. That lapse should not of course be mistaken for indifference to the constitutional text. Jefferson strove mightily to bind the nation to a strict interpretation of the Constitution from his days as President Washington's Secretary of State to his own years as President—his staggering decision to purchase the Louisiana Territory to the contrary notwithstanding. But neither should we overlook the fact that the principal figures of the founding generation thought that the Constitution was in *need* of explication. In construing it in accord with its "genuine meaning," or as we might say today, its original intent, they looked not so much to its legislative history—the Federal Convention had met in secrecy, and Madison's *Notes* on its proceedings would be published only posthumously—but to the arguments of *The Federalist*. Publius's reflections were required to defend and explain the choice that the delegates to the Convention, and later the people of the United States, had made in favor of the Constitution. Although the American founding, in contrast to ancient foundings, was the work of many great men rather than of one lawgiver (as Publius emphasizes in *Federalist* 38), to be made intelligible and respectable it seemed to require the reason of one man: of Publius, whose explication of the Constitution is also a guide to its interpretation; is, in fact, an interpretation that draws out the reasoning latent in the text and completes it with the reasoning of Publius—making the Constitution into an expression not only of the popular will but of a rational will.

To be sure, in the beginning is the text of the Constitution, but in the course of refuting its opponents' arguments and advancing his own in defense of it, Publius teaches his readers a way of understanding what a written constitution is and what it requires of the citizens who live under it. To make the provisions of the document into a harmonious whole (as harmonious as it can be, given the institution of slavery; see *Federalist* 54), Publius shows us the Constitution in light of its ends; he shows us, in short, that the Constitution requires *constitutionalism* if the American experiment in republican government is to be crowned with success. "Societies of men" cannot govern themselves well without insisting that the rule of the people be made compatible with the rule of law and with the dictates of prudence. But the doctrine of constitutionalism must itself be inculcated in the opinions of the governed, whose consent authorizes the government in its institution and operation. The fountainhead of such civic education in America is *The Federalist.*

Accordingly, it takes a special effort to remind ourselves of the differences between the literal text of the Constitution and Publius's Constitution, that is, the Constitution as one understands it after having read *The Federalist.*[4] It has become second nature for us to confound the two, which is exactly what Publius intended. The text of the Constitution, for example, says nothing concerning the "separation of powers," an "energetic" executive, or "judicial review." There is nothing in the document itself to prevent Congress from using its power of impeachment to override the President and the Supreme Court at will, on ordinary policy questions, whenever a sufficiently numerous faction is so moved. The very way in which the powers of government are shared by the branches—especially the Senate's participation in the executive power of appointment through the requirement of advice and consent, and its entire possession of the judicial power to try cases of impeachment—might suggest, as indeed it did to the Anti-Federalists, that the principle of separated powers is openly flouted in this Constitution. And where does it say anything about the power of the Court to strike down congressional statutes by declaring them unconstitutional and void? That power—as well as the energetic character of the executive and the responsible understanding of the separation of powers—is expounded only in *The Federalist.*

THE POLITICS OF *THE FEDERALIST*

Publius's interpretation of the Constitution proved persuasive not only to the generation that ratified it but to subsequent generations that have lived under it, whose constitutional expectations and experience have been shaped by *The Federalist*'s precepts. But as we have seen, Publius's influence has not grown ineluctably, without argument. In fact, his view of the Constitution—his constitutionalism—has been at the center of American political controversy from the beginning, sometimes explicitly, more often implicitly. Before the Civil War, the papers on the nature of the Union, on federalism, loomed behind the arguments between the nationalists and the secessionists of both North and South. It was against Publius's case for an extensive Union and an effective separation of powers in the national government that John C. Calhoun directed his profound critique, offering the doctrine of the concurrent majority as both a necessary and desirable substitute for *The Federalist*'s Constitution. After the Civil War, Progressive intellectuals, social critics, and politicians began to distill their impatience with the course of American politics into an indictment of the eighteenth-century mechanisms of the Constitution. Frank Goodnow, J. Allen Smith, Charles Beard, and, perhaps most importantly, Woodrow Wilson blamed the reactionary spirit of the Constitution, especially as infused by Publius, for the failure of political reform to keep pace with economic and social problems, and proposed as a remedy nothing less than a rebirth of American freedom under the tutelary spirits of Darwin and Hegel.

In various ways both the Southern and the Progressive critiques of *The Federalist* live on in contemporary American conservatism and liberalism. Perhaps the simplest way to account for this is to note that, while conservatives tend to revere the Constitution but to deprecate the Declaration, and liberals prefer to celebrate the Declaration but are impatient with the Constitution (excepting the Bill of Rights), neither acknowledges the essential relation between the two that is embodied in *The Federalist*. Neither sees, on the one hand, that without the fixed ends of government proclaimed in the Declaration, the Constitution cannot provide a stable, enduring, and dignified form of government; nor, on the other hand, that the principles of the Declaration require a constitutional form and a doctrine of constitutionalism to perfect that form.

So today, as in the past, *The Federalist* is in the middle of the debate over the national character, over the meaning and purposes of American life. The essays gathered herein disagree on many vital points in interpreting Publius and in understanding American politics. Although many of the contributing authors would proudly call themselves "conservatives" or "neoconservatives" (some, however, would definitely eschew both labels), if this book is "conservative" it is because it tries to take the past seriously. Unlike many contemporary analyses of Publius, it reads rather than raids him, taking care to try to understand him as he understood himself, because it is possible that he grasped certain political truths as well as—perhaps better than—we do today.

Which brings us to what some may regard as a stylistic crotchet, our gentle insistence on referring to the author of *The Federalist* as Publius rather than as (depending on the paper under discussion) Hamilton, Madison, or Jay. It is true that after a century's disputation, the authorship of nearly every paper has been determined (a few remain uncertain as between Hamilton and Madison); and that much has been made over the years of the alleged "split personality" of Publius, differences between Hamilton's and Madison's contributions having been magnified in the light of their famous falling-out in the 1790s. But we have adopted the practice of referring to "Publius" out of fidelity to the intention of the actual authors. They chose to write under a pseudonym to prevent their personalities and political reputations from distracting their readers from the arguments that were being advanced. Until we have assured ourselves of grasping Publius's arguments in all of their subtlety, and as arrayed in his masterly rhetoric, it would be premature to resort to a diagnosis of schizophrenia. Like many other neuroses so easily discovered today in great books, this malady may well be the result of a superficial acquaintance with the patient or even of the physician's own incompetence. We know that neither Hamilton, Madison, nor Jay was entirely satisfied with the new Constitution, nor particularly optimistic about its long-term prospects. But the "miracle" at Philadelphia was that a group of delegates had been able to agree on a reasonably good plan of government at all; the union of the diverse opinions of Hamilton, Madison, and Jay under the auspices of Publius was only a continuation of that "miracle" by other means.

A GUIDE TO THIS VOLUME

The essays that follow will therefore identify *The Federalist*'s author as Publius, allowing for a few exceptions where the identification of the flesh-and-blood author is essential to an argument. All references to *The Federalist* are to the handy edition of Clinton Rossiter's published by the New American Library, New York, in 1961. The chapters follow roughly the order of the topics addressed by Publius, so that it is possible to use our volume as a companion to the reading of the original. But for the reader who is interested in specific topics, it will perhaps not be out of place to provide a brief overview of the present volume.

In chapter 1, I examine the prevailing interpretation of *The Federalist*'s political science, which traces its distinctive features to the political philosophy of Machiavelli, Hobbes, Locke, and Montesquieu—i.e., to modern political philosophy in contradistinction to ancient. The centerpiece of this interpretation is *Federalist* 10's argument for an extensive republic, in which a multiplicity of interests effectively cancels out the possibility of majority tyranny, though at the cost of a diluted patriotism and a predominant tone of self-interestedness in the new society. I argue that treating *Federalist* 10 as an epitome of the whole *Federalist* is a mistake, but that, properly understood, it prepares the opinions and habits of republican citizenship—the moral seriousness of which in America has been called into question by the prevailing interpretation.

In some ways this controversy is a continuation of the original debate over the ratification of the Constitution, and no book on *The Federalist* would be complete, or fair, without granting a hearing to Publius's opponents, the Anti-Federalists. After examining the parts of *The Federalist* that respond directly to the criticisms of particular Anti-Federalists, Murray Dry, professor of political science at Middlebury College and co-editor (with the late Herbert J. Storing) of *The Complete Anti-Federalist*, reproduces the other side of the founding dialogue over the ratification of the Constitution. The issue here is not merely the comparative advantages of small versus large republics, but the kind of citizen that the new American should be. By examining the arguments of two of the most influential Anti-Federalists—

the Federal Farmer and Brutus—Professor Dry limns the serious alternative to the new Constitution, and canvasses the Anti-Federalists' grave doubts about what they regarded as the inflated power of the aristocratic few in the national government, and the baneful influence of commerce on the national character.

In chapter 3, we hear *The Federalist*'s vigorous rebuttal of these charges, not excluding Publius's sometimes dour speculations on the motives of his opponents. The case for Publius's view of federalism is cogently argued by David Broyles, professor of political science at Wake Forest University and the author of a forthcoming commentary on *The Federalist*. In addition to reviewing the vexed questions of states' rights and the protection of minority rights under the Constitution, he charges the Anti-Federalists with misprizing the moral and political significance of the high-toned government for which Publius contends.

Patrick Garrity, a foreign policy scholar at the Naval Postgraduate School, writes on yet another dimension of the debate over the Constitution's ratification—the foreign policy of *The Federalist*. As opposed to the separation of idealism and realism that typifies contemporary debates on foreign policy, Publius grounds his discussion in a prudent unity of morality and utility. To this Garrity adds some important reflections on the phenomenon of bipartisanship in foreign policy: if bipartisanship is to be stable and respectable, it must reflect an underlying consensus on the unity of morality and utility; but doesn't it require, he asks, an act of farseeing partisanship (such as Publius's arguments) to bring bipartisanship into being?

In chapter 5, William Kristol, on leave from Harvard's John F. Kennedy School of Government and currently serving as chief of staff to Secretary of Education William Bennett, breathes life into a frequently read but seldom understood part of *The Federalist*: the papers on the separation of powers, Numbers 47–51. Over the past few decades, the extended sphere argument of *Federalist* 10 has eclipsed federalism and the separation of powers as the principal topic of theoretical interest in the book; but Kristol's meticulous reading of Numbers 47–51 redirects our attention to the separation of powers as *The Federalist*'s greatest contribution to political science. What he shows is how radically the principle of separated powers cuts across the democratic (or republican) principle, and therefore to what extent the American regime may be understood as an approximation under modern conditions of the classical idea of the mixed regime. In other words, the separation of powers makes the American form of government more aristocratic than it otherwise would—perhaps could—be, which in turn affects, however indirectly, the character of the American people.

What concerns William B. Allen, professor of government at Harvey Mudd College, is not so much the famous "auxiliary precautions" of the Constitution but what they are auxiliary to—namely, the American people. His essay explores the status of majority rule in *The Federalist* and in the thought of James Madison, and shows why Publius (Madison) was confident that "a coalition of a majority of the whole society could seldom take place on any other principles than those of justice and the general good." Following up that line of inquiry, Thomas G. West, professor of politics at the University of Dallas, explores *The Federalist*'s view of legislative power and the rule of law. Why, he asks, in a regime that claims to be wholly popular, are the people completely excluded from the administration of the government? Why, in short, does "wholly popular" turn out to mean "wholly representative"; and why, if the people are the fountain of all legitimate authority, must they acknowledge the authority of the Constitution?

With chapters 8 and 9 we turn to the consideration of the second branch of the new national government, the executive. Harvey C. Mansfield, Jr., professor of government at Harvard University and author of *The Spirit of Liberalism* and *Machiavelli's New Modes and Orders*, offers a wide-ranging interpretation of Publius's papers on the executive, Numbers 67–77. Against the background of previous republican theory, he sees *The Federalist*'s distinctive contribution to republicanism to be the domestication of the executive power. For the first time, a strong, "energetic" executive and republican freedom could keep house together, despite the traditional republican fear of monarchical power. In fact, Mansfield argues, it is only this achievement—the "republicanizing" or "constitutionalizing" of the executive—that permits republican government over the extensive territory of the United States to be responsible government.

The other side of executive power with which we are familiar today is the federal bureaucracy. *The Federalist* has almost nothing to say about bureaucracy—there was, happily, very little of it to speak of in American government until this century—and it falls to Jeremy Rabkin, assistant professor of political science at Cornell, to explain Publius's becoming silence. He does so by comparing the modern science of administration—rooted in the political philosophy of Kant, the sociology of Max Weber, and (in America) the pioneering studies of Woodrow Wilson and other first-generation academic American political scientists—with the political science of *The Federalist*. He concludes that the modern, value-free, "realistic" science of administration is starkly at odds with Publius's view of good government, which was eminently political, and not at all divorced from questions of "value" or principle, much less from considerations of the consent of the governed.

Following the order of Publius's exposition, we come now to the judicial branch, which James Stoner, assistant professor of political science at Goucher College, explicates in chapter 10. Stoner sees judicial review as the linchpin of the Constitution, despite or actually because of the fact that it is not mentioned in the Constitution. Its absence, or rather its need to be inferred, suggests how dependent our system of government is on the premises and practices of the great unwritten tradition of constitutionalism known as the common law. The philosophical issue involved is the status of judging

in a democracy. Judging is to be distinguished from willing, which is something that democracies are very good at. How is it that democracies can be
taught to appreciate the virtues of judging well, and how can the American
people be confident that the judges themselves will respect the difference
between judging and willing? This issue figures also in Ralph Rossum's
discussion of *The Federalist* and the Bill of Rights. Publius was, of course,
opposed to adding a bill of rights to the Constitution, because he considered
such bills to be dangerous both to men's rights and to stable government.
Many conservatives have today come to the conclusion that he was right; and
many liberals, who defend the Bill of Rights, do so on grounds that are
utterly opposed to those of its original proponents. Rossum, the Alice Tweed
Tuohy Professor of Government and Ethics at Claremont McKenna College,
defends Publius's confidence in the Constitution as a functional bill of rights,
and explains how Madison nevertheless came to be the leader of the successful fight for the Bill of Rights in the first Congress.

Chapters 12 and 13 explore the fate of *The Federalist* in the years after
the Constitution's ratification. Jack N. Rakove, professor of history at Stanford University and author of *The Beginnings of American National Politics*,
traces the use of *The Federalist* in the political, constitutional, and historical
debates of the antebellum period. It is a measure both of Publius's influence
and of the limits of his influence that he was cited as an authority by both
sides in the controversies leading up to the great secession winter of 1860–
61. Dennis J. Mahoney, assistant professor of political science at California
State University, San Bernardino, and assistant editor of *The Encyclopedia
of the American Constitution*, carries the story of Publius forward to the
present, or more precisely, to the period when the contemporary view of
The Federalist was formed—namely, the Progressive era. It was in those
years that criticism of the Constitution and perforce of *The Federalist* became established as a staple of academic political science. Mahoney shows
persuasively how the contemporary retreat from the Constitution in our
constitutional law was prepared, and to some extent directed, by the earlier
retreat from the Constitution in American political science.

Lest after so much reflection on the choice made by the American
founders and their posterity we should be tempted to forget the role that
accident and force played then and must continue to play in political life, we
offer in the final chapter Edward C. Banfield's sage reconsideration of the
role of chance in the founding. The ineradicable power of accident and force
was a fact of which Publius was well aware, as Banfield, the George D.
Markham Professor of Government Emeritus at Harvard and author of
(among many fine books) *The Unheavenly City* and *The Democratic Muse*,
explains.

After examining the history of the Federal Convention's deliberations,
he concludes that the Constitution itself, not to mention the achievement of
moderate government under its provisions, was either the result of a wildly
improbable series of accidents, or the design of a superintending provi-

dence. From the human point of view, of course, it is impossible to distinguish the two. Such a reflection ought to give pause to those in the academy and in politics who continue to advocate the jettisoning or wholesale rewriting of the Constitution to bring it in line with the latest pronouncements of the *Zeitgeist*. These visionaries are misguided, for reasons that *The Federalist* made clear two centuries ago; but what is most striking is how obstinately ungrateful they are two centuries later. After so much experience of life, liberty, and happiness under the Constitution, surely there is much to be grateful for, even as there is much to continue to strive for.

The Revolution that gave life to the American republic gave it liberty as well—the liberty to save or condemn, to honor or disgrace itself by its own words and deeds. Every generation of Americans is thus charged with saving the Revolution. That is, one might say, the American vocation, the highest and most demanding calling of American citizenship. The American Revolution, to borrow a line, ain't over till it's over, and it will never be over so long as a single American soul loves the cause of truth.

1

Federalist 10 and American Republicanism

CHARLES R. KESLER

It has been said that the oldest word in American politics is "new." Even the United States Constitution, at age 200 by far the oldest written constitution in the world, was once new, and had to be defended against charges that it was an unnecessary and unrepublican innovation. *The Federalist* was keenly aware of the novelty of the Constitution's enterprise— the attempt to establish "good government from reflection and choice"—but boldly turned it to account. "Hearken not to the voice which petulantly tells you that the form of government recommended for your adoption is a novelty in the political world," Publius admonished. For why should "the experiment of an extended republic" be rejected "merely because it may comprise what is new?" If the "leaders of the Revolution" had blindly followed precedent and tradition, the American experiment might have failed ingloriously—and the American people might already be suffering under one of those forms of government "which have crushed the liberties of the rest of mankind." But "happily for America, happily we trust for the whole human race, they pursued a new and more noble course."[1]

Yet not a perfect course. New things are noble because they are difficult; so one should not be surprised that mistakes were made in the American people's first efforts at self-government, both in the state constitutions and "in the structure of the Union." To correct these was the object of the proposed Constitution, whose superiority to the state constitutions and to the Articles of Confederation was based not only on its framers' good fortune but on their superior knowledge of political science. For as Publius declared, "the science of politics . . . like most other sciences, has received great improvement," even as measured against the high standard of the political science of the classics. "The efficacy of various principles is now well understood, which were either not known at all, or imperfectly known to the ancients," he claimed.[2]

It is as a product of this new science of politics, of the modern as opposed to the ancient understanding of man, that *The Federalist* is principally known today. Broadly speaking, we owe this view of Publius and of the Constitution to the political scientist Martin Diamond—and to a lesser extent, to the historian Douglass Adair—who in a series of remarkable essays spelled out the thesis of *The Federalist*'s thoroughgoing modernity. Publius himself named five ingredients of the improved science of politics in *Federalist* 9: "the regular distribution of power into distinct departments; the introduction of legislative balances and checks; the institution of courts composed of judges holding their offices during good behavior; the representation of the people in the legislature by deputies of their own election"; and, finally, "the ENLARGEMENT of the ORBIT within which such systems are to revolve."[3] But it was Diamond's great achievement to expound the central importance of the last principle to the republicanism of *The Federalist*.[4]

Interpreting *The Federalist*

Without neglecting the importance of the separation of powers, legislative checks and balances, the independent judiciary, and the principle of representation, Diamond nonetheless insisted that the Constitution's success in curing the ills of republican government depended "utterly upon the last item in Publius's science"—upon his "most novel and important theoretical teaching"—the extended sphere.[5] The doctrine of *Federalist* 10 was therefore at the heart of the American regime. Seen in all its ramifications, it marked a decisive break between the theory and practice of classical, and the theory and practice of modern politics. For while *The Federalist* rejects "'the chains of despotism,' i.e., the Hobbesian solution to the problem of self-preservation," Diamond wrote, "it nevertheless seems to accept the Hobbesian statement of the problem." The novel solution to that problem contained in *Federalist* 10 does not issue in a liberalism and republicanism that are "the means by which men may ascend to a nobler life; rather they are simply instrumentalities which solve Hobbesian problems in a more moderate manner." To put it differently, Diamond showed that Publius's republicanism becomes merely a means to his liberalism, to the doctrine of individual rights and freedom bounded only by the dictates of (comfortable) self-preservation.[6]

To protect men's rights, it is necessary to design a republicanism that avoids the characteristic malady of republican government—majority faction. To do this, according to *The Federalist*, it is necessary to ensure that the government, with its elaborate structure of separated powers, a bicameral legislature, and so forth, can endure any siege that a factious majority might mount. But even the daunting parapets of the Constitution can be overrun by a majority that is sufficiently persistent. Therefore, the majority must be weakened *before* it can close the siege ring around the government. Publius proposed to accomplish this by dividing the majority—which in all hitherto existing societies had been, as Diamond noted, "the great mass of the little propertied and the unpropertied," i.e., "the many"—into many different and competing interests that would serve to check one another. To encompass this "saving multiplicity of factions," republican government must be extended over a large territory; and the territory must be rich and variegated enough to support a vigorous commercial society. The "first object of government" must therefore be the protection of the diverse faculties of men from which arises "the possession of different degrees and kinds of property."[7] The requirements of commercial society exact a moral and political price, however, by encouraging "the aggressive private pursuit by all of immediate personal interests." This emancipation of acquisitiveness risks "magnifying and multiplying in American life the selfish, the interested, the narrow, the vulgar, and the crassly economic"; but this "is precisely the substratum," Diamond emphasized, "on which our political system was intended to rest and where it rests still."[8]

The resulting society is "solid but low," that is, it offers an elementary "decency if not . . . nobility." Accordingly, *The Federalist*'s republicanism abstracts "from politics the broad ethical function of character formation" that had been the chief concern of the ancient science of politics. "Other political theories," Diamond declared, "had ranked highly, as objects of government, the nurturing of a particular religion, education, military courage, civic-spiritedness, moderation, individual excellence in the virtues, etc. On all of these *The Federalist* is either silent, or has in mind only pallid versions of the originals, or even seems to speak with contempt."[9] Insofar as Publius shuns the traditional goal of character formation, he also abandons the traditional emphasis on the teaching of political opinions—on the education of citizens' habits and tastes—as a part of the shaping of character. While "from the classic perspective, *the* political task is to refine and improve a regime's opinion of what is advantageous and just," Diamond explained, "Madison instead turns away almost in horror from the human 'zeal for different opinions concerning religion, concerning government.'" It is not that higher concerns will not manifest themselves in America. The cultivation of virtue and opinion will instead be left to society, which will by and large be a realm of bourgeois virtue and even of a species of republican virtue. But these virtues, however high they may soar, will not lose touch with their base, which is self-interest, albeit enlightened self-interest or self-interest rightly understood. In America, virtue will always be colored by its origins, by the horizon established in the founding and perpetuated by the Constitution: the horizon set by the attempt to supply "by opposite and rival interests, the defect of better motives." For even when "better motives" can be found, when statesmen of virtue and wisdom are at the helm, their virtue will not be regarded as *indispensable*—and so their nobility will never command the awe and deference that it deserves. Publius's system "has no necessary place and makes no provision for men of the founding kind," Diamond concluded.[10]

This interpretation of *The Federalist*—and of America—has over the course of the past few decades come to prevail in most sectors of the academy, and has molded several generations of students who have gone on to employ it, as citizens and as scholars, in the making and analysis of American public policy.[11] But then the influence of Diamond's work is not in question. As an interpretation of *The Federalist*, it must be regarded as a stunning breakthrough—the starting point of all future inquiries—as revolutionary in its own way as the famous constitutional iconoclasm of Charles Beard. In fact, the scholarly lines through which Diamond broke had been marked out by Beard in 1913 in *An Economic Interpretation of the Constitution of the United States*. As Douglass Adair has shown, Beard was the first to realize that *Federalist* 10 is the key to *The Federalist* as a whole, the first to thrust *Federalist* 10 into the spotlight as an authoritative guide to the character of American politics.[12]

But Beard fastened upon the tenth *Federalist* not because of its argument for an extensive Union but because it appeared to be "a masterly statement of the theory of economic determinism in politics." Indeed, Beard lauded *The Federalist* as "the finest study in the economic interpretation of politics which exists in any language." In recapitulating Publius's argument in Number 10, Beard did not overlook the case for the extended sphere, but he regarded its true importance to be as a part of the larger argument on the role of economics in politics. The genius of Publius lay in his acknowledgment that "the chief business of government, from which, perforce, its essential nature must be derived, consists in the control and adjustment of conflicting economic interests."[13] Beard insisted in the original text and in his Introduction to the 1935 edition that he regarded this "theory of economic determinism" only as a hypothesis—though as the most powerful and successful one hitherto devised. That it was devised by him, however, he never claimed, always insisting that he was following in the footsteps of Madison, Harrington, Aristotle, and, to be sure, of Marx.[14]

It was this connection between the theory of economic determinism and the history of political philosophy that Adair took up. While not rejecting Beard's focus on the role of economic interests, Adair understood the clash of these interests to be not a continuation of the class struggle between the rich and the poor, the few and the many, but rather an alternative to that struggle: the conflict of interest groups cut across class lines, thereby allowing prudent statesmen to craft a moderate politics based on an equilibrium of interests. But such an equilibrium was possible, Adair maintained, only in an extensive republic that embraced a multiplicity of factions and an intricate, layered system of representation. Publius's patronage of interest groups was therefore in the service of something more fundamental—his argument for the extended sphere, in particular, and the ability of political theory to guide political life, in general. Whereas Beard had thought that abstract political ideas had little influence compared to economic factors—even the abstract idea of economic determinism was, after all, only a hypothesis—Adair sought to restore the independence and something of the dignity of political theory, even if it was only from the historical point of view. Republican government in a vast country—an idea that Adair traced back from Publius to David Hume—would produce the stable middle-class regime that had been the desideratum for thinkers on government since Aristotle. Thus Adair, too, saw Publius's argument as part of a tradition stemming from Aristotle; but he identified the extended sphere as Publius's special contribution to that tradition, and implicitly rejected Marx, an advocate of class war and of economic determinism, as being altogether outside it.[15]

Diamond pursued this same connection between *The Federalist* and the tradition of political thought, but brought to his efforts a much wider and deeper acquaintance with the history of political philosophy. Like Adair, he rejected Beard's economic determinism but retained *Federalist* 10 as the centerpiece of his interpretation of the book. But now the doctrine of the extended sphere was not only not an anticipation of Marx, but emphatically a refutation of him. Diamond viewed *Federalist* 10 as *the* modern answer to the threat of class struggle and violent revolution: the politics of regulating the "various and interfering interests" of an extensive commercial society would defuse the war between the rich and the poor, and avoid the ideological fanaticism that in the past had led to religious tyranny, and in the twentieth century to totalitarianism. At the same time, Diamond argued that ancient political philosophy was in the decisive respect superior to the modern political philosophy on which Publius drew, for the ancients had been able (at least in theory, and Diamond acknowledged that their practice fell short of their theory) to aspire to political nobility without abandoning the solid ground of decent, constitutional politics.

But in the modern world, Diamond insisted, men had to choose either the nonideological, low-but-solid politics of interest groups, or the ideological fanaticism and tyranny of the Nazis and Communists. In this context, his interpretation of *The Federalist* made perfect sense not only as a gloss on the Constitution but as a guide to the fundamental tendencies of contemporary American politics. *The Federalist* (especially Nos. 10 and 51) helped to explain how Franklin D. Roosevelt had steered the country between the Scylla and Charybdis of right-wing reaction and incipient socialism, preserving the rights of property and of minorities along the way. For the genius of F.D.R.'s approach was precisely his bravura use of interest-group politics to assemble a vast middle- and lower-class coalition in defense of American democracy. His incremental, pragmatic, nonideological approach was a perfect demonstration of the effective use of the political system described by Publius. And the soundness of Publius's "sober expectations" was driven home to Diamond again in the 1960s as he watched the New Left attempt to shake down the system bequeathed by the New Deal and invented by *The Federalist*.[16]

Yet despite its influence, its helpful insights, and its intellectual and political provenance, Diamond's view of the founding—and of Publius in particular—is terribly one-dimensional. His rejection of ideological politics is sound as far as it goes, but it does not properly distinguish between political ideology and political philosophy; it imagines that all efforts to form citizens or to inform public opinion on the basis of abstract truths are (at least since the seventeenth century?) *eo ipso* pernicious; it does not acknowledge (to speak of the present case) that interest-group politics cannot be defended apart from the ends that it is intended to serve and that therefore legitimize it, which ends must exist in public *opinion*, the special care of the greatest statesmen. The articulation of these ends is the task of political philosophy, whether undertaken by public or private men, by politicians or by academics. In short, if modern American politics is not to be cut off completely from the wellsprings of the Western tradition and from the first principles of our own founding, the rejection of ideology must be accompanied by the reassertion of the authority of political philosophy; and the politics of interest groups must be justified by and incorporated into the larger politics of public opinion.[17]

What Diamond neglected was the prudent political science of the founding, the political science that left room for and indeed regarded as indispensable the virtue of prudence, in the old-fashioned sense of the term: the virtue of the man who is adept at deciding what is the best thing to be done under the circumstances, who can determine what is the best way to get from here to there (and who therefore must know where he is going, the goal for which to strive), who can instruct public opinion without either scorning its backwardness or flattering its vanity or enflaming its passions. This is prudence in the traditional sense, the virtue that crowns the political art and is an indispensable part of political science. It is not a virtue that is especially needful in a regime of interest-group politics, where sobriety, calculating realism, and skill in maneuver suffice. But in a republican regime in which public opinion is everything, it is the one virtue most needful.[18]

To put it differently, from the standpoint of the "new science of politics"—of the political philosophy of Machiavelli and Hobbes and, so Diamond asserted, *The Federalist*—prudence properly speaking is dethroned; and alongside that, republicanism is made into the valet of liberalism, the obedient and invisible servant of interest-group pluralism. Yet *The Federalist* says nothing of this "new science of politics." That term belongs to Alexis de Tocqueville—and it is even a question how "new" is the science that he calls for to understand "a world itself quite new."[19] *The Federalist* speaks only of an *improved* science of politics that will supply the "means" by which the "excellencies of republican government may be retained and its imperfections lessened or avoided." As readers of cereal boxes know, "new" and "improved" are not the same, and hence cereal companies like to use both terms to communicate the sheer magnificence of their work. Publius, on the other hand, claims only to have added new elements to an already existing science, to have improved but not remade it. His improvements relate only to "means" and not to ends—the ends of *republicanism*, whose "excellencies" he wishes to *retain* and whose imperfections he wishes to lessen or avoid.[20] One should not forget that the authors of *The Federalist* are not embarrassed to write under the pen name of an ancient Roman statesman, one of the founders of the Roman republic.[21]

Let us then have a fresh look at what has been regarded as the centerpiece of the new political science in America, the argument of *Federalist* 10.

THE PLAN OF *THE FEDERALIST*

The Federalist is divided into two main parts, corresponding to the two volumes in which the collected papers were first published. The first thirty-six papers are a discussion of the Union, or more precisely, as Publius lists the topics in *Federalist* 1, of "the utility of the UNION to your political prosperity," "the insufficiency of the present confederation to preserve that Union," and "the necessity of a government at least equally energetic with the one proposed, to the attainment of this object."[22] Following the discussion of the Union, Publius turns to the particular "merits of this Constitution." It is this part of the book (Papers 37–85) that discloses "the conformity of the proposed Constitution to the true principles of republican government." We may say provisionally, then, that Publius discusses the matter of the new nation in the first part of *The Federalist*, and the form of the new nation in the second.[23]

Although the first section begins with Publius's inspiring announcement that "It has been frequently remarked that it seems to have been reserved to the people of this country, by their conduct and example, to decide the important question, whether societies of men are really capable or not of establishing good government from reflection and choice, or whether they are forever destined to depend for their political constitutions on accident and force," it is not until the second part of *The Federalist* that one hears very much about what the framers have chosen in the new Constitution, not to mention why they have chosen it. The first part of the book concerns rather the inextirpable power of "accident and force" in America's affairs. Its argument ranges over the many necessities, domestic and foreign, that require Union. The qualities of "good government," and the relation between the ends of good government and the form of republican government, are topics that are not examined systematically in Papers 1–36. Instead, Publius turns first to the lowest and most solid basis for all government, the force of necessity.

"Nothing is more certain than the indispensable necessity of government," he declares in *Federalist* 2, and in the ensuing papers proves that in

America necessity requires a government of the whole Union, not separate confederacies of states. The reason for this is not Providence or even deference to the judgment of the "wise and experienced men" of the Convention, but safety. "Among the many objects to which a wise and free people find it necessary to direct their attention, that of providing for their *safety* seems to be first." And so Papers 2–5 expound the necessity of the Union to protect against external dangers, and Papers 6–10 the necessity of the Union to guard against domestic dangers to our safety.[24] The low horizon of the first part of *The Federalist* is firmly established in the beginning numbers: the case for the Constitution seems to rest entirely on the case for the Union, and the latter depends upon the "natural course of things" or the "natural and necessary progress of human affairs," arising from man's consideration of his natural weakness and his need to make himself secure at all costs. This Hobbesian reasoning ignores the differences among forms of governments and reduces politics to the questions of self-preservation and sovereignty, which are really the same question. "Safety from external danger is the most powerful director of national conduct," Publius advises. "Even the ardent love of liberty will, after a time, give way to its dictates."[25]

It is in the second part of *The Federalist* that the case for the Constitution on its merits is propounded. The concluding paragraph of the first part promises that what is to follow will be different in character: Publius declares that "a further and more critical investigation of the system will serve to recommend it still more to every sincere and disinterested advocate for good government." This "more critical and thorough survey of the work of the convention," as he calls it in Number 37, occupies the rest of the book, and is addressed to "the candid and judicious part of the community," those who "add to a sincere zeal for the happiness of their country, a temper favorable to a just estimate of the means of promoting it." With the shift in subject matter comes a shift in rhetorical mode: rather than teaching men to understand their passions so that they may satisfy their fundamental passion for self-preservation—rather than using necessity as an effective substitute for moderation—Publius chooses to speak in moderate tones to moderate men. For the "sincere and disinterested advocate for good government" will not be satisfied with proofs of the necessity of the plan. Morality, and especially the supreme political morality of framing and ratifying a constitution, involves choice; and what "the candid and judicious part of the community" wants to know is whether the new Constitution is worthy of choice. Whereas in the first part Publius strives to show the American people that they have no choice (in any rational sense) but to preserve the Union by adopting the Constitution, in the second part he attempts the very different task of persuading moderate men not only of the "expediency" but of the "propriety" of choosing the Constitution. And so he exclaims, in the transition to the second part, "Happy will it be for ourselves, and most honorable for human nature, if we have wisdom and virtue enough to set so glorious an example to mankind!"[26]

The Union may be necessary for our "political prosperity," but as depicted in the first part of *The Federalist*, i.e., when prescinded from the principles informing the Constitution, the Union is not "most honorable for human nature." It becomes honorable only in the light of the Constitution. The glory and honor of America—the principles and form of the new government—become visible only in the second part of Publius's argument. By initially teaching his readers the limits that necessity places on human choice, Publius prepares them to choose wisely when "the merits of this Constitution" are finally presented in their own terms. For the fact that choice is not completely free means that men must respect its conditions and anticipate its consequences if they are to choose well. Publius shows his readers that the truly necessary choice *is* to choose well.[27]

THE IMPROVED SCIENCE OF POLITICS

If the two parts of *The Federalist* are thus united by a common intention, we should expect that the first part's argument from necessity would have to provide some account of or room for human freedom. The danger to freedom is obvious, as Publius explains in Number 8: "The violent destruction of life and property incident to war, the continual effort and alarm attendant on a state of continual danger, will compel nations the most attached to liberty to resort for repose and security to institutions which have a tendency to destroy their civil and political rights." But Publius does not draw the Hobbesian conclusion of absolute monarchy from the continual perils of this state of war. Instead, in Papers 9 and 10, he presents a defense of the Union that rises above the level of necessity, that anticipates and prepares the way for the argument in the second part of the book: free or republican government is possible based on the advantages of a "firm" (No. 9) and "well-constructed" (No. 10) Union.

The Union is made "firm" by being a confederate or federal republic, combining the "internal advantages" of a small republic with the "external force" of a monarchical government. Publius's authority for this argument is "that great man" Montesquieu, from whom he quotes extensively to prove that the proposed government of the United States would fulfill Montesquieu's recommendations, and that the much discussed distinction between a confederated and a consolidated government is therefore "more subtle than accurate." But Montesquieu is introduced only in response to the circumstance that "the opponents of the PLAN proposed here, with great assiduity, cited and circulated" his observations; he is not presented as an independent authority for the Constitution on his own terms, despite the fact that in the preceding paragraph Publius had remarked the "great improvement" that the science of politics, like most other sciences, had achieved when compared to the ancients. "It is impossible to read the history of the petty republics of Greece and Italy," Publius remarks, "without feeling sensations of horror and disgust at the distractions with which they were continually agitated, and at the rapid succession of revolutions by which they were kept in a state of perpetual vibration between the extremes of tyranny and anarchy." It is from such accounts that the "advocates of despotism" have drawn arguments not only against the republican form of government but against "the very principles of civil liberty." "If it had been found impracticable to have devised models of a more perfect structure," Publius concludes, "the enlightened friends to liberty would have been obliged to abandon the cause of that species of government as indefensible."[28]

The improved science of politics is introduced in *Federalist* 9, in short, as a means of persuading "the enlightened friends to liberty" to become republicans. The lovers of "civil liberty" must be taught to cherish political liberty or self-government, and to accomplish this Publius appeals to their "enlightened" fondness for devising "models" and their confidence in "improvement," in "wholly new discoveries" or discoveries that "have made their principal progress towards perfection in modern times."[29] It is because the opponents of the Constitution have "cited and circulated" Montesquieu's views on confederacies that Publius considers it important to answer them in kind; but what is at stake is the allegiance of the "enlightened friends to liberty," who as such are inclined to regard that "enlightened civilian," Montesquieu, as an authority. On the merits of the question, it would apparently have been possible to pronounce without recourse to him. Publius admits that "the utility of a Confederacy, as well to suppress faction and to guard the internal tranquillity of States as to increase their external force and security, is in reality not a new idea"; and Montesquieu himself cites ancient Lycia as a worthy example.[30]

By his carefully hedged employment of the improved science of politics, which, after all, he invokes with some fanfare in the same number, Publius suggests the limitations of that science. However important it is for political science to devise "models of a more perfect structure" for the better securing of liberty—however useful are such devices as the separation of powers, legislative checks and balances, an independent judiciary, and so forth, for the sake of civil liberty—they must finally be understood to serve the purposes of a prudent republicanism. "They are means, and powerful means"— but only means—"by which the excellencies of republican government may be retained and its imperfections lessened or avoided." It is precisely the continued importance of republicanism that connects the political wisdom of *The Federalist* with that of the ancients, that connects the American Publius with the Roman Publius. Although our Publius endorses Montesquieu's description of a confederate republic as "a kind of constitution that has all the internal advantages of a republican, together with the external force of a monarchical, government," Publius never specifies in Number 9 what those "internal advantages" are. To do so, following Montesquieu, would require him to distinguish between republicanism (whose principle is, according to

Montesquieu, virtue) and honor. But as we learn only later, Publius's case for the Constitution depends crucially upon connecting honor and republicanism, upon vindicating "the honorable title of republic."[31] This is the deeper reason why the new science of politics, the science of Machiavelli, Hobbes, and Montesquieu, is rejected in favor of the old science improved by prudence, experience, and new instrumentalities suited to modern conditions.

The most famous of these new means or instrumentalities is the "extended sphere" or "the ENLARGEMENT of the ORBIT" of republican governments. Publius introduces this topic in Number 9 and explicates it in Number 10. In the course of introducing it, he changes his description of the valuable improvements in the science of politics. From being virtually new principles or indeed "wholly new discoveries," they become a "catalogue of circumstances that tend to the amelioration of popular systems of civil government." As a consequence of their status as means, they become "circumstances" that are interesting only insofar as they are the conditions of something better or good in itself, only insofar as they "tend" to a certain end. To this "catalogue" Publius, now speaking in his own name, ventures "to add one more" circumstance, "however novel it may appear to some."[32] As "circumstances" these means or instrumentalities seemed to be almost beyond human choice, to be "givens" in the sense of the ineluctable conclusions of science. But as parts of a "catalogue" Publius reminds us that they are in fact subject to human choice, which he underscores by emphatically adding an item to the catalogue. The founders of "popular systems of civil government" must choose from this "catalogue" when trying to improve their regimes, but their choosing must adapt itself to the character and circumstances of particular peoples; they cannot simply apply or implement "models of a more perfect structure." So we are prepared when, after the long excursus on Montesquieu's view of confederations, Publius takes up the discussion of "the ENLARGEMENT of the ORBIT" in Number 10 in his own name and without any reference to Montesquieu or any other philosophical authority.

THE PROBLEM OF FACTION

"Among the numerous advantages promised by a well-constructed Union," Publius announces at the beginning of Number 10, "none deserves to be more accurately developed than its tendency to break and control the violence of faction." Whereas a "firm" Union will act "as a barrier against domestic faction and insurrection," apparently by its ability to "repress" such outbreaks, a "well-constructed" Union will tend to "break and control the violence of faction." That is to say, it will not put an end to faction but will control it by breaking its violence or perhaps breaking it of its violent habits; if the violence of faction can be controlled it will not be necessary to "repress" faction because it will not threaten to become an "insurrection." This is an advantage of Union, and so is properly discussed in the first part of *The Federalist;* but it is not a tendency of the Union simply, but only of a "well-constructed" Union, and so suggests the need to transcend the first part's terms of discussion. A well-constructed Union is a firm Union but also something more. Its parts are not only put together well, but are well interpreted and regulated by the Constitution and by Publius. The "well-constructed" Union, like a well-constructed or well-construed Constitution, is the product of wise interpretation.[33]

Montesquieu cannot be the basis of the argument for the extended sphere because, as Publius shows in Number 9, on Montesquieu's authority the larger American states were already too large to be proper republics. With some reduction in the extent of these states, his argument did not, *mutatis mutandis*, rule out a confederated republic for the United States; but it did place the opponents of the Constitution—the defenders of the existing states—in an embarrassing position. From this standpoint, Number 10's argument is as necessary to rescue them from their predicament as it is to defend the new Constitution. In short, by severing his opponents' political interest from their philosophical authority, Publius prepares and gradually encourages them to connect their interest to his authority, and to elevate their gaze to "the greatness or happiness of the people of America," rather than by "the multiplication of petty offices" to seek to extend their influence in "the narrow circles of personal intrigue."[34]

The problem of faction provides the leverage needed to pry the respectable part of the opposition away from their present convictions, because the "dangerous vice" of factionalism disturbs both "the friend of popular governments" who is "alarmed for their character and fate," and "our most considerate and virtuous citizens," who share with the former an anxiety over the state governments' instability and injustice but add to it a concern for the common good. Both those who love the form of popular government and those who love the end of all good government (the common good) will have reason to study *Federalist* 10, which goes as far toward reconciling the form of republican government and the end of good government as is possible in the first part of the book, before the thematic discussion of the separation of powers and of "the true principles of republican government." That the state governments cannot realize these hopes is implied in the fact that they have failed to cure the "mortal diseases" of popular governments; the implication is that they are dangerously close to expiring, despite the fact that their improvements on ancient and modern models, Publius says, "cannot certainly be too much admired." Of course, their failings could be excused if the extended sphere were necessary to solve the problem of faction. It is only in the discussion of the separation of powers in the second part of *The Federalist* that we discover that the state constitutions were inherently flawed—and, literally, "cannot certainly be too much admired."[35]

Publius must show his fellow republicans that justice, stability, and liberty can be at home in a large territory; and he must persuade his countrymen who are less concerned with popular government than with the common good that the good of the whole will be sought after and secured in the new regime. All of these considerations are provisionally united in the definition and remedy for faction proposed in Number 10. "By a faction," Publius writes, "I understand a number of citizens, whether amounting to a majority or minority of the whole, who are united and actuated by some common impulse of passion, or of interest, adverse to the rights of other citizens, or to the permanent and aggregate interests of the community." As if to emphasize his distance from Montesquieu and from previous republican theory, Publius states his definition in the first person ("I understand") and makes clear that unlike the older Latin use of the term (*factio*), a faction can consist not only of the few but of the many. This will, in fact, turn out to be the danger above all to be feared. A certain parallelism might be inferred from his disjunctions: perhaps majority factions (which are mentioned first) are more often united and actuated by some passion that is "adverse to the rights of other citizens," whereas minority factions are usually the creatures of an interest directed against "the permanent and aggregate interests of the community." The inference does not of course preclude the existence of factions that cut across the categories; but the definition does make clear that factions must be "united and actuated," i.e., that to exist they must enjoy both "the impulse" and "the opportunity" provided by a common passion or interest. By the clear implication of this carefully wrought definition, a majority or minority united and actuated by a common *opinion* does not qualify as a faction. Nor does *Federalist* 10 ever propose a multiplicity of opinions as a solution to the problem of faction. It is true that Publius will soon establish the reciprocal relation between opinions and passions, thereby implying that a multiplicity of passions would breed a multiplicity of opinions, and vice versa. But he never explicitly connects this implication with his definition of faction, or with his later solution to the problem.[36]

REMOVING THE CAUSES OF FACTION

"There are two methods of curing the mischiefs of faction," Publius explains, "the one, by removing its causes; the other, by controlling its effects." Before, the "well-constructed" Union was said to have the tendency to break and control "the violence of faction." Now it seems possible to accomplish something else: not only to break and control faction's violence, but to cure its mischiefs as well. Perhaps the violence of faction is not its worst feature, though it may well be its most alarming. If the mischiefs of faction (understood in a comprehensive sense) can be cured, then the Union's restraint on faction's violence may be unnecessary or at least of only secondary importance, because the conditions that lead to the outbreak of violence will have been ameliorated. In any case, Publius says that there are two methods of curing these mischiefs. He does not say (although he implies) that either the one or the other must be chosen; that is, he does not explicitly exclude the possibility that both may prove useful. Of the two methods, he remarks of the second that it "must derive" an "efficacy" from the Union. He never claims that the first method—removing the causes of faction—derives an efficacy from the Union.[37]

"There are again two methods of removing the causes of faction," Publius continues, "the one, by destroying the liberty which is essential to its existence; the other, by giving to every citizen the same opinions, the same passions, and the same interests." Publius rejects the first method as a cure worse than the disease: to destroy liberty in order to abolish faction would be like wishing the annihilation of air in order to eliminate fire. The analogy is complicated by Publius's specification that liberty "is essential to political life" just as air "is essential to animal life." But liberty can be abolished, air cannot; men can only "wish the annihilation of air." "Political life" is in this crude sense weaker than "animal life," but only because political life is distinctively human, i.e., it involves the capacity for reflection and choice. Man can choose to abolish liberty; neither he nor the other animals can choose to annihilate air. Men who would choose to abolish liberty do not understand the distinctiveness of human life: they do not appreciate what they have in common with all mankind but not with the other animals. Publius's rejection of this first method of removing the causes of faction teaches those men—the few—who would be tempted to deny the human claim to liberty based on the equal rights of man (perhaps acting in the name of the common good), that they are but men, and cannot afford to dispense with the rights to which their humanity entitles them.[38]

Even as the first method was denounced as "unwise"—an apt rejoinder to those who think themselves wise—so the second is dismissed as "impracticable." To give every citizen "the same opinions, the same passions, and the same interests" is impracticable because no government is so powerful as to be able to blot out the natural inequalities among men, which inequalities take two forms. In the first place, there is the connection between men's opinions and their passions. "As long as the reason of man continues fallible, and he is at liberty to exercise it, different opinions will be formed. As long as the connection subsists between his reason and his self-love, his opinions and his passions will have a reciprocal influence on each other; and the former will be objects to which the latter will attach themselves."[39] Despite the "reciprocal influence" of opinion and passion, Publius does not state that men's passions will be objects to which their opinions will be drawn, only that their opinions will furnish the objects of their passions. That is, he maintains a certain independence and even dignity for opinion: men are divided in their opinions not so much on account of the influence of passion but due to the fallibility of reason. To be sure, one cause of the fallibility of human reason may well be the obscurantism of the passions; but Publius emphasizes that fallible men typically make mistakes in their reasoning or cannot quite grasp the truth, not that they are biased or unjust. This refusal to reduce opinions or reason to the effect of prerational or subrational causes is characteristic of *Federalist* 10's argument, and lays the groundwork for the politics of public opinion—of republicanism—that *The Federalist* is constructing.

The second reason why giving to every citizen "the same opinions, the same passions, and the same interests" is "impracticable" reveals more fully the character of the argument. It is especially the democrats—the many—or at least their most vociferous partisans, who think that the inequalities among men can be erased. So even as Publius's argument to the few emphasized that abolishing liberty is "unwise," so this argument, directed particularly to the many, emphasizes that radical egalitarianism is "impracticable." He addresses each in terms that are dear to their own passions or interests (to the few: don't show your unwisdom; to the many: don't show that despite your number you are weak) but in so doing corrects the partial opinion of justice held by each. Without appealing directly to their opinions regarding who should rule, Publius teaches them that neither claim to rule is sufficient. What is true in the claims of the few and the many will be preserved and enhanced not in the regimes of aristocracy or direct democracy but in Publius's own federal republic, in the regime of the Constitution. But refuting the claim of the many takes longer, partly because in a regime based on the consent of the governed the majority deserves a full hearing; but also because in a republic the majority is the most powerful, hence the most dangerous, political group.

The proposed uniformity of opinion and passion is quickly disposed of, but Publius essentially devotes the rest of Number 10 to considering the proposed uniformity of interests. Democrats may easily be persuaded that the liberty to hold opinions should be protected, inasmuch as it is an aspect of their own claim to equal freedom. Interest is another matter; it smacks of wealth, the principle of the (oligarchical) few. But interest is not the same as wealth: it is a kind of combination of wealth and freedom, of the desire or right to get wealthy with the freedom or right of every man to choose his own path or to be judge in his own cause. Publius's discussion of interests is thus part of his effort to combine the few and the many: the discussion of interests is part of his education of public opinion or to public opinion, i.e., to the creation of an American public formed by the Constitution and its principles.

"The diversity in the faculties of men," Publius maintains, "from which the rights of property originate, is not less an insuperable obstacle to a uniformity of interests. The protection of these faculties is the first object of government." Publius had said in *Federalist* 3 that "safety" was the first object of a people's attention; later he will define the object of government as the higher and more comprehensive one of "the safety and happiness of society," "the common good of the society," "the happiness of the people."[40] The protection of "the diversity in the faculties of men, from which the rights of property originate" lies in between protecting the safety and securing the happiness of society, between the alpha and the omega of political life. It corresponds to the place of *Federalist* 10 in the overall argument of *The Federalist*. To understand any part of that argument one must see it in relation to the structure of the book as a whole. This consideration would save many commentators on *The Federalist* from the mistake of identifying the "first object" with the final object of government, as well as the corollary mistake of identifying the purposes of the Union—e.g., as stated in *Federalist* 23, "the common defense of the members; the preservation of the public peace, as well against internal convulsions as external attacks; the regulation of commerce with other nations and between the States; the superintendence of our intercourse, political and commercial, with foreign countries"—with the purposes of government or of the Constitution.[41]

"From the protection of different and unequal faculties of acquiring property, the possession of different degrees and kinds of property immediately results; and from the influence of these on the sentiments and views of the respective proprietors ensues a division of the society into different interests and parties." If the acquisitive faculties are protected, then society will necessarily be divided into "different interests and parties." The relation between interest and opinion, which Publius had not mentioned in his discussion of passion and opinion, now comes to the fore. With the division of society into interests one gets "parties" or politics, and only then the invocation of "nature": "the latent causes of faction are thus sown in the nature of man; and we see them everywhere brought into different degrees of activity, according to the different circumstances of civil society." Politics arises from the differences in men's opinions and interests, not from the conflict of their passions per se. From the diversity in men's faculties and the consequent diversity of property—or, considering men as themselves a kind of property arising from their faculties, from the diversity in the degrees and kinds of men—arise certain "sentiments and views" that produce the division of society into interests and parties. Again Publius places opinions first: it is opinions that give rise to interests and to politics; opinions themselves arise from (fallible) reflection on unequal human conditions, broadly speaking. The "latent causes of faction" are thus sown in the liberty of man's reason, in his self-love, and in his diverse faculties, including particularly his faculty for holding opinions concerning what is rightly his or what is his due. For it is not so much man's "faculties of acquiring property" but "the diversity in the faculties of men" from which the "rights" of property originate that stimulates faction and political conflict.[42]

But not all politics is factious. The latent causes of faction become activated "according to the different circumstances of civil society." "A zeal for different opinions concerning religion, concerning government, and many other points, as well of speculation as of practice" is mentioned as the first of these "different circumstances." This use of the term "circumstances" perhaps recalls Number 9's "catalogue of circumstances that tend to the amelioration of popular systems of civil government." Perhaps the "circumstances" of political science can ameliorate the "circumstances of civil society." It is certainly true that until zealous opinions concerning religion and government are separated and moderated, it is unlikely that "the regulation of . . . various and interfering interests" will be the "principal task of modern legislation": so mild a preoccupation presupposes that the prior and divisive question of who should rule has been decided and consented to. Publius's task is to answer that question in, and through, his exposition of the Constitution. His task is complicated by the fact that the Constitution is a means to an end, to the ends of government proclaimed in the Revolution, which means particularly in the Declaration of Independence; and complicated further by the fact that a constitutional form of government is essential to the realization of those ends, and so is itself a kind of end. In other words, Publius must persuade his readers not only that the people should rule but that the people's rule can—indeed must—be constitutional. If republican government is to be "rescued from the opprobrium under which it has so long labored and be recommended to the esteem and adoption of mankind," Publius must show that the rule of the people will take place only through the rule of law, rather than through force, sheer will, or the tyrannical passions of the greatest number.[43] Concretely, this means that the people must not only rule *through* the law, but be ruled *by* the law: they must come to love the law, and in particular the fundamental law, the Constitution, more than they love their own sovereign authority. Or, more precisely, they must come to identify their rule with the majestic authority of the Constitution.

So Publius cannot remedy the factions caused by "a zeal for different opinions concerning religion, concerning government" by attempting to multiply those contending opinions. While he does endorse a "multiplicity of interests" and "multiplicity of sects" to provide security for "civil rights" and "religious rights," he never advocates a multiplicity of opinions to protect political rights. There must be a uniformity of opinion underlying the multiplicity of interests and sects; otherwise the result would not be pluralism but civil war or anarchy, not America but Lebanon. Pluralism, then, is not enough; before men can be divided by interests and sects they must be united by citizenship. Far from "turn[ing] away almost in horror from the human 'zeal for different opinions,'" Publius himself inculcates an opinion; far from eschewing zealous politics, Publius concludes Number 10 by declaring, "And according to the degree of pleasure and pride we feel in being republicans ought to be our zeal in cherishing the spirit and supporting the character of federalists."[44]

VIRTUE AND INTERESTS

To be sure, that zeal is restricted to a republicanism embodying the "spirit" and "character" of federalists, and presumably of the chief federalist, Publius. It is only when that zeal has replaced the factious zeal "for different opinions" that the pluralistic politics of interest groups becomes possible. For "the most common and durable source of factions," Publius explains, "has been the various and unequal distribution of property." The unequal distribution comprises "those who hold and those who are without property," as well as creditors and debtors; the various distribution includes the landed, manufacturing, mercantile, moneyed, and other lesser interests that "grow up of necessity in civilized nations." Civilized nations are those that protect the diverse faculties of men; they are to that extent commercial nations.

To the extent that the Constitution secures more than the diverse faculties that give rise to property, insofar as it secures the people's "safety and happiness," it exists for the sake of more than a merely commercial nation.[45] One should not forget that in the thematic discussion of commerce in *Federalist* 6, Publius depicts it as a source of dissension and war: "Has commerce hitherto done anything more than change the objects of war? Is not the love of wealth as domineering and enterprising a passion as that of power and glory?" Against those "projectors in politics" who maintain that "the genius of republics . . . is pacific" and that "the spirit of commerce has a tendency to soften the manners of men"—against Montesquieu, Kant, and Hume, among others—Publius asks, "Have republics in practice been less addicted to war than monarchies? Are not the former administered by *men* as well as the latter?" To answer these questions, he appeals to experience, and cites examples ancient and modern. In Number 7 Publius affirms the "unbridled spirit" of commercial enterprise in America, and in Number 11 attests that the "adventurous spirit, which characterizes the commercial character of America," has already "excited uneasy sensations in several of the maritime powers of Europe." Plainly commerce does not promise "perpetual peace" between the United States and the rest of the world; why should it be the handmaid of civil harmony within the United States? The multiplicity of interests becomes conducive to peaceful, nonfactious government within the United States only when commerce itself has been tamed or shaped by Publius's constitutionalism, by the opinions taught in *The Federalist*. After the discussion of the extended republic in Number 10, the importance of the Union to commerce is said to be "one of those points about which there is least room to entertain a difference of opinion," inasmuch as "the prosperity of commerce is now perceived and acknowledged by all enlightened statesmen to be the most useful as well as the most productive source of national wealth." From this new point of view, even the "often-agitated question between agriculture and commerce" has "received a decision which has silenced the rivalship that once subsisted between them" and proved "that their interests are intimately blended and interwoven."[46]

But the harmony of interest that underlies the multiplicity of interests that "grow up of necessity in civilized nations" is not itself a necessity: it must be taught and it must be learned. *Federalist* 10 suggests a common opinion about the value of commerce or of commercial prosperity that justifies it not as an end in itself but as a means to the public good, and therefore allows the peaceful division of society into competing economic interests. This opinion is "perceived and acknowledged by all enlightened statesmen" and has "commanded the most general assent of men who have any acquaintance with the subject," but it must be taught to and enforced upon men whose "general assent" is not sufficient to moderate their own particular interest. "The regulation of these various and interfering interests forms the principal task of modern legislation," Publius continues, "and involves the spirit of party and faction in the necessary and ordinary operations of government." But the whole purpose of Publius's inquiry in Number 10 is to find a way to remedy "the unsteadiness and injustice with which a factious spirit has tainted our public administration."[47] If a factious spirit is necessarily involved in the ordinary operations of government, how can there be any cure for the "unsteadiness and injustice" of our politics?

One must pay careful attention to Publius's words. "The regulation of these various and interfering interests forms the principal task of modern legislation"—Publius says nothing about those aspects of government that are not particularly modern (even as he has said nothing concerning "wise" as opposed to "enlightened" statesmen), nor does he bring up modern execution or judgment. The discussion in *Federalist* 10 seems to take place entirely on the level of the legislative power, as if the legislature were the whole government. Publius has not yet separated the powers of government, which will happen only in the second part of the book. The solution to the problem of faction proposed in Number 10 is a partial solution, one that needs to be supplemented by Publius's consideration of the principle of separation and the powers of the particular branches in Papers 47–83. If the legislature were to be tainted by the spirit of party and faction, then the importance of the executive and judiciary in preventing "unsteadiness and injustice" would be all the greater. What is more, *Federalist* 10's discussion proceeds without discriminating the legislature into two houses; the importance of the Senate would, *ceteris paribus*, also be enhanced by this analysis.

A closer consideration reveals, however, that the problem of faction in the legislature is the epitome of politics in general. "No man is allowed to be a judge in his own cause," Publius writes, "because his interest would certainly bias his judgment, and, not improbably, corrupt his integrity. With equal, nay with greater reason, a body of men are unfit to be both judges and parties at the same time; yet what are many of the most important acts of legislation but so many judicial determinations . . . ?" Republican politics, after all, consists in self-government, and self-government implies that men can take responsibility for judging themselves as parties to their own causes. Indeed, men *are* their own causes, particularly in the state of nature, where the fact that each is the sole judge of himself leads to anarchy. The problem of judging one's own cause seems merely to have been transferred from the state of nature to civil society, from individuals to parties and factions of men. For as Publius comments in Number 51, "In a society under the forms of which the stronger faction can readily unite and oppress the weaker, anarchy may as truly be said to reign as in a state of nature, where the weaker individual is not secured against the violence of the stronger. . . ."[48]

With this thought we reach the heart of the problem: so long as factions exist in society, and in particular so long as a majority faction threatens, the state of nature has not been overcome. It is not just that rights are insecure, but that men still act as if their passions (or their reason acting, so to speak, on the orders of their passions) and not the law were the measure of right. These men are not yet citizens; they lack the virtues that make them worthy of citizenship. The studied ambiguity in Publius's language evinces the problem. He speaks in Number 51 of "the stronger faction" oppressing "the weaker," as if there were no nonfactious groups in society at all. Yet justice "ought to hold the balance between them," and justice is "the end of government" and of "civil society." Surely justice cannot be obtained by replacing the anarchy of the state of nature with the regulated anarchy (such paradoxical terms are necessary) of a civil society that does nothing for, or to, its members other than encouraging their appetites with a view to what has been called the "saving multiplicity of factions"—so many that no one faction (a majority faction) can consistently rule. The difficulty with this thesis, however, is that Publius never speaks of a "multiplicity of factions"; he speaks of a "multiplicity of interests."[49]

Now, it is true that a majority or minority united and actuated by an *unjust* interest is a faction. But not all interests are unjust. Publius plays on the ambiguities of the term "interest" by using it sometimes as almost a synonym for faction, sometimes as meaning a legitimate claim under the rules of justice. The problem, in brief, is to lift unjust interests up to justice, or at least to see to it that factious interests are not simply checked but so checked as to allow nonfactious interests to predominate, thus encouraging the former to become more reasonable in order to be more successful.[50]

Although self-government inevitably requires parties to judge their own causes, this is not fatal to good government if the parties are virtuous, and part of Publius's effort is to inculcate a certain kind of virtue in American citizens. In keeping with the respect for law and especially for the Constitution that he teaches them, Publius will elevate the status of the judiciary in the new government by confirming or inventing its power to review laws for their constitutionality. By separating the partisan or factious politics of the legislature from the judging of the Supreme Court, he reminds citizens of their obligation to be more than partisans of factions, and helps to insulate the government against the people's weaker moments. In the same manner, while deprecating the "vain" notion that "enlightened statesmen will be able to adjust these clashing interests and render them all subservient to the public good," for the sensible reason that "enlightened statesmen will not always be at the helm," he admonishes the people not to count on the intervention of others to save them—thus encouraging them to be mindful of their own responsibility. "Nor, in many cases, can such an adjustment be made at all without taking into view indirect and remote considerations, which will rarely prevail over the immediate interest" of the parties. Publius himself is the great tutor in the importance of "indirect and remote considerations," and in the second part of *The Federalist* readers learn the wisdom of having a senate, an energetic executive, and an independent judiciary precisely to emphasize these considerations to the people. The quick dismissal of statesmanship as an answer to the problem of faction reflects the low horizon of necessity that characterizes the argument in the first part of the book. It is not Publius's final word on the subject, but it is an ironic depreciation of his own function that accords with the rhetorical needs of the whole work and his own pseudonymous character: the Roman Publius Valerius, from whom the American Publius borrows his name, was renowned for renouncing his own power and emphasizing "the majesty of the democracy"—consequently increasing his own authority over the democrats, and providing *bona fides* for future republican magistrates.[51]

CONTROLLING THE EFFECTS OF FACTION

After canvassing the possible methods of eliminating the causes of faction, Publius turns to the second half of his argument. "The inference to which we are brought is that the *causes* of faction cannot be removed and that relief is only to be sought in the means of controlling its *effects*." If the faction is a minority, the republican principle of majority rule provides a remedy. If the faction is a majority, the problem is acute; the very "form of popular government . . . enables it to sacrifice to its ruling passion or interest both the public good and the rights of other citizens." The republican form, reduced to the principle of majority rule, is incapable of securing private rights and the public good. This too is in keeping with the horizon of the book's first part: the republican form has not been seen in relation to the true ends of republican government, of good government. Accordingly, from the assumption that the "first object of government" is the protection of men's diverse faculties, the ends of government in Number 10 appear to be "the public good and private rights," two separate but related goals—separate, because the faculties of men are diverse, i.e., some are spirited and political while some are acquisitive and private; related, because the manipulation of the latter seems essential to gratifying the former. But when the end of government is seen as the "safety and happiness of society" (as in the second part of *The Federalist*), then private rights and the public good become two aspects of a single common good.[52]

Having been brought to the "inference" (not a demonstrated conclusion) that the causes of majority faction cannot be removed, Publius takes up the possibility of controlling its effects. Two means present themselves: "Either the existence of the same passion or interest in a majority at the same time must be prevented, or the majority, having such coexistent passion or interest, must be rendered, by their number and local situation, unable to concert and carry into effect their schemes of oppression." Either the "impulse" or the "opportunity" must be prevented. But for all its familiarity Publius's reasoning is genuinely puzzling: if "giving to every citizen the same opinions, the same passions, and the same interests" is a way of curing the causes of faction, would not preventing "the existence of the same passion or interest in a majority" amount to the same thing? Does not preventing the "impulse" mean dealing with the *causes* rather than the *effects* of faction? And is not preventing the "opportunity" merely another way of treating the causes of faction by abolishing or restricting the liberty that is faction's precondition? Publius is careful again not to say that the existence of the same *opinion* in a majority is to be prevented, nor that a majority's opportunity to act on the basis of that opinion ought to be prevented. Publius is teaching the majority (not necessarily "every citizen") a common opinion that will check majority faction, and that is necessary even for the extended sphere to control factions based on interest. The majority should not attempt to rule in its own name; for the sake of the success and honor of republican government, the many must yield to the law—to the Constitution. This opinion will be cultivated in the course of the second section of *The Federalist* until it becomes clear that the people must not only acquiesce in but revere or venerate the Constitution. In practice, therefore, the people must also respect the offices established under it; they must try to select the best men for the job, or, in the case of those officers selected indirectly (the president, senators, and Supreme Court justices), the people must recognize the special virtues or functions of the offices that justify the indirect selection.[53] Thus the people's own impulses are recruited to the regime's assistance, and the majority is persuaded of the justice and advantage of representative rather than direct government.

Publius deals with causes while seeming to deal only with effects: he teaches informally, and shapes the character of American citizens indirectly. This is appropriate to his own status as a literary rather than (like the Roman Publius) an actual statesman; and as an unelected or unauthorized interpreter of the fundamental law, which (unlike Roman law) does not claim to be divine.[54] Insofar as Publius removes the causes of faction, the "efficacy" of the cure for the mischiefs of faction comes not from the Union but from the Constitution and its interpreter, Publius himself. Publius's respectful indirection thus leads to the topic of representation, and to his famous distinction between republican and democratic government. "From this view of the subject" he declares, "it may be concluded that a pure democracy, by which I mean a society consisting of a small number of citizens, who assemble and administer the government in person, can admit of no cure for the mischiefs of faction." "From this view of the subject," but perhaps not from a more political or constitutional view. In contrast to a "pure" democracy, a republic is a popular government "in which a scheme of representation takes place." But this definition proves somewhat elusive. Publius had called the democracies of Greece and Italy "petty republics" in Number 9, and in Number 63 he repeats the error, calling Sparta, Rome, and Carthage republics, and noting that "the difference most relied on between the American and other republics consists in the principle of representation." He admits, however, that "the position concerning the ignorance of the ancient governments on the subject of representation is by no means precisely true in the latitude commonly given to it." Even in "the most pure democracies of Greece," there was representation, and "similar instances might be traced in most, if not all, the popular governments of antiquity." Publius concludes, then, that "the true distinction between these and the American governments lies *in the total exclusion of the people in their collective capacity* from any share in the *latter*, and not in the *total exclusion of representatives of the people* from the administration of the *former*." He reveals the "true distinction" only after his account of the principle of separated powers, only in the second part of *The Federalist*. In Number 10 he obscures this distinction, preferring to "heighten the advantages" of the Union or of republicanism based upon the Union by setting up the straw man of "pure democracy." Once "pure democracy" is discredited as the standard for popular governments, Publius can defend the American republic as "wholly popular" despite the fact or rather because of the fact that it is exclusively representative. In Number 10, speaking especially to the "friend of popular governments," he confines himself to the distinction between the republican form and "pure democracy"—and it is the former alone that can admit of a cure for "the mischiefs of faction," because it alone derives an "efficacy" from the Union.[55]

REPRESENTATION AND THE EXTENDED SPHERE

The cure depends upon the two "great points of difference" between the two forms of popular government: in a republic the government is delegated to "a small number of citizens elected by the rest," and (therefore) a republic may extend to a "greater number of citizens and greater sphere of country." At first glance the differences seem to be entirely numerical, in keeping with the democratic or popular character of the distinction under discussion, and with the fact that in Number 10 representation turns out to be a derivative advantage. Representation will "refine and enlarge the public views by passing them through the medium of a chosen body of citizens, whose wisdom may best discern the true interest of their country and whose patriotism and love of justice will be least likely to sacrifice it to temporary or partial considerations." When the "public voice" is passed through the "medium" of the representatives, it "may well happen" that it is "more consonant to the public good than if pronounced by the people themselves, convened for the purpose." We thus see that representation, working through the forms of the Constitution, turns interests into "views" that can be shaped to the "public good." Interests cease to be factious insofar as they become based on opinions of what is due to one within the limits of a common or ruling opinion of justice. When interests adopt "public views" they have been constitutionalized; and as part of the "public good" they can be both represented and regulated. Thus the "public voice" is a rational expression or set of expressions that can be harmonized; it is not a tumult. It appears then that representation is especially for the sake of the public good (rather than the rights of individuals) and is a kind of substitute for or rehabilitation of the "enlightened statesmen" dismissed earlier. It offers the few, who have already been shown the insufficiency of their claim to rule, a place and a calling under the Constitution, without injuring the equal rights of other men. It therefore plays a role in preventing minority faction. But representation also helps to prevent majority faction, insofar as it prevents the "opportunity" by excluding the people from playing any collective role in the administration of the government, and prevents the "impulse" by allowing the people to look to, and to heed, their representatives' wisdom, patriotism, and love of justice.[56]

The aristocratic tones of the latter are too much for "the friend of popular government" to bear, however, and so Publius quickly retreats from representation to the extended sphere as the cure for the mischiefs of faction. "On the other hand," he observes, "the effect may be inverted." Rather than men of wisdom, patriotism, and justice, the people may find themselves saddled with "men of factious tempers, of local prejudices, or of sinister designs." We note that faction appears, from the standpoint of representation, as a problem of character or of the soul: "men of factious tempers" have usurped men of wisdom. To ensure that the effect is not inverted, Publius seeks the greatest probability of electing "proper guardians of the public weal"; his question is "whether small or extensive republics are more favorable" to this outcome. And the question is "clearly decided in favor of the latter," he holds, "by two obvious considerations." Republics are now the only defensible kind of popular government; "pure" democracy, which now appears not as pure but as debased, as popular government without a constitution, is returned to where Aristotle had left it, a bad form of government, and the republic or constitutional democracy becomes the standard of good popular government. The debate between "pure democracy" and the republican form is thus transformed into a debate between small and large republics, and the latter is settled on the same basis as the former. In both cases, the question of representation, which is linked to the structure of government, is absorbed into the question of size, which turns upon the Union. Whereas initially it had appeared that representation would prevent the "impulse" to majority faction and the extended sphere would prevent the "opportunity," it is now up to the sphere to prevent both.

The two "obvious considerations" that decide in favor of the large republic are, however, far from obvious. In the first place, Publius argues that in a large republic the probability of making a "fit choice" for office will be greater because the people will choose, other things being equal, from a greater pool of "fit characters." But even if Publius's conditions are granted, his conclusion assumes that the people will take advantage of the wider choice, that they will choose well; for surely there is also a greater pool of *unfit* characters in the competition. In the second place, Publius argues that with larger electoral districts, it will be more difficult "for unworthy candidates to practice with success the vicious arts by which elections are too often carried." But in larger districts new arts of advertising, image making, and public relations may spring up to replace the "vicious arts" of old. Nonetheless, Publius makes explicit his assumption that when the suffrage of the people is "more free," they are more likely to pick men of "the most attractive merit and the most diffusive and established characters." By collapsing the issue of representation into the question of size, Publius shows his readers the democratic bent of the argument for the extended sphere, and underlines the emphasis on the legislature that pervades Number 10. He gives no hint of what he will later discourse on at length, the tendency of the offices established by the Constitution, particularly the presidency and the Senate, to attract men "pre-eminent for ability and virtue." In Number 10, the explanation remains on the level of the Union.[57]

The other great difference between a democracy and a republic, then, is "the greater number of citizens and extent of territory" that the latter may encompass; "and it is this circumstance principally which renders factious combinations less to be dreaded in the former than in the latter." Publius's reasoning is brisk and impressive: "The smaller the society, the fewer probably will be the distinct parties and interests composing it; the fewer the distinct parties and interests, the more frequently will a majority be found of the same party; and the smaller the number of individuals composing a majority, and the smaller the compass within which they are placed, the more easily will they concert and execute their plans of oppression." Publius summons his famous conclusion: "Extend the sphere and you take in a greater variety of parties and interests; you make it less probable that a majority of the whole will have a common motive to invade the rights of other citizens; or if such a common motive exists, it will be more difficult for all who feel it to discover their own strength and to act in unison with each other."[58]

This second solution to the problem of majority faction is Publius's way of revisiting and rehabilitating the second method of removing the causes of faction. Even as representation is, in one view, a way of restricting the people's liberty, so preventing the majority from having the same interest is a way of giving everyone a "common motive" to conceive of himself as a minority, as one whose rights are endangered. Through such an opinion, it is, as Publius remarks in Number 11 in a different connection, possible to "take away the motive to such combinations by inducing an impracticability of success." As presented by Publius, the extended sphere is an automatic governor that restrains our politics by nonpartisan or mechanical or indeed virtually quantitative means. That it raises no partisan claim—more precisely, that it checks democratic claims by democratic means, encouraging various interests to flourish freely—and that its operation seems automatic, only serves to commend it more highly to "the friend of popular government." But its seemingly ineluctable working becomes a kind of self-fulfilling prophecy, militating against both the ardor and the injustice of a potential majority faction.[59]

Still, thinking of oneself always as a threatened minority is as little suitable for decent republican politics as a faction's constant self-aggrandizement. It is, of course, necessary to ensure in a republic that majorities are moderate and just—are *constitutional*, in the profoundest sense of the term. But to the extent that majority rule is the republican principle, majorities must rule: the political life of the regime must be lived. "In the extended republic of the United States," Publius declares in Number 51, ". . . a coalition of a majority of the whole society could seldom take place on any other principles than those of justice and the general good." On the basis of the prevailing interpretation of *Federalist* 10, however, it is hard to see how any majority, especially a just one, could be formed athwart the various and interfering factions. When it is seen that Publius is contending not for a multiplicity of factions but of interests, and these informed by a common opinion, the way from *Federalist* 10 to republican politics (and to the rest of *The Federalist*) opens up. To indicate that the citizens of America are not to be regarded simply as members of factions or as legislative claimants, Publius speaks to his readers as fellow founders: "Extend the sphere and *you* take in a greater variety of interests and parties," he tells them; "*you* make it less probable that a majority of the whole will have a common motive to invade the rights of other citizens. . . ." The "friend of popular governments" can join with "our most considerate and virtuous citizens" in the act of founding a republican government that is purged so far as possible of the danger of majority faction. But that partnership in founding becomes a common citizenship in the course of *The Federalist*'s whole argument.[60]

This common citizenship is based on common principles, on the principles of the Revolution especially as they are embodied in the Constitution. The veneration of the Constitution and its principles is the form that this citizenship takes in common opinion. For in the last analysis, the security of the people's rights depends "altogether . . . on public opinion, and on the general spirit of the people and of the government." But that public opinion is itself partially a product of the "general spirit" of the people and their government, of the Constitution that Publius urges them to respect. Republican government cannot rest on opinion alone, but it cannot be either safe or happy without having its ruling public opinion anchored in the Constitution and dedicated to its perpetuation. Publius writes to "fortify" this opinion by inculcating certain truths about republican constitutionalism that many previous republicans and many of the opponents of the Constitution had either denied or overlooked.[61]

   This purpose is not fulfilled in *Federalist* 10 or in the first half of *The Federalist*, but these papers prepare the way for the actual discussion of the Constitution in the second part. The qualifications that the latter imposes on *Federalist* 10 have been indicated, but they deserve to be restated plainly: Number 10 overstates the case for the extended sphere, though for good rhetorical purposes. In expounding the Senate in Number 63, Publius confesses what he had refused to say in Number 10, that "the same extended situation which will exempt the people of America from some of the dangers incident to lesser republics will expose them to the inconveniency of remaining for a longer time under the influence of those misrepresentations which the combined industry of interested men may succeed in distributing among them." The extended sphere does not provide a fully effective "republican remedy for the diseases most incident to republican government." Although a large republic is necessary to alleviate faction, it is not only not sufficient to the purpose, but can actually make the problem worse. The root of the problem is that Publius has not yet shown what are "the true principles of republican government"; hence the republican diseases have been inadequately diagnosed and the "republican remedy" too easily prescribed. Publius reiterates the importance of a large republic in Number 63, but he subordinates it to the proper kind of representation—in this case, to a properly constructed Senate—because the mischiefs of faction are now described as "misrepresentations," and their proper cure is good representation. "It adds no small weight to all these considerations," he writes, "to recollect that history informs us of no long-lived republic which had not a senate," and he proceeds to consider the examples of Sparta, Rome, and Carthage. Those "petty republics" whose "transient and fleeting brilliancy" had engaged Publius's attention in Number 10 turn out to include "long-lived" republics that, though in some respects "repugnant to the genius of America," nonetheless had managed prudently to "blend stability with liberty."[62]
   Whereas in Number 10 representation had been for the sake of the extended sphere—and the Constitution for the sake of the Union—in Number 63 the sphere is for the sake of the right kind of representation: the size of the Union allows the exclusion of the people from the administration of the government to have its full salutary effect. To put it differently, when the principle of separated powers is finally established in Papers 47–51, its primary constitutional effect is to allow and encourage the people to venerate the Constitution by removing it from their grasp, by elevating it above their factious passions and interests. But in this manner it becomes the object to which the people's passions and interests are harnassed by the opinion concerning the Constitution's goodness—and concerning the proper conduct of good government under its provisions—that Publius does so much to foster. In this great achievement the extended sphere plays an indispensable but still a subordinate role: it ministers to what Abraham Lincoln would later call our political religion.

2

Anti-Federalism in *The Federalist:* A Founding Dialogue on the Constitution, Republican Government, and Federalism

MURRAY DRY

The Federalist is usually studied standing alone, as the definitive account of the Constitution. After all, Alexander Hamilton and James Madison, the two major authors, were both members of the Federal Convention, and Madison is generally regarded as the "Father of the Constitution." Moreover, *The Federalist's* full explanation of the Constitution's provisions, as well as its argument for a strong government, remain impressive and instructive today.

Both the form and the substance of the work, however, suggest that it can best be studied in conjunction with the Anti-Federalist opposition. Not only was most of *The Federalist* first published in the form of newspaper essays supporting the Constitution's ratification, but much of the text is directed against the opponents' arguments. Indeed, Publius promises "to give a satisfactory answer to all the objections which shall have made their appearance that may seem to have any claim to your attention."[1] One might not discern this, however, from *The Federalist's* scant seven references to Anti-Federalists by name—all occurring in the last eighteen essays on the executive and judicial branches. In Number 67, Publius devotes the entire essay to critizing Cato's mistaken notion that the president's power to make temporary appointments, while the Senate is in recess, extends to senators as well. In Number 68, he refers to Federal Farmer's approval of the election of the president. In Number 69, he disagrees with Tamony on the source of the English king's prerogative. In Number 73, he mentions Abraham Yates as an opponent who first opposed the executive's veto but later supported it. In Number 78, while supporting judicial independence as a way of guarding the Constitution and the rights of individuals, he professes his attachment to the people's right to alter or abolish their government. Here he chides the Pennsylvania Minority and Luther Martin for allegedly opposing that right. The last two references, in Number 83, criticize the Constitution as then drafted for failing to secure trial by jury. Only here do Publius's specific references to the Anti-Federalists—in this case to the reports of the Pennsylvania Minority and the Massachusetts Convention— involve a serious objection.[2]

I am not sure why these items were selected for attribution to the Anti-Federalists, since virtually every important objection that was made to the Constitution is taken up in *The Federalist.* For example, the argument of the famous tenth Federalist is directed against the common view, pressed by the Anti-Federalists, that republics can exist only within a small territory having a small population. The argument for the complex version of separation of powers embodied in the Constitution, in Numbers 47–51, replies to distinct Anti-Federalist challenges to that arrangement. And the case for judicial review, as it is made in Number 78, takes issue with the Anti-Federalist Brutus's very fine argument against it. Finally, the most fundamental Anti-Federalist critique concerns federalism, and, as we shall see, Publius engages in a virtual dialogue with Brutus and Federal Farmer on both the definition of federalism (Numbers 9 and 39) and on the extent of the legislative powers, especially the tax and war powers (Numbers 23–36). In general, one imagines that Publius did not consider it rhetorically effective to give recognition to his opponents, especially where they had a strong case; although on the question of the jury trial, Publius may have concluded that his opponents had been making headway and that a response showing the limitations of their own proposals could be useful.

This essay examines the parts of the ratification debate that preoccupied Publius—republican government and federalism. In the first place, this is necessary because the Federalists were often responding to the Anti-Federalists, and so the opponents' arguments must be made clear in order to understand the argument for Constitution. A second point concerns the Anti-Federalists' own contribution. Herbert Storing, whose authoritative edition of the Anti-Federalist writings facilitates our full understanding of this debate, has argued that the Anti-Federalists "played an indispensable if subordinate part in the founding process."[3] Storing saw the Anti-Federalists as expressing sound moral reservations about the possibility that republican self-government could prosper by relying so fundamentally on "enlightened self-interest" and ambition checking ambition. The argument of this essay, while in agreement with Storing, will concern itself with the constitutional alternatives offered by the Anti-Federalists.

I have chosen the two best Anti-Federalist writings as the counterpart to *The Federalist:* the "Letters of Brutus" and the "Letters of the Federal Farmer." The eighteenth-century practice of writing under pseudonyms was intended to highlight the importance of reasoned argument. Unfortunately for the Anti-Federalists' claims to fame, their identification remains uncertain even today. For example, the essays of Brutus were attributed by Paul Leicester Ford to Robert Yates of New York, but on little evidence. Yet Brutus is surely more open to the proposed Constitution than was Yates, on the basis of the latter's opposition to the Virginia Plan in the Federal Convention and his subsequent brief "Reasons of Dissent," co-authored by John Lansing, his Convention colleague. The Federal Farmer has been identified as Richard Henry Lee, but the only evidence is one contemporary reference. Storing, William Winslow Crosskey, and Gordon Wood all came to doubt this identification, partly because Lee's public letter of opposition does not emphasize the same argument that Federal Farmer does, and partly because if Lee had been the author of these well-known and highly regarded Letters, it is surprising that he never acknowledged authorship. Nor did Lee's grandson and early biographer attribute the "Letters of the Federal Farmer" to Lee.[4]

These Anti-Federalist writings were published in New York newspapers during the publication of *The Federalist,* and in many cases it is clear that Publius is replying directly to Brutus or to Federal Farmer.[5] To place this "debate" on republican government and federalism in its proper context, I shall begin with three related points of departure: how each side understood the issue facing the country; how each side viewed the other; and what each thought about foundings in general and the Convention's compromises in particular.

I. STARTING POINTS FOR THE TWO PARTIES

Publius begins *Federalist* 1 by linking the fate of the new Constitution with the existence of the Union and "the fate of an empire, in many respects the most interesting in the world." He concludes by saying that "we already hear it whispered in the private circles of those who oppose the new constitution," that the country is too large for "any general system," and that resort must be had to separate confederacies (p. 36). This charge, which Publius repeats at the beginning of *Federalist* 2 (p. 37), was not true of Brutus, Federal Farmer, or even Patrick Henry. Moreover, aside from a statement of Luther Martin's in the Federal Convention that he would favor dissolution of the Union if equality of the states was abandoned, there seems to be no evidence that the Anti-Federalists favored separate confederacies.

On the contrary, both Federal Farmer and Brutus begin by acknowledging the country's critical period, demonstrating that the assessment was not the creation of later Federalist historians.[6] Federal Farmer even admits "that our federal system is defective, and that some of the state governments are not well administered." Both emphasize the importance of full deliberation, however, because "when the people once part with power, they can seldom or never resume it again but by force," and hasty and blind changes will wear down the better part of the community and cause it to accept despotism.[7] For these writers, the question is not union versus separation, but confederation versus consolidation—or more precisely, whether the proposed Constitution is compatible with confederation, and hence with republican government. They feared that it was not, at least in its present form. "The plan of government now proposed is evidently calculated totally to change, in time, our condition as a people. Instead of thirteen republics, under a federal head, it is clearly designed to be one consolidated government."[8]

Publius obviously prefers to begin *The Federalist* with a discussion of the utility of union rather than with the question of federalism versus consolidation. It would have been difficult for him to do that if he had conceded that the opponents accepted the importance of union.

Both sides agree that the times are critical, that something must be done, and that disinterested, public-spirited deliberation is in order. They disagree over which side benefits most from interested parties. Publius refers to attachments to state governments (No. 1, p. 34), while Federal Farmer refers to "those who expect employment under the new constitution" as well as "those weak and ardent men who always expect to be gainers by revolutions."[9] Publius pretends to be unaware of such motives when he argues that the crisis excuses the "predetermined patron" but the predetermined opponent "must be culpable" (No. 37, p. 225).

Moving from interested parties to his true addressees, Publius, again in the first essay, gives an excellent description of the two sides' principles (especially from his perspective) and the manner in which they are misrepresented.

An enlightened zeal for the energy and efficiency of government will be stigmatized, as the off-spring of a temper fond of despotic power and hostile to the principles of liberty. An overscrupulous jealousy of danger to the rights of the people, which is more commonly the fault of the head than the heart, will be represented as mere pretense and artifice; the bait for popularity at the expense of public good. [*Federalist* 1, p. 35]

The first position, with which Publius soon expresses agreement, is sound, since "the vigour of government is essential to the security of liberty." The Anti-Federalist position, however, is misguided, if well intentioned, and dangerous, since "a dangerous ambition more often lurks behind the specious mask of zeal for the rights of the people than under the forbidding appearance of zeal for the firmness and efficiency of government" (No. 1, p. 35).

I have not found a comparable Anti-Federalist description of the principles of both parties. In light of the following statement of Federal Farmer, I think he might adopt Publius's formulation—as it relates to energy and efficiency versus republican jealousy—but draw a different conclusion.

> In viewing the various governments instituted by mankind, we see their whole force reducible to two principles—the important springs which alone move the machines, and give them their intended influence and control, are force and persuasion: by the former men are compelled, by the latter they are drawn. . . . Our true object is to give full efficacy to one principle, to arm persuasion on every side, and to render force as little necessary as possible.[10]

Our final preliminary topic concerns foundings and the work of the Federal Convention. Brutus urges caution, since "when the people once part with power, they can seldom or never resume it again but by force." He also identifies a full declaration of rights with "forming a government on its true principles."[11] Publius, on the other hand, in *Federalist* 37 and 38, argues against rejecting the Constitution in the name of a perfect but impracticable solution. He introduces theoretical speculations concerning nature, man, and speech to explain why political boundaries cannot be drawn precisely. Then, reflecting on all the divisions in the Federal Convention, Publius notes that the "man of candor" must experience "astonishment" that they were surmounted, while "the man of pious reflection . . . perceive[s] in [the Convention's unanimity], a finger of that Almighty hand which has been so frequently and signally extended to our relief in the critical stages of the revolution" (No. 37, pp. 230–231). Since Madison saw many of his important proposals rejected in the Convention—e.g., the national negative, the council of revision, proportional representation in the Senate—we may conclude that Publius's candor does not prevent him from appealing to the faithful on their own terms. Publius goes on, in *Federalist* 38, to compare the Federal Convention's work favorably to ancient foundings, to attribute whatever errors may be found to lack of experience, and to charge the opponents of the Constitution with an inability to agree on any other plan (No. 37, pp. 234–237).

The framers dealt with the major divisions in the country so successfully that those divisions were not prominent in the ratification debate. In addition to the "Great Compromise" between the large and the small states, the Convention had to deal with the sectional division in the country. This was taken up in the apportionment rule for the lower house, which also affected the election of the executive; and in a compromise over navigation acts and slave importation. By the first, the infamous "three-fifths" clause aimed at giving the South rough parity in representation; by the second, the South allowed the North a right to pass tariffs, without requiring a special majority for this act of commercial regulation, in exchange for a twenty-year guarantee of slave importation.[12] While Brutus briefly objected to counting slaves in the apportionment,[13] the sectional compromises generated little opposition.

Furthermore, since they conceded the need for a stronger government, Brutus and Federal Farmer did not emphasize the legal objections to ratification. Those who did—Luther Martin was the most prominent—could point not only to the limited authorization from Congress to make proposals "for the sole and express purpose of revising the Articles of Confederation," but also to the requirement, in the thirteenth article of that constitution, that amendments pass Congress and *every* state legislature.[14] Federal Farmer expresses regret over "the non-attendance of eight or nine men who were appointed," but he also acknowledges that the plan is one "of accommodation, and that it is in this way only, and by giving up a part of our opinions, that we can ever expect to obtain a government founded in freedom and compact."[15]

Both sides, then, promise a candid discussion of the Constitution, and the most thoughtful Anti-Federalists concede the need for a strengthening of the federal Constitution. Brutus and Federal Farmer even agree that the proposed Constitution provides a better starting point than the Articles of Confederation. But the Anti-Federalist focus on federalism and the threat of a consolidation of all power in the national government—in contrast to Publius's emphasis on the needs of union—highlights the major division. Before we turn to the debate on federalism, however, it will be useful to examine what lies behind that debate: two different views of republican government.

II. REPUBLICAN GOVERNMENT

Brutus begins his discussion of republican government shortly after asking whether the United States "should be reduced to one great republic," which is the meaning of "consolidation," or "whether they should continue thirteen confederated republics."[16] He quotes the following passage from Montesquieu's *Spirit of the Laws:*

> It is natural to a republic to have only a small territory, otherwise it cannot long subsist. In a large republic, there are men of large fortunes, and consequently of less moderation; there are trusts too great to be placed in any single subject; he has interest of his own; he soon begins to think that he may be happy, great and glorious, by oppressing his fellow citizens; and that he may raise himself to grandeur on the ruins of his country. In a large republic, the public good is sacrificed to a thousand views; it is subordinate to exceptions, and depends on accidents. In a small one, the interest of the public is easier perceived, better understood, and more within the reach of every citizen; abuses are of less extent, and of course are less protected.[17]

In Montesquieu's republic—as opposed to monarchy, which is another form of free government—the public good takes precedence over individual liberty. Both equality and frugality support it, and the small size facilitates citizen oversight. In addition, a certain homogeneity is important. "In a republic," Brutus writes, "the manners, sentiments, and interests of the people should be similar."[18] In that connection, Federal Farmer questioned the Constitution's liberal qualifications for election to office, which included only age, residency, and citizenship for a certain number of years. "It can be no objection to the elected, that they are Christians, Pagans, Mahometans, or Jews; that they are of any colour, rich or poor, convict or not. Hence, many men may be elected who cannot be electors."[19]

The Anti-Federalists depart from Montesquieu's account of republican government in two ways, however. First, Montesquieu makes no reference to representation in his discussion of republics, and, with one notable exception—Maryland Farmer, who advocated direct citizen voting analagous to the Swiss cantons—the Anti-Federalist "small republic" argument is joined to an argument for substantial representation. Second, the Anti-Federalists, in agreement with the Federalists, start with liberty, not virtue (as Montesquieu does) as the principle of republican government.[20] However, the Anti-Federalists embrace a view of liberty that gives greater emphasis to mild government and to citizen participation than Publius does.

Federal Farmer, for example, describes "the essential parts of a free and good government" as "a full and equal representation of the people in the legislature, and the jury trial in the vicinage in the administration of justice." And in his next letter, he writes

> The great object of a free people must be so to form their government and laws, and so to administer them, as to create a confidence in, and respect for the laws; and thereby induce the sensible and virtuous part of the community to declare in favor of the laws, and to support them without an expensive military force.[21]

Substantial representation and jury trial, in civil as well as criminal cases, and on issues of law as well as fact, "are the means by which the people are let into the knowledge of public affairs—are enabled to stand as the guardians of each others' rights, and to restrain, by regular and legal measures, those who otherwise might infringe upon them."[22] Federal Farmer could have gone further in his advocacy of jury trial, since, while a substantial representation gives more citizens experience in government than a smaller representation does, every citizen can expect to serve on a jury from time to time. Hence every citizen learns about government by sharing in public deliberation and decision making.

Now let us turn to Publius's account of republican government. Noting that "no other form would be reconcilable with the genius of the people of America," he offers this definition in *Federalist* 39:

we may define a republic to be, or at least may bestow that name on, a government which derives all its powers directly or indirectly from the great body of the people; and is administered by persons holding their offices during pleasure, for a limited period, or during good behavior. It is *essential* to such a government, that it be derived from the great body of the society, not from an inconsiderable portion, or a favored class of it; otherwise a handful of tyrannical nobles, exercising their oppressions by a delegation of their powers, might aspire to the rank of republicans, and claim for their government the honorable title of republic. It is *sufficient* for such a government, that the persons administering it be appointed, either directly or indirectly, by the people; otherwise every government in the United States, as well as every other popular government that has been or can be well organized or well executed, would be degraded from the republican character. [No. 39, pp. 240–241]

In his recent book on *The Federalist*, David Epstein notes that this definition would encompass Hamilton's plan in the Federal Convention (with its governor and senate for good behavior). He also points out that Publius presents a narrower statement, in *Federalist* 37, according to which "'the genius of republican liberty,'... seemed to require short terms and a large number of officers."[23] While Epstein is apparently satisfied with Publius's main definition, the Anti-Federalists are not. I think the reason for this is that Epstein agrees with Publius on the importance of ambition for political life.[24] The constitutional arrangement that is expounded and defended so ably in *The Federalist* assumes the legitimacy of interest and ambition, and constructs a system of elective offices that channels interests and ambitions into public service. A brief review of some of the major *Federalist* arguments illustrates this point.

The argument of *Federalist* 10 is based on two principles that reveal a different approach to republican government from the Anti-Federalists'. First, the protection of diverse faculties among men, specifically, "different and unequal faculties of acquiring property," "is the first object of government" (No. 10, p. 78). Second, the republican principle, which is majority rule, is so established in America that constitution makers must focus on restraining its abuses in order to secure the other objects of good government, "the rights of other citizens and the permanent and aggregate interests of the community" (No. 10, p. 78). These principles form the basis for an argument for the "large republic," which shifts the locus of power from the states to the national government, and, within that government, from the legislature as a whole to the senate and the executive branches, and, one should add, to an independent judiciary. Moreover, the argument stands on its own, without any reference to the exigencies of union; that is, unlike the discussions (considered below) of the need for adequate powers for the national defense, this argument claims that nothing will be lost and everything will be gained, in terms of republican government, by the larger sphere.

By drawing on diversity as it does, Publius's argument assumes and even fosters inequality and a separation of the people from the government. For example, when Publius defines republic in terms of representation, in contrast to democracy (we would say, direct democracy), he notes that the resulting refinement of a republic—that the people do not govern directly but through others—can have good or ill effects. But will the effects be better in the small or the large republic? He answers that it will be better in the latter case, since there will be greater competition for the proportionally fewer places, assuming that the people will choose the fit characters and not be deceived by capable demogogues. To this answer there are two noteworthy Anti-Federalist responses. First, assuming Publius is right about the people's capacity to judge, in the few cases where a demagogue succeeds on the national level, he will do greater damage than at the state level. Second, even if the refinement works as predicted, it may well establish a permanent division between the governors and the governed. This will be so if the effect of a large population and extended territory is that only a certain class is capable of winning. To have the right to vote for one's governors is not the same as governing; nor does it guarantee confidence in government, and hence a mild government, if the people are not familiar with the individuals elected and if the elected are not substantially like the people.

Publius's first reply to the Anti-Federalist argument is to deny that what they wanted is possible, meaning consistent with popular elections. "The idea of an actual representation of all classes of the people by persons of each class is altogether visionary. Unless it were expressly provided in the Constitution that each different occupation should send one or more members the thing would never take place in practice" (No. 35, p. 214). Publius proceeds to sketch out a tripartite "trickle down" theory of representation: mechanics and manufacturers will be represented by merchants, who uphold the commercial interest; small landholders will be represented by large landholders, with whom they share a common interest vis-à-vis objects of taxation; and the lawyers and other men of the learned professions will act as arbitrators (No. 35, p. 216).

There is an element of deference in this prescription that is not likely to overcome the Anti-Federalist suspicion of a conflict between the few in government, or the few who influence it, and the many, who are outside it and without influence. This is especially true when one considers that large landholders' interests will often diverge from small landholders' interests, and that the former may be better clients for the lawyers than the latter.

Publius returns to this subject in *Federalist* 57, where he responds to the charge that those elected "will be out of sympathy with the mass of the people" and likely to "sacrifice . . . the many to the aggrandizement of the few." Publius describes this as "the most extraordinary" objection to the Constitution. While it "is leveled against a pretended oligarchy, the principle of it strikes at the very root of republican government" (No. 57, p. 350). Since Publius was aware of the more restricted definition of republic, and since he knew that his extended sphere argument departed from the traditional assumptions about republican government, his expression of shock must be taken with a grain of salt. Publius begins by reminding his readers that the Constitution establishes no special class or standards for electors or elected—other than age, citizenship, and residency, in the latter case, or what the states set for themselves, in the former. After discussing duty, gratitude, interest, and ambition as cords that bind the representative to his constituents, Publius remarks that the difference between federal and state districts is roughly the difference between five to six thousand and as many hundred constituents. "Will it be pretended that this difference is sufficient to justify an attachment to the State Governments and an abhorrence to the Federal Government?" He replies to his own question that with so many to choose from, "a fit representative would be most likely to be found." This is part of the argument of *Federalist* 10. The Anti-Federalist reply is that skillfulness in elections may go together with dishonesty or a lack of sympathy for the common citizen. After appealing to the British experience with representation in the House of Commons (the Anti-Federalists could distinguish this case, by referring to the class-based character of British bicameralism), Publius cites examples of states—including New York—where the same number of voters are found in state and federal districts. The reason is that these states have multimember districts. When Publius gets around to mentioning this fact, which seems to go against him, he turns it around, arguing that surely one good representative can be found if the states can find four or five (No. 57, p. 355). Publius closes by arguing that in the most refined statewide elections, i.e., for senators and executives, there has not been the abuse of authority that opponents fear. But now he has moved away from the most popular branch of government, the one charged with representing the people.

Publius's arguments may not be convincing, but they do point to a certain indeterminateness in the Anti-Federalist position as presented so far. How many classes or orders in society are there, and how are they to be represented consistent with popular elections? Federal Farmer answers these questions in his VIIth letter, where he aggregates the different occupations into two major classes, the natural aristocracy and the natural democracy.[25] Farmer identifies the political and professional elite of the country (he offers the number "four or five thousand men") as the natural aristocracy, and he distinguishes them from the more moderate merchants, traders, and landholders, whom he calls the natural democracy.

> Men of the first class associate more extensively, have a high sense of honor, possess abilities, ambition, and general knowledge; men of the second class are not so much used to combining great objects; they possess less ambition, and a larger share of honesty; their dependence is principally on middling and small estates, industrious pursuits, and hard labour, while that of the former is principally on the emoluments of large estates, and of the chief offices of government.[26]

Federal Farmer sees a qualitative difference in state versus federal representation, whereas Publius sees merely 500 versus 5,000 constituents. It follows that representation of the democratic or middling class will always be found to a greater extent in the state governments than in the federal government. Furthermore, Federal Farmer implies, and Melancton Smith, who makes the same argument in the New York Convention, makes clear, that the yeoman middling class, the natural democracy, is the most important class for republican government. For that reason, Federal Farmer, who argues that the federal representation needs to be increased, would continue to insist on limitations on federal powers over armies and taxes.

The difference between the Anti-Federalist "small republic" and the Federalist "large republic" is also relevant to each side's discussion of the Constitution's separation of powers. Here too, as with representation, the distinction is between "reflection" and "refinement," or, to use Publius's terms, between the republican form on the one hand, and energy and stability, on the other (No. 37, p. 226). The version of separation of powers that Publius defends in *Federalist* 47–51 uses the following means to weaken the more popular branch at the expense of the others: the legislature is divided, the executive is given a participation in the legislative power, and the Senate is given a share, with the executive, of two important powers—treaty-making and appointments—in which arguably the entire legislature should participate. After all, these are not clearly executive functions, unless, of course, one identifies executive functions with the prerogatives of the British monarch. Publius argues that "ambition must be made to counteract ambition," but such checks are always aimed either at weakening the more popular branch (No. 48, p. 309) or removing the people, in their collective capacity, from government altogether (No. 63, p. 387). Publius makes this last argument when he defends the Senate's six-year term. The Anti-Federalists criticized the term as too long, and many, including Federal Farmer, proposed instead a three- or four-year term, along with rotation and recall, which they argued would make the Senate more responsible.[27]

Publius reverses the ordinary meaning of responsibility in order to defend the long term. Instead of answerability, it becomes capability: institutions must permit their members enough time to do their tasks. Since some tasks of government take time, an institution such as the proposed Senate is necessary (No. 63, pp. 383–384). And the case for the reeligibility of the unitary executive is made on the basis of the need to support inducements to good behavior with the prospect of reward (No. 71, pp. 437–438). Federal Farmer did not object to a unitary executive, although he favored a council of appointment, or the executive's qualified veto, but he and most Anti-Federalists objected to the president's reeligibility.[28] Finally, Publius argues for the good behavior tenure of federal judges to gain the benefits of "integrity and moderation [in] the judiciary," as well as the learning necessary to have legal precedents understood and followed (No. 78, pp. 470–471). Brutus agreed with the tenure provision, but he objected to the provision in Article III that implied judicial review. If the judicial power did not extend "to all cases, in law and equity, arising under this Constitution," then the legislature would have the final say on the meaning of the Constitution and the courts would be limited to interpreting the laws.[29]

To the Anti-Federalists, then, the high-toned separation of powers only accentuated the basic problem, that under the proposed Constitution the powers of government were separated from the substantial representation of the people, which could only be found in the states. For that reason, the debate over federalism, to which we now turn, is more than merely terminological or legal.

III. FEDERALISM

Our examination of federalism involves two related topics. The first concerns definition: the question is whether the Constitution is consistent with federalism. The second concerns the scope of the legislative powers, particularly the powers to tax and raise armies.

A. *Federalism Defined and Redefined*

The federalism issue was complicated by an ambiguity in usage during the Confederation period, and then by the work of the Federal Convention. Herbert Storing explained the ambiguity by showing how "federal" referred at first to measures designed to strengthen the federal authority, as opposed to state authority, but at the same time presupposed state supremacy.[30] That is, the proponents of "federal measures" took the Articles of Confederation for granted as the constitutional framework; without disturbing state equality and state sovereignty, they proposed to give Congress a limited power to tax imports. The standard means of raising taxes and armies was for Congress to vote for them, with nine states necessary to pass such measures; and then the state governments were responsible for raising their proportional share. These measures were called requisitions, and it was the view of most of the framers that such measures had failed. In the Federal Convention, therefore, the "federal" principle referred to congressional reliance on requisitions, in contrast to the national principle of direct governmental authority over individuals.[31] Since the Constitution eliminated requisitions and departed from state equality in the House of Representatives, it went beyond the federal principle, according to the Anti-Federalists. Hence, the Anti-Federalists claimed to be the true federalists.[32]

Hamilton provides the first discussion of this subject in *Federalist* 9.[33] He attempts to use the Anti-Federalist authority on this topic, Montesquieu, in support of his contention that the distinction between confederacy and consolidation is "more subtle than accurate." According to Montesquieu, men form an assemblage of societies or confederacy for the sake of security. "As this government is composed of small republics, it enjoys the internal happiness of each, and with respect to its external situation it is possessed, by means of the association, of all the advantages of large monarchies."[34]

Hamilton constructs a three-part definition of confederacy drawn from his opponents' statements. His intention is to demonstrate, with reference again to Montesquieu, that the definition does not hold up and therefore must be rejected.

> The essential characteristic of [a confederacy] is said to be the restriction of its authority to the members in their collective capacities, without reaching to the individuals of whom they are composed. It is contended that the national council ought to have no concern with any object of internal administration. An exact equality of suffrage between the members has also been insisted upon as a leading feature of a confederate government. [*Federalist* 9, p. 75]

Hamilton then cites Montesquieu's discussion of the Lycian confederacy: each city did not have an equal vote, and the common council appointed all the judges and magistrates of the several cities—yet Montesquieu called it a model confederacy. Hamilton ignores the matter of requisitions, or the federal authority's reliance on the governmental parts for arms and money. In *Federalist* 15, Hamilton argues that "the great and radical vice in the existing Confederation is the principle of LEGISLATION for STATES or GOVERNMENTS, in their CORPORATE or COLLECTIVE CAPACITIES, and as contradistinguished from the INDIVIDUALS of whom they consist" (No. 15, p. 108). If we put the two passages together, we have Hamilton asserting that the great vice of the existing Articles of Confederation is also the essential feature of confederacies, and yet the distinction between confederacy and consolidation is "more subtle than accurate."

Federal Farmer presents a more candid account of federalism and consolidation in his first letter. He distinguishes "three different forms of free government under which the United States may exist as one nation." They include: (1) "Distinct republics connected under a federal head," or a federal plan; (2) a complete consolidation, which involves the elimination of the state governments; or (3) a partial consolidation, which means "consolidat[ing] the states as to certain national objects, and leav[ing] them severally distinct independent republics, as to internal policy generally."[35] Of the federal plan, Federal Farmer writes, "I do not think much can be said in its favor: The sovereignty of the nation, without coercive and efficient powers to collect the strength of it, cannot always be depended on to answer the purposes of government." Of the two remaining, he "once had some general ideas that the second plan was practicable," but after "long attention" concluded that the third plan, partial consolidation, "is the only one we can with safety and propriety proceed upon."[36]

When he began his "Additional Letters," however, Farmer decided to claim the name federalism for his preferred middle position.

Some of the advocates [of the Constitution] are only pretended federalists; in fact they wish for an abolition of the state governments. Some of them I believe to be honest federalists, who wish to preserve *substantially* the state governments united under an efficient federal head; and many of them are blind tools without any object. Some of the opposers also are only pretended federalists, who want no federal government or one merely advisory. Some of them are the true federalists, their object, perhaps, more clearly seen, is the same with that of the honest federalists; and some of them, probably have no distinct object. We might as well call the advocates and opposers tories and whigs, or any thing else, as federalists and anti-federalists. To be for or against the constitution, as it stands, is not much evidence of a federal disposition; if any names are applicable to the parties, on account of their general politics, they are those of republicans and anti-republicans.[37]

What Farmer previously had described as federalism and criticized, he now identifies with opponents of the Constitution who are only "pretended federalists," because they want no federal government "or one merely advisory." The position previously described as partial consolidation is now identified with federalism.

In his XVIIth letter, Farmer tries to justify the shift in definition by emphasizing each state's retention of control over its internal affairs. Requisitions on the states remain a characteristic of federalism in that sphere at least.[38] Thus the Federal Farmer has already accepted the necessity of moving away from a traditional federal arrangement. He and Brutus both agree with Hamilton's criticism of the Articles of Confederation. But they both remain committed to state control of internal affairs.

Unlike Hamilton, Madison does not attempt to describe the Constitution as wholly federal. Rather, in *Federalist* 39, he presents an elaborate five-part examination of the Constitution to prove that it is "partly federal and partly national." Thus Madison adopts the position of the "moderate" nationalists, or compromisers, in the Federal Convention, whom he had opposed when they had advanced that slogan to argue for state equality in the Senate. At the time, he argued that the proposed government was entirely national, since it would act directly on the people and not on them through the states.[39] Now, Madison makes use of the compromise that was forced upon him and he introduces four additional criteria, besides the one he had used in the Federal Convention, to demonstrate the Constitution's mixed character. The five criteria are: (1) "the foundation on which [the government] is to be established"; (2) "the sources from which its ordinary powers are to be drawn"; (3) "the operation of those powers"; (4) "the extent of them"; and (5) "the authority by which future changes in the government are to be introduced" (No. 39, p. 243). In his examination of the Constitution in terms of these criteria, Madison's unstated assumption is that any recognition of the states as states is a sign of federalism. This is the original "new federalism."[40]

As for the Constitution's ratification, Madison calls it "a federal act," because the people ratify in the states (No. 39, p. 243). But this argument ignores the two, perhaps three, essential departures from the existing constitution's amending provision: unanimity was dropped; popular conventions in the states, not the legislatures, were to vote on the Constitution; and the existing Congress was not asked to approve it, but only to pass it on to the states. Recourse to ratification conventions, whose mode of selection the states were free to choose (and about half were popularly elected), had been defended by Madison in the Convention as essential to establish the legal supremacy of the Constitution over the states.[41] Madison goes on to note that each state must give its own consent before it is bound, but he fails to acknowledge that the choice of nine states as the number necessary for ratification offered a better chance that all the states would ratify than would either a simply majority or unanimity. When ratification is considered in light of the preamble's reference to "We the People," (rather than Patrick Henry's "We the States,")[42] it seems more accurate to call the government's foundation primarily, if not wholly, national.

Madison identifies the sources of authority, his next criterion, with mode of election, thus permitting him to conclude that the sources are mixed, both federal and national. But in light of the preamble, again, and the supremacy clause, it seems odd to describe the government's powers as emanating even partly from the states. Furthermore, a truly federal senate would have voted by state delegation, and the state legislatures would have retained their right of recall, as they did under the Articles of Confederation.

Madison concedes that the operation of the government is national, as he had argued in the Convention, but he argues that the extent of the powers is federal, because of the enumeration of legislative power.

Finally, Madison argues that the amending power, since it requires an extraordinary majority but not unanimity, is partly federal, partly national.

Both sides, then, shifted their definitions of federalism away from state supremacy and the exclusive reliance on requisitions. This was true for Brutus and Federal Farmer because they recognized that the proposed Constitution was a better basis for discussion then the existing Articles. What the Anti-Federalists insisted on was a partial recognition of the federal principle of requisitions in the sphere of internal affairs. This brings us to the debate on the powers of government.

B. The Extent of the Powers

The powers of government are discussed in *Federalist* 23–36 (Hamilton) and 41–44 (Madison). During the same time that Hamilton's essays were published in the New York papers, Brutus published his letters V–X.[43] Both writers examine the enumeration of powers in general, and the power to raise armies, control the militia, and tax, in particular. Hamilton's treatment begins with a general argument about how the powers are to be granted (*Federalist* 23), and proceeds to a discussion of the war powers (24–29) and the tax powers (30–36). The latter discussion includes a treatment of the necessary and proper clause (33). Brutus begins with the most general clauses, such as the preamble, taxing and spending for the general welfare, and the necessary and proper clause; and then he proposes alternatives, more limited than the Constitution's grants, for the tax power (V–VII), the power to borrow money (VIII), and the war power (VIII–X). Except for his discussion of the necessary and proper clause, Madison does not add much to Hamilton's discussion of the key powers.

The debate on the powers of government may be viewed under two headings: a disagreement about the scope of the powers vested in Congress; and Brutus's argument for limited grants of power over armies and money, followed by a defense, by Hamilton, of the Constitution's full grant of power.

In both his first and his fifth letters, Brutus argues that the necessary and proper clause, combined with the taxing and spending power, the supremacy clause, and the preamble, gives Congress a virtually unlimited grant of legislative power. "All that is reserved for the individual states must very soon be annihiliated, except so far as they are barely necessary to the organization of the general government."[44] He argues later on that this power will be brought home to the people "through the medium of the judicial power."[45]

There are two *Federalist* replies to this argument, and neither one settles the matter. According to Hamilton, "it is expressly to execute these [enumerated] powers, that the sweeping clause, as it has been affectedly called, authorizes the national legislature to pass all *necessary* and *proper* laws" (No. 33, p. 203). And Madison, perfecting an argument he first made in the Federal Convention in favor of an enumeration so long as it was not unduly confining, argues against reliance on any definitive listing, be it of powers or prohibitions. This meant rejecting the qualifier "expressly," which had been used in the Articles of Confederation (Article II). Madison contends that silence would have conveyed the same power: "wherever a general power to do a thing is given, every particular power necessary for doing it, is included" (No. 44, p. 285). But what is the meaning of necessary? Is it "convenient and useful," or "without which the enumerated power is nugatory?"[46] Suffice it to say that the Constitution's enumeration of powers is not presented by either Hamilton or Madison as describing a clearly delimited amount of power. The Anti-Federalists wanted such limitations, in the name of federalism.

But the argument that produced the most instructive debate concerns the scope of the powers actually given. In *Federalist* 23, Hamilton argues that a Constitution "at least equally energetic with the one proposed" is required for the preservation of the union. This follows from an application of the maxim that the means must be proportional to the ends, i.e., to the principal purposes of union: "Shall the union be constituted the guardian of the common safety? Are fleets and armies and revenues necessary for this purpose? The government of the union must be empowered to pass all laws, and to make all regulations which have relation to them" (No. 23, p. 155). Since "the powers are not too extensive for the objects of Federal administration," a choice must be made: adopt this Constitution, in order to preserve the union, or separate.

> For the absurdity must continually stare us in the face of confiding to a government, the direction of the most essential national interests, without daring to trust it with the authorities which are indispensable to their proper and efficient management. Let us not attempt to reconcile contradictions, but firmly embrace a rational alternative. [No. 23, p. 157]

This is the most difficult challenge for the Anti-Federalists, and Storing thought that they were unable to meet it. This may be so, especially since the Anti-Federalists disagreed among themselves. Still, the proposals of Brutus and Federal Farmer merit consideration. They are the strongest alternatives; and notwithstanding the Constitution's ratification, subsequent practice stayed close to them for some time.

Brutus argues that the national government's unlimited taxing power could deprive the states of an independent source of revenue.[47] Hamilton replies, in *Federalist* 32, by discussing concurrent taxation, but Brutus is concerned about how the states will make out if both governments tax the same commodity. He thinks the Constitution "should have marked the line in which the general government should have raised money, and set bounds over which they should not pass, leaving to the separate states other means to raise supplies for their own governments, and to discharge their respective debts."[48] Drawing on the former colonies' controversy with England, Brutus proposes "the distinction between external and internal taxes." The former refers to "impost duties on all imported goods," and it can be collected "in few places and from few hands with certainty and expedition." The latter refers to excise taxes within the country and direct, i.e. head, taxes. Brutus also thought that a limited duty on exports could be levied, if necessary.[49]

Restricting the federal tax power to external taxes was an important and common Anti-Federalist proposal. It was offered as a constitutional amendment by six state ratification conventions, including New York.[50] Federal Farmer's version of the proposal was to require the use of requisitions, if it became necessary for the federal government to levy internal taxes.[51] In defense of his proposal along these lines, Brutus replies to Hamilton's argument about the means being proportional to the end, objecting that the government's end is not simply "the common defense and general welfare of the union." For "besides this, the state governments are to be supported, and provision made for the managing of such of their internal concerns as are allotted to them."[52]

Hamilton replies to Brutus in *Federalist* 30. He repeats his axiom, now called a "fundamental maxim of good sense and sound policy," "that every POWER ought to be proportioned to its object," and argues, further, that "*in the usual progress of things, the necessities of a nation in every stage of its existence will be found at least equal to its resources*" (No. 30, p. 190; emphasis in the original). As for the suggestion that deficiencies could be provided by requisitions on the states (which Federal Farmer proposed after publication of this essay, but Luther Martin had proposed in the Federal Convention), Hamilton dismisses it as proposing to rely on what was an admitted failure.

We turn now to the war power.[53] Both Brutus and Federal Farmer objected to the legislative power to raise and support armies, subject to new appropriations every two years, on the grounds that standing armies in times of peace are dangerous. In addition, Federal Farmer expressed concern about federal control of the militia; he wondered why there was no reliance on a *posse commitatus*.[54]

Brutus begins his discussion as follows. "I take it for granted, as an axiom in politics, that the people should never authorize their rulers to do any thing, which if done, would operate to their injury."[55] He seems opposed to standing armies, even if they are maintained in the states, and he and Hamilton disagree on precisely what the practice was in the states and for Congress under the Articles. Brutus argues that the Confederation itself prohibited the states from keeping standing armies, aside from what was needed to protect forts; and while the legal position with respect to Congress's power was unclear, the states exercised ultimate control anyway.[56]

In reply to this objection, Hamilton asks about the need to defend against Indians (No. 24, p. 161) and about the extent of the prohibition— does "keeping them up" also include "raising" armies (No. 25, pp. 164– 165)? The first question is easier for Brutus to answer; the garrisoning of forts and frontiers is a permissible exception. On the second point, Hamilton argues that once you concede the need to prepare for emergencies, Congress must judge what is to be done; and it is very difficult to distinguish peaceful times that do require raising an army, and hence having it "standing," from those which do not. Brutus acknowledges the argument, but he maintains the distinction between the "exigencies" of impending war, and peace, or between a limited and an unlimited discretion.[57] Brutus therefore proposes that "since standing armies are dangerous to liberty, and have often been the means of overturning the best constitutions of government," they shall not be raised, except in the cases noted (guards for arsenals, garrisons to posts on frontiers), unless two-thirds of both houses concur.[58]

Hamilton's reply to this is implicit in the above discussion. If Brutus's key distinction breaks down, one is left with the choice of violating the provision to defend the country, or prohibiting even the raising of armies in time of peace. Hamilton calls this latter prospect "the most extraordinary spectacle, which the world has yet seen—that of a nation incapacitated by its constitution to prepare for defense, before it was actually invaded" (No. 25, p. 165). As for the militia, Hamilton notes that "the steady operations of war against a regular and disciplined army, can only be successfully conducted by a force of the same kind" (No. 25, p. 166).

Finally, Federal Farmer argues against a select militia, which he thought would be composed of "the young and ardent part of the community, possessed of but little or no property," and who could become a threat to the rest. For this reason, he favors a *posse commitatus* "for executing the laws of the union."[59] Hamilton responds directly to Federal Farmer in *Federalist* 29. His argument is twofold: first, nothing in the Constitution prevents the calling of a *posse commitatus;* and second, a select militia is more economical than complete reliance on the people at large, and it will "lessen the call for military establishments" and stand as the best security against government oppression (No. 29, p. 185).

This concludes our examination of federalism. If the Anti-Federalists had the better of the argument on definition, inasmuch as they remained faithful to the states, the Federalists had the better argument on the powers, certainly on the war power. Put another way, Publius would risk the states for union and the other side would risk union for the states. We have seen that the Anti-Federalist conception of republican government gives the states an importance that they do not have in the Federalist formulation. It is true that there are occasional references in *The Federalist* to the people's affections siding with the states and to the "few and defined" delegated powers (No. 17, p. 119; No. 45, p. 292). But if the first argument is read in conjunction with Publius's later statement about the people ultimately being won over by the government that is best administered, which he clearly thought would be the federal government (*Federalist* 27 and 16), and if the second argument is read in conjunction with his characteristically liberal interpretation of the powers of government (*Federalist* 23, 30, and 31), I think it is fair to conclude that the federalism of *The Federalist* was predominantly nationalism.[60]

IV. CONCLUSION

The Anti-Federalist conception of republican government emphasized the need for a substantive link between the great body of the people and their government. The authors of *The Federalist* stood on what they regarded as the solid ground of election, which directly or indirectly linked the people to their governors. Where the opponents feared oppression from an elective aristocracy in a government that could not represent the middling class, Publius emphasized energy and stability and the need to secure individual rights. And each argument on republican government was connected to federalism. The Federalists emphasized the needs of union, and thus the importance of granting powers liberally. The states were secured because they were established as part of the structure of government. The Anti-Federalists wanted the states to remain more than mere administrative units of the federal government. Hence they argued for a line-drawing approach to the key powers of government, raising armies and money.

The Anti-Federalist demands for amendments to the Constitution— which led to a Federalist promise on the subject, later fulfilled under Madison's leadership in the First Congress—are best viewed in light of this debate over federalism. The Anti-Federalists wanted a Bill of Rights to curb governmental power. When the Federalists denied the necessity of a federal bill of rights on the grounds that whatever power was not enumerated in the Constitution could not be claimed by the government it established, the Anti-Federalists pointed to the Constitution's supremacy and to the extensiveness of its enumerated powers. Paradoxically, however, this argument resulted in the passage of a Bill of Rights that confirmed the new federalism, with its extended republic. The Anti-Federalist proposals to institute rotation and recall for the senate, rotation for the president, and a special council of appointments, were not accepted. Nor were their proposals to restrict the taxation and war powers or the "necessary and proper" clause (by adding "expressly" to what became the Tenth Amendment).[61]

The ratification of the Constitution did not end this founding debate on either republican government or federalism. It simply shifted the argument to different interpretations of the new fundamental law. Partisans of both sides should appreciate this fact, since however strong the Anti-Federalist reservations were, and still might be, concerning this new form of republican government, their own proposals respecting the key powers were unlikely to provide for the purposes of union—particularly the common defense, the common welfare, and the blessings of liberty. To find elements of the Anti-Federalist view of republican government today, one could look to the opposition to "big government," particularly to a strong presidency and an extensive administrative state. In addition, the Anti-Federalist interest in homogeneity and civic responsibility, as reflected in their concerns about qualifications for office, jury trial, the militia, and the *posse comitatus*, bears some relation to the contemporary interest in referenda and the "communitarian" critique of our traditional emphasis on individual rights.[62]

The most important Anti-Federalist legacy concerns federalism. One obvious explanation for this lies in the text of the Constitution itself. The states are guaranteed some form of political existence, and, notwithstanding the expectations of Publius,[63] they can try to retain the attachments of the people. And while Brutus seems to have seen clearly how some future Supreme Court Justice was going to interpret the necessary and proper clause, the enumeration of powers permits, and has produced, a variety of interpretations of the limits of the federal government's authority.

Another reason why the debate did not end with the Constitution's ratification concerns the sectional compromises, which temporarily muted the deepest division in the country. There is more than a hint of the tensions between a heterogeneous commercial society and a homogeneous landed society in the Federalist and Anti-Federalist discussions about republican government and representation. Since that division was bound up with slavery, however, it was not fully explored. Perhaps the sectional aspect of the commerce question explains Madison's shift to strict construction in 1790, when Secretary of Treasury Hamilton proposed a national bank. It is difficult to imagine the major arguments of *The Federalist* supporting anything but a strong government to regulate the "various and interfering interests" (No. 10, p. 79). Perhaps the sectional division also explains why, notwithstanding *The Federalist's* candid and powerful arguments for unlimited powers of taxation, the federal government relied on imposts, or at least excise taxes, for a hundred years. And then it needed a constitutional amendment to facilitate the collection of an income tax, since otherwise the government would have had to collect the money by state quotas. As for the war power, the first conscription act appears to have been in 1863; before then, the government relied on the militia and volunteers.[64]

Today, our constitutional federalism resembles the Federalist formulation more than the Anti-Federalist. Given the requirements of modern government, it is hard to imagine it otherwise. Still, since 1976, we have seen a revival of interest in the tenth amendment as a source of constitutional, and hence judicial, protection of state's rights, and for nearly one hundred years the Supreme Court has interpreted the eleventh amendment as a source for the states' claim to sovereign immunity from otherwise valid law suits by individuals in federal courts.[65] The constitutional history of American federalism may therefore be described as a continuation of the founding debate, only within the bounds of the Constitution.

3

Federalism and Political Life

DAVID BROYLES

> It has been a principal aim of these papers to inculcate that the danger
> which most threatens our political welfare is, that the State Governments
> will finally sap the foundations of the Union.
>
> *Federalist* 33

INTRODUCTION

The great Goldwater rout of 1964 proved not to be the final triumph of
unrestricted nationalism for which many had hoped. While it *was* a defeat
for strict constructionism, this was really nothing new, since Jefferson himself had refused to follow his campaign rhetoric, and instead purchased
Louisiana—to the manifest advantage of the Union. Goldwater's successors,
especially Presidents Carter and Reagan, profited greatly from vigorously
opposing the interfering pretensions of the Washington establishment; that
is, they profited from the old argument that big government is nonrespon-
sive government. And this was more than campaign eyewash.

American federalism blooms perennially as the people indulge the hope
that their supposed sovereign power can be used to get control over way-
ward politicians. As Harry Jaffa has argued, an ambiguity lies at the heart of
the American system that sustains state and local loyalties as well as national.
Each government, national and state, implies the existence of the other as a
matter of permanent constitutional necessity.[1] The Constitution is not "our
social compact" in the sense of establishing national sovereignty in a numerical majority of the American people. There is an ambiguity about whether
the national majority is *the* majority. It is striking that the Constitution's
national government cannot come together at all without elections that re-

quire the active cooperation of the states. On the other hand, neither does our Constitution recognize the states as competent sovereignties. Thus Jaffa properly reminds us of the greatest of our trials of federalism—the Civil War—with the observation that "every attempt . . . to present the right of secession as a constitutional right . . . [has been] hopelessly entangled in self-contradiction." The states cannot secede and even their very legitimacy, their republican form, must be guaranteed from outside.

That the people's sovereignty found expression in the ambiguity of federalism was not unintended. Or if it was originally unintended, there are convincing reasons for thinking that it was a fortuitous accident, turned to their own purposes by the founders. Federalism was like other institutions which, as Martin Diamond has emphasized, found their way into the Constitution after being adapted to it.[2] For by the time of the ratification, federalism was vigorously defended in the great synthesis of proratification arguments, *The Federalist*. There, federalism is routinely criticized as the favorite theory of Anti-Federalist forces and is often condemned as unrealistic. But it is also defended, when properly understood, as part of the national system rather than as an enemy of it.

Publius supports vigorous state governments at crucial points of his argument because they are essential to his new system. In the early numbers of *The Federalist*, his rhetorical strategy dictates delaying discussion of specific institutions as much as possible. Despite this, however, it is hard even to conceive of the great argument for an extended republic in *Federalist* 9 and 10 without supposing that the variety of local interests and sects, advanced as a mainstay of the new system, would not require active state governments to support them. Publius's later argument in *Federalist* 39 is even more explicit on the importance of the states. There the states are said to be essential to any process of ratifying or amending the Constitution. Furthermore, support for (or, as we might say today, "legitimacy" for) the national government's operations is said to come from the people acting in their capacity as citizens of states (No. 39, p. 244). And of great importance to those Anti-Federalists who feared "consolidation" and the loss of all reserved liberties,[3] Publius argues that the national government is not to be possessed of "an indefinite supremacy over all persons and things, so far as they are objects of lawful government." Instead, he repeatedly makes clear that "the proposed government['s] . . . jurisdiction extends to certain enumerated objects only" (No. 39, p. 245). His argument presumes that a great range of legitimate objects of government will remain in the care of the states.

It is the people, says *The Federalist*, who are to exercise that continuing sovereignty over all government which is presumed by the Declaration of Independence, and which is most readily associated with John Locke's contract theory of government. As the sovereign authority, the people not only judge the performance of each government, but they also judge what is the proper balance between the states and the nation. Thus Publius says that, in any contest between the two levels of government, "everything . . . must be left to the prudence and firmness of the people" (No. 31, p. 197). Furthermore, the people's choice will be rooted in a primitive instinct to sustain their own sovereignty. It will thus favor the government that is most responsive to them. And so, Publius adds, if "the Federal Government [is not] sufficiently dependent upon the people . . . it will not possess the confidence of the people, and its schemes of usurpation will be easily defeated by the State Governments; who will be supported by the people" (No. 46, p. 300).

In practice, the people decide where to place their confidence in the light of some particular issues that are in the public eye, and that are seen as crucial to the republican spirit in critical elections. Either the nation or the states are usually right about the issues. The decision about federalism is thus always open to an erroneous interpretation that its purpose is more to decide a specific policy than to decide between governments. When Governor George Wallace blocked federal officers at Alabama's schoolhouse door, was he more the states' righter or the segregationist? Was he representing the whole people on an issue of federalism, or a region on a policy toward civil rights? Any interpretation of such questions that is based on policy choices alone, and that ignores the voters' expression of confidence in their nation and/or states, may purchase a false reputation for realism at the expense of overlooking something very important. A series of crucial policy choices may amount to peacefully exercising a right of revolution—may amount to the peaceful substitution of a new government for the old one.

While federalism survives to our day as a fundamental constitutional principle, we should observe also that the consequences of the choice for federalism have become ever more obscure to the voter. Very different men, such as Jimmy Carter and Ronald Reagan, have been chosen as its champions within a short space of time. Voters seem to lack confidence that a choice for national politics is a choice for healthy politics. But on the other hand, they disagree regarding its alternative. To some it seems that a choice for local government is a choice for grass-roots, participatory democracy. They are seeking active citizenship and voting. To others, it is a choice for standing pat and enjoying a rich local tradition. They are seeking a community based on traditional lifestyles. Confronted by these ambiguities and more, we do well to seek clarification about federalism from the writers of the Constitution, who saw clearly its implications during their contest with the Anti-Federalists.

THE GENESIS OF ANTI-FEDERALISM

Federalist and Anti-Federalist opinions concerning constitutional questions took shape in the amorphous situation following the Revolution. In that environment, similar events prompted different reactions among equally thoughtful individuals; but more importantly, there was also a variety of profoundly learned opinion about what was essential to good government. As a result, the debate on ratification was rich as well as varied.

Both sides agreed on one thing, though, that the situation was critical and in need of reform. Herbert Storing emphasizes this in a comment which he directs against some contemporary historians. It is irrelevant, says Storing, to make a hindsight judgment that the period of the revolution was not in fact a critical one. This did not affect the issues being debated. "Few Anti-Federalists," Storing writes, "would in fact have objected to the designation of 1787 as the 'critical period,' and many used that or synonymous phrases."[4]

As to the desirable corrective, the Federalist argument has been given authoritative voice for all time by the most able leaders of their movement, writing in *The Federalist*. For the Anti-Federalists, however, reconstruction of their arguments is necessary. Some scholars, most notably Storing in our day, have insisted that the Anti-Federalist position is developed best by taking them at their own self-estimate.[5] On the other hand, Publius makes a powerful case that the Anti-Federalists were unclear about their own premises. In this controversy I support Publius, who seems to me to understand the Anti-Federalists better than they understood themselves.

Publius judged that the final import of the Anti-Federalist position was not a proper federalism, as was claimed, but a mistaken support of disunion. Accordingly, I will maintain that the founders of the American nation must be judged to be those Federalists who defended the union and wrote the Constitution, and not (even partially) their Anti-Federalist opponents.

Publius introduces *The Federalist* by giving his estimate of Anti-Federalism. He reminds his readers of something that may require contemporary readers to exert some effort of historical imagination to recall. He reminds us that many Americans in the aftermath of the Revolution quietly argued that union was undesirable. "The fact is," he says,

> that we already hear it whispered in the private circles of those who oppose the new Constitution, that the thirteen States are of too great extent for any general system, and that we must of necessity resort to separate confederacies of distinct portions of the whole. [*Federalist* 1, p. 36]

This opinion was never satisfactorily extinguished, even upon the ratification of the Constitution. It was carried forward most notably by John C. Calhoun, who said of the North and South, "indeed it is difficult to see how two peoples so different and hostile can exist together."[6] Calhoun worked to exaggerate this difference from the beginning of his career, and his efforts were made easier by the survival of a legacy of Anti-Federalism. To this legacy Calhoun owed the appearance that his campaign for a slave-based society was a conservative one. To this legacy he also owed the opinion that slavery was not merely a necessary evil but a "positive good."

Publius calls those who oppose the union, or at least their hard-core leaders, self-interested. He mentions the "obvious interest of a certain class of men in every State" who already enjoy the privileges of state office. And he also mentions the "perverted ambition of another class," who will hope to "aggrandize themselves by the confusions of their country, or will flatter themselves with fairer prospects of elevation from the subdivision of the empire into several partial confederacies" (No. 1, pp. 33–34).

Opposition motives are thus described without naming names and detailing specifications. It is not Publius's purpose to accuse. Instead, he quickly admits that it would be wrong to resolve every opposing view into interest and ambition. "Candor," he says, "will oblige us to admit that [those who oppose the Constitution] may be actuated by upright intentions." Publius sees clearly that many of his Anti-Federalist opponents agree with "A Georgian," and that they, like him, seek "that very government intended by our glorious Declaration of Independence."[7] But the important thing for upright Anti-Federalists to see is that their mistaken reasoning supports the causes of men with very bad motives. It may even support the Calhouns of their time, and this is an important sign that, although Anti-Federalist motives may be "upright," they cannot be fully the best.

According to Publius, correct reasoning leads men to support the Constitution and the union, which alone offer "the safest course for [America's] liberty . . . dignity, and . . . happiness" (No. 1, p. 36). What prevents the upright Anti-Federalists from properly perceiving this end to which unbiased reason should direct them? Publius does not modify his description of them as "upright," but he suggests that their motives are not a sufficient safeguard against prejudices. Their "preconceived jealousies and fears" interfere with reason. Such prejudices prevent an adequate grasp of the first principles (the "self-evident truths," in the language of the Declaration) that support the Constitution. While they know that America is sick, they don't know what it would be like if it were truly healthy (No. 38, pp. 234–235). Publius's disagreement with such Anti-Federalists, then, is not apparently over the end, union, but over choosing the right means to that agreed-upon end. But the disagreement is one which arises from the fact that Publius's opponents do not grasp the end—political health—with sufficient firmness, because their motives are not the best. They do not really take the Declaration to heart with sufficient force to correct their biases.[8] Is the Constitution the best means to union, or is something else, possibly a division of the union or an amendment to expand Congress' powers under the Articles of Confederation? To Publius's thinking, only a thorough review of America's first principles of natural law and right, a review that he undertakes in *The Federalist*, can possibly supply an adequate foundation for agreeing on the correct answer.[9]

In his description of Anti-Federalism, Publius calls it naive and unsympathetic. He says, perhaps to the surprise of contemporary readers, that the Anti-Federalist bias is more "of the head than of the heart." This is true, he says, even though the Anti-Federalists see themselves differently. They see themselves as full of sympathy for individual liberty and the common man, the "yeoman farmer," who, they insist, "ought to have the same measure of justice as the rich."[10]

To Publius, this Anti-Federalist intellectualizing amounts to a false sympathy, because it is shallow, and comes out of an unwillingness to grapple with the realities of political life. It is characteristic of "political doctors, whose sagacity disdains the admonitions of experimental instruction" (No. 28, p. 178). Thus Anti-Federalists confusedly reason toward an end outside of everyday experience. They may well be called apolitical, because their thinking is super- (or occasionally sub-) political. Most often they tend to be dreamy utopians who imagine that training in "republican virtue" can make men into near angels.[11] Or paradoxically, occasionally they are misanthropes.[12] Either posture, however, takes its bearings from another world, so that Publius accuses them of speaking with an "unnatural voice."

The other-wordly perspective of the Anti-Federalists leads them to be mostly critical of realistic politics. As Publius says, they choose to "dwell on the inconveniences which must be unavoidably blended with all political advantages; and on the possible abuses which must be incident to every power or trust of which a beneficial use can be made" (No. 41, p. 255). And this is inherent in Anti-Federalism. It is not forced on them because they had to react to Federalist initiatives. The fact is that, despite the best efforts of outstanding modern scholars, the positive side of Anti-Federalism is still obscured by its more obvious negative side.

As to what the Anti-Federalists were for, Publius's analysis suggests that their thinking was guided by a confusion about the souls of men. Were they angels or animals? To resolve this uncertainty Anti-Federalists tried to separate honest people from ambitious leaders, tending always to deny that leaders could be honest, or that the people were ambitious. There were times when Anti-Federalists could be heard insisting puritanically that only harsh coercion could control popular appetites. But it was more characteristic of them to expect that common men could govern themselves, and that they only required something like the convenience of administrative agents to execute the community's rules. They did not think of the people as political men do—that the people need to protect themselves against their own momentary delusions. Nor did they think that public debate and campaigning are essential, and that political give-and-take is needed to give public definition to opinions of justice and right.

On the other hand, the Anti-Federalists' inordinate suspicion of all power and of the ambitious men it attracts showed itself when they talked about Federalist purposes for the union. These purposes, they insisted, required the creation of a new commercial aristocracy of the "wealthy and wellborn."[13] Centinel expanded on this view in a familiar charge which, in a later day, might have been directed not against Madison's republic, but against his avenue:

The merchant, immersed in schemes of wealth, seldom extends his views beyond the immediate object of gain; he blindly pursues his seeming interest and sees not the latent mischief; therefore it is that he is the last to take the alarm when public liberty is threatened. . . . [Merchants] do not consider that every concern of individuals will be sacrificed to the gratification of the men in power, who will institute monopolies and shackle commerce with every device of avarice, and that property of every species will be held at the will and pleasure of rulers.[14]

Thus the Anti-Federalist bias was always against the powerful, and they feared, as Tocqueville did later, a commercial or industrial aristocracy.[15] They did not agree with Publius that statesmen could serve the public good if safeguards were enacted to make sure that their ambitions would be satisfied only upon doing their duty. And the opponents of the Constitution thought it was altogether unlikely that elected representatives would be men "whose wisdom may best discern the true interest of their country and whose patriotism and love of justice will be less likely to sacrifice it to temporary or partial considerations" (No. 10, p. 82).

Even when the necessity of political leadership was conceded by the Anti-Federalists, their bias showed itself in a continuing hostility to "monocrats" of the executive branch, and in a partiality for legislators because they more closely resembled the people. Maryland Farmer traced what is for him the inevitable consequence of national power institutionalized in an independent executive:

> The rule of any one man who is elevated to a pre-eminence of power is always surrounded by those vile minions and favorites, who bask in the sunshine of courts, deify the object of their adoration with the venal incense of flattery, intercept every avenue to truth, and who never can be satisfied until they reduce the people to the slavery of the ancient Persians. . . . In all governments in which there is sown the smallest seed of the rule of one man, no checks, no bars can prevent its growing into a monarchy, or a despotism if the empire is extensive.[16]

By and large, the Anti-Federalists approved of the House of Representatives but thought it would be even better if expanded. The Senate, on the other hand, many thought would be made into a tool of the executive. Even the judiciary was attacked, insofar as it appeared open to elite professional domination and a diminished reliance on the jury system.

Such thinking led many Anti-Federalists to favor a continuation of the Articles of Confederation, albeit with slight alterations. When they did find reasons for approving the Constitution, it was usually as nothing more than a necessary means to achieve utilitarian goals. Martin Diamond notes that the Federalist forces exploited this argument at the Philadelphia Convention to bring many Anti-Federalists over to their side.[17] In Diamond's words, many "'pure federalists' . . . admitted how broad the governing powers must be to achieve the blessings of union." But other "pure federalists" were unwilling to concede that the Constitution was necessary as drafted, and added what they considered safe proposals for modifying the Constitution's power. The counsel of Agrippa is characteristic testimony to their intransigence. His "be careful to give [Congress] only limited revenue," appears at least by hindsight to be quite incompatible with any demand that the nation encourage commerce and defend itself against European rivals.[18]

Publius viewed these proposals to modify the Constitution as especially dangerous. Anti-Federalists favored "parchment barriers," he said, and doctrines that owed their support to vestigial prejudices of the community rather than to their logical derivation from true political axioms. These parchment barriers and vestigial rules were awkward mechanical contrivances, like what have come to be called "administrative rules." Storing's comment on this subject catches well what Publius was alarmed about. He says, speaking especially of Agrippa, that his "formulation emphasizes the *facilitating* character of federal political power, in contrast to the governing power that seemed to be provided in the Constitution."[19]

To succeed, administrative rules attempt to profit all parties equally, and thereby to appear to be "neutral." But they can appear to be neutral only because they are described as saving the beleaguered people from an attack by oppressive governors. Administrative rules characteristically ignore the possibility that elected officials might be loyal republicans. They are proposed as guards against politicians who are presumed to be single-mindedly bent on usurpation.

In fact, of course, in a democracy such rules serve to arbitrate between citizens competing among themselves for limited goods. Therefore, Publius argued that such rules could not be what they were made to appear by the distortions of Anti-Federalist bias; they would necessarily serve unforeseen and unwanted purposes. In attempting to overcome parchment barriers and accomplish the purposes for which it was instituted, government would have to resort to extra-legal action. Thus, he warns gravely of an inevitable transgression against the republican faith:

> Every breach of the fundamental laws, though dictated by necessity, impairs that sacred reverence which ought to be maintained in the breast of rulers towards the constitution of a country, and forms a precedent for other breaches where the same plea of necessity does not exist at all, or is less urgent and palpable. [*Federalist* 25, p. 167]

Publius further charges that the preference for noncontroversial administrative rules arises from a bias or prejudice prompted by utopianism, that is, by an unrealistic yearning for peaceful sociability, "facilitated," as Storing says, and not "governed." The arch enemy of such peaceful sociability was this-wordly power and circumstance. Maryland Farmer gave simple expression to what Publius deplored in anti-federalism when he said, "should we not reflect that quiet is happiness?—That content and pomp are incompatible?"[20]

All administrative rules, Publius said, attempt to avoid political give-and-take and the necessity to arrive at the best prudential judgment among a welter of conflicting advantages and disadvantages. They try to substitute rules for politics. "Where annual elections end, tyranny begins" is a good example (No. 53, p. 270), as is the oft-repeated prejudice against standing armies. So also were their formulas to separate legislative, executive, and judicial powers by defining them as mutually exclusive, rather than by more realistic means. And so also was their proposal to regulate national powers by a Bill of Rights.

This last Anti-Federalist proposal has proven to be a key one in a program of continuing anti-federalism. Today's Bill of Rights is somewhat different from the original, but often is praised nevertheless as a development from the best of anti-federalism. Thus Storing disagrees profoundly with the Federalist view that a Bill of Rights would dangerously expand national power, and says that "the debate over the bill of rights was an extension of the general debate over the nature of limited government, and at this level the Anti-Federalists can perhaps claim a substantial, though not unmitigated, accomplishment."[21] In accordance with this view, the Bill of Rights has now been given a greater prominence in national politics than the Anti-Federalists ever intended. And for this reason the full implications of the original Anti-Federalist position can now be seen better than they were earlier. The contemporary program supplies evidence that Publius was right in cautioning the Anti-Federalists about the dangerous tendency of their suggestions.

Publius said the Bill of Rights might be appropriate against monarchies, but not against popular governments (No. 84, pp. 512–513). Furthermore, it implied not a decrease, but an increase of national power over matters that had been properly left by the founders to the people and their state governments. It was not merely an unnecessary redundancy in the Constitution, but a positive threat to limited government:

> Men disposed to usurp[ation] . . . might urge with a semblance of reason, that the constitution ought not to be charged with the absurdity of providing against the abuse of an authority, which was not given, and that the provision against restraining the liberty of the press afforded a clear implication, that a power to prescribe proper regulations concerning it, was intended to be vested in the national government. This may serve as a specimen of the numerous handles which would be given to the doctrine of constructive powers, by the indulgence of an injudicious zeal for bills of rights. [*Federalist* 84, p. 514]

Publius's forecast has come true more and more in recent years, as the Supreme Court has tried to solve national problems like civil rights by insisting, contrary to the framers' intentions, that the Bill of Rights restricts laws enacted by the states. The national government has acted more and more in the spirit of the so-called "incorporation doctrine." Local zoning for public morals is under attack, local schools and hospitals are being administered by the national judiciary, and in other more subtle ways, too, the national administration has begun to control intimate matters that were formerly left to local government.

Now, the Anti-Federalists clearly did not foresee, as the founders did, that the Bill of Rights might be used like many other administrative regulations to violate the constitutional division of national and state politics. Even more to their dislike, it can be imagined, would be its contemporary use to reshape community tastes and standards on a national scale. The national judiciary has accomplished exactly this, however, by bringing state regulation of such things as unpatriotic expressions and obscene language under national control.

These changes were first introduced as restrictions on government "censorship," but they finally took shape as a substantive doctrine of what constitutes acceptable public speech. As the courts denied the power to regulate such traditional objects as unpatriotic or obscene expressions, they undercut any public recognition that such standards were useful or valid criteria in evaluating the worth of new ideas. They implied, and sometimes said, that patriotic and moral standards were not worth upholding—not serious and important. In the "marketplace of ideas," to use Supreme Court terminology, all ideas should be given a hearing so that society could make "progress."

In practice, this meant that certain kinds of heretofore unheard-of ideas should henceforth be heard as worthy contributions to public debate. A defense of tyranny was now to be given an equal hearing, whereas before it had been considered unpatriotic. And "sincere expressions" were to be honored even if they encouraged licentious sexual behavior. By this means the character of public debate was radically altered. The old criteria by which speech was judged good or bad, progressive or reactionary, were lost one by one. And with them, as a matter of course, was lost the old appreciation of what was good and bad in general. New general standards marking "social progress" necessarily replaced the old ones to constitute a new national creed. New "lifestyles" were to be preferred to old ones, irrespective of whether they were unpatriotic or obscene. A caricature of the Anti-Federalist Brutus's insistence on a similarity of "manners, sentiments, and interests"[22] among a republican citizenry has thus gained national recognition as a community standard, enforced much like the sumptuary laws of old.

The Anti-Federalists were certainly right on one thing that escapes the contemporary judiciary. They saw clearly the incompatibility between adequate standards of "republican virtue" and truly national purposes. As the Anti-Federalists saw the national government, it could not take adequate care of virtue because of America's heterogeneity. Yet the Anti-Federalists favored the indefinite continuation of a great variety of interests and sentiments in America.[23] If the national government were to attempt to impose standards of "republican virtue," the Anti-Federalists reasoned, it would require monarchical powers, which could only be coercive, since there could be little if any genuinely enthusiastic citizen participation in its policies.

The paradox of Anti-Federalist politics stems from the fact that the peaceful administrative politics that they desired cannot be realized at the national level without resort to the monarchical power they deplored. This becomes ever more evident when their kind of "republican virtue" is attempted on a national scale. The similarity of interests and opinions to which they looked is now being imposed not on individual citizens of a small locality but on vast regions and, inevitably, only with great force and citizen disaffection.

But on the other hand, the founders always said that Anti-Federalist virtue was unsatisfactory. It was incompatible with the highest responsibilities of republican citizenship; it was incompatible, that is, with the Declaration's promise of natural rights. The founders offered a better way, involving a diverse population in their own self-government at the national level. Their solution put great value on exactly what the Anti-Federalists feared, on an "extended republic" and its complement, a popular, unitary executive. The workability of these measures depended in turn on a new approach to federalism and to limited national government.

The Founders' Federalism

It should be remembered that following the Revolution the states had done much to deserve the criticism that came from all kinds of public-spirited men, and not just from headstrong nationalizers. Under the Articles of Confederation, irresponsible states were blocking national measures for which there was widespread support. Furthermore, there was inflation and general insecurity of property within the states. But, most importantly, as Diamond notes, states were being untrue to republican principles by passing biased legislation to the advantage of favored classes of society.[24]

In this post-Revolutionary crisis, the best course the Anti-Federalists could recommend was a return to a modified Articles of Confederation. They wanted to return to an association rather than a government, Publius argues in *Federalist* 15–22—a league whose limited charter for defense and commerce in no way intruded on the domestic felicity of the smaller member states. As for those who took the weakness of the Articles more seriously, they were troubled, as Publius says, by "preconceived jealousies and fears" about a strong national government. These prompted them to advocate a new Constitutional Convention or else a variety of modifications to the recommended frame of government. Again, these were intended to preserve the felicity of local institutions. Thus Publius complains that the Anti-Federalists who proposed modifying his Constitution were always asking the wrong questions about it. Following stubborn habit, they belabored the extent to which local sovereignty might be restrained; and consequently could not pay sustained attention to his argument that not the states but the new nation was truly responsive to the popular will.

The founders, by contrast, regarded the post-Revolutionary crisis as fundamental. Their hostility to the state's political principles was encouraged by mounting evidence that state democracies were deteriorating into legislative tyrannies dominated by rubber-stamp representatives of self-serving factions.[25] They foresaw that the logic of state politics dictated the continuation of this legislative bartering among powerful interests, because the states lacked those great objectives that could inspire a national government, and because they lacked the variety that would characterize the "extended republic" of the union. To the founders, the Constitution was a wonderful new invention that redeemed the suffering cause of the states' republicanism (No. 14, p. 104).

The founders were realistic in establishing proper new foundations for republicanism. They appreciated that the national government needed support from the most powerful motives compelling men to submit to society's constraints. The desire for self-preservation, Publius argues in *Federalist* 23–36, animates men to give plenary powers to the national government for two principal purposes, to provide defense and the kind of taxation that could bring secure prosperity. Unless this is done, nothing more is possible. "Opinions and supposed interests" which are at variance with this necessity must be "stifled by the more powerful sentiment of self-preservation" (No. 38, p. 234).

Publius's fuller view of national powers follows naturally from this necessary beginning. At one point he describes these as follows:

> The several powers conferred on the Government of the Union . . . may be reduced into different classes as they relate to the following different objects:—1. Security against foreign danger; 2. Regulation of the intercourse with foreign nations; 3. Maintenance of harmony and proper intercourse among the States; 4. Certain miscellaneous objects of general utility; 5. Restraint of the States from certain injurious acts; 6. Provisions for giving due efficacy to all these powers. [*Federalist* 41, p. 256]

The list shows that Publius expects the nation to supervise the states in important respects. He also assumes as a matter of course that all non-specified powers remain with the states. The character of these powers is suggested in other passages of *The Federalist* by fragmentary references to "domestic police," by which Publius means such things as "administration of private justice," and "internal encouragement of agriculture and manufactures" (No. 17, p. 118; No. 34, p. 209). These references are only fragmentary and suggestive, because, in principle, state powers are limited only by the fact that they must be governmental and not private. However strange it may sound, Publius clearly expects the national government, using a few specified powers, to supervise the states' use of their many unrestricted ones.[26]

National powers thus go much beyond merely insuring self-preservation. National and state powers may sometimes sound as though they are the same, but national powers are understood to have a special character. That they establish the fundamentals of American economic life by protecting and fostering commerce and competition in agriculture and industry is well established. It is obvious from a casual reading of Article I, Section 8, of the Constitution, which clearly presupposes private property and a market economy. But that national powers decisively affect even the domain of morals is not so obvious. The Anti-Federalist view was that this was impossible, that national powers could only corrupt morals, in fact. Publius's view was exactly the opposite. Thus founders and Anti-Federalists differed fundamentally on the moral character of national powers and on their relation to state powers.

On this key question concerning federalism, differences showed themselves especially in opinions about which was of higher quality, local or national life. For Anti-Federalists, even for those who might accept the Constitution on pragmatic grounds, idealized small republics were much to be preferred, with their simplicity and public-spiritedness, and with the uniformities of attitude and behavior which they called "republican virtue." It is just this kind of republicanism that Publius rejects for the nation, however, when he resists "giving to every citizen the same opinions, the same passions, and the same interests" (No. 10, p. 78). For the founders, republican virtue is described properly as a "vigilant and manly spirit." Their emphasis is on the spirit in which opinions and actions are judged, rather than on believing and acting in common.

The two views agree on many things, but are nevertheless at odds. Federalism would agree with anti-federalism that citizens must agree on definitions of obscenity, libel, and other such community standards. To this extent, they agree that common opinions and behavior must cement society. Also, anti-federalism would agree with federalism that a proper standard must inspire common opinions for them to be valid. The difference between the two shows itself, however, when the spirit must give way to common opinions, or vice versa. For anti-federalism, a common viewpoint is the necessary basis of proper communal life and true republicanism, even if it sometimes means sacrificing the highest standards to communitarian values. For federalism, what is most important is the willingness to subject a great variety of accepted views to sometimes destructive criticism in the light of the highest, i.e., the national, standards.[27]

As Publius sees it, the great problem of government is to encourage the formation of a variety of opinions and tastes, but of the right kind. Publius's principal enemy is not heresy, but faction. And faction arises from reasoning that succumbs to self-interest (No. 10, p. 78). Such reasoning is the source of opinions that are defended as property would be—biased opinions that give rise to "mental passions" and hence "ought to be controlled by government." When they are properly controlled and regulated, as in Publius's republic, the anticipated result is a rule of reason. "It is the reason, alone, of the public, that ought to control and regulate the government" (No. 49, p. 317).

Publius goes on to add that "the most common and durable source of factions has been the various and unequal distribution of property." This is particularly true in the modern world of "industrious habits," as distinguished from the warlike classical republics of Greece and Rome (No. 8, p. 69). Publius's solution to the problem of modern faction is to curb its excesses, particularly its economic excesses, so that good, i.e., reasonable, opinions can assert themselves, even though they are weaker. Under the right circumstances, Publius believes, spirited self-interest can be encouraged to seek an object beyond self-aggrandizement. This is evident in the Constitution's provision for patent laws. But patent laws are just the beginning. Self-interest can even be "instructed" to be just and reasonable, and to defer to natural law and natural right.

Publius's view of the inherent defect of state governments becomes clearer in the light of these considerations. A desirable environment for combating factions is substantially denied due to the limited size of the states, even of the larger states, which allows their governments to be easily captured by their larger economic interests. As a consequence the states fall victim to tyrannizing elites who impose their own self-interested standards on the whole community.

On the other hand, at the national level, reason and the common good will assert themselves aided by the spirited pursuit of honorable objects. Matters of national character and dignity will usually come to the forefront, since sufficient steady purpose and military might will support the pursuit of grand objectives. With this in mind, Publius forecasts that the national military will "vindicate the honor of the human race," particularly as it protects commercial projects (No. 11, p. 91). Given this protection, economic science and its instrument, a vigorous national commerce, can lead the way to an economy which dignifies and rewards all forms of the pursuit of human happiness, whether from the mind of a genius of the natural *aristoi* or from the hands of common people. Thus national pride will advance together with individual, both being guided by those high standards that are the likely objects of America's challenging pursuits.

The special character of national powers amounts to this: they combine the honorable pursuit of man's natural fulfillment with the necessities of defense and prosperity. In one place, Publius speaks of the national powers as being "commerce, finance, negotiation and war" (No. 17, p. 118). Regarding the last two, their character can be seen especially well as they come to life in legislation developing a military establishment capable of enforcing economic hegemony. Publius's thinking connects military preparedness with economic greatness, and he says that the latter grows out of moral as well as physical "necessity":

> Under a vigorous national government, the natural strength and resources of the country, directed to a common interest, would baffle all the combinations of European jealousy to restrain our growth. This situation would even take away the motive to such combinations by inducing an impracticability of success. An active commerce, an extensive navigation, a flourishing marine would then be the inevitable offspring of moral and physical necessity. We might defy the little arts of little politicians to control or vary the irresistible and unchangeable course of nature. [*Federalist* 11, p. 87]

Publius's policy is clearly designed to construct (and defend with honor) channels for economic activity which are expressions of human nature. National policy is to oppose the unnatural behavior encouraged by "the little arts of little politicians." Here as throughout *The Federalist* Publius displays his conviction that natural law is the proper guide to behavior, particularly as it expresses itself in the modern commercial activity of the common man. Conversely, unnatural behavior is a result of persuading men to defy nature, and especially of falsely persuading them to bottle up commercial life.

Publius speaks of the national power over finance and commerce in a similar vein. His tone suggests a statesman's pride in his skill at enticing men to higher callings.[28] The purposes which are to guide national statesmen in pursuing these objects are indicated in passages like the following:

> By multiplying the means of gratification, by promoting the introduction and circulation of the precious metals, those darling objects of human avarice and enterprise, [commerce] serves to vivify and invigorate all the channels of industry and to make them flow with greater activity and copiousness. The assiduous merchant, the laborious husbandman, the active mechanic, and the industrious manufacturer,—all orders of men look forward with eager expectation and growing alacrity to this pleasing reward of their toils. [*Federalist* 12, p. 91]

Gratification is channeled to be not an end in itself, but a means to encourage labor and industry and advance the common good.[29] Publius's emphasis here is on encouraging the kind of activity, labor, and industry, which entails such character traits as temperance (in economic terms, "deferred gratification") and courage ("adventurism," "entrepreneurship"). Thus it is fitting for him to speak of the national taxing power (Publius's key to managing the national economy) as if it were a power to free the whole range of human activity from "oppressive expedients":

> There is no part of the administration of government that requires extensive information and a thorough knowledge of the principles of political economy so much as the business of taxation. The man who understands those principles best will be least likely to resort to oppressive expedients, or to sacrifice any particular class of citizens to the procurement of revenue. [*Federalist* 35, pp. 216–217]

This passage almost goes to the extent of saying that a proper national tax policy will be of itself sufficient to prevent oppression of the human spirit. Publius seems convinced that unnatural elites cannot impose their will on society without economic support. Had his view been retained into the nineteenth century, when it became necessary to deal with the growing slave power, the national government might have preempted the Civil War by properly managing the national economy.[30]

On the foundation of such national policy, public morals could soar, Publius tells us, especially when responding less to legislative initiatives and more to leadership from his new invention, the popular presidency. The president represents the nation in the environment of international challenge. He "holds the sword of the community" when executing his distinctive powers as commander in chief, while in domestic affairs he "dispenses [its] honors" (No. 78, p. 465). Publius's national government, especially that part most feared by his opponents, is evidently intended to encourage the "free and gallant" citizen body which "republican government presupposes . . . in a higher degree than any other form" (No. 46, p. 300; No. 55, p. 346).

As an important part of his characterization of national powers, Publius insists that their scope can, and must in fact be limited to these high purposes.[31] With good rhetorical irony, he expresses his own incredulity at the suggestion that Article I, Section 8, of the Constitution is open to a constructive powers interpretation:

> A power to destroy the freedom of the press, the trial by jury or even to regulate the course of descents, or the forms of conveyances, must be very singularly expressed by the terms "to raise money for the general welfare." [*Federalist* 41, p. 209]

Publius's words may sound strange to modern ears, which have been attuned to the notion that historical changes, particularly industrialization, have outmoded the original constitutional limits, and that no original principle now supports the Constitution. But the truth is that the founders were really uninterested in exercising the powers that are now often thought to be so important, because their view of government's purposes had little to do with achieving "historical change." On the contrary, it was precisely because of *limited*—not unlimited—power that the national government was competent to achieve the objectives that they thought proper for political life.

Publius's attitude toward state powers is a complement to his pride in the nation. He is perhaps too candid in showing that state powers interest him little and occasionally even evoke from him a scornful comment:

> Allowing the utmost latitude to the love of power which any reasonable man can require, I confess I am at a loss to discover what temptation the persons intrusted with the administration of the general government could ever feel to divest the States of authorities [which it might be judged proper to leave with the States for local purposes]. The regulation of the mere domestic police of a State appears to me to hold out slender allurements to ambition. [*Federalist* 17, p. 118]

All this is not to deny, however, that Publius concerns himself about local matters. The founders had every incentive to encourage strong states, since their republicanism depended on a citizen body actively consenting to their government, and state political life in the constitutional system is a means of drawing citizens into the national scene.

Furthermore, affections centered about familiar local customs constitute the great "cement of society." Publius is fully aware that most of the time national policies are remote matters to the average citizen. And he agrees with the Anti-Federalists about something of which many contemporary Americans, who think of themselves as being sympathetic to anti-federalism and its Bill of Rights, have lost sight. He agrees that local, not national, laws must give expression to communitarian "manners, sentiments and interests." They must prohibit obscenity and libel, for example, in accordance with local standards.

Publius says further, that state police powers are more attractive to citizens, because they are the kind that can be used to satisfy more common desires. The general rule is presented in one of Publius's favorite metaphors based on natural science:

> In every political association which is formed upon the principle of uniting in a common interest a number of lesser sovereignties, there will be found a kind of eccentric tendency in the subordinate or inferior orbs by the operation of which there will be a perpetual effort in each to fly off from the common center. [*Federalist* 15, p. 111]

The prose rendition of this oft-repeated metaphor is given in one place as follows:

> The State governments will have the advantage of the federal government, whether we compare them in respect to the immediate dependence of the one on the other; to the weight of personal influence which each side will possess; to the powers respectively vested in them; to the predilection and probable support of the people; to the disposition and faculty of resisting and frustrating the measures of each other. [*Federalist* 45, pp. 290–291]

It is by nature that the state governments will possess an advantage over the national because of the kind of powers they exercise:

> There is one transcendent advantage belonging to the province of the State governments, which alone suffices to place the matter in a clear and satisfactory light,—I mean the ordinary administration of criminal and civil justice. This, of all others, is the most powerful, most universal, and most attractive source of popular obedience and attachment. It is that which, being the immediate and visible guardian of life and property, having its benefits and its terrors in constant activity before the public eye, regulating all those personal interests and familiar concerns to which the sensibility of individuals is more immediately awake, contributes more than any other circumstance to impressing upon the minds of the people, affection, esteem, and reverence towards the government. This great cement of society, which will diffuse itself almost wholly through the channels of the particular governments, independent of all other causes of influence, would insure them so decided an empire over their respective citizens as to render them at all times a complete counterpoise, and, not unfrequently, dangerous rivals to the power of the Union. [*Federalist* 17, p. 120]

To modify the force of what Publius calls "antecedent propensities" so that they do not favor local governments at the expense of the national, the national government has only one recourse—"good administration."

> I believe it may be laid down as a general rule, that [the people's] confidence in and obedience to a government, will commonly be proportioned to the goodness or badness of its administration. [*Federalist* 27, p. 174]

Publius believes that good administration can come from his new republican politics, which unifies men of diverse backgrounds in a common project to elect the best men. His differences with the Anti-Federalists come into sharp focus when he talks about representation and the capacity of citizens to defer to the best in their communities (No. 57, pp. 350–353).[32] This the Anti-Federalists thought was impossible. They thought only "brilliant talents" could characterize such representatives,[33] and they preferred instead a system in which representatives would be simple duplicates of their constituents; or that they would be different only in technical skills of service to legislators, but not in opinions and desires. Anti-Federalist legislators would be rubber-stamp representatives only. For Publius, such legislators were to be encouraged only at the local level. They could not provide what he meant by "good administration."

In sum, then, it is the people's willingness to judge local standards in the right spirit that makes possible their electing national representatives "whose wisdom may best discern the true interest of their country and whose patriotism and love of justice will be least likely to sacrifice it to temporary or partial considerations" (No. 10, p. 82). Without this spirit, voters will simply demand a carbon copy of themselves just as they do, Publius implies, at the local level.

The superiority of the national administration, which Publius anticipates, owes much to the fact that there is a larger pool of men who reason about politics and government from which the national government can draw. These men take note of the fact that national powers are concentrated on the limited set of objectives that the Constitution identifies as essentially political, and that Publius identifies as worthy of proud statesmen. There can be little doubt that the founders did in fact expect such men to emerge periodically, and that they expected them to see to it that the better administration of the people's more distant national concerns would entice the people away from the states:

> Unless we presume . . . that the powers of the general government will be worse administered than those of the State government, there seems to be no room for the presumption of ill-will, disaffection, or opposition in the people. [*Federalist* 27, p. 174]

At its best, nature provides a rare kind of man who is to be a special object of choice. He will be attracted to national politics more than to local:

> The benefits derived from [the national government] will chiefly be perceived and attended to by speculative men. [*Federalist* 17, p. 120]

While most men live by "national sentiment," speculative men may enjoy contemplation of the nature and tendency of [military (and other)] institutions, fortified by the events that have happened in other ages and countries. [*Federalist* 26, p. 169]

Thus Publius suggests that America's best representatives, its rare presidents perhaps, may be not only men of good character and reputation, but also of a philosophic temperament. They will be such men as could have written the Declaration of Independence. The Constitution, it appears, aims at the rule of law and reason even in the statesmen it promotes.

Observers generally agree that the national government has succeeded to a remarkable degree in attracting talent.[34] Whether it has been able sufficiently to counteract "antecedent propensities" is another matter. The case has been well made that contemporary national politics is deteriorating toward the local model. As was noted, the Bill of Rights has been used in modern times to enforce national sumptuary laws. It is also true, according to many observers, that the Congress has "localized" national powers by increasingly ignoring policy matters and devoting its energies to serving "clients" with economic advantages in the way that was formerly characteristic of the states.[35]

The strength of local politics in contemporary life owes a debt to a confusion about federalism as the founders understood it. This confusion has its roots in the academy. Academic readers of *The Federalist* often misconstrue the import of Publius's argument and overemphasize his concern with national commerce and the taxing power, while dismissing his concern to influence the moral life of the nation. Such a view might be supported by another common contemporary viewpoint, which interprets Publius as a student of John Locke, encouraging materialism for political ends.[36] Supporters of this view often go so far as to insist—against evidence as fresh as the Civil Rights movement—that the national government "can't legislate morals." But such a view argues against America's long history of great statesmen who have viewed the national powers as implacably hostile to such things as slavery, polygamy, pornography, and libel. Like these statesmen, Publius saw that "vigorous plants [would be] flourishing in the soil of federal as well as of State legislation" (No. 35, p. 217). Publius saw that, in the sense of recognizing "merit of every description" (No. 52, p. 326) without prescribing local sumptuary laws, national legislation would be decisively moral.

Such academic distortions of *The Federalist*, and of history, are nurtured by a contemporary pessimism that cannot attribute to leaders a public-spirited attachment to "sacred honor." A contemporary anti-federalism persists in a tacit bias regarding honor that is self-serving in the last analysis.[37] It persists in siding with Patrick Henry who thought that "harm is more often done by tyranny of rulers than by the licentiousness of the people."[38] And it persists against all experience in maintaining that the Constitution was established by and for the "wealthy and wellborn." Attention to constitutional provisions like the one prohibiting titles of nobility, or to the history of the Constitution in operation, should quiet these fears, but never succeeds in doing so because they are motivated by desires stubbornly based upon "preconceived prejudices."

Will the founders' view of federalism prevail, or will it be undermined by a hostile interpretation of their work? In the final analysis, the founders believed, everything depends upon the "prudence and firmness of the people" (No. 31, p. 197) and the leaders they appoint. That is to say, everything depends on the loyalty the people and their leaders show to the higher purposes of the nation, and the strength they show in resisting the attractions of a utopian local politics of "republican virtue."

CONTEMPORARY ANTI-FEDERALISM

Many, if not most, of today's conservative and liberal partisans simply reject the founders' understanding of federalism and the kind of politics it entails. Instead, they adopt a form of anti-federalism. Thus many contemporary conservatives rely on arguments from ancestral and prescriptive authority when they support such causes as prayer in school or restrictions on abortion. Their sentimental nostalgia involves them in a preference for regulating details of everyday life with the weight of custom, not political authority. Their position differs from the Anti-Federalists', however, insofar as the latter took their stand not for the purpose of revering the ancestral as such but of sustaining a politics of small republicanism. On the other hand, many contemporary liberals support grass-roots, participatory democracy with arguments that are also akin to anti-federalism. Unlike the Anti-Federalist small republicans, however, these liberals sacrifice what might be preferred in the (idealized) present to programs advanced in the cause of progress.

Thus for these partisans, both liberal and conservative, there is a common ground that is a product of the academy. This ground was prepared by Rousseau and cultivated by his many followers. It is the ground of "culture" (or "society"), by which is meant a world devoid of harsh political struggle. Although they emphasize different and even incompatible aspects of this apolitical world, both liberals and conservatives believe that it is the realm where human happiness is to be realized: both liberals and conservatives therefore reject the founders' opinion that a new human excellence is to be realized in national politics. In today's academy, this opinion is systematically ignored by a liberal political science that is passionately indifferent to the distinction between high things and low,[39] and also by a kind of conservative, Straussian scholarship to which the national government seems suspect because of its supposed inattention to the high things. Such partisan pedantry supports many conservatives and liberals when they decide that the Anti-Federalist view has been demonstrated to be correct, after all.[40]

In the light of these arguments, any claim that the nationalizing founders appreciated matters of the spirit is quickly dismissed. Only the Anti-Federalists are said to have been sensitive to such matters. Even the sympathetic label "federalist" is denied to the founders, for it is a favorite tenet among these scholars that, for rhetorical advantage, the nationalists shrewdly but illegitimately coopted the name "Federalist," while, ironically, the real federalists were called "Anti-Federalists." In fact, the term "federalist" had become synonomous with "unionist" by the time the Constitution was written, so that the founders rightly thought it belonged to them, not the Anti-Federalists, whom they deemed to be "disunionists." According to the founders, the union of the Constitution was federal because the states remained "sovereign" in the sense that their separate organization could not be abolished, even though it was true that they possessed only "exclusive and very important portions of sovereign power" (No. 9, p. 76). Today's scholars deny the founders' contention that the Anti-Federalists were ultimately disunionist, even as they side with the Anti-Federalist claim that "republican virtue" can flourish only in small republics.[41]

This academic bias toward a new anti-federalism was given classic expression when Martin Diamond sympathetically restated what he called the "small republic" argument in his famous text.[42] Diamond went so far as to imply that there was a moral superiority to the Anti-Federalist argument. The small republic advocates were convinced to adopt the Constitution, he said, only by an argument for the *advantages* of union, not for its superiority in principle. Madison "drove them to admit that what they wanted from union could only be supplied by *an essentially national government.*"[43] It should be noted that this was Diamond's sympathetic restatement of the Anti-Federalists' explanation of their own actions, not the Federalists' account of them. Diamond nowhere seriously considers the Federalist charges that the Anti-Federalists were greedy, power hungry, and irresponsible.

An academic and political partisanship follows Diamond's lead. Conservative academics elaborate on certain of the Anti-Federalists' ends by praising their supposed allegiance to traditionalism—to one's own family and land—and by supporting decentralization and "territorial democracy," to use Russell Kirk's phrase, which he adopted from Orestes Brownson and Alexis de Tocqueville. These conservatives fear that community feeling will lose its definition in the glare cast by abstract and universal political theories, and they want to counterbalance this loss with a great variety of traditionalist communities, especially those identified by a distinctive religious life and distinctive traditions of artistic excellence.[44] In a democracy, they argue, real localism is eroded by majorities demanding uniformity and equality even to the extent of sacrificing liberty. These are the so-called "Jacobin" majorities, which pursue a superficial and transitory politics of petty desires—which would freely engineer society without remembering that men's habits of heart and mind change only slowly. Thus the federal government's administrative technocrats are seen by conservatives as the instruments of national majorities demanding equality above all else.[45]

Today's liberal academics often agree with their conservative counterparts when they magnify the significance of local government, but of course for different reasons. Although they are known best for their internationalist concerns, liberals are also quite active on the local scene. They portray the national government as trapped by interest-group democracy, and accordingly try to encourage "grass-roots" democracy in cooperation with a national administrative apparatus. Robert Dahl, for example, decries the alienation of citizens from their national government and their lack of "confidence" in it. His ideal model is a direct or "grass-roots" democracy.[46] In such a state, intensity of personal feeling develops out of fraternity and commitment to clear-cut programs for social reform and for advancing the so-called performing arts. In the liberal view, this is the only adequate expression of public-spiritedness available in the modern world.

Liberals are fearful of conservative discipline, however, and are always on guard against the danger of local majorities giving expression to the wrong kind of politics. Such majorities are thought to be drummed up by zealots with a religious commitment, who threaten the proper free interplay of cultural values. Liberals typically want to prevent such a development by the all too familiar means of the federal judiciary, newly armed with a creative interpretation of the Fourteenth Amendment.

As these academic partisans battle over the spoils of a national government reduced to the status of mere facilitator, what remains unnoticed is the position taken by the founders when they debated the Anti-Federalists. What remains unnoticed, in other words, is the founders' defense of the Constitution's true federalism.

4

Foreign Policy and
The Federalist

PATRICK J. GARRITY

In the first volume of his memoirs, Henry Kissinger reflects upon those traditions of American foreign policy that stand in the way of a more realistic approach to the preservation of U.S. national interests. Because of our geographic remoteness and the shield provided by British sea power during the nineteenth century, Kissinger tells us, "Americans came to consider the isolation conferred by two great oceans as the normal pattern of foreign relations. Rather arrogantly we ascribed our security entirely to the superiority of our beliefs rather than to the weight of our power or the fortunate accidents of history and geography." The United States' belated interventions in the two great Eurasian wars of this century are said by Kissinger to have come about more from passion and idealism than from a cool calculation of the imperatives of the balance of power. Even the post-1947 American policy of containing the Soviet Union suffers according to Kissinger's standards: "This [American] definition of containment treated power and diplomacy as two distinct elements or phases of policy. It aimed at an ultimate negotiation but supplied no guide to the content of those negotiations." The incoherence of American foreign policy became apparent with the breakdown in the domestic consensus on containment caused by the Vietnam War: "The internationalist Establishment . . . collapsed before the onslaught of its children who questioned all its values."[1]

But the former Secretary of State grants that there was one period in U.S. history when American policy makers were able to act reasonably in the pursuit of American national interest: "Ironically, our Founding Fathers

The views expressed herein are those of the author, and not necessarily those of the Department of the Navy or any U.S. government agency.

were sophisticated statesmen who understood the European balance of power and manipulated it brilliantly, first to bring about America's independence and then to preserve it." Later generations would unfortunately forget "the statecraft by which the Founding Fathers had secured our independence; disdained were the techniques by which all nations must preserve their interests."[2]

Among those Founding Fathers whom Kissinger praises are Thomas Jefferson (for engaging Britain's enemies on the colonies' side during the American Revolution) and John Jay (for later securing recognition from Britain and "liquidating the residual problems of our war with England"). It should be noted, however, that Jay's latter accomplishment—"liquidating the residual problems" with Britain through the so-called Jay's Treaty—was vehemently opposed by Jefferson precisely on the grounds that it threatened American independence. In fact, the founders were deeply divided on a number of critical foreign policy questions, before, during, and after the ratification of the Constitution. The national debate over Jay's Treaty was just as heated and divisive as were subsequent controversies in American history—e.g., the Treaty of Paris (1898–1899), the Treaty of Versailles (1919), and the SALT II Treaty (1979). If wisdom was a hallmark of the founding generation, ordinary political consensus was not.

This is not to deny the importance of the views of the founding generation on foreign affairs; the creation and preservation of the Union during the late eighteenth and early nineteenth centuries are surely testimony to their genius. Behind the obvious and impassioned disagreements there must have been some fundamental consensus on the international environment and America's place in it, or the young nation could not have survived its turbulent beginnings. We are thus justified in looking for policies and documents—Washington's Farewell Address (1796) and the Monroe Doctrine (1823) being the two most prominent examples—in which that consensus might be revealed.

The effort to understand that consensus is not merely an indulgence in antiquarian curiosity, despite such obvious considerations as that ballistic missiles and nuclear weapons did not then exist. The actions and thoughts of the founders are rich with insights into the nature of man and politics, insights that are not limited to a particular time and place, insights that Henry Kissinger correctly calls to our attention. Also, by comprehending the basic divisions of opinion about foreign relations in the 1780s and 1790s, we may better understand the divisions that exist today.[3] Perhaps most importantly, American political leaders of the founding period recognized that major foreign policy disagreements must at times be reconciled if the safety and well-being of the regime were not to be put in immediate or long-term jeopardy. At the same time, they were not afraid to pursue the truth as they saw it, to seek political victory rather than consensus if that seemed necessary for the good of the regime.

The obvious danger with any search for consensus is that it will follow the lowest-common-denominator principle—i.e., an agreement for the sake of agreement, incorporating the weakest and least relevant portions of the contending arguments.[4] But three of the most important Founders—Alexander Hamilton, James Madison, and John Jay—demonstrated that this need not be so in their monumental literary collaboration to support ratification of the new Constitution.

The Federalist does not contain a complete elaboration of the theory and practice of international relations, because that was not the authors' purpose. But Publius does reveal many of the key assumptions about international affairs that informed the making of the Constitution and that guided early American foreign policy—even though two of the authors (Madison and Jay) had been bitterly at odds during the previous two years about the latter's negotiations with Spain over the Mississippi River, and even though two of them (Madison and Hamilton) would be at each other's throats during the next decade over almost every significant international question.

It is precisely these differences, clearly thought out and articulated in other forums and at other times, which make the consensus of *The Federalist*, however temporary, especially worthy of close study. Neither the form nor the substance of these differences was ultimately sacrificed to the necessities of the ratification debate, whatever temporary accommodations had to be made. None of the authors surrendered his prior or future policy preferences because of his intellectual and political participation in the joint project (although both Hamilton and Madison did later have certain passages from *The Federalist* cited against them). And above all, the profound threat to American security stemming from the weakness of the Confederation was dealt with, thereby providing the means to contend with other dangers—and to continue the debate over the true character of American national interest. This suggests that neither the search for political consensus nor for geopolitical truth alone represents the best approach to the formation of American foreign policy.

THE NATURE OF INTERNATIONAL POLITICS

The Federalist divides the globe into four political/geographic regions—Europe, Asia, Africa, and America—each of which is said to have a distinct set of interests. Unfortunately, at the present time, Europe, "by her arms and by her negotiations, by force and by fraud, has in different degrees extended her dominion over them all." Some attribute this European success to the superiority of her inhabitants, casting doubt upon the natural ability of the other regions to challenge Europe's global mastery. ("Men admired as profound philosophers . . . have gravely asserted that all animals, and with them the human species, degenerate in America—that even dogs cease to bark after having breathed awhile in our atmosphere.") Publius admits that "[f]acts have too long supported these pregnant pretensions of the European."[5]

Nevertheless, Europe's worldwide glory came from the collective successes of several nations, not just the singular excellence of one. Among themselves, the kingdoms of Europe struggle for commercial and military advantage, both inside and outside the continent. It is this struggle for national power which characterizes international politics. *The Federalist* makes this point most strongly when it argues that conflict, and not cooperation, would mark the American states if they ceased to come under the aegis of a national government. Despite their common language, geography, and preference for republican government, the demands of national interest would quickly divide them as surely as they had divided France and Great Britain.[6]

According to *The Federalist*, all nations have distinct interests that are of sufficient importance to be defended or advanced through war or the threat of war. Publius speaks of two principal factors that determine these interests. First, there is the effect of geography and the requirement to defend national territory. Nations that border on one another tend naturally to be rivals: ". . . it has from long observation of the progress of society become a sort of axiom in politics that vicinity, or nearness of situation, constitutes nations natural enemies."[7] Propinquity leads to territorial disputes, which "have at all times been found one of the most fertile sources of hostility among nations."[8] Along this same line, *The Federalist* distinguishes between continental and insular situations—nations that have land borders with other nations (e.g., France, Prussia, and Austria) automatically inherit "natural" geographic rivals, unlike nations that are surrounded by water or an otherwise benign environment (e.g., Great Britain).[9]

The second major determinant of national interest is commerce: "Diffent commercial concerns must create different interests. . . ."[10] *The Federalist* reflects that the great wars between Britain and France "have in great measure grown out of commercial considerations—the desire of supplanting and the fear of being supplanted, either in particular branches of traffic or in the general advantages of trade and navigation, and sometimes even the more culpable desire of sharing in the commerce of other nations without their consent." Further, Publius notes that the violent character of international relations has not changed since commercial interests and disputes became relatively more important: "Is not the love of wealth as domineering and enterprising a passion as that of power and glory? Have there not been as many wars founded upon commercial motives since that has become the prevailing system of nations, as were before occasioned by the cupidity of territory or dominion?" This is not to say that "the love of power or the desire of pre-eminence and dominion" has ceased to be a driving force in international relations—merely that the impulse to maximize national power tended to manifest itself in wars or diplomacy based on the search for commercial advantage.[11]

According to *The Federalist*, then, the major factors that determine national interest (geography, commerce, national or kingly ambition) tend toward conflict rather than conciliation among nations. "To judge from the history of mankind, we shall be compelled to conclude that the fiery and destructive passions of war reign in the human breast with much more powerful sway than the mild and beneficent sentiments of peace."[12] To reinforce this case about the "realistic" character of international politics, Publius describes the pernicious influence of "unrealistic" factors: Nations make war for advantage ("whenever they have a prospect of getting anything by it"), but "absolute monarchs will often make war when their nations are to get nothing by it, but for purposes and objects merely personal, such as a thirst for military glory, revenge for personal affronts, ambition, or private compacts to aggrandize or support their particular families or partisans."[13]

The latter point suggests that *The Federalist* has neglected a rather obvious factor affecting national interest: the nature of the regime. Surely monarchies are more aggressive than republics? But Publius takes pains elsewhere to demonstrate that peoples (and republics) have in practice been no less addicted to war than monarchs, that "aversions, predilections, rivalships, and desires of unjust acquisitions . . . affect nations as well as kings." Again: "There have been, if I may so express it, almost as many popular wars as royal wars."[14] *The Federalist* makes this point strongly in order to emphasize that the traditional balance of power politics, based on the conflict of nations, will not be replaced by some other, less conflict-ridden international system.[15]

As noted above, disputes over commerce had to a large extent replaced conflicts over territory as the mechanism that drove the European national and imperial competition, according to *The Federalist*. But at the time of the Revolution and during the Confederal period, some Americans argued that the combination of commerce (based on free international trade) and the spread of the republican form of government would lead to a very different kind of relationship among nations. Specifically, Publius refers to those who favored a dissolution of the Union and to their argument that several small commercial American republics would enjoy peace and prosperity with each other. This principle of commercial cooperation was also expected by some to create a similar relationship among the nations of the world. As *The Federalist* characterizes this view:

> . . . there are still to be found visionary and designing men, who stand ready to advocate the paradox of perpetual peace between the States though dismembered and alienated from each other. The genius of republics (say they) is pacific; the spirit of commerce has the tendency to soften the manners of men, and to extinguish those inflammable humors

which have so often kindled into wars. Commercial republics, like ours, will never be disposed to waste themselves in ruinous contentions with each other. They will be governed by mutual interest, and will cultivate a spirit of mutual amity and accord.

Publius's rejoinder is harsh:

. . . what reason can we have to confide in those reveries which would seduce us into an expectation of peace and cordiality between the members of the present confederacy, in a state of separation? Have we not already seen enough of the fallacy and extravagance of those idle theories which have amused us with promises of an exemption from the imperfections, the weaknesses, and the evils incident to society in every shape? Is it not time to awake from the deceitful dream of a golden age and to adopt as a practical maxim for the direction of our political conduct that we, as well as the other inhabitants of the globe, are yet remote from the happy empire of perfect wisdom and perfect virtue?[16]

The crucial point for Publius is that the United States cannot expect that international politics will somehow be transformed into something other than what observation reveals—the struggle for the advantage and survival of individual nations. Neither trade nor the development of republics (in the United States or elsewhere) will change the character of international relations. The new Constitution will not change, and was not intended to change, this situation. Publius emphasizes that the question of "peace or war will not always be left to our option, that however moderate or unambitious we may be, we cannot count upon the moderation, or hope to extinguish the ambitions of others. . . . To model our political systems upon speculations of lasting tranquillity would be to calculate on the weaker springs of human character."[17] More specifically, the United States must expect "that a firm union of this country, under, an efficient government, will probably be an increasing object of jealousy to more than one nation of Europe. . . ."[18]

Having made this grim observation, however, *The Federalist* does not counsel despair or the abandonment of republican government in favor of some other form better suited to the conduct of war and the defense of territory. Rather, Publius concludes that republican government, properly constructed, can provide security in this hostile international environment—and more importantly, that in doing so a republican government can bring domestic prosperity and well-being to its people. Here the Constitution, and the policies of those who drafted and supported the Constitution, were expected to play the crucial role in vindicating the worth and viability of self-government in international relations.

THE UNITED STATES AND WORLD POLITICS

Much of *The Federalist's* discussion of foreign policy is devoted to the question of safety—i.e., how the United States could preserve its national independence in the face of severe domestic and foreign pressure. This argument was made partly for ordinary political effect in the ratification debate; raising the British (or Spanish or Indian) threat garnered votes for the new Constitution, insofar as that threat seemed to have come about because of the inadequacies of the Confederation. But Publius seems to have much more in mind when making this argument. The most thoughtful supporters of the Constitution believed that the weakness of the Confederal government reflected an even larger political deficiency. The Constitution was written (as was *The Federalist*) with the hope of helping to define a sense of American nationhood that otherwise seemed incomplete. In a world of powerful and avaricious states, the United States was required to present itself to the world as a nation that understood and was capable of defending its interests. Any significant internal differences on this point were bound to be exploited by unfriendly powers. External danger, then, constituted an important unifying (centripetal) element for American nationalists.[19]

The Federalist was very explicit about the types of foreign dangers then confronting the United States. Britain and Spain held possessions on and around the North American continent from which attacks against U. S. territory could take place. (The British and the Spanish could strike directly with their own forces, or indirectly through support of the Indian tribes resisting the westward migration of American settlers.) This threat of military aggression against the United States was only part of the problem, however. America's domestic and international trade, which was vital to national prosperity, had been placed in jeopardy by the policies of the European empires. For example, Spain had closed the Mississippi River to Americans in 1784, thus shutting off the easiest route of trade from the emerging West to the rest of the states. Britain had imposed Orders in Council that effectively removed most of the lucrative trading advantages that the colonies had enjoyed while a member of the British Empire. Nor was the economic threat strictly a European one; for example, pirates from the Barbary Coast threatened to destroy American shipping in the Mediterranean.[20]

Publius thus insists that American independence had by no means been assured merely because of the peace treaty with Britain. Isolation from the quarrels of Europe was not a foregone conclusion in 1787. Hostile nations schemed to take advantage of American domestic weakness by convincing certain peripheral areas of the Confederation (Vermont, the West) that their interest lay in separation from the United States, if not formal alignment with Britain or Spain. Weakness at the periphery was unfortunately compounded by weakness at the center—or more precisely, because of the lack of a center ("weakness and divisions at home would invite dangers from abroad").[21] State governments by and large ignored the efforts of Congress to address the immediate dangers to the territorial and economic security of the Union. By following their own particular interests while sabotaging those of the entire nation, the states had drawn both the contempt and the wrath of Britain and Spain.

This line of argument was sympathetically received by many who had resented or suffered from the indignities borne by the United States during the Confederal period. But the requirements of safety were essentially negative in character. Foreign dangers could only go so far in creating a sense of national identity and interest; once the immediate danger had ceased—or when one state or faction tried to turn the threat to its narrow advantage—the artifice of cohesion would break down. Everyone could presumably agree upon the point that the American nation should not be held hostage to the whims of European despots, but what exactly did that principle mean in practice? Was it the interest of the West in free navigation of the Mississippi, or the interest of the East in enhanced trade with Spain (which might require an agreement with Madrid to forego navigation of the Mississippi, at least for some time)? What were the positive aspects of American nationhood that could unite those people who resided in American territory, and that could give energy and direction to the affairs of state in a dangerous and demanding world?

If these are not easy questions today, much less were they during the troubled years during and immediately after the Revolution. *The Federalist* is in part a description of the political and institutional process by which American national interests could be satisfactorily (and safely) defined. In the judgment of Publius, the Articles of Confederation had manifestly failed at this most essential task. That task was then conferred upon the Constitution, in combination with the Union.

The formation of positive national interests, however, is viewed by Publius as depending upon much more than properly structured institutions of government. Many American interests were derived from the fact that the United States existed at a particular place and time, and that it existed in a specific international environment that was largely beyond American control (but not beyond prudent manipulation). For instance, *The Federalist* noted that the occupants of American territory have a certain genius which must be taken into account in the formation of American institutions and policies. Among other traits, there is the "unequaled spirit of enterprise, which signals the genius of the American merchants and navigators and which is in itself an inexhaustible mine of national wealth."[22]

The devotion to commerce that marks the American character is buttressed by a natural inclination to Union. Publius remarks in Federalist 2 that "[t]his country and this people seem to have been made for each other," and that "independent America was not composed of detached and distant territories, but that one connected, fertile, wide-spreading country was the portion of our western sons of liberty." The people were united because they had descended "from the same ancestors, speaking the same language, professing the same religion, attached to the same principles of government, very similar in their manners and customs, and who, by their joint counsels, arms, and efforts, fighting side by side throughout a long and bloody war, have nobly established their general liberty and independence."[23]

Unfortunately, according to *The Federalist*, neither commercial enterprise nor affection for Union had prospered under the weakness of the Articles of Confederation. As a consequence of this weakness, the United States found it impossible to cope with the threat of aggression described above or to promote international or domestic commerce. The obvious failings of the Confederation undermined the popular ties that bound the Union together, and encouraged hostile foreign powers to restrict trade and otherwise meddle in internal American affairs, with the hope of breaking up the Union (or, in the case of Britain, recovering her imperial status). Thus the lament in *Federalist* 6:

> Let the point of extreme depression to which our national dignity and credit have sunk, let the inconveniences felt everywhere from a lax and ill administration of government, let the revolt of a part of the State of North Carolina, the late menacing disturbances in Pennsylvania, and the actual insurrections and rebellions in Massachusetts, declare—![24]

Publius warns that this depressing situation will lead to its logical conclusion—the frustration of commerce and the break-up of the Union, due in large part to foreign pressure—unless the substantial reforms undertaken by the Constitution are adopted. Once these reforms are achieved, *The Federalist* anticipates the outline of an approach to foreign policy that would provide security and prosperity to the American regime, along the lines that would satisfy the peculiar genius of the people. This outline, not surprisingly, contains many of the elements that would later appear in Washington's Farewell Address and the Monroe Doctrine. *The Federalist* does not argue that the United States can or should change the international environment radically to secure American interests; a global revolution on behalf of free trade or republican government does not seem to be necessary to the prosperity and security of the American regime. Rather, Publius suggests that the United States, if properly governed and prudent, can exempt itself from much of the turmoil caused by European conflicts. Indeed, American statesmen might well gain diplomatic leverage because of the mechanics of the European balance of power, thereby permitting the United States to gain positive economic and strategic advantages without exposing the United States to undue risks.

The central geopolitical objective of the United States is set out in *Federalist* 8. Here Publius makes the distinction between insular and continental states on the basis of the frequency with which nations are subject to invasion. Great Britain is described as falling within the first (insular) category because of its geographic location and its powerful navy. If the United States remains united and energetic, "we may for ages enjoy an advantage similar to that of an insulated situation. Europe is at a great distance from us. Her colonies in our vicinity will be likely to continue too much disproportioned in strength to be able to give us any dangerous annoyance." On the other hand, division of the Union would place the remaining states or confederacies "in a short course of time, in the predicament of the continental powers of Europe," both with respect to each other and to the European empires, which would then represent a much greater threat.[25]

We should note that the geopolitical objective established by *The Federalist*—insularity, or isolation—is a conceivable but not necessary consequence of the geographic separation between the Old and New World. That is, insularity for the United States, while feasible, is not automatic. To achieve this preferred position, the United States requires a positive program to maintain and strengthen the Union, provide adequate military capability to deter or conduct war, and remove European influence from American domestic councils and eventually from threatening positions in the Western Hemisphere. If the United States fails on this score, it will become "the instrument of European greatness." If the United States succeeds, however, it will be "superior to the control of all transatlantic force or influence and be able to dictate the terms of the connection between the old and the new world." The United States "may hope, erelong, to become the arbiter of Europe in America, and to be able to incline the balance of European competitions in this part of the world as our interest may dictate."[26]

The Federalist's understanding of the "balance of competition" can be reduced to this axiom: America rules in America, or Europe rules in America. (The United States, we should note, seeks to play upon the European balance of competition "in this part of the world"—i.e., America does not seek to become the arbiter of Europe in Europe.) By remaining united, the American states can play upon the inevitable conflicts among the European empires; the distinguished historian Samuel Flagg Bemis referred to this concept as "America's advantage from Europe's distress."[27]

How exactly does *The Federalist* propose that the United States gain advantage from Europe's distress? Military action is an obvious conclusion, but it is not the one that Publius reaches. Keeping in mind the peculiar commercial genius of the American people, *The Federalist* holds out trade as the preferred tool of American diplomacy. We recall his earlier observation that European disputes over commerce had supplanted to some extent the previous pattern of disputes over territory.[28] By playing in this commercial game—at the economic, not the military level—with its not inconsiderable resources, the United States might expect to gain leverage over competing European powers. "By prohibitory [discriminatory] regulations, extending at the same time throughout the states," Publius writes, "we may oblige foreign countries to bid against each other for the privilege of our markets." American markets were thought especially attractive to the Europeans because the U.S. economy was then, and seemed likely to remain, predominantly agricultural in character; European traders thus had several million potential customers whose needs for manufactured goods could not be satisfied in the domestic American marketplace.[29]

The Federalist describes briefly how a commercially based foreign policy might work, using the often-discussed British example:

> Suppose, for instance, we had a government in America capable of excluding Great Britain (with whom we have at present no treaty of commerce) from all our ports; what would be the probable operation of this step upon her politics? Would it not enable us to negotiate, with the fairest prospect of success, for commercial privileges of the most valuable and extensive kind in the dominions of that kingdom? . . . A mature consideration of the objects suggested by these questions will justify a belief that the real disadvantages to Great Britain from such a state of things, conspiring with the prepossessions of a great part of the nation in favor of American trade and with the importunities of the West India islands, would produce a relaxation of the present [British] system and would let us into the enjoyment of privileges in the markets of those islands and elsewhere from which our trade would derive the most substantial benefits. Such a point gained from the British government . . . would be likely to have a correspondent effect on the conduct of other nations, who would not be inclined to see themselves altogether supplanted in our trade.[30]

American commercial leverage over the European nations would be strongest when the latter were at war and in desperate need of trade. This interest increased the incentive for the United States to remain neutral and reap the benefits from all of the belligerents while suffering the wrath of none. The commercial approach to foreign policy also explains the long-standing American interest in the trading rights of neutrals in international law and practice, an interest which the Founding generation very much shared.

The inability of the Confederation to develop and enforce such a national economic policy was one of the major marks against the old system. As a result of this failure, Publius claims, commercial affairs tended to divide rather than unite the states and the people. The East-South debate over the question of the Mississippi, with its immense foreign policy repercussions, provided only one of many examples of this deplorable trend. The commercial genius of the American people, being frustrated, had manifested itself in dangerous ways—e.g., separatist trends and flirtation with foreign powers in the West, the flouting of Congress's requests for cooperation on trade legislation. A breakup of the Union would leave matters even worse:

> The spirit of enterprise, which characterizes the commercial part of America, has left no occasion of displaying itself unimproved. It is not at all probable that this unbridled spirit would pay much respect to those regulations of trade by which particular States might endeavor to secure exclusive benefits to their own citizens. The infractions of these regulations, on one side, the efforts to prevent and repel them, on the other, would naturally lead to outrages, and these to reprisals and wars.[31]

The Federalist suggested that the new constitutional system, and an intelligent geopolitical approach to American security, would channel this potentially divisive commercial energy and ambition into policies aimed to strengthen the bonds of Union, increase the general prosperity, and maintain security from external threats. Here is at least part of the positive national interest that the Founders were attempting to cultivate.[32]

Military power—at least as defined in terms of war and conquest—is not put forward by Publius as an object of positive interest to the American regime. *The Federalist* goes into great detail about how the Constitution and Union will decrease the likelihood of foreign aggression, whether the causes of the attack were just or unjust.[33] Publius is by no means indifferent to the importance of strategy or complacent about the military requirements of foreign policy; he notes that "[w]ar, like most other things, is a science to be acquired and perfected by diligence, by perseverance, by time, and by practice." The romantic image of the citizen-farmer leaving his plow to defeat the invader is unrealistic in the era of modern, professional warfare.[34] *The Federalist*, however, sees American military competence put to its best use not on the battlefield, but on occasions when it would deter a European power from contemplating war against the United States. In particular, the United States should be in a political and military position to maintain its neutrality, and its overseas commerce, during a war among European powers that does not immediately threaten American security.

Publius emphasizes that preference alone will not allow the United States to maintain its neutrality: "The rights of neutrality will only be respected when they are defended by an adequate power. A nation, despicable by its weakness, forfeits even the privilege of being neutral." To this end, a federal navy would be the most efficacious military tool with which to influence European behavior. That navy would not necessarily have to match the capabilities of the great British or French fleets to be effective, given the geographical advantages of operating an American navy in the Western Hemisphere, and the narrow margin of combat between the European maritime powers. In the not-too-distant future, the United States should be able to create a navy that would

> . . . at least be of respectable weight if thrown into the scale of either of two contending parties. This would be more particularly the case in relation to operations in the West Indies. A few ships of the line, sent opportunely to the reinforcement of either side, would often be sufficient to decide the fate of a campaign on the event of which interests of the greatest magnitude were suspended. Our position is in this respect a very commanding one.[35]

The Federalist here is not arguing that the United States should seek opportunities to conduct naval warfare; under these circumstances, the United States could probably avoid war and still maintain and promote its essential national interests. By combining American military forces with the usefulness of American military supplies to a European power operating in the New World, the United States would be able "to bargain with great advantage for commercial privileges. A price would be set not only upon our friendship, but upon our neutrality."[36]

The Federalist does not argue that military power alone, any more than preference alone, is the best way to maintain a useful neutrality for the United States. A positive American "correlation of forces" is best built on a broader base of national power and unity: "America united, with a handful of troops, or without a single soldier, exhibits a more forbidding posture to foreign ambition than America disunited, with a hundred thousand veterans ready for combat."[37] Publius puts this case forward in *Federalist* 4:

> If they [foreign nations] see that our national government is efficient and well administered, our trade prudently regulated, our militia properly orga- nized and disciplined, our resources and finances discreetly managed, our credit re-established, our people free, contented, and united, they will be much more disposed to cultivate our friendship than provoke our resentment.[38]

To sum up: like all other nations, the United States seeks to survive and prosper as a nation; to that end, Publius argues that it should seek to accu- mulate power and freedom of international action along the prudent lines described above. But national survival and prosperity are not comprehen- sive guides to the proper ends of national power. Commercial genius and inclination to Union are not sufficient descriptions of the American char- acter, because the same might be said of peoples under a monarchy or mixed regime. *Federalist* 39 points to another crucial aspect of the American way of life: "It is evident that no other form [than strictly republican government] would be reconcilable with the genius of the people of America; with the fundamental principles of the Revolution; or with that honorable determina- tion which animates every votary of freedom to rest all our political experi- ments on the capacity of mankind for self-government."[39]

What special requirements, if any, does the republican form of govern- ment place on American foreign policy? We earlier noted *The Federalist's* observation that there seemed to be no difference between monarchies and republics when it came to such crucial points as the pursuit of international commerce and the propensity to war. This observation must be qualified at least to the extent that, according to *The Federalist*, all other attempts at self-government to that date had been fatally flawed, and that only the American experiment fully grasped the true requirements of republican rule. To this extent, the United States may have interests and pursue pol- icies that differ from those of all other nations, both monarchical and quasi- republican.

One might also be able to formulate republican foreign policy by making a strict separation between the requirements of domestic politics (self-gov- ernment) and the demands of international relations (*Realpolitik*). The Pre- amble to the Constitution apparently gives equal weight to "the common defense," "a more perfect Union," "Justice," "domestic Tranquility," "the general Welfare," and "the Blessings of Liberty." In theory, one could avoid questions of priority by assuming that defense applies only to external matters and the rest strictly to internal affairs. But *The Federalist* does not permit that distinction to be made quite so easily, and indeed posits a very close relationship among these various goals of the regime. To recall points already made: a strong Union and domestic tranquility are essential to an effective foreign policy, while an effective foreign policy creates an environment in which American commerce can prosper without fear of external or internal European interference.

More importantly, *The Federalist* also stresses that the success of American foreign policy is essential to the preservation of American liberty. The character of any regime depends to a great extent on its place in the world. Again recurring to the distinction between insular and continental powers, Publius makes the point that those nations which are constantly exposed to the danger of invasion must maintain large standing armies to repel sudden invasion, and that "the liberties of Europe, as far as they have ever existed, have, with few exceptions, been the price of her military establishments."[40]

> The perpetual menacings of danger oblige the government to be always prepared to repel it; its armies must be numerous enough for instant defense. The continued necessity for their services increases the importance of the soldier and proportionately degrades the condition of the citizen. The military state becomes elevated above the civil. The inhabitants of territories, often the theater of war, are unavoidably subjected to frequent infringements on their rights; and by degrees the people are brought to consider the soldiery not only as their protectors but as their superiors.[41]

Unfortunately, according to Publius, some opponents of the Constitution have concluded too much from the unhappy condition of the continental European powers. To be specific, many Anti-Federalists objected to the lack of a Constitutional prohibition against a standing army as being a fatal flaw in that document—the first step toward an American despotism. *The Federalist* counters this argument directly on the grounds that a standing army as such need not lead to tyranny; clearly, given the importance of a constant defense of the frontier and the seacoast, some sort of permanent military force will be necessary.[42] Publius makes this part of his more general argument that it is foolish, indeed counterproductive, to limit in advance those powers of the government (e.g., to ensure public safety from external invasion) that cannot be limited in practice:

> How could a readiness for war in time of peace be safely prohibited, unless we could prohibit in like manner the preparations and establishments of every hostile nation? The means of security can only be regulated by the means and the danger of attack. They will, in fact, be ever determined by these rules and by no others. It is vain to oppose constitutional barriers to the impulse of self-preservation. It is worse than vain, because it plants in

the Constitution itself necessary usurpations of power, every precedent of which is a germ of unnecessary and multiplied repetitions. If one nation maintains constantly a disciplined army, ready for the service of ambition or revenge, it obliges the most pacific nations who may be within reach of its enterprises to take corresponding precautions.[43]

To support this essentially negative argument about military power, Publius develops a much more optimistic theme: the American military establishment will prove compatible with republican government because a prudent foreign policy can decisively affect (though it cannot absolutely prohibit) "the preparations and establishments of every hostile nation." By indirectly reducing the threat, an American government can thus minimize the necessary size and importance of its own armed forces. In contemplating their verdict on the fate of the Constitution, the people should not assume that the continental situation will or should obtain for the United States; an insular condition is both desirable and possible. (An insular nation, we recall, is one that is not ordinarily jeopardized by the constant threat of foreign invasion.) Britain here is proof of what the combination of favorable geography and sensible foreign policies can achieve: "Being rendered by her insular situation and her maritime resources impregnable to the armies of her neighbors, the rulers of Great Britain have never been able, by real or artificial dangers, to cheat the public into an extensive peace [time military] establishment."[44]

To enjoy "the same happy security" as her former colonial master, the United States must follow the British pattern of security, or "the face of America will be but a copy of that of the continent of Europe. It will present liberty everywhere crushed between standing armies and perpetual taxes."[45] That pattern for Publius included maintaining the Union, and developing an effective maritime (naval) capability to defend against seaborne invasion, protect American commercial shipping, preserve America's rights as a neutral, and (in the modern vernacular) project military power if such became necessary. In geopolitical terms, an emphasis on the navy was a cheap way to purchase a great deal of diplomatic and economic leverage; by denying a potential European enemy the ability to supply land forces in North America or to hold American coastal cities hostage, the United States would enjoy a potentially decisive military advantage, and hence discourage attack in the first place.

In political terms, a strong navy was much less offensive to republican liberty than a standing army; in Publius's words, the "batteries most capable of repelling foreign enterprises on our safety [i.e., the navy] are happily such as can never be turned by a perfidious government against our liberties."[46] Naval competence would imply a reduction in the size of the army, that force which is most feared by republican governments: "When a nation has become so powerful by sea that it can protect its dockyards by its fleets, this supersedes the necessity of garrisons for that purpose. . . ."[47]

In summary, *The Federalist* does not anticipate any dichotomy between the requirements of "power" and "principle" in American foreign policy. A due regard to republican liberty (which necessitates Union and a properly constructed national government) and to the requirements of geopolitics are seen as being complementary, not contradictory. The approach that made the most strategic sense—the active pursuit of insularity (isolation) with an emphasis on strengthening America's position in international commerce— would also create a domestic environment that would support the preservation and maturation of self-government. This was about as comprehensive a definition of the national interest as one could possibly achieve.[48]

CONCLUSION

To return to our earlier question: how could three men, who were able to collaborate on such a brilliant exposition of political rhetoric and political theory as *The Federalist*, disagree so strongly over the direction of the American regime in the decade following ratification of the Constitution? The consensus articulated in the name of Publius—that insularity and the pursuit of commerce represented the essential American national interest toward the rest of the world—proved impossible to maintain in practice. Neither Hamilton nor Madison, nor their respective followers, ever repudiated this basic goal of American foreign policy, but they interpreted the means to that goal (and indeed, the goal itself) in vastly different lights. This observation is not intended to revisit the political terrain of the Hamilton-Madison split, which has been well staked-out by other and far wiser scholars. But it is intended to produce reflection concerning the meaning and purpose of reaching a consensus about American foreign policy.

For those attending the national security conference circuit in the Washington–New York–Boston triangle, one familiar topic is today discussed virtually without fail: how can the American political community reestablish a bipartisan consensus on foreign affairs similar in form—but almost certainly not in substance—to that which existed during the so-called Cold War? This project, unfortunately, is hampered by the general lack of clarity about the fundamental assumptions and goals that underlie various foreign policy options now being discussed. Perhaps it is this lack of clarity, and not the lack of consensus, which lies at the root of our security problem.

When one examines the historical record to identify the "golden years" of the anti-Soviet consensus, one will search almost in vain. There were significant differences of policy and purpose about the American doctrine of containment from the beginning; the original "father" of containment, George Kennan, would later deny paternity for virtually the entire enterprise. Harry Truman and Dean Acheson, now heroes for much of the conservative movement, were not heroes to the right when they were in office. George Marshall, the architect of American victory in World War II, somehow managed to "lose" China and was later vilified on the floor of the Senate as "an errand boy, a front man, a stooge, or a co-conspirator for this [Truman] administration's crazy assortment of collectivist cutthroat crackpots and Communist fellow-traveling appeasers."[49]

This is not to deny that one can identify, in retrospect, critical agreements about the national interest from 1947 to the late 1960s, just as one can identify certain points of consensus in 1787, or today for that matter. If these points—often unspoken and even unrecognized—did not exist, then the American regime would have collapsed at some point. But such specific or general areas of concurrence have not been, and are not now, a complete blueprint for U. S. national security. A consensus on the ends of American foreign policy, if that were intellectually possible, would provide no guarantee of a consensus on the means to achieve those ends. (Nor would the fact of a consensus guarantee that it would work in the real world.) A consensus on certain means (e.g., the MX missile and the small ICBM), if that were politically negotiable, would very likely not be supported by a common purpose.

Such is the pattern of American history, and there is little reason to believe it will change. There is no magic solution to resolve differences over the proper approach to the Soviet Union, over the morally and strategically correct nuclear doctrine, over the efficacy of sanctions against the government of South Africa. We will in all likelihood continue to muddle along, knowing that it is not the best we could do, but that it will have to do.

Still, for those who are interested in doing better, in improving the contemporary content of American foreign policy, a reappraisal of the experience of the founders is most instructive. Publius demonstrated in the 1780s the fruits of collaboration; Hamilton and Madison demonstrated in the 1790s the limits of that collaboration, and their belief that it was more important to demonstrate the alternatives then open to the American regime than to remain in shallow agreement for the sake of consensus and political tranquillity. We are richer for both experiences, not only because the founders were sophisticated, but because they worked hard to make serious arguments about their deeply held convictions, and to understand fully their own position and that of their political adversaries (or allies). Over the past two centuries, we have taken liberally from each vision—from each set of policies—that which suited us. We have profited from both the harmony and the discord. The search for consensus is not always the best approach, and certainly not the only approach, to improving our understanding of the national interest.

5

The Problem of the Separation of Powers: *Federalist* 47–51

WILLIAM KRISTOL

Experience has instructed us that no skill in the science of government has yet been able to discriminate and define, with sufficient certainty, its three great provinces, the legislative, executive and judiciary; or even the privileges and powers of the different legislative branches. Questions daily occur in the course of practice which prove the obscurity which reigns in these subjects, and which puzzle the greatest adepts in political science. [*Federalist* 37, p. 228]

One of the principal objections inculcated by the more respectable adversaries to the Constitution is its supposed violation of the political maxim that the legislative, executive and judiciary departments ought to be separate and distinct. . . . No political truth is certainly of greater intrinsic value, or is stamped with the authority of more enlightened patrons of liberty than that on which the objection is founded. [*Federalist* 47, p. 301]

As these quotations suggest, the separation of powers was for Publius a principle of both great authority and considerable obscurity.

The authority both for the founders and for us of this "political maxim"—not to say "sacred maxim" (No. 47, p. 308)—is clear. Consider the text of the Constitution under which we live. There the principle of the separation of powers seems not to require a defense or even an exposition; it is simply presupposed. Just as it seems to be assumed that government should be established by "We the People," so the separate existence of the three

100

powers that constitute the separation of powers appears to be taken for granted; the Constitution merely "vests" each of these powers in a certain institutional arrangement. The fact of the separation of powers, and of each of the three powers, seems to be something accepted by "We the People" rather than established by us. One could say, simply from a reading of the bare text of the Constitution, that the separation of powers is to be one of the two underlying principles of its structure (along with federalism), just as the principle of republican government underlies its overall form.

Yet, despite (or perhaps because of) its importance, both the grounds for the authority of the principle of the separation of powers, and the principle's meaning, remain obscure. The Constitution gives only minimal guidance as to the character of each of the three powers, and even less guidance as to grounds for the separation and distribution of the powers in the first place. And Publius's account of the separation of powers in *Federalist* 47–51 is terse, and seems primarily intended to refute an objection rather than to clarify the basis of the principle. At most, one could say that while it is relatively clear *that* power must be separated, it is unclear *why* power should be separated into these three powers, each with its particular features. There seems to be no explicit discussion anywhere in *The Federalist*—and precious little elsewhere in the writings of the founders—of just what the principle is by which the three powers are separated and distributed, or of just what the intrinsic character of each of the powers is. In *Federalist* 48, Publius writes

> After discriminating, therefore, in theory, the several classes of power, as they may in their nature be legislative, executive, or judiciary, the next and most difficult task is to provide some practical security for each, against the invasion of the others. [*Federalist* 48, p. 308]

But where does the prior task of discriminating the powers in theory take place?

A commentary on Publius's general discussion of the separation of powers in *Federalist* 47–51 may at least help to sharpen our understanding of the problem—or the several problems—that surround the concept of the separation of powers in the American Constitution. Among these are the following: What is (are) the principle(s) by which the powers are separated and distributed? What is the character and purpose of each power? What is the relationship of the principle of the separation of powers to the principle of republicanism? Why is Publius so hesitant about confronting these questions directly—and why does there seem to be something particularly indirect or opaque about the principle of the separation of powers as a whole? By giving some idea of the complexity and subtlety of Publius's understanding, this commentary may provide a starting point for the further thought and investigation that these questions deserve.

FEDERALIST 47

Publius arrives at the topic of the separation of powers in *Federalist* 47: "Having reviewed the general form of the proposed government [Nos. 39–40], and the general mass of power allotted to it [Nos. 41–46], I proceed to examine the particular structure of this government, and the distribution of this mass of power among its constituent parts." The particular structure is discussed in *Federalist* 47–51, or more strictly in *Federalist* 48–51, after Publius has answered an objection in Number 47.[1] The key to the particular structure of the government is thus the separation of powers and the principles underlying it. This discussion of the government's structure occupies a central position in *The Federalist* between the discussion of the general form and the mass of power of the federal government, and the discussion of its different branches or parts;[2] it is the link between the general form of the government and its parts. Indeed, the central question of *The Federalist* might be said to be the relationship between the "general form" of the government and its "particular structure." For both the general form—republican, i.e., "dependent on the people." (No. 46, p. 300)—and the particular structure—informed by the principle of the separation of powers—are presented by Publius as principles or standards by which the Constitution must be judged. And each of these principles seems independent of the other—and in some tension with the other. For while dependence on the people is *the* principle of republicanism, and from this point of view the standard by which the Constitution should be judged (No. 46, p. 300), we learn in Numbers 47–51 that dependence on the people can be a problem for liberty and good government. The separation of powers helps to solve the problem of republican government in a way that does not apparently violate the principle of republican government.

The discussion of the particular structure of the federal government is introduced by Number 47, which consists of a response to an objection. The practical character of *The Federalist* is reflected in Publius's unwillingness directly to address theoretical questions; just as *The Federalist* as a whole presents itself as at least in part a response to objections to the Constitution (see No. 1, p. 36), so the most theoretical sections of *The Federalist* are provoked by the need to respond to objections. Though wise politicians may resist, they cannot help appealing to theory, to "more general inquiries" (No. 52, p. 325) beyond this particular constitution to defend the Constitution. But Publius is sparing and circumspect in his general inquiries; he is reluctant to lay bare the theoretical foundations of the Constitution in general, and of the separation of powers in particular. While the Constitution (and *The Federalist*) clearly rests on certain theoretical principles, Publius is not eager to lay out those principles in broad daylight. Somehow Publius wishes the Constitution to appear to stand on its own as much as possible, to appear, as it were, as self-sufficient as possible. As we shall see, the separation of powers is peculiarly conducive to this sort of apparent self-sufficiency.

What is the objection that provokes Publius's discussion of the separation of powers?

> One of the principal objections inculcated by the more respectable adversaries to the Constitution is its supposed violation of the political maxim that the legislative, executive and judiciary departments ought to be separate and distinct. In the structure of the federal government no regard, it is said, seems to have been paid to this essential precaution in favor of liberty. The several departments of power are distributed and blended in such a manner as at once to destroy all symmetry and beauty of form, and to expose some of the essential parts of the edifice to the danger of being crushed by the disproportionate weight of other parts. [*Federalist* 47, p. 301]

These respectable adversaries of the Constitution believe that politics can embody symmetry and beauty of form; they therefore believe that the different departments can be kept separate and distinct. They do not understand or appreciate the difficulty of distinguishing explained by Publius in Number 37; politics cannot live up perfectly to political maxims.

Publius readily concedes that "no political truth is certainly of greater intrinsic value or is stamped with the authority of more enlightened patrons of liberty than that on which the objection is founded" (p. 301). Before appealing to the authority of these patrons, Publius briefly elaborates on this "political truth." "The accumulation of all powers legislative, executive and judiciary in the same hands, whether of one, a few, or many, and whether hereditary, self appointed, or elective, may justly be pronounced the very definition of tyranny" (p. 301). Publius goes out of his way to indicate that each of the three traditional forms of government may be free or tyrannical; the separation of powers which preserves liberty replaces what was traditionally understood to distinguish each of these forms from their perverted versions, a concern for the common rather than a partial good. All three forms seem compatible with the separation of powers and therefore with liberty; the difference among the forms seems from this point of view relatively unimportant. The separation of powers appears to be a standard separate from the different forms of government, which would moderate or guide each of these forms toward the common end of liberty, understood at first in its simplest sense of non-tyranny. In the preceding paper, Number 46, Publius reminded the adversaries of the Constitution, and us, that under the Constitution "the ultimate authority, wherever the derivative may be found, resides in the people alone" (p. 300). The separation of powers in a republican regime would then have the purpose of checking the accumulation of power in the hands of the people.

Were the federal Constitution really guilty of a tendency toward the accumulation of power, "no further arguments would be necessary to inspire a universal reprobation of the system." Republicanism without the separation of powers is indefensible. But Publius persuades himself "that it will be made apparent to every one, that the charge cannot be supported, and that the maxim on which it relies has been totally misconceived and misapplied" (p. 301). Everyone is attached to the separation of powers if it is understood as necessary for the sake of liberty, and everyone can be made to see that the maxim has been misunderstood.

To investigate the meaning of the maxim, Publius turns to "the oracle who is always consulted and cited on this subject," the celebrated Montesquieu. When discovering the meaning of a republic, Publius had rejected recurring to authorities, and had offered—indeed, asserted—his own definition of the republican form (No. 39, pp. 240–241). Here, by contrast, Publius does not speak in his own name, saying that the accumulation of all powers in the same hands "may justly be pronounced the very definition of tyranny" (p. 301), and he resorts to an authority or even an oracle to learn the meaning of the maxim. If the republican principle reflects our claim to be able to govern ourselves, the separation of powers seems to reflect a truth beyond our choosing to which we must accommodate ourselves; Publius accordingly recurs to an authority above us to find its meaning. But Publius's recurrence to authority to establish the meaning of the separation of powers does not obviate the need for us to pronounce the definition of tyranny, or to interpret the "oracle" who teaches the maxim; as we know from Number 37, even the meaning of the words of the Almighty is unclear to men; the authority to which Publius recurs does not speak for itself.

Publius endeavors "in the first place" to ascertain his authority Montesquieu's meaning. But he does so not by turning directly to Montesquieu but rather by turning to Montesquieu's source, the British Constitution. The source of the maxim of the separation of powers is the British Constitution; and the British Constitution is, as we were reminded by Publius in Number 39, not a republican one. This invaluable precept is not only not limited to republican regimes; its source is a nonrepublican regime.

But Montesquieu did not recur to the British Constitution as such, but rather, "to use his own expression," to the British Constitution "as the mirror of political liberty." As Homer is "the perfect model" for the epic art, the British Constitution is a mirror of political liberty. It is surely questionable whether there is such a thing as the "epic art" outside of the epics of Homer and other poets; Homer seems to be the founder of the epic art which seems wholly conventional. Must political liberty be seen in a mirror because it is only an image, and images look real in a mirror? Montesquieu at least seems to suggest that this might be the case in *The Spirit of the Laws*, Book XI, chapter 6: the citizen's political liberty is a spirit of tranquillity that comes from an opinion of security; it is not security itself; it is only an opinion, and its status is questionable from the philosophic point of view or from the point of view of philosophic liberty.[3] If the citizen's opinion of his security or his liberty is not warranted, if it is a poetic fiction, then Montesquieu is being kind to that opinion by finding it in the British Constitution and claiming that that constitution is a mirror of something real; in fact the British Constitution, insofar as it claims to be based on nature, beautifies nature; it is more like Homer than a mirror. Politics must claim to be a mirror of nature but cannot be based on nature; thus in Number 39 Publius claims to be recurring to principles but in fact asserts his own political definition of a republic; thus Publius here recurs to Montesquieu as his mirror, in the spirit of Montesquieu, rather than trying to look directly at the separation of powers. Looking directly at the separation of powers might cast doubt on the possibility of the liberty it is designed to secure.

The political implication of the fact that politics cannot be based on a recurrence to nature is that political communities cannot recur directly to the people. Publius's recurrence to the source of the separation of powers in the British Constitution rather than to first principles in nature perfectly mirrors the way in which the separation of powers operates, as we shall see in Number 49, to prevent or discourage a recurrence to the people, or to first principles, in the American regime. It does this for the sake of the people's liberty. In the American republic the people claim to be their own first principle, to govern themselves; this claim is moderated by the separation of powers—for first principles are perhaps not so supportive of human liberty as republicans presume. To prevent the need for a recurrence to the people, the separation of powers will be made as self-sufficient as possible; when forced to look beyond the separation of powers, Americans will look to the explanation of Publius, who will become our authority, even as Montesquieu was his. Publius will do for the American Constitution what Montesquieu did for the British: he will use it as a mirror for the principles of political liberty.

Publius therefore takes a brief look at the British Constitution, and discovers that the three departments there are not totally separate and distinct. He infers from this fact that Montesquieu's meaning can amount only to this: "that where the *whole* power of one department is exercised by the same hands which possess the *whole* power of another department, the fundamental principles of a free constitution, are subverted." Publius's interpretation of Montesquieu merely sets forth the minimal requirements of the separation of powers; to what do we look for guidance in the ordering of the different branches? Publius is reluctant to confront this question in *Federalist* 47–51. Furthermore, Publius ignores the weight Montesquieu puts on the importance of the person of the executive being sacred, or of one house of the legislature consisting of hereditary nobles; his deference to Montesquieu on the separation of powers and his obscuring of the non-republican character of Montesquieu's analysis lead us to wonder what in America might substitute for those elements that Montesquieu thought important to prevent the existence of what he called "an unfree republic."[4] The novel American judicial power (see especially No. 78) and the energetic American executive power (see especially No. 70) seem particularly important in this context.

Publius further appeals to "the reasons on which Montesquieu grounds his maxims" to support "the meaning which we have put on this celebrated maxim of this celebrated author." Publius uses Montesquieu to support the meaning he, Publius, has put on Montesquieu's maxim; the meaning is Publius's, but it requires support in the authority of Montesquieu. Here, Publius seems to act as a judge, interpreting the meaning of the maxim by recurring to its author and his source and reasons. It is appropriate that Publius act as a judge in interpreting the separation of powers, for the separation of powers is not something simply chosen by us, but a standard to which our government must conform for the sake of liberty. Publius seems to give us here a model for how a judge might behave in interpreting the American Constitution; he would look at its oracle, and his source and reasons, rather than directly at the first principles themselves; the separation of powers, which seems to depend peculiarly on the judiciary and even to culminate in the judiciary, is established by Publius in a judicial manner.

Publius next turns to the state constitutions as his other authority for the minimal understanding of what the separation of powers requires. In these constitutions, "notwithstanding the emphatical, and in some instances the unqualified terms in which this axiom has been laid down, there is not a single instance in which the several departments of power have been kept absolutely separate and distinct" (p. 304). Publius quickly examines all of the state constitutions to prove his point. Publius makes progressively clearer as he goes through the state constitutions that in practice the violations of the separation of powers are in the direction of legislative supremacy; the state constitutions, despite or because of their belief in the pure separation of powers, and their refusal to consider the necessity of mingling the different powers, have allowed for a sort of legislative supremacy. This difficulty is the theme of Number 48.

At the end of Number 47 Publius warns, "in citing these cases in which the legislative, executive and judiciary departments, have not been kept totally separate and distinct, I wish not to be regarded as an advocate for the particular organizations of the several state governments" (p. 307). Publius has appealed to the authority of the state constitutions to support his interpretation of the separation of powers; now he begins to undermine that authority. Here, however, Publius excuses the state framers: among their many excellent principles, the state constitutions "carry strong marks of the haste, and still stronger of the inexperience, under which they were framed" (p. 307).

Publius concludes:

> What I have wished to evince is, that the charge brought against the proposed constitution, of violating a sacred maxim of free government, is warranted neither by the real meaning annexed to that maxim by its author; nor by the sense in which it has hitherto been understood in America. This interesting subject will be resumed in the ensuing paper. [*Federalist* 47, p. 308]

Publius appeals both to the now nameless author of the maxim, and to America, as support for "the real meaning" of the separation of powers: the "meaning which we have put on this celebrated maxim" is now its "real meaning," supported as it is both by Montesquieu, i.e., by the British Constitution, and by the American state constitutions. One might say that the separation of powers can be found both in the nonrepublican British regime and the too narrowly republican (as we shall soon learn) state constitutions. We should note that while Publius will in the next paper criticize the state constitutions, he never criticizes Montesquieu or the British Constitution's embodiment of the separation of powers. By contrast, in Number 39 Publius had distinguished the republican American Constitution from the British and allied it with the state constitutions. Does the American Constitution strike a mean between the republicanism of the state constitutions, which lack a well-functioning separation of powers, and the well-constructed but unrepublican separation of powers of the British Constitution?

We should also note that at the end of Number 47 the separation of powers is promoted to a "sacred maxim" from a mere "political truth" or "precept in the science of politics." This is in accord with Publius's earlier reference to Montesquieu, who, "if he be not the author" of this precept is at least "the oracle." Yet right after calling the maxim "sacred," Publius calls Montesquieu "its author." Its source is human; the sacred maxims of politics have human authors, human beginnings; one cannot treat the separation of powers as something sacred and therefore pure, refusing to mix the powers at all; the separation of powers requires human support and contrivance; human liberty requires an understanding of the human origins of political principles. On the other hand Publius does in a way defer to the notion that this maxim is sacred, and his method of presenting it in these papers is that of a faithful believer: Publius does not question or investigate the grounds of the separation of powers. Politics requires a kind of reverence, and in America that reverence is directed toward the Constitution and particularly toward the principle of the separation of powers embodied in the Constitution. Publius thus denies the sacred character of the separation of powers without challenging its authority: the separation of powers seems to stem from a nondivine or quasi-divine standard above us that supports liberty; and the Constitution with the separation of powers in it seems to have a status on the one hand not divine, but on the other hand not merely the product of popular choice. In *Federalist* 78, Publius shows that judicial review depends on the fact that the Constitution is more than an expression of popular will, that it is both the expression of popular will and a reasonable such expression (see the movement in No. 78 from "will" to "intention"). But our reverence for the reasonable Constitution cannot simply be based on reason: Americans must respect the separation of powers without fully understanding its grounds.

FEDERALIST 48

While in Number 47 Publius had appealed to authorities to clear the Constitution of the charge against it, Publius now begins his own exposition: "I shall undertake in the next place, to show that unless these departments be so far connected and blended, as to give to each a constitutional control over the others, the degree of separation which the maxim requires as essential to a free government, can never in practice, be duly maintained." Some connection is required to support the separation required for free government. Publius will focus in his discussion on maintaining the separateness of the powers, on preserving their separation which is for the sake of free government, rather than on the correct distribution of power. But we shall see that in the course of his discussion Publius cannot but indicate some of what informs the particular structure of the government beyond the need to keep the powers separate—some of what accounts for the particular ordering and distribution of power in the different departments.

Thus Publius begins by reminding us that "it is agreed on all sides" that no department ought to administer the powers of another, or to have "directly or indirectly, an overruling influence" over the others. Nor will it be denied, Publius continues, "that power is of an encroaching nature, and that it ought to be effectually restrained from passing the limits assigned to it." And Publius concludes with the statement:

> After discriminating therefore in theory, the several classes of power, as they may in their nature be legislative, executive, or judiciary, the next and most difficult task is to provide some practical security for each, against the invasion of the others. What this security ought to be, is the great problem to be solved. [*Federalist* 48, p. 308]

Now Publius does not attend in *Federalist* 48–51 to the task of discriminating in theory the several classes of power. Indeed, Publius seems to wish to turn our attention away from this first question. That this task has been accomplished is presumed, and Publius moves on to "the next and most difficult task" of providing security for the different powers. Publius proceeds as if this first task of discrimination were simple or evident, despite his statement in Number 37 that "no skill in the science of Government has yet been able to discriminate and define, with sufficient certainty, its three great provinces, the legislative, executive and judiciary." Or is it precisely the great difficulty, even the impossibility, of making this theoretical determination, of discovering the "nature" of each class of power, that accounts for Publius's method in Numbers 48–51? If there is no evident support in nature for the separation of powers, if "the limits assigned" to power are assigned by men, must we nonetheless believe that the separation of powers is quasi-natural, if not quite sacred? We might note that whatever its source, the separation of powers is presented as having a status independent of human making, independent of the republican principle; it is something to which we have to conform for the sake of our liberty. Publius gently teaches us this necessity, and therefore obscures the more radical question of whence the separation of powers is derived.

Thus Publius focuses on preserving the separateness of the separate powers for the sake of liberty or free government. The ordering or discriminating of the several classes of power would presumably be for the sake of good government, each branch performing the functions it is best suited to perform. Just as the security for the separation of powers presumes the prior distribution of those powers, so the end of that separation—liberty or security for individuals—presumes the possibility of an order which allows for liberty or security. But as the phrase "separation of powers" suggests, the liberal regime focuses our attention on the separateness of the powers for the sake of our security or liberty, rather than on the prior distribution of powers whose continued separateness we secure. The first question—the proper discrimination of the several classes of power—cannot be the first question for us. Attending to the first question would perhaps be inimical to our honorable determination to govern ourselves and to live freely; it might reveal to us the problematic status of human liberty, or that the claim of liberty seems to collapse either into the need to anticipate necessity, on the one hand, or into the need for good government (human liberty depending on human wisdom), on the other. The separation of powers in its ordering, in particular in the executive and judicial branches, seems to acknowledge this truth, but to do so in a way that does not destroy the claims of political liberty.

Publius considers in Numbers 48–50 three methods of providing for the security of the separation of powers. Only after showing the insufficiency of those methods does Publius introduce his own solution in Number 51; Publius's reasons for rejecting these methods are therefore important for understanding the meaning of the American separation of powers.

The first method of securing the separation of powers, which is discussed in the remainder of Number 48, is "to mark with precision the boundaries of these departments in the Constitution of the government, and to trust to these parchment barriers against the encroaching spirit of power." This solution would suppose that mere legislation is sufficient to stand up against the encroaching spirit of power. But ironically (or appropriately) the legislative solution would be particularly ineffectual against legislative encroachments. The legislative solution of parchment barriers will have to be supplemented with devices making the separation of powers, as it were, self-executing and self-judging; it is already self-legislating, insofar as the proper discrimination of the powers does not seem to depend on the people.

Publius tells us that parchment barriers are "the security which appears to have been principally relied on by the compilers of most of the American Constitutions" (p. 308). But we know from experience that the efficacy of this provision was greatly overrated, "and that some more adequate defense is indispensably necessary for the more feeble, against the more powerful members of the government. The legislative department is everywhere extending the sphere of its activity, and drawing all power into its impetuous vortex" (p. 309). The compilers of the state constitutions seem to have ignored the fact that certain of the departments are naturally more powerful or more feeble than others; their understanding was too formal, ignoring the different character of the different powers, indeed the different power of the different powers, in a republic.

Publius respectfully but firmly criticizes the state constitutions, one of his authorities in Number 47. "The founders of our republics have so much merit for the wisdom which they have displayed, that no task can be less pleasing than that of pointing out the errors into which they have fallen." Publius apologizes for criticizing these founders, having already excused them for their haste and inexperience in Number 47; he practices what he teaches in Number 49 about the need for reverence even or especially in a republic. But a "respect for truth" obliges Publius to remark that these Founders seem never to have recognized the danger to liberty from legislative usurpation rather than from an hereditary monarch. The state founders seem not to have grasped that the threat to the separation of powers in a republic comes from the *legislature*. They thought of the separation of powers as a support for, rather than a check on, the power of the legislature.[5]

Indeed, the errors of the state founders were apparently due to their unfamiliarity with the novel regime of a "representative republic." For in a government where a monarch has extensive prerogatives, the executive is justly viewed as the source of danger, "and watched with all the jealousy which a zeal for liberty ought to inspire." The general form of the government affects the relative power of the different departments; the separation of powers must be adjusted to counteract the natural propensities of the different forms. And in a "representative republic," where the executive is limited, and where the legislative power is exercised by an assembly, the legislature ought to be feared. For the legislature is "inspired by a supposed influence over the people," and is sufficiently numerous to feel the passions of a multitude but sufficiently small to be capable of pursuing the objects of its passion by means which reason prescribes. "It is against the enterprising ambition of this department, that the people ought to indulge all their jealousy and exhaust all their precautions." Representation in the legislature, far from being the solution to the problem of popular government, as suggested in Number 10, creates new dangers, since the legislature at once has the mantle of popular authority and is capable, unlike the people, of rationally pursuing the objects of its passions. Representation must be supplemented by the separation of powers. We note that Publius's definition of the republican form in Number 39 (pp. 240–241) makes all three branches equally republican—though not in fact equally close to the people—and thus legitimizes the separation of powers that is directed against the legislature.

Publius says that he has appealed to our experience for the truth of his argument; but he refers in particular "to the example of two States, attested by two unexceptionable authorities." Publius's "unexceptionable authorities," i.e., authorities with republican credentials, are Thomas Jefferson for Virginia and the council of censors for Pennsylvania. After taking these as his authorities in Number 48, Publius criticizes their solutions for maintaining the separation of powers in Numbers 49 and 50, though without calling attention to this fact. Thus in the course of Numbers 47–50, Publius discredits all the authorities to whom he appeals (except for Montesquieu); in Number 51 Publius will appeal to no authorities, and the separation of powers will be presented as if it were self-sufficient, independent of any author and even of any particular place.

Publius's first example in Number 48 is Virginia, which proclaims the separation of powers in its constitution, and his authority is Jefferson. Publius quotes Jefferson at some length to the effect that all the powers in Virginia had devolved to the legislature, and consequently the state was tending toward an "elective despotism." In short, the elective principle, "the characteristic policy of republican government" (No. 57, pp. 350–351), is insufficient to prevent despotism.

The other state Publius takes as an example is Pennsylvania, and the other authority the council of censors, which met to inquire whether the Constitution had been preserved. This council found that the legislature had flagrantly violated the Pennsylvania Constitution in a variety of ways.

Publius offers a formal statement of his conclusion: "a mere demarcation on parchment of the constitutional limits of the several departments, is not a sufficient guard against these encroachments which lead to a tyrannical concentration of all the powers of government in the same hands." This restatement is formal because he fails to remind us that the parchment barriers in a republic are particularly insufficient against the legislature's encroaching hands. This formal conclusion to some extent masks, as does the separation of powers as a whole, the real impact of the separation of powers in a republic. But if a demarcation on parchment is insufficient to secure the separation of powers, what is sufficient?

FEDERALIST 49–50

The possibility of resorting to the people to preserve the separation of powers is explored in Numbers 49–50. By rejecting this alternative, Publius makes clear the radical implications of Number 48: it is not simply that parchment barriers are insufficient—but that rule by the people, the republican principle, is itself in tension with both the maintenance and the end of the separation of powers.

Publius begins Number 49 by remarking that "the author of the 'Notes on the State of Virginia,' quoted in the last paper," added to that work a draft constitution he had prepared for the state. The named authority of Number 48 thus becomes the unnamed and criticized author of Number 49. Publius quotes Jefferson's "original" proposal: whenever two of the three branches concur by a two-thirds vote that a convention is necessary to alter or to correct breaches in the Constitution, a convention shall be called for the purpose.

Inasmuch "as the people are the only legitimate fountain of power," Publius remarks, "and it is from them that the constitutional charter, under which the several branches of government hold their power, is derived, it seems strictly consonant to the republican theory to recur to the same original authority" (pp. 313–314), not only to alter the powers of government but whenever one department encroaches on another. Republican theory seems to require recurring to the people as the legitimate source of authority to preserve the Constitution. But we shall see that it is necessary, if the republican claim is to be vindicated, that the limits of that claim be acknowledged, if only indirectly; so American government begins from the people, but will not return or recur to them. The reasons for not recurring to the people limit the truth of the claim that the people can be the "original authority" in the full sense. The refusal to recur to the people will have the effect of separating the author from the authority; the Constitution becomes an authority over the people who are its source; and the principle of that Constitution is the separation of powers. We may say that the American regime moves from its republican origins and form to its structure of the separation of powers; the structure is not derived from the authority of the people, though it is implemented by authority of the people. The regime thus combines the claim that the people are the supreme and original authority, and an acknowledgment of the limits of that claim in the separation of the government from the people. That separation is enforced above all by the judiciary, which protects the Constitution in the name of the people and obviates the need to return to the people; and in protecting the Constitution, it makes clear that the Constitution derives its dignity both from being an act of the people and from embodying standards of good government outside their will.

Publius acknowledges that there is "great force" in the reasoning that suggests an appeal to the people; and "it must be allowed . . . that a constitutional road to the decision of the people, ought to be marked out, and kept open, for certain great and extraordinary occasions" (p. 314). The Constitution can provide for an appeal beyond itself, to the people, on extraordinary occasions; but extraordinary occasions need not and indeed should not guide the provisions for the ordinary. For the force of the reasoning suggesting an appeal to the people cannot overcome "insuperable objections against the proposed recurrence to the people, as a provision in all cases for keeping the several departments of power within their constitutional limits" (p. 314). What are those insuperable objections?

After discussing a less important objection, Publius sets forth one that "may be considered as an objection inherent in the principle": "as every appeal to the people would carry an implication of some defect in the government, frequent appeals would in great measure deprive the government of that veneration, which time bestows on everything, and without which perhaps the wisest and freest governments would not possess the requisite stability" (p. 314). A frequent recurrence to the original authority would destroy the veneration of that authority for its creation. Veneration requires "time" which allows the people to forget that the Constitution is merely their creation. But veneration also requires, as Publius indicates, a belief in the absence of defect in the object venerated; one does not venerate old defective things; one only venerates what is without defect, self-sufficient; the people will only venerate the government if they are made to forget its dependence on them, indeed if it is made independent of them. But it must be more than independent: it must be admirable, something to be looked up to. Time is perhaps necessary for veneration, and therefore the Constitution must not be easily changeable; but a belief in the independence and even superiority of the thing seems necessary in addition; the Constitution must be seen as independent of and superior to the people at the same time that it is the product of the will of the people. Of course, the Constitution is most visibly venerated as the expression of the people's will, as the embodiment of mankind's capacity for self-government. But this requires that the capacity lay dormant after the founding or be understood to be embodied in the workings of the government. The people can venerate a government based on the people only if that government is separated from them so that their original act is unique; after the founding the government is self-sufficient. Publius's ascription of the grounds of veneration to "time" tends to obscure the way in which the operation of the separation of powers not only protects the government from changes by the people, but also elevates it above the will of the people.

Why is veneration required for stability?

> If it be true that all governments rest on opinion, it is no less true that the strength of opinion in each individual, and its practical influence on his conduct, depend much on the number which he supposes to have entertained the same opinion. The reason of man, like man himself, is timid and cautious when left alone, and acquires firmness and confidence, in proportion to the number with which it is associated. When the examples which fortify opinion are *ancient* as well as *numerous,* they are known to have a double effect. [*Federalist* 49, pp. 314–315]

The American regime tries to combine two bases for this public opinion—time and numbers, by combining the republican form which grounds the government in the people and a structure that does not necessitate a recurrence to the people. The American regime will be supported by the "double effect" of a popular origin and the lack of recurrent appeals to the people; this double effect depends on the double ground of the Constitution in its republican form and its structure of the separation of powers.

Publius concludes this paragraph:

> In a nation of philosophers, this consideration ought to be disregarded. A reverence for the laws would be sufficiently inculcated by the voice of an enlightened reason. But a nation of philosophers is as little to be expected as the philosophical race of kings wished for by Plato. And in every other

> nation, the most rational government will not find it a superfluous advantage to have the prejudices of the community on its side. [*Federalist* 49, p. 315]

One might have thought that in a nation of philosophers, reverence for the laws would be unnecessary; such a nation could live by reason, by a reasonable attachment to reasonable laws alone. But this is not so. A nation of philosophers would realize, by enlightened reason, the insufficiency of reason to support any set of laws. Even or especially a nation of philosophers would realize that men cannot live simply according to their self-legislation—that men need to acknowledge something higher than themselves, higher than human choice. In the American regime this higher principle is embodied in the separation of powers, which indirectly, and especially through the judiciary, teaches us that men cannot simply govern themselves as they wish. Men have to limit their attempts to govern; the people must accept the limited Constitution which limits the legislature and even the people, ultimately in the interest of the people and their liberty.

Publius next turns to "a still more serious objection against a frequent reference of constitutional questions, to the decision of the whole society." This objection is based on "the danger of disturbing the public tranquillity by interesting too strongly the public passions" (p. 315). Like the previous objection, this objection is based on the importance of stability or tranquillity. Stability requires at once a common opinion and a dampening of passion. This is difficult, for "As long as the reason of man continues fallible, and he is at liberty to exercise it, different opinions will be formed. As long as the connection subsists between his reason and his self-love, his opinions and his passions will have a reciprocal influence on each other; and the former will be objects to which the latter will attach themselves" (No. 10, p. 78). The judiciary seems to some degree to abridge the liberty of citizens to exercise their fallible reason by upholding the Constitution that teaches a common opinion, and by preventing a recurrence to the people's fallible reason; it teaches a common opinion which however does not much interest the passions. The reason and the self-love of the people are disconnected by the separation of the Constitution from the people, and by the separation within the Constitution of the judiciary from the legislature. Public passions are channeled into the legislature, but a common opinion is taught by the judiciary, which is distant from the people and relatively safe from public passions.

Publius has to support his contention that recurring to the people would interest too strongly the public passions, given the recent recurrences to the people within the states: "notwithstanding the success which has attended the revisions of established forms of government and which does so much honor to the virtue and intelligence of the people of America, it must be confessed that the experiences are of too ticklish a nature to be unnecessarily multiplied" (p. 315). One can wonder how successful these revisions have been, since admittedly all power in the states is falling into the legislative vortex. Publius does not address this question here. Rather he distinguishes between previous and future recurrences to the people:

> We are to recollect that all the existing constitutions were formed in the midst of a danger which repressed the passions most unfriendly to order and concord; of an enthusiastic confidence of the people in their patriotic leaders, which stifled the ordinary diversity of opinions on great national questions; of a universal ardor for new and opposite forms, produced by a universal resentment and indignation against the ancient government; and whilst no spirit of party connected with the changes to be made, or the abuses to be reformed, could mingle its leaven in the operation. The future situations in which we must expect to be usually placed do not present any equivalent security against the danger which is apprehended. [*Federalist* 49, p. 315]

We "are to recollect" that conditions could not have been better for the founders of the state constitutions. Whereas Publius in Number 47 had excused their mistakes because of the haste and inexperience under which they labored, we now see clearly that their mistakes must have been due to failures in understanding rather than to unfortunate circumstances. Even the good conditions now outlined by Publius did not produce wise decisions; they perhaps did at least repress the public passions. What will substitute for these conditions in the future? The danger that repressed the passions will perhaps be replaced by the extended sphere that diffuses the passions; the confidence of the people in their patriotic leaders, which stifled the usual diversity of opinions, will be replaced by a common opinion in the worth of the Constitution; the ardor for new forms will be replaced by reverence for the old Constitution; and the absence of the spirit of party will be replaced by involving the spirit of party in the operations of the government, through the separation of powers.

Publius considers the different situations of the departments. The members of the executive and judiciary, few in numbers, will be personally known only to a small part of the people. The judges, "by the mode of their appointment, as well as by the nature and permanency of it, are too far removed from the people to share much in their prepossessions" (p. 316). This "permanency," a term used again in Numbers 51 and 78, is of course an exaggeration—judges can be impeached; but it suggests that the judicial power is to be as permanent as possible under the republican form, and therefore as independent as possible from the prepossessions of the people. The mode of appointment and the tenure of the judiciary are crucial to understanding its character; but the character and purpose of the judicial power are never addressed explicitly.[6] In the American regime, and in *The Federalist*'s presentation of it, the nature and purpose of the different departments never seem to be openly addressed; they must be inferred from the reasons given to support particular provisions for appointment and removal, and from the particular powers given to the different departments; and the particular provisions and powers of each department are not comprehensively discussed in their relations to each other. The different "powers" of the separation of powers only indirectly reveal their character and object; they present themselves, we might say, as "powers," though to understand the characteristics of the different powers one has in fact to look to the purpose and character of each. And so Publius here, typically, treats the different prepossessions of the judges as a consequence of their mode of appointment and tenure rather than as the *purpose* of their mode of appointment and tenure.

The executive and judiciary, Publius continues, will ordinarily be an "adverse party" to the legislature, and as long as the legislature is understood to be peculiarly the guardian of the people's rights, the other branches will be overwhelmed in an appeal to the people. One can see the importance of establishing the principle that all three departments are coordinate and equally representative of the people, and of supporting this by preventing recurrences to the people and indeed by casting the judiciary as particularly the guardian of popular rights. One could say that the solution of the separation of powers not only separates the judicial power from the legislative power, but separates the people's legislating of the Constitution from the executing and judging of the Constitution.

Publius next turns to the most important aspect of his greatest objection to recurring to the people's judgment. It might sometimes happen, Publius acknowledges, that appeals would be made under circumstances less adverse to the executive and judiciary departments. The legislative usurpations might be flagrant; a part of the legislature might take the side of the other branches; the executive might be a favorite of the people. "In such a posture of things, the public decision might be less swayed by prepossessions in favor of the legislative party. But still it could never be expected to turn on the true merits of the question" (p. 317). The decision should be one on the true merits, not simply one that would happen to restore the equilibrium. The limits on popular knowledge seem to be the highest ground for Publius's refusal to recur to the people.

Publius gives three reasons why a decision on the merits is "never" to be expected in an appeal to the people. The decision would be connected with the spirit of preexisting parties or parties springing out of the question itself; it would be affected by influential persons; and it would be pronounced by men who had been involved in the measures to which the decision would relate. These reasons why a popular decision on the merits is never to be expected would seem to cast doubt on the capacity of mankind to govern itself reasonably, which is to cast doubt on the capacity of mankind for self-government: For "the *passions*, therefore, not the *reason*, of the public would sit in judgment. But it is the reason, alone, of the public, that ought to control and regulate the government. The passions ought to be controlled and regulated by the government" (p. 317).

This is a striking statement. It stops short of proclaiming the right of wisdom rather than of consent to rule in two respects: it refers to the "reason of the public" rather than to reason simply, and it says not that the reason of the public should rule the passions but that the reason of the public should control the government which in turn should control the passions. This is nonetheless the clearest and boldest statement in *The Federalist* that self-government implies good government, that the rule of the public implies that the reason of the public will sit in judgment.

How is "reason" to be brought together with or derived from "the public?" And how is the reason of the public to control the government? The answers to these questions are related, and both point to the judiciary. For the "reason of the public" is embodied not in the people but in the judiciary, and in the separation of powers in general; the reason of the public cannot be the reason of the people though it must be derived from the people. The reason of the public can only prevail if there is no appeal to the people, to the original authority. The republican claim that the people are the only legitimate fountain of power can be accommodated to the requirement of reasonable government by, on the one hand, confining the people to the original exercise of their authority, and, on the other hand, by not trying to impose the direct rule of reason but rather contriving that it control and regulate the government. The reconciliation of the republican claim with that embodied by (and hidden in) the separation of powers is possible because the republican claim of government by consent, i.e., self-government, ultimately must recognize the necessity of wisdom or must become the claim of good government; the right of mankind to self-government depends on the capacity of mankind for self-government, of government by reflection as well as choice.

But at the same time, the claim of wisdom has to acknowledge its limits in the necessity of consent; even a nation of philosophers would need laws and reverence for those laws; reason cannot rule directly in politics, so reason is justly limited to controlling the government. The principles of consent and wisdom are brought together through the mixture of the republican form and the separation of powers. The fact that the separation of powers is somehow independent of the people reflects the fact that the capacity of mankind for self-government does not come from mankind, and that the people are incapable of securing their own liberty simply by their own legislation. But the possible compatibility of the separation of powers with the republican form reflects the fact that mankind can choose or consent to the separation of powers, to what is reasonable, despite the inability of reason to rule directly.

Publius turns in Number 50 to a second possible way of preserving the constitutional demarcation of powers: rather than occasional appeals to the people, periodical appeals may be "the proper and adequate means *of preventing and correcting infractions of the Constitution*" (p. 317).

But if the fixed periods are short intervals, the measures will be recent and will give rise to all the difficulties that disqualify the proposal for occasional revisions. If the periods are distant, the previous objections will still hold for recent measures, and to the degree that the remoteness of some measures may allow dispassionate review of them, there are counter-balancing inconveniences. Publius mentions three: a distant prospect of public censure would be a feeble restraint on power compared with the urging of present motives; the abuses might have completed their mischievous effects before the remedy could be applied; or they might at any rate be of long standing and deeply rooted. We should note that all the arguments of Numbers 49 and 50 are based on the unspoken premise that normal elections are insufficient to preserve the separation of powers. Indeed elections, and the republican form, are part of the problem rather than part of the solution, since they are the cause—or at least the corollary—of the excessive power of the legislature as against the other two branches. But if elections do not work, why should "periodical appeals" to the people work? What are elections but periodical appeals? The tension between the republican principle and the separation of powers is almost made explicit here, but by casting his discussion as a criticism of Jefferson's and then of Pennsylvania's solutions, Publius to some extent masks the fundamental nature of that tension. It is gentler, and more reverent of the republican principle, to reject the idea of recurrence to the people when it is presented as the plan of Jefferson and the Pennsylvania council of censors, rather than in its own right. Publius's indirect method here is indicative of the indirection of the separation of powers, which moderates and modifies the republican principle without confronting it head on.

We should remark especially the third of the five problems that Publius cites in Number 50 as characterizing Pennsylvania's experiment. The deliberations of the council of censors were marked by a split between two fixed and violent parties. Every unbiased observer can see that "unfortunately, *passion*, not *reason*, must have presided over their decisions. When men exercise their reason coolly and freely on a variety of distinct questions, they inevitably fall into different opinions on some of them. When they are governed by a common passion, their opinions, if they are so to be called, will be the same" (p. 319).

This reassertion of the limits of human reason is in contrast to the calm statement of Number 49 that the "reason of the public" should control the government. The reason of the public is not every man exercising his own reason, for that leads to diverse opinions. And the usual source of a common opinion is a common passion. Publius's task is to foster a necessary common opinion that will not, however, simply reflect a common passion, but will somehow reflect the "reason of the public." Can a common opinion be taught through the separation of powers that acknowledges the limits of the people's reason or of the capacity of men directly to rule themselves? Can the reason of the public and a common passion necessary to support it be brought together in an opinion that reveres the Constitution both as the product of the people and the embodiment of the reasonable separation of powers?

So, "this censorial body, therefore, proves at the same time, by its researches, the existence of the disease, and by its example, the inefficacy of the remedy" (p. 320). But even if the facts of this experiment are "a complete and satisfactory illustration" of Publius's reasoning, his reasoning heretofore has not provided an efficacious remedy. We turn for a solution to Number 51.

FEDERALIST 51

Parchment barriers are insufficient to maintain the separation of powers; a force beyond the Constitution, beyond the law, is necessary to support the law. What force shall we choose? The most obvious choice in a republic would be to rely on the people, but this is rejected in Numbers 49 and 50. Though the people are the source of power, they cannot secure or maintain the government they set up. So to what expedient does Publius finally resort for maintaining in practice the necessary partition of power among the several departments laid down in the Constitution? "The only answer that can be given is, that as all these exterior provisions are found to be inadequate, the defect must be supplied by so contriving the interior structure of the government as that its several constituent parts may, by their mutual relations, be the means of keeping each other in their proper places."

Publius proposes to contrive the "interior structure" of the government so that the parts keep each other in their proper places: the government is a whole with parts, but with no apparent ruling part or principle, except for the preservation of the system itself. Number 51 continues, after the manner of the previous papers, to present the separation of powers as a separation simply for the sake of liberty, ignoring the purposes or principles that govern the distribution of the powers. The "relations" of the different parts of the government keep each part in its proper place, but there is no visible ordering principle of what is the proper place for the parts. The relations do not happen naturally; they must be contrived; but we are not explicitly told with an eye to what they are contrived.

Publius says he will not presume to undertake a full development of this important idea, but will "hazard a few general observations, which may perhaps place it in a clearer light, and enable us to form a more correct judgment of the principles and structures of the government planned by the convention." Publius is reluctant to address the theoretical grounds of this "important idea," but he must in order to defend it. In Number 47 Publius had introduced his discussion of the separation of powers by saying that his investigation will be "in order to form correct ideas on this most important subject. . . " (No. 47, p. 301). Perhaps it is not possible for politics to be based on "correct ideas"; therefore Publius does not fully develop the important idea of Number 51, but rather offers enough so we will be able "to form a *more* correct judgment. . . ." And what we have to judge more correctly are "the principles and structure of the government planned by the convention"; the Convention, selected by us, planned the government; and we the people can judge it. We note that the government has "principles" rather than one principle; is this related to the fact that it can only be *more* correctly judged by us, rather than correctly understood, since the government embodies two or three principles that cannot fully be reconciled? We could form correct ideas, perhaps, if the government were based on one principle. Our need to judge, and the limits on our judgment, both stem from the fact that politics requires reconciling different principles that must be mixed in the structure of the government.

Publius's "general observations" in Number 51 consist of three observations developed in only five paragraphs of tightly argued explication; these are followed by "two considerations particularly applicable to the federal system of America." The discussion in Number 51 of the grounds of the America separation of powers is on a very general and theoretical level, without the mention of a single proper American name. The truth of the separation of powers is not particularly American; the principles of the separation of powers provide a standard by which to judge the government planned by the Convention; and these general principles must then be brought together with particularly American considerations.

Publius begins:

> In order to lay a due foundation for that separate and distinct exercise of the different powers of government, which to a certain extent, is admitted on all hands to be essential to the preservation of liberty, it is evident that each department should have a will of its own; and consequently should be so constituted that the members of each should have as little agency as possible in the appointment of the members of the others. [*Federalist* 51, p. 321]

Each department should have a will of its own. In Number 78 we learn that will can be said to be the principle of the legislative department; each department has to have a legislative aspect—an independent will. Each department has an aspect that is common to all the departments—their having a will—and an aspect that differentiates it according to its own character and purpose.

If each department is to have a will of its own, the members of each should have as little agency as possible in the appointment of members of the others. Publius points out that "were this principle rigorously adhered to, it would require that all the appointments for the supreme executive, legislative, and judiciary magistracies should be drawn from the same fountain of authority, the people, through channels having no communication whatever with one another" (p. 321). Publius acknowledges that perhaps a plan of constructing the departments by separate channels from the people would be less difficult in practice than it may appear in contemplation: the objection to adhering to this plan is not primarily practical. But "some difficulties however, and some additional expense, would attend the execution of it. Some deviations therefore from the principle must be admitted." The "execution" of a plan reveals its difficulties, the difficulties of adhering strictly to one principle. Publius's discussion seems to portray the separation of powers at work, as it were: the legislature legislates a plan based on a general principle, the executive modifies it in light of difficulties which the general principle does not take into account, and, as we are about to see, the judiciary judges the principle and modifies it not in light of practical difficulties but in light of its limitation by other principles. The attempt to execute a principle shows that some deviations "must be admitted," regardless of our wishes. But the example Publius gives of a deviation is not one of execution but of a more fundamental kind: "In the constitution of the judiciary department in particular, it might be inexpedient to insist rigorously on the principle" (p. 321). The constitution of the judiciary reveals the limits on the expediency of this principle of separate wills for each department, in light of the end of the judiciary—in light of the character of the judicial power rather than its mere separateness.

The principle is inexpedient "first, because peculiar qualifications being essential in the members, the primary consideration ought to be to select that mode of choice, which best secures these qualifications." This is a radical statement: the "primary" consideration with regard to the judiciary is to secure qualified members, not to respect the republican principle of selection by the people, or the principle of independent wills for each department. The primary consideration for the judiciary "in particular" is not the source of its authority but a mode of choice which selects the best men; who is to be selected, rather than who is to select, is primary for the judiciary. This is much less the case—it cannot be primarily the case—for the legislature. The constitution of the judiciary reflects its purpose, and suggests also how the judiciary is to choose—with a view to the end—as opposed to how the legislature characteristically or primarily chooses—with a view to the source of its power, to expressing the popular will. The primary consideration for the judiciary is a nonrepublican one—qualifications—and therefore the mode of choice is nonrepublican; Publius does not bother explicitly to remind us that he is assuming that the people cannot judge who will be a good judge. One could say that in constituting the judiciary the Convention appears to have acted judicially—judging with a view to its end—whereas in constituting the legislature, it seems to have acted legislatively—looking first to the source of authority, to who chooses. There *is* an element of judging in the constitution of the legislature, and Publius will later explain why we can hope for good legislators. His discussion of the House of Representatives ascends from the legislature's duty to express the popular will to the legislature's duty to make wise choices[7]; and there is an element of the legislative in the judiciary, indirectly chosen by and removable by the people, and with, as we are about to see, a will of its own. But the primary consideration for each is different; and the separation of powers as a whole includes both considerations.

The second reason not to insist rigorously on the principle is that "the permanent tenure by which the appointments are held in that department must soon destroy all sense of dependence on the authority conferring them" (p. 321). "Permanent tenure" is taken to be the *de facto* meaning of tenure of good behavior, the phrase that is used in the definition of the republican form in Number 39 (p. 241). Publius here appeals to the judges' "permanent tenure" as evidence that the judges will be independent of the president and Senate; insofar as permanent or near-permanent tenure is presented as for the sake of securing the judiciary against the other branches, it can be made acceptable to republicans. But it is striking that permanent tenure is here simply presumed; we only learn the grounds for it in Number 78. Permanent tenure is presented here as a fortunate fact that allows the modification with regard to appointments to be safe from the standpoint of the principle of separate wills. As we have said, Publius avoids giving a coherent account of any of the powers, always presuming one feature while defending another. In this case, the presumption of permanent tenure allows him to justify the fact that the primary consideration for the judiciary should be a wise choice of judges, not a republican one. One distinctive and questionably republican feature of the judiciary—permanent tenure—is used to reassure us about the effect of another—the mode of choice—in the context of the agreed-upon need for each department to have a will of its own.

Publius tells us that the judges' permanent tenure must destroy "all sense of dependence on the authority conferring them." This authority means at first the president and Senate; but permanent tenure will presumably also destroy all sense of dependence on the authority indirectly conferring appointments on the judges: the people. Once the judges are appointed, the permanent tenure of the judiciary would seem to constitute it something close to a will independent of society, independent of the people who are the fountain of authority.

Publius's second general observation supplements his first: "It is equally evident" that the members of each department "should be as little dependent as possible" on members of the others for their salaries. Were the executive or judges dependent on the legislature in this respect, "their independence in every other would be merely nominal." Neither in this case nor in the first is simple independence possible: the members "should be as little dependent as possible"; (p. 321) the limits on the independent will and support of each department reflect the limits on the self-sufficiency of the separation of powers as a whole, and the fact that the separation of powers still depends ultimately, in a republic, on the will of the people.

"But the great security against a gradual concentration of the several powers in the same department," though perhaps not so evident as the first two, "consists in giving to those who administer each department the necessary constitutional means and personal motives to resist encroachments of the others" (pp. 321–322). It is not enough to give each department a will and support of its own; each must be able to defend itself against the others. One might say that if the first two observations had to do with giving each department its own legislative aspect, this third observation has to do with giving each department an executive aspect. "The provision for defense must in this, as in all other cases, be made commensurate to the danger of attack. Ambition must be made to counteract ambition. The interest of the man must be connected with the constitutional rights of the place" (p. 322).

Each department must be able to defend itself; in each department, ambition must connect the interest of the man to the rights of the place. Interest can be brought to support right, and right can elevate or guide interest; ambition seems to yoke right and interest. Neither uninformed interest, the uninformed assertion of interest without regard to the rights of the place, nor a mere assumption of rights, unsupported by and undefended by interest, is sufficient to defend each department, or perhaps, more broadly, to defend human liberty. Ambition seems to be the crucial link in the American regime between man's interest and his rights, bringing his interest to the support of his rights; this is done, I believe, particularly by the executive, who takes account of man's interest in light of natural necessity, but who can then turn interest to the support of human rights. This ambition, we should note, is defensive in character: ambition is turned from the attempt to rule over man to the defense of rights or the linking of interest and rights.

Having set down this general principle, Publius now responds to the unspoken objection, that this is a sorry reflection on human nature. Publius acknowledges that "It may be a reflection on human nature that such devices should be necessary to control the abuses of government. But what is government itself but the greatest of all reflections on human nature?" (p. 322). The separation of powers seems to embody both "devices" to control the government, and government itself; it reflects the claim of human beings to govern themselves, to be self-sufficient, and the limits of that claim. Through the separation of powers the interests of man are connected to an understanding of his rightful place; ambition is crucial for this—the human pride in being distinctive, the ambition of human beings to be free and to rule themselves. Men can therefore assert their liberty through a separation of powers which reflects human nature; we even take a kind of pride in the separation of powers for reflecting human nature.

Publius continues with the famous observation that if men were angels, no government would be necessary and "If angels were to govern men, neither external nor internal controls on government would be necessary" (p. 322). Men need government because they are not angels; government needs to be controlled because governors are not angels. As we have suggested, both the need for government and the need for control of government reflect the facts of human nature. The vindication of the capacity of mankind for self-government therefore requires the separation of powers which controls mankind's self-government; the separation of powers in its checking and balancing aspect disabuses men of their angelic pretensions.

Thus, "In framing a government which is to be administered by men over men, the great difficulty lies in this: You must first enable the government to control the governed; and in the next place oblige it to control itself" (p. 322). Publius writes, "*You* must first. . . ." Publius addresses the reader as a fellow framer; in doing so, Publius gratifies our ambition. Every American can think of himself as a framer of the government, thanks to the republican form; we can all take pride in our framing of a separation of powers that reflects human nature. Insofar as we are co-framers, we can be persuaded of the need to reflect on human nature; as framers, we must embody the reason of the public that controls the government. The republican form can be used to teach a kind of responsibility by encouraging citizens to think of themselves as founders, or as judges who reflect *on* human nature rather than legislators who simply reflect human nature.

After appealing to us as framers of the government, Publius says that "a dependence on the people is no doubt the primary control on the government; but experience has taught mankind the necessity of auxiliary precautions" (p. 322). Republicanism is insufficient; Publius appeals on the basis of common experience to the necessity of auxiliary precautions. The people are capable of appreciating the insufficiency of a dependence on the people, as long as the separation of powers is presented as primarily for the sake of liberty and as an auxiliary precaution to the republican principle—as long, we might say, as the extent to which it modifies the republican claim is obscured. Republican citizens can thus become partisans of the separation of powers if they think of themselves as founders and judges rather than simply as legislators.

"This policy of supplying, by opposite and rival interests, the defect of better motives, might be traced through the whole system of human affairs, private as well as public" (p. 322). Publius finds the principle of American government in the whole system of human affairs, as if securing natural support for the framers' work. It seems necessary to find support for politics outside politics; indeed Publius here seems to claim that politics mirrors the whole system of human affairs; the separation of powers somehow mirrors the way things are. Politics cannot be separated from opinions about the whole; the American separation of powers must bring with it or claim to have support in a certain view of human nature and of the human whole.

The "inventions of prudence" that characterize subordinate distributions of power, Publius concludes, "cannot be less requisite in the distribution of the supreme powers of the state" (p. 322). These are inventions of "prudence," not of the new science of politics. But prudence does not rule; it invents a system of distributing powers that apparently runs itself, in which private interest is apparently sufficient to guard public rights. The distributions of power, much as they seem to reflect human nature or the whole system of human affairs, are inventions, not simply reflections of an arrangement that "might be traced" everywhere. The separation of powers is an invention which however claims to be a mirror of nature; it is not presented as a contrivance of prudence but as a quasi-natural system of checking and balancing for the sake of liberty.

Having fixed the separation of powers in human nature and in the whole system of human affairs, Publius returns to political concerns, picking up from his comment that the provision for defense must be commensurate with the danger to any department. He observes that it is not possible to give each department an equal power of self-defense: "In republican government the legislative authority, necessarily, predominates. . . ." The remedy for this inconvenience caused by the republican form is to divide the legislature into different branches, "and to render them, by different modes of election and different principles of action, as little connected with each other as the nature of their common functions and their common dependence on the society will admit" (p. 322). The second limit on the difference between the two legislative branches would limit the separation of powers as well: a pure separation of powers would seem to imply a mixed regime, in which different departments would have "different modes of election" as well as "different principles of action" or functions. We are reminded that the judiciary was singled out in the second paragraph as having a different mode of election, and that its permanent tenure eliminates its dependence on the authority conferring the judges' appointment, thereby destroying its dependence on the society. What is more, the judiciary seems to share far fewer "common functions" with the other branches than they share among themselves. The judiciary seems the most distinctive part of the separation of powers, the branch least affected by the common republican form.

The splitting of the legislature may not be sufficient, then; further precautions may be necessary to guard against legislative encroachment. "As the weight of the legislative authority requires that it should be thus divided, the weakness of the executive may require, on the other hand, that it should be fortified" (pp. 322–323). If Publius earlier provided especially for the judiciary, he now provides for the executive. In a republic the legislative branch needs no special provision; the other two branches have to be strengthened against the legislature and against the tendency of the republican form. An absolute veto at first appears to be the "natural defense with which the executive magistrate should be armed." But the seeming "natural defense" would perhaps "be neither altogether safe, nor alone sufficient" (p. 323). The separation of powers must be contrived by prudence; it is not natural or a simple reflection of what might seem natural. For on "ordinary occasions," an absolute veto might not be exercised firmly enough; and "on extraordinary occasions," it might be abused. An absolute veto is both too weak and too strong. Publius's rejection of the absolute veto seems to reflect his rejection, or modification, of a Machiavellianism which would teach that government is fundamentally execution and that absolute power is required for security. The Machiavellian solution seems to try to assimilate ordinary to extraordinary situations; but it therefore fails to provide adequately for either. Publius admits the Machiavellian solution seems the "natural" one, but he rejects it; the executive cannot have absolute security; in a sense this is because men cannot have and should not seek absolute security. The policy of supplying the defect of better motives through giving each department the motives and means to resist the others was necessary because one cannot count on motives; mere parchment barriers or legislation is insufficient. But Publius also rejects the opposite possibility—exemplified by an absolute executive veto—that since one cannot count on motives, men need to strive for absolute security in self-defense through a complete reliance on their own arms. Publius rejects, or rather supplies the defects of, both of these understandings of politics.

"If the principles on which these observations are founded be just, as I persuade myself they are, and they be applied as a criterion to the several state constitutions, and to the federal constitution, it will be found that if the latter does not perfectly correspond with them, the former are infinitely less able to bear such a test" (p. 323). Publius's observations are based on principles which serve as a criterion for the Constitution; they provide the standard by which the Constitution is judged. Could one call this appeal to just principles above the Constitution a kind of dependence on exterior provisions? The Constitution cannot simply be defended at the level of the interior structure of the government; that structure must be based on principles outside the government. The Constitution's dependence on these principles or Publius's resort to these principles in Number 51 replaces a recurrence to the people. The structure of the government is derived from principles not made by us, though we are the source of the government's power. What is implied in Number 51's exception for the judiciary is to an extent true of the whole regime: a primary consideration is its correspondence to certain principles, as well as its deriving from the will of the people.

After completing his general observations, Publius turns to "two considerations particularly applicable to the federal system of America, which place that system in a very interesting point of view." The first consideration particularly applicable to America is that in a "single republic" all power surrendered by the people is to a single government; usurpations are guarded against by the separation of powers. But in the "compound republic" of the United States, the power surrendered by the people is divided between two governments, and then each portion is subdivided among separate departments. "Hence a double security arises to the rights of the people. The different governments will control each other, at the same time that each will be controlled by itself" (p. 323). America is a "compound republic" with regard to the federal system. One can wonder if the effect of mixing the federal principle with the republican principle is to check the power of the people—without mixing in a source of power other than the people—by dividing their power between the two governments. It becomes easier to move the federal government further away from the people because of the role of the states, in which the people manage their local affairs.

The second particular consideration is the extended sphere that is made possible by the federal system of America. Publius begins by reminding us that "it is of great importance in a republic, not only to guard the society against the oppression of its rulers, but to guard one part of the society against the injustice of the other part" (p. 323). Not just liberty but justice is required. But does the separation of powers merely guard society against the oppression of its rulers, as Publius implies here? Does it not in fact guard against the oppression of the legislature, which is capable of oppression because close to the people, i.e., close to the majority of the people? Does the separation of powers not guard one part of society against the oppression of another part by checking the legislature? Publius wishes formally to distinguish the purpose of the separation of powers—to prevent governmental tyranny—and the purpose of the extended sphere—to prevent majority tyranny; but he has made it clear that the type of governmental tyranny to be feared in a republic is a form of, or the result of, majority tyranny. The formal separation of the ends of the separation of powers and the extended sphere conceals the extent to which the separation of powers supplements the extended sphere, which by itself is insufficient.

Publius now restates the argument of Number 10, but with significant changes. "Different interests necessarily exist in different classes of citizens." But:

> If a majority be united by a common interest, the rights of the minority will be insecure. There are but two methods of providing against this evil: the one by creating a will in the community independent of the majority—that is, of the society itself; the other, by comprehending in the society so many separate descriptions of citizens, as will render an unjust combination of a majority of the whole very improbable, if not impracticable. [*Federalist* 51, pp. 323–324]

These two methods seem to correspond to or to replace the two solutions of Number 10 to the problem of faction, representation and size: a will independent of society replaces representation, or is an extension of the tendency of representation to separate the government from the people. We have learned that the structure of the representative government of the United States is based on the principle of the separation of powers; is the separation of powers not a sort of will independent of society? And is this solution not necessary to supplement the fundamentally republican solution of extending the sphere?

Now this first solution—a will independent of society—is "at best, a precarious security; because a power independent of society may as well espouse the unjust views of the major as the rightful interests of the minor party, and may possibly be turned against both parties" (p. 324). But this abstracts from the particular character of this "will" or "power" independent of society. If the power can be prevented from having a distinctive will, as is the case with the separation of powers as a whole and especially with the judicial power, perhaps this danger is minimized; to say nothing of the fact that this power is mixed with the republican principle, a mixing that Publius does not explicitly acknowledge to be possible in this discussion. The judiciary was, in the second paragraph, said to lack "all sense of dependence" on the authority which appoints it, which as we pointed out would imply a lack of dependence on the people or on society; the judiciary may therefore be said to be a kind of will, or a power, independent of society. Publius appears at first to reject a will independent of society in favor of the republican solution of the extended sphere; in fact, he shows how the two are in a way combined in the United States. It is true that it is the second solution of an extended sphere that will be "exemplified in the federal republic of the United States" (p. 324). This first method of a will independent of society is not "exemplified" in the United States; but does it not exist? Indeed, would not a combination of the two methods—a possibility Publius never explicitly brings up in this paragraph—be a true double security for the people of the United States?

In the second method exemplified in the United States, all authority will be derived from and dependent on society, but society will be broken into so many interests that the rights of individuals or of the minority will be in little danger from the majority. Publius explains this second method of providing against majority faction: "In a free government, the security for civil rights must be the same as for religious rights." A republic must be made a free government; and how is this security to be attained?

> It consists in the one case in the multiplicity of interests, and in the other in the multiplicity of sects. The degree of security in both cases will depend on the number of interests and sects; and this may be presumed to depend on the extent of country and number of people comprehended under the same government. This view of the subject must particularly recommend a proper federal system to all the sincere and considerate friends of republican government. [*Federalist* 51, p. 324]

This democratic view—that numbers are sufficient for security—is that of Number 10, and "this view of the subject" is designed to convince "the sincere and considerate friends of republican government" of the merits of a federal system. "This view," that the second method of size is sufficient, is not necessarily Publius's view, but it is a view congenial to the friends of republican government. And it is this view that will be exemplified in the United States; the separation of powers drops out of sight in this paragraph, because the separation of powers is less congenial to the friends of republican government than to patrons of liberty or of good government (*Federalist* 47, p. 301; No. 37, p. 224).

Publius continues: "Justice is the end of government. It is the end of civil society. It ever has been and ever will be pursued until it be obtained, or until liberty be lost in the pursuit" (p. 324). The stability and independence of a member of the government must be increased to the extent that the extended sphere is insufficient, because men pursue justice: men are willing to sacrifice their republican claim of self-government in favor of a will independent of society for the sake of justice. Men look—or should look—first and foremost to the end of government and of society; the end is as fundamental as the desire to be the source of the government. Justice limits the republican principle; self-government must be for the sake of achieving justice.

Justice appears to be understood by Publius here as security against oppression, as security of rights: "In a society under the forms of which the stronger faction can readily unite and oppress the weaker, anarchy may as truly be said to reign as in a state of nature, where the weaker individual is not secured against the violence of the stronger" (p. 324). And, Publius continues, as in the state of nature even stronger individuals are prompted to submit to a government which would protect the weak as well as themselves, so in society the more powerful factions will be gradually led to wish for a government that will protect all parties. Insofar as we all realize our weakness, we all seek justice, understood as security. It is useful that we all realize our potential weakness for the sake of justice, but the pursuit of justice on the basis of our weakness can lead to the loss of liberty: men pursue justice until it is obtained, or until liberty be lost in the pursuit. Can justice be obtained? Or will not the unremitting pursuit of justice lead to the loss of liberty? Men have to be satisfied of their security even if in fact that security is not fully attainable; otherwise their pursuit of justice will endanger liberty—the liberty, it seems, of self-government. For individuals to preserve their independent wills, the claim of society must be tempered; the popular claim must be transformed from one of direct to indirect rule, acknowledging the limits on the capacity of men directly to govern themselves.

Publius concludes that "it is no less certain than it is important, notwithstanding the contrary opinions which have been entertained, that the larger the society, provided it lie within a practicable sphere, the more duly capable it will be of self-government." Again this proportional statement suggests the incapacity of any society for full self-government, due to the limits of a practicable sphere. But "happily for the *republican cause*, the practicable sphere may be carried to a very great extent by a judicious modification and mixture of the *federal principle*" (p. 325).

By the end of *Federalist* 51 the topic of this section, the separation of powers, has disappeared; in moving from general to particularly American considerations, we have moved first to the separation of powers plus federalism, and then to the extended sphere that federalism allows. At the end of Number 51 Publius brings republicanism to the fore again, and obscures the extent to which the republican principle was modified in

Federalist 47–51. He thereby shows how the separation of powers can be inconspicuously accommodated to the republican form of the American regime.

We learn more about the separation of powers from Publius's discussion of the particular powers in *Federalist* 52–83. Indeed, we learn much about the character of each of the powers from the substance and manner of Publius's presentation of each one. And we are taught in more detail how the principles of the separation of powers can be incorporated into the republican form of America so as not to disturb the republican cause—indeed so as to vindicate the republican cause, or what is true in that cause. In learning this, in reading and studying *The Federalist*, we are able to learn something not merely about America but something of the nature of politics in general, and indeed something of "the whole system of human affairs." We therefore become, thanks to Publius, more capable of vindicating "that honorable determination which animates every votary of freedom to rest all our political experiments on the capacity of mankind for self-government" (No. 39, p. 240).

6

Justice and the General Good: *Federalist* 51

W. B. ALLEN

James Madison said it:

> In the extended republic of the United States, and among the great variety of interests, parties, and sects which it embraces, a coalition of a majority of the whole society could seldom take place on any other principles than those of justice and the general good. [*Federalist* 51, p. 325]

Elsewhere (*Federalist* 63), Madison made clear that the rare occasion on which some other kind of coalition could take place would be the end of the extended republic of the United States. Accordingly, we must regard it as Madison's rule that, so long as the extended republic of the United States endures, it operates on the basis of the formation of majority coalitions grounded in principles of justice and the general good. Further, we must note that the condition for its so enduring is that restraints upon the majority do not reach so far as to transfer power to any minority—which the requirement of a super-quorum in the legislature would do.

> In all cases where justice or the general good might require new laws to be passed, or active measures to be pursued, the fundamental principle of free government would be reversed. It would be no longer the majority that would rule: the power would be transferred to the minority. [*Federalist* 58, p. 361]

His definition of the general good therefore implies this: a form of social life wherein the weaker party may forcefully maintain its claims of right within the very structure and processes of the government. Under these conditions, political and social contradictions (e.g., class conflict) are eliminated. The majority confirms and protects the rights of the weaker party because the stronger party can exercise its powers only on behalf of the public good. Accordingly, there is "no pretext" for defending minority rights (qua *minority* rights) in a well-constituted republic.

This essay is a meditation upon the Madisonian vision of the dynamics of the American republic, setting forth the argument in a detail that the richly schematic and emblematic structure of *Federalist* 51 was required to forego. It further offers the argument that more impoverished versions of Madisonianism—typically presented as the doctrine of a multiplicity of interests within an extended republic—fail systematically to express the correct foundations of Madison's founding principle because they fail to take seriously *Federalist* 51's invocation of justice. The operative analogy throughout is that justice inheres as fully in the arguments of *The Federalist* as piety inheres in the *Torah*, although neither is frequently mentioned in either.[1]

THE MADISONIAN PROJECT

Madison most fully reveals his idea of a decent regime in *The Federalist*. But Madison's draft of a "farewell address" for President Washington in 1792 merits consideration alongside *The Federalist* as a kind of commentary on the implications of its republican nationalism. In that address Madison spoke in unrestrained terms of America's providential advantages and achievements. He found the "theatre of our fortunes" well adapted to every important national consideration.

> All its essential interests are the same: while its diversities arising from climate, from soil, and from other local & lesser peculiarities, will naturally form a mutual relation of the parts, that may give to the whole a more entire independence than has perhaps fallen to the lot of any other nation.[2]

His efforts to construct a democratic nationalism had since 1780 been bent precisely to the search for this "entire independence." To that end, nothing was so essential as the elaboration of a national interest or identity even if, finally, it was constructed on the foundation of mutually interlocking particular interests.

Madison identified the popular establishment of a "common government, . . . free in its principles" and "intended as the guardian of our *common right* and the patron of our *common interests*" as the decisive event in the achievement of the goal he sought. This work, the provision for amendment being admitted, "must approach as near to perfection as any human work can aspire. . . ." Madison, we can see, did not underrate the achievements of the founding. What is less apparent is that this express claim— made at the very height of his efforts on behalf of the Republican party press in 1792—leaves no doubt that Madison imagined a common good to be framed in the new regime.

We may render this last conclusion even more convincing, however. And in the process we shall demonstrate that *Federalist* 51 stands at the very center of the Madisonian project, as much in 1792 as in 1787. The purpose in demonstrating this is to insist upon the political relevance of an interpretation of Madison's "Publius" contributions, and to indicate the range of interpretation to which *Federalist* 51 must be subjected before we can speak definitively of the Federalists' project.

At some point, probably in 1792, Madison seems to have envisioned writing a regular treatise on the foundations of government. His notes exhibit a plan to set forth the fundamental principles at stake in the party contests of that era; the editors of the Madison Papers have entitled these fragments, "Notes for the National Gazette Essays," and dated them between December 19, 1791, and March 3, 1792.[3] The foundation of their educated guess on both scores seems to have been that the notes contain direct passages and the obvious first drafts of other passages that appear in six of Madison's *National Gazette* essays, which were published contemporaneously.

Madison, however, published seventeen *National Gazette* essays, extending from November 19, 1791, through December 22, 1792. Further, of the eleven essays not reflected in these notes, three fell within the period assigned for the notes' composition. Those three are the essays on "Charters," "Universal Peace," and the "Spirit of Governments." If Madison's notes were merely first drafts of the essays composed during this period, it would be difficult to conceive why these three important essays were not included, especially since the notes do not correspond exactly with the essays. That is to say, some notes under one heading, "Public Opinion" for example, do not appear in the essay of that title but in another, namely "British Government." Consequently, the organization of the notes departs significantly from the organization of the essays.

The three omitted essays are distinguished by the fact that they discuss principles or theories at the heart of the development of European political philosophy. "Charters" opens with the words, "In Europe," and proceeds to distinguish the notions of contract prevalent east and west of the Atlantic. "Universal Peace" tempers the spirit of Rousseau, and "Spirit of Governments" broadens the understanding received from Montesquieu. The main work of these essays, therefore, seems to be to correct mistakes that might be made if Enlightenment thought were simply applied to the American scene with main force. I submit, accordingly, that the notes reflect only the essays that they do ("Public Opinion," "Government," "Parties," "British Government," "Government of the United States," and "Republican Distribution of Citizens") precisely because Madison had set about organizing a separate and independent work, a principled response to the questions at issue between Federalists and Republicans—questions about the necessary relations of the parts of American government, rather than about philosophical antecedents.

What Madison's outline for a treatise on the foundations of government contributes to the present discussion is a solid indication of how *Federalist* 51 should be read. Madison's notes deserve a full exegesis in their own right; here, however, I limit myself to a summary in order to come to the main point—namely, the centrality of *Federalist* 51. Because my discussion must be limited, I will reproduce Madison's outline (without annotation, and indicating his pagination) so that the reader may more easily see the comprehensive scope of his work.

[PART A]

I. Influence of the size of a nation on Government. page 1
II. Influence of external danger on Government. page 10
III. Influence of the stage of society on Government. page 16
IV. Influence of Public opinion on Government. page 22
V. Influence of Education on Government. page 30
VI. Influence of Religion on Government. page 35
VII. Influence of Domestic slavery on Government. page 40
VIII. Influence of Dependent dominions on Government. page 46

[PART B]

IX. Checks devised in democracies marking self-distrust. page 49
X. True reasons for keeping the great departments of power separate. page 55
XI. Federal Governments. page 65
XII. Government of United States. page 75
XIII. Best distribution of people in Republic. page 82

Before turning to Madison's discussion of these matters, I hasten to forestall the easy assumption that Madison, metamorphosing from Federalist to Republican, had set out to redo *The Federalist*. For in the course of his inquiry he not only invokes "Federalists No. X et alia," but he also cites explicitly *Federalist* 7, 30, 51, as well as volume one's discussion of federal governments. Furthermore, he tacitly relies on *Federalist* 43 at the very heart of this outline (in chapter VII), making explicit what he had cautiously discussed in 1788 as the "natural majority."[4] The only portion of *The Federalist* he seems directly to call into question was written under a professed veil in any case, and that is Number 47, in which Madison aimed to express the meaning of Montesquieu and then only by describing Montesquieu's British model. Accordingly, he now promises to reveal the "*true* reasons for keeping great departments of power separate." I confine the implications of this statement to *Federalist* 47—and absolve *Federalist* 51— because under the section on the "Government of the United States" Madison refers the reader to the entire *Federalist*, but "particularly No. 51." The division Madison himself makes tells us that Number 51 in its true bearings is less a discussion of separation of powers than of the governing of the United States.

Madison goes beyond *Federalist* 51 in making his conclusion explicit. "Partitions and internal checks of power" deserve high praise but not the highest praise. For "the chief palladium of constitutional liberty" is its "authors" and "guardians," the people. They are called upon to signal, judge, and "repel aggressions on the authority of their constitutions."[5] Madison later provides the reason why this is so, as the character "Republican" responds to "Anti-Republican," debating the question, "Who are the Best Keepers of the People's Liberties?"

> The people themselves. . . . The centrifugal tendency then is in the people, not in the government, and *the secret art lies in restraining the tendency, by augmenting the attractive principle* of the government with all the weight that can be added to it.[6]

This is in Madison's eyes the real subject of *Federalist* 51. Through it he aims to explain how the essence of a "representative republic" is to "*chuse* the wisdom, of which hereditary aristocracy has the *chance*," while avoiding the oppression incident to the latter.[7]

To achieve this goal, the government must be brought more fully under the power of "public opinion," which means in the first place under the power of the natural majority to the extent possible.

> In proportion as slavery prevails in a state, the government, however democratic in name, must be aristocratic in fact. The power lies in a part instead of the whole; in the hands of property, not of numbers. . . . In Virginia . . . the slaves and non-freeholders amount to nearly ¾ of the State. The power is therefore in about ¼. Were the slaves freed and the right of suffrage extended to all, the operation of the government might be very different.[8]

While "property" and "numbers" contend for political power in every state, and thereby influence it either toward aristocracy or toward democracy, Madison does not reduce the question of the character of the representative republic to the mere question of interests. Public opinion and not cash is the nexus, and the question is, in what "proportion" the government is influenced by public opinion in the true sense—the opinion of the whole instead of a part.[9]

Here Madison relies on Aristotle to authorize his conclusion. He reads the discussion of the cycle of regimes in *Politics*, Book V, to suggest that the cycle is not an iron law and is alterable by changes in opinion. Aristotle had arrayed three good forms of regime against their respective opposites: monarchy versus tyranny, aristocracy versus oligarchy, and polity versus democracy. The order represented an order of descent in terms of relative excellence. The forms were defined primarily by the number of persons participating in office and secondarily by the objective of their rule—that is to say, rule in the private interest of the ruler or rulers, or rule in the interest of the common good. He indicated, however, that the two bad regimes, democracy and oligarchy, each presented a partial view of justice, insisting on the one hand that the free born should rule and on the other hand that only the well-to-do should rule. Madison's reading yields an untraditional emphasis. Above all, by regarding the defenders of oligarchy as lovers of justice (they do not think it just that those who contribute unequally should share equally) instead of as lovers of money, Madison teaches that by replacing a partial view of justice with a whole view, one can provide the motive force for a change of regime which is not a corruption but an improvement.

> Government is instituted to protect property of every sort; as well that which lies in the various rights of individuals, as that which the term particularly expresses. This being the end of government, that alone is a *just* government, which *impartially* secures to every man, whatever is his *own*.[10]

This, then, is the subject of *Federalist* 51 and the heart of the Madisonian project. Simply by making Virginia a part of a true federal republic, and thereby reducing the effect of the number of slaves as a part of the whole, one may effect a change in the regime contrary to the iron cycle. Enhancing the republican character of the whole is necessary to perpetuate that salutary motion. And the question, how the system may operate so as to preserve and enhance its republicanism, is the burden not only of Madison's career as a partisan but of his analysis in *Federalist* 51. In undertaking an exegesis of that paper, we are assured only of one thing, that it "is a perversion of the natural order of things, to make *power* the primary and central object of the social system, and *liberty* but its satellite."[11]

REPRESENTATION AND THE SEPARATION OF POWERS

A reasonable objection to the approach I take here would be that I am giving short shrift to the role of the discussion of separation of powers in preparing a context for the exegesis of *Federalist* 51. I believe that the ultimate result of this discussion will justify my approach. Nevertheless, I shall add here a summary discussion of that principle, in order that those familiar with standard interpretations may judge how the interpretation to follow fits in with them.

Separation of powers forms a valid principle only by virtue of its goal, which is precisely the same as that of the system of balances and checks. The latter system renders the former an efficacious tool in ameliorating the evil consequences of popular government: the system of balances and checks provides the interior controls that supplement the partitions among the powers, in themselves insufficient controls. The interior structure of the government, then, is so arranged as to render each department an agent in keeping the others "in their proper places." Additionally, the officeholders in each branch are provided with "the necessary constitutional means and

personal motives to resist encroachments of the others. . . . The interest of
the man must be connected with the constitutional rights of the place. . ."
(No. 51, pp. 321–322). That such a system is necessary is certainly "a reflection on human nature," but, then, government itself is the greatest of such
reflections. In the system of *Federalist* 51 "you must first enable the government to control the governed; and in the next place oblige it to control
itself" (p. 322). When this situation obtains, the American federal system
boasts as much security as can be provided, with the added benefit of a
further partition "between two distinct governments" that renders it still
more secure than "a single republic."

Next, the role of the judiciary in sustaining the separation of powers is
regarded as crucial. Fortunately for Publius, the need for an independent
judiciary was not much questioned. Nevertheless, he is still required to
elaborate its mode of appointment and term of office, revealing one of the
decisively modern aspects of the Constitution. Not even Montesquieu—
from whose principles the implication can well be drawn, Publius asserts—
had raised "the standard of good behavior" as a requirement for the tenure
of judges. But it is not too difficult to see that this strengthens the independence of judges and provides an "excellent barrier to the encroachments and
oppressions of the representative body."

> [In a government of separated departments] the judiciary, from the nature
> of its functions, will always be the least dangerous to the political rights of
> the Constitution; because it will be least in a capacity to annoy or injure
> them. . . . [T]he judiciary is beyond comparison the weakest of the three
> departments of power. . . . I mean so long as the judiciary remains truly
> distinct from both the legislature and the executive. For I agree that 'there
> is no liberty if the power of judging be not separated from the legislative
> and executive powers' . . . as all the effects of such a union must ensue
> from a dependence of the former on the latter. . . . [*Federalist* 78, pp. 465–
> 466]

The very nature of a "limited Constitution" encourages this particular construction of a judiciary that must "declare all acts contrary to the manifest
tenor of the Constitution void."

Lastly, in judging the republicanism of the new Constitution, Madison
explains that republican government must be derived from the great body of
the people, "not an inconsiderable proportion or a favored class" (*Federalist*
39, p. 241). All, or practically all members of the society must be citizens
even if all—women, for example—do not exercise the immediate rights of
citizenship—for example, voting. Montesquieu erred—Publius hesitated to
say it but is forced to by the nature of the case—in considering that a fairly
large "proportion" is sufficient to render a society republican. But he rejects
Montesquieu in this particular case in order to exclude the possibility that "a
handful of tyrannical nobles, exercising their oppressions by a delegation of
powers, might aspire to the rank of republicans and claim for their govern-

ment the honorable title of republic" (*Federalist* 39, p. 241). A republic, deriving its power from the whole society as nearly as possible and administering through persons appointed directly or indirectly by the people and serving for various terms, creates and thrives upon a dependence on the people. This dependence in turn protects a sovereignty that is indivisible, despite the fact that citizens alienate their collective legislative capacity (*Federalist* 63).

A broadly based principle of representation mirrors the founding itself: it is the power in the people which, by means of consent, flows from the people. In the first instance, the people *exercise* their power in founding the system; in the second instance this very exercise of power *delegates* its administration to representatives. Thus the nature of representation is that all power must flow from the people as directly as possible. "The streams of national power *ought* to flow immediately from that pure, original fountain of all legitimate authority" (*Federalist* 22, p. 152, emphasis added).

An apparent exception to this argument, namely, the Senate—whose members were elected by the state legislatures for six-year terms—reveals how considerations of the safety of the republic and the safety of the government work together. Two great desiderata compelled the creation of the Senate. The first was the need to include the states in their political capacities in the formation of the government. So far as this may expose the Union

> to the possibility of injury from the State legislatures, it is an evil; but it is an evil which could not have been avoided. . . . If this had been done it would doubtless have been interpreted into an entire dereliction of the federal principle, and would certainly have deprived the State governments of that absolute safeguard which they will enjoy under this provision. [*Federalist* 59, p. 364]

As for the second desideratum, one need only consult the histories of Rome, Sparta, and Carthage to discover the value of some body that will provide stability in a government all too prone to momentary passions. "The cool and deliberate sense" of the people must ever serve as a command for their representatives and agents; but the latter must always reflect just such sense rather than the spontaneous rages of the people. The examples cited are not intended as models for America, but they are "very instructive proofs of the necessity of some institution that will blend stability with liberty when compared with the fugitive and turbulent existence of other ancient republics." Nor, again, may one take comfort in the great extent of the country, since that alone will not render it immune to "infectious passions." To this real advantage it is necessary to add "auxiliary precautions," in the form of balances and checks and the separation of powers (*Federalist* 63).

Auxiliary precautions once provided, the benefits of an extended territory may be placed in proper perspective. The great diversity in the "state of property, genius, manners, and habits of the people" from the various parts of the country will reproduce itself in the government through the "dispositions in their representatives." The prevailing interest in each part will be reflected in the government, and there will be a sufficient variety to avoid the predominance of any single interest (*Federalist* 60). Secondly, the states can expect very material increases in population and diversification of interests, which will necessitate a yet "fuller representation." Next, the effect that an extensive territory has in thwarting foreign attacks will similarly thwart the designs of ambitious officeholders (*Federalist* 28). Finally, no greater protection can be afforded minorities than the extended republic, without which they would be all too easily threatened by clear and intractable majorities (*Federalist* 51). Evidently, to the degree one compresses the size of the territory, one augments the probability of injustice, therefore demanding for justice's sake a corresponding increase in the "stability and independence" of governing institutions. Hence discussions of the relative worth of liberty and justice are constrained by the necessity to take into account circumstances, as well as human passions and character. The "extended republic" of America renders it highly improbable that a viable majority could ever occur except on principles of "justice and the general good."

In this way we arrive at the central conclusion of Publius, even in the standard interpretation: a full determination of the worth and fitness of a government can be made on but one principle, "the public good, the real welfare of the people." No government is worthy except insofar as it is adapted to that end (*Federalist* 43). We threaten to lose sight of the fact, however, that the means to this end are not at all entirely clear at this point. Let us agree, then, that there are two requirements for a good government: faithfulness to the happiness of the people, and sufficient wisdom to attain that object. Concede that there has rarely existed a government that fulfilled the first requirement, and that many acknowledge neither. The key for us is the claim that until now, "American governments have paid too little attention to the last." Thus the new Constitution provides not only for the public happiness, but for the wisdom to attain it (*Federalist* 56). That wisdom is a wisdom as to means; and if the claim of Publius is to be vindicated, our exegesis must reveal not only the structures and general principles of the regime, but the peculiar means that will produce this excellent result. Let us therefore return to the exegesis of *Federalist* 51 in an attempt to discern how the standard interpretation of it omits something that may deepen significantly our understanding of the founding.

THE ARGUMENT OF *FEDERALIST* 51

The fifty-first *Federalist* follows the forty-fourth as logically as the fortieth could well precede the thirty-ninth.[12] When Madison closed the forty-fourth *Federalist* with the claim that only the propriety of a regime such as the proposed one remained to be discussed, he was partly right, partly wrong.

Although it is true that the "mass of power" delegated had been discussed—and its particular arrangements remained to be discussed—it was not true that he had completely demonstrated that this government invested with energy and stability could act with safety. The fifty-first *Federalist* responds precisely to that question—the *safety* of the regime as a whole, once set in motion and without respect to the operation of one branch vis-à-vis another. In this sense the paper logically follows the general conclusion of *Federalist* 40–44, and the whole is the prelude to any particular consideration of the branches or offices of government. This is in keeping with the outline that opens the forty-first *Federalist*.[13]

The great desideratum that results from the emphatic defense of a regime of character and power sufficient to secure the public good is the necessity to account for its being *confined* to pursue the public good or "justice."[14] The strictly formal argument from the separation of powers seems to provide the account sought, which is why the papers detailing the separation of powers intervene between 44 and 51. But the formal account itself poses a problem. As *Federalist* 41–50 reveal, the separation of powers raises a pretext for constitutional adjudication of the powers—and abuses of power—of government. But the deeper question beneath the doubt as to who properly must do what is the question, what remains to give a regime thus impeded the impulse to do anything? The question of the safety of the regime is really a question of its safety in operation, safety in motion when all the parts move together. (It is correct to say "regime" rather than "government" here, for when the whole moves together its deeds are presumably determined by its character as a regime. What Aristotle means when he defines "regime" as an arrangement of offices is more than just an institutional framework; he means the human characteristics that predominate in a society and give it its decisive character.) The regime might be envisioned as some unchained behemoth, in keeping with that modern appreciation of politics, which denies that the essential judgment of political life is founded on a judgment of the character of human beings as distinguished from beasts. No one would voluntarily unchain the behemoth without reassuring himself at least of the possibility of keeping it on a path of safety. In this manner the fifty-first paper continues the defense of the regime.

Federalist 51 specifically repeats key themes from Papers 40–44 at least five times. Beginning with an invocation of that "fountain of authority, the people," which recalls Papers 40, 42, and 43, and passing by way of a remark echoing Number 44 to the effect that the states are to be created anew by the Constitution,[15] the paper concludes with an emphatic rejection of the mere rule of the stronger, which possibility was raised in Number 43.[16] The fifty-first paper serves to disprove that the regime of *Federalist* 40–44 will be victim to any of the common illnesses of regimes. Its purpose is far wider than the opening claim would indicate.

> To what expedient, then, shall we finally resort, for maintaining in practice the necessary partition of power among the several departments as laid

down in the Constitution? . . . as all these exterior provisions are found to be inadequate the defect must be supplied, by so contriving the interior structure of the government as that its several constituent parts may, by their mutual relations, be the means of keeping each other in their proper places.[17]

Madison himself licenses the view that he will not pursue this narrow question when he immediately adds that he will only "hazard a few general observations"—rather than undertake a "full development" of this theme— sufficient *both* to make it "clearer" and to "enable us to form a more correct judgment *of the principles and structures*" (No. 51, p. 321) of the regime as a whole.

The actual "general observations" on the "mutual relations" of the separate departments of government are preceded by the recognition that the purest separation would surely arise from distinct popular appointment of each branch. Each would accordingly have "a will of its own"—that is, each would exercise the will of the people on the basis of a distinct authorization. This purity is attained only to some degree, however, because of practical difficulties. It is more nearly a question of the character of the branches than of the representatives themselves; but the succeeding question involves the character of the men as such, and introduces one of those "auxiliary precautions" that necessarily supplement the "primary control," dependence on the people.[18]

Madison drew the distinction here so finely that to fail to recognize it is to fail utterly to comprehend the essay. The regime must invoke the character of the representatives in order to supplement a separation (which cannot be absolute) of the branches of government.

> . . . the great security against a gradual concentration of the several powers in the same department consists in *giving to those who administer* each department the necessary *constitutional means and personal motives* to resist encroachments. . . . Ambition must be made to counteract ambition. The interest of the man must be connected with the constitutional rights of the place. [No. 51, pp. 321–322, emphasis added]

This is not a discussion of interests or factions in the society itself (except perhaps indirectly). This is an invocation of that "ruling passion," fame, and perhaps, though surely to a lesser extent, of avarice.

The passions or interests that will make representatives in this government into "sentinels of public rights" are not the same passions or interests that will set the regime in motion. While the latter "enable the government to control the governed," the former "oblige it to control itself." The people are rendered amenable to government by means of those very private passions and interests that incline them to seek to win the influence of power to their causes, whereas representatives, driven by ambition, are charged with mastering those diverse private passions and interests as the price of maintaining their public standing. The representative must then at one and the same time satisfy the clamant interests of his constituents as far as possible, while fighting off the clamant interests of the constituents of fellow representatives as far as possible. In doing so, his regard is less for the interests at risk than for the office or station he holds. Accordingly, though it "might be" possible to trace "this policy of supplying, by opposite and rival interests, the defect of better motives . . . through the whole system of human affairs," it is not necessary to trace "these *inventions of prudence*" beyond the "distributions of power." "Better motives" are wanted for the public good. Their absence—the "defect of better motives"—must be supplied not in the people but rather in those who would govern or, perhaps, administer the government.

This analysis does not pretend that the motives of representatives are less pure than those of the people. It is rather the case that, once the full force of separation of powers is admitted and the predominant "legislative authority" of republican government is safely left to be wielded by the people only indirectly, the defect of better motives in the people is far less dangerous than in the representatives. Madison insisted more than once that "force and right are not *necessarily* on the same side in republican governments."[19] The definition of tyranny—the concentration of all the powers of government in the hands of the one, the few, or the many—militates most strongly against the people's *direct* legislative authority.

The discussion of the "mutual relations" of the branches of government occupies but the first half of the paper. The second half examines the safety to be derived from the "federal system of America." Here Madison offers "two considerations." The first repeats the argument that the "compound" relationship of the general government and the states will operate to the same effect as the separation of powers among the branches of government, thus offering "a double security" to the people's rights. The entire discussion takes only four sentences. The remainder of the paper discusses the further question: after a society is guarded "against the oppression of its rulers," how is "one part of society" to be guarded against the injustice of the other part?

This argument is of peculiar interest not only because of its restatement (not merely a repetition) of *Federalist* 10. It is of peculiar interest because Number 51 had opened by invoking that "foundation of authority," society, as the "primary" ruler in republican government. Insofar as the people do indeed rule, the protection of one part of the people from the other is still a protection against the oppression of rulers—the critical problem of majority faction, which we find in *Federalist* 10 and think the only problem to be solved, inasmuch as minority faction would be handled by the "republican principle." But now, equally important, we see that once the people's *direct* authority has been qualified, it becomes important to protect one part of the people, namely, the ruling majority, against the violence or injustice of another part—namely, the minority or the few, since Madison writes explicitly of only two parts, "one part" and "the other part." But this, it seems, is identical to *our* original question: Once the regime has been made safe—impeded in its movement—how can it again be made to move, to attain the end sought from the government, the public safety? Madison seems to say that this is something more than the familiar "deadlock" conundrum hackneyed in contemporary analysis.[20] For representatives as such, even with the defect of better motives supplied, seem insufficient to the task.

What sets the regime in motion—what will make the representatives *do something*—will be the clamant interests of the "different classes of citizens." I repeat: this is not the argument from *Federalist* 10, where the multiplicity of interests will *prevent* the action of a factious majority. Those interests have a second function, which is not merely to become the primary subject of "modern legislation" but themselves to set the agenda of modern legislation, thus setting the regime in motion. But what will make this motion safe? Auxiliary precautions would be no barrier to a majority that rules. And *the point* of this essay is that the people will rule! We are working with a distinction between the "opposite and rival interests" that must be *supplied* to the representatives and the interests that *exist of necessity* in "different classes of citizens." These more fundamental interests— *Federalist* 10 interests—may have to be worked with (or regulated), perhaps even manipulated; but they do not have to be created.

Precisely because the people do rule, "if a majority be united by a common interest, the rights of the minority will be insecure." The danger in this regime is in fact identical to the danger the natural majority[21] poses to every republic. It is inconsistent with republican principles to erect a "will in the community independent of the majority—that is, of the society itself." This means the minority is left exposed to the violence of the majority, which *appeared* to be the problem we were handed. So here Madison reaffirms the *Federalist* 10 solution, though it is still unclear how "one part" of the society is protected against "the other part." The reaffirmation does no more than assure that no minority "will" or veto is permissible. And the minority cannot otherwise be expressly defended without arresting the motion of the regime.

Hence, the minority must be left theoretically exposed. Majority rule must govern, but in such fashion that the minority no longer requires protection. The remedy in this regime, as under natural circumstances, is to render the majority unfit for concerted action in pursuit of unjust ends. Because the defect of better motives cannot be supplied, the only recourse will to be a diversity or confusion of motives. Suspicious self-interest must limit the seeking after extra advantages to the degree that minorities will benefit. This method "will be exemplified" in the new regime.

> . . . in the federal republic of the United States. Whilst all authority in *it* will be derived from and dependent on the society, the society itself will be broken into so many parts, interests and classes of citizens, that the rights of individuals, or of the minority will be in little danger. [No. 51, p. 324]

The question, however, had been, given this hobbling of the majority, how could it then protect itself from minority violence? Madison's obtuse return to the question of preventing majority violence begins to be vexing, until, that is, this reiterated theme takes on another voice. The "multiplicity of interests" is a natural occurrence that is artificially encouraged in a "proper federal republic." The point is to avoid government under the majority's "unjust views." *That alone is at stake.* Not the majority's power, but its injustice is curtailed; hence it remains able to defend itself against minority violence.

The republican operation of the regime itself defends against minority-inspired injustice:

> . . . justice is the end of government. It is the end of civil society. It ever has been and ever will be pursued until it be obtained, or until liberty be lost in the pursuit. [No. 51, p. 324]

The interest of justice is served by distinguishing right and might. Where "the stronger faction can readily unite and oppress the weaker, anarchy may as truly be said to reign as in a state of nature." The rule of the stronger faction, even a majority, is implicitly distinguished here from majority tyranny. The definition of tyranny applies most forcefully in democracy, where the actual separation of powers is not possible. The rule of the stronger faction, likened to the anarchy of the state of nature, is however not founded in the abuse of power as such. It is grounded in the denial that anything beyond force legitimizes the claim of right. It is a denial of a genuine public good, wherein the weaker maintain a claim of right as forcefully as the stronger.

While essentially democratic tyranny affirms the bonds of citizenship, essentially undemocratic anarchy denies the bonds of citizenship. Anarchy, the rule of the stronger faction, is rule by a will independent of the society. It has more in common with "governments possessing an hereditary or self-appointed authority" than it has with either democracy or tyranny.[22] The provision for republican safety, the method for avoiding the evil of a majority united by a common factional interest, is to confine the formation of majority views to principles of "justice and the general good." This unexpected result comes from one source only: namely, the necessity for republicanism, *a conscious attachment on the part of the citizens to republican principles and processes*, in order to impart motion to the regime. This result is unexpected precisely because it had appeared that the regime would be set in motion by the diverse interests forcefully asserting their respective claims. Upon reflection, however, it would seem that no self-interested endeavor could be confined to channels so pure as those Madison described—"justice and the general good"—unless the self-interested agent was at the same time of the opinion that some principle either of right or necessity *obliged* him to have recourse to the prescribed channels. Majority rule, in short, is not just the republican mode; it is the mode for making republicans. Majorities there must be, at least formally. Accordingly, one cannot speak of rendering majorities as such powerless or impossible.

REPUBLICANISM AND THE COMMON GOOD

Another element of Madison's solution is to confine majority sentiment to salutary principles.

> In the extended republic of the United States, and among the great variety of interests, parties, and sects which it embraces, a coalition of a majority of the whole society could seldom take place on any other principles than those of justice and the general good. . . . [No. 51, p. 325]

It is a further refinement, once concession is made to the "fountain of all authority," to pose "justice and the general good" as the necessary *means* of action. Through this device, the *majority* is confined as nearly as possible to pursuit of the public good. The pursuit of self-interest is not incompatible with this result, so long as the road to profit runs through a "coalition" of do-gooders.

But how is the public good defined? Publius offers a negative characterization: It is that condition in which the weaker part of society may forcefully maintain its claims of right within the very structures and processes of government. Insofar as that condition obtains, political and social contradictions are eliminated. The majority confirms and protects the rights of the weaker party when and only when the majority party can exercise its power in behalf of the public good.[23] Accordingly, there is "no pretext" for separately defending minority rights in a well-constructed republic. And the absence of these special precautions is itself evidence of a public good that animates the regime. What Publius calls self-government is then government by the majority for the sake of the public good without recourse to "a will independent of society." This he regarded as "the *republican cause*" which is made possible, made realizable by "judicious modification and mixture of the *federal principle.*" This is, in other words, democratic nationalism—the regime quality—the character of public opinion—necessary for the protection and consecration of natural right in republican government.

We are within our rights to wonder exactly how far Madison was willing to carry his scheme. His 1792 outline suggests that he would carry it quite far indeed. We may take a more direct measure, however. For Madison himself returned to this subject—in some ways the most consistent theme of his lifework—at a time when he was confident that he would never hold office again, and in a manner that reveals lingering doubts about his solution.

More than thirty years later, Madison resurrected an argument he had raised in the 1787 Philadelphia Convention and wrestled with it anew. On August 7, 1787, the Convention had debated the report from the committee of detail, scrutinizing the fourth article's provision to leave in the hands of the states the rule of suffrage for choosing the national legislature. The leading alternative was a freehold or property qualification—and Madison was tempted by it, given the circumstances of the country. "The freeholders of the country would be the safest depositories of Republican liberty."[24] Above all, such a provision would guard against the abuses of power by a propertyless majority. Somewhere around 1821,[25] however, Madison re-thought his contribution to the debate of August 7. On his own testimony, his speech had been too much colored "by the influence of Virginia" on his mind. That is to say, the problem he had originally set forth, presumably including the original note he appended to it in his records of the Convention debate, had not taken sufficient account of the distinctively American solution to this problem.

In the original formulation, a property qualification had been a safe-guard against a *future* propertyless majority. But even then Madison had hastened to note that "this does not satisfy the fundamental principle that men cannot be justly bound by laws in the making of which they have no part."[26] The true solution, he had maintained, would assure security both for persons and property. Nevertheless, this rule had been breached only in principle and not in fact, and therefore Madison had been willing to suffer the violation in a society in which "conflicting feelings of the class with, and the class without property" were not yet mature. Originally he had been content to rely on enlarging "the sphere of power without departing from the elective basis of it" as a sufficient safeguard, as the best mode of forestall-ing the anticipated breach.

Thirty years later Madison thought it wise to advance beyond that ex-pressly provisional formulation. His re-evaluation of his earlier discussion begins by admitting the problem:

> These observations [see Debates in the Convention of 1787, August 7th] do not convey the speaker's more full and matured view of the subject, which is subjoined.[27]

In his note Madison restates the problem, this time with clarity: "The right of suffrage is a fundamental article in republican constitutions." From here he proceeds to describe the "peculiar delicacy" touching this right, namely, that to secure the right with recourse to persons could leave property ex-posed, and vice versa. In the nature of civil life, property requires as much to be safeguarded as every other essential right. Accordingly, a "just and free government" accomplishes both of these fundamental objectives. But how? Universal suffrage leads to severe problems; but then so does suffrage tied to a property qualification.

The correct solution depends on comprehending the nature of the prob-lem in its details. Madison distinguishes the *degree* of exposure to danger in the two cases, namely, when property alone is represented and when per-sonhood alone is represented. He notes that property holders participate in common with others in the rights of persons; but nevertheless a suffrage confined to freeholders creates tendencies that make it imperative that "the poor should have a defence." Similarly, because groups of men feel the sting of interest no less than individuals—and are "less controlled by the dread of reproach"—property needs protection.

> Who would rely on a fair decision from three individuals if two had an interest in the case opposed to the rights of the third? Make the number as great as you please, the impartiality will not be increased, nor any further security against injustice be obtained, than what may result from the greater difficulty of uniting the wills of a greater number. [28]

To avoid the dangers either on the side of majority rule or on the side of a will "independent of the society," Madison turns to an examination of "the characteristic excellence" of the American system—its particular arrangement of powers—which secures "the dependence of the Government on the will of the nation" and at the same time provides protection against majority factions.

In addition, the United States enjoyed in 1821 the advantage that "the actual distribution of property" and "the universal hope of acquiring property" produced a situation in which perhaps "a majority of the nation are even freeholders, or the heirs or aspirants to freeholds." That advantage, however, would not continue forever and therefore is cause for special concern in a regime "intended to last for ages."[29] Hence, the fateful question, "what is to secure the rights of property against the danger from an equality and universality of suffrage, vesting complete power over property in hands without a share in it," when the moment of reckoning shall come? Madison is particularly worried by the dependence of more and more propertyless persons on the wealth of a few.

> In the United States the occurrence must happen from the last source; from the connection between the great capitalists in manufactures and commerce, and the numbers employed by them . . . such being the enterprise inspired by free institutions, that great wealth in the hands of individuals and associations may not be unfrequent. But it may be observed, that the opportunities may be diminished, and the permanency defeated, by the equalizing tendency of our laws. [30]

Against the equalizing tendency of the laws, there was the permanent and natural tendency of mankind to form into parties, above all along the line between those who own and those who do not own property.

Madison tests five possible "modifications" that might offer some security to the propertied minority. The first four seem to approximate progressively the final modification, out-and-out "universal suffrage and very short periods of elections."[31] At last, then, Madison embraces the feared prospect:

> the security for the holders of property, when the minority, can only be derived from the ordinary influence possessed by property, and the superior information incident to its holders; from the popular sense of justice,

enlightened and enlarged by a diffusive education; and from the difficulty of combining and effectuating unjust purposes throughout an extensive country. . . .[32]

Madison, in the end, is thus willing to confront the future, not quite sanguinely, but with a determination to rely upon the principles of *Federalist* 51. "If the only alternative be between an equal and universal right of suffrage . . . , and a confinement of the *entire* right to a part of the citizens, it is better that those having the greater interest at stake, namely that of property and persons both, should be deprived of half their share in the government, than, that those having the lesser interest, that of personal rights only, should be deprived of the whole."

Yet eight years later Madison seems to have qualified even this conclusion. He produced yet another statement on the subject, this time during the Virginia Convention called to amend the state constitution. One must pay close attention to the context, however. Again Madison opens with an affirmation that "the right of suffrage [is] of vital importance," and he proceeds from there to deal with the immediate question, namely, the extension of that right to "housekeepers and heads of families." In other words, in Virginia Madison is now defending a broadening of the suffrage! No longer under the influence of the "situation in Virginia"—slave-holding Virginia— as he had been at the 1787 Constitutional Convention, he undertakes the task of bringing the state into line with the broadened basis of republicanism that he had done so much to create in the nation at large. He reassures the Virginians, however, that even if "an unlimited" extension of the suffrage were attempted in the "present circumstances," it would "vary little the character of our public councils."[33]

Accordingly, Madison encourages efforts to widen the franchise as the surest means to regulate the changes sure to follow. In effect, in 1829 Madison seeks to produce what he had promised in 1792, namely, that Virginia's inclusion in the larger republic would ameliorate the dangerous situation in which Virginia then found itself, concentrating the franchise in the hands of one-quarter of the people subject to its laws.

> What is to be done with this unfavored class [the other three-quarters] of the Community? If it be, on the one hand, unsafe to admit them to a full share of political power, it must be recollected, on the other, that it cannot be expedient to rest a republican government on a portion of society having a numerical and physical force excluded from and liable to be turned against it, and which would lead to a standing military force, dangerous to all parties and to liberty itself.[34]

Accordingly, Madison silently invokes the problem of the "natural majority," first set forth clearly in *Federalist* 43, and demonstrates the true nature of the solution he had envisioned in the beginning. The genius of the people is to be cultivated to the point where it can embrace as citizens all of the people subject to the laws. Thus, the images of disfranchised and unpropertied masses, constantly increasing in population, serve not to foreclose extension of the suffrage but to defend a prudent extension of it. The result is to "embrace in the partnership of power every description of citizens having a sufficient stake in the public order, and the stable administration of the laws." Joining them to the "owners" of the country would serve to increase the numbers of those who would benefit from "the political and moral influence emanating from the actual possession of authority, and a just and beneficial exercise of it."

Many practical considerations may affect and qualify the instant application of this principle, but it *is* the unqualified tendency of the laws encouraged by Madison. His project—the heart of *Federalist* 51—is to generate that attachment to republicanism that alone can safeguard the regime. To that end he recommended such changes as would foster in the motion of the regime a further motion toward its ultimate salvation. His words alone can describe the desired result: "To the effect of these changes, intellectual, moral, and social, the institutions and laws of the country must be adapted, and it will require for the task all the wisdom of the wisest patriots."[35]

7

The Rule of Law in *The Federalist*

THOMAS G. WEST

The Federalist proudly claims that the government established by the Constitution is "strictly republican," and that it must be so if it is to be reconcilable "with the fundamental principles of the Revolution" (*Federalist* 39, p. 240). Those principles are stated in the Declaration of Independence. The Declaration is quoted and cited as an authority by *Federalist* 40 (p. 253), and *Federalist* 43, in a near-quotation, speaks of "the transcendent law of nature and of nature's God, which declares that the safety and happiness of society are the objects at which all political institutions aim and to which all such institutions must be sacrificed" (p. 279).

The Federalist does not discuss as a theme the "fundamental principles of the Revolution" because those principles were unanimously approved of by all prominent Americans of the day, and had little immediate bearing on the great controversy between Federalists and Anti-Federalists over the proposed national government. Today, however, it is needful to spell out those principles in order to understand why and in what sense the founders promoted the rule of law in the American Constitution. We can reconstruct their view by reflection on several occasional but weighty remarks scattered throughout *The Federalist*.

The Declaration of Independence appeals to the "laws of nature and of nature's God" to justify the United States' break with Britain and to declare to a candid world the basis of the political order that will take its place. The purpose and limits of political life are determined by the rule of a higher law in the divine and natural order. It could be said that God and nature, in the founders' understanding, are man's supreme legislature. This natural standard of right, which transcends all human laws and constitutions, directs politics in two ways. First, it shows politics its proper end, namely, the safety and happiness of the people. Second, it indicates the human source of political authority: the consent of the governed. And by doing these two things, the laws of nature also define political injustice: policies that do not secure safety and happiness, and government that rules without consent.

That is why, in the discussion of slavery in *Federalist* 54, even the hypothetical Southerner quoted there must admit that slaves have "rights which have been taken away" by the laws, and that those rights, if acknowledged, would give the Negroes "an equal share of representation with the other inhabitants." When Publius admits that slaves are considered by the laws "in the *unnatural* light of property" (my emphasis), he implies that they are *naturally* free and equal. *The Federalist* therefore follows the self-evident truth of the Declaration that "all men are created equal." It is not by nature but by the slavery laws that the blacks have been "degraded from the human rank, and classed with those irrational animals which fall under the legal denomination of property." The difference between men and beasts, then, is that between rational and irrational animals, by which Publius clearly implies that *rational animals share by nature the same rank.* Rationality involves responsibility for good and bad actions, and even the slave, Publius points out, insofar as he is held legally responsible for his crimes, is treated "as a member of society, not as a part of the irrational creation; as a moral person, not as a mere article of property."[1]

Why should rational animals be equal? The statements just quoted imply that since all share in *reason,* no one can claim that his own rationality justifies governing another as if he were an irrational beast. Further, all men, being animal as well as rational, have a share in *passion* as well as reason. And since all share in passion, no one can claim that his own reason is entirely exempt from the imperfection of animal passion. Men are not angels, and their reason will generally be influenced by their passions (*Federalist* 51, p. 322; No. 10, p. 78). So "all men are created equal" in the sense that no one is the natural ruler of another by virtue of a transcendent superiority in regard to reason. Thus all share a natural right to life and liberty; no one has a right by nature to take away another's life or enslave him.

Men are naturally equal, but government means inequality: some rule, others are ruled. How can the two be reconciled? Only when government is established by the consent of the governed is this possible. The Declaration: "[To] secure these rights, governments are instituted among men, deriving their just powers from the consent of the governed." *The Federalist:* "The fabric of American empire ought to rest on the solid basis of THE CONSENT OF THE PEOPLE. The streams of national power ought to flow immediately from the pure original fountain of all legitimate authority" (No. 22, p. 152). And government is consequently also limited by the people's right to revolution, "that fundamental principle of republican government which admits the right of the people to alter or abolish the established Constitution whenever they find it inconsistent with their happiness" (*Federalist* 78, p. 469).

Furthermore, consent is needed not only in the founding of government, but also in its operation once founded. Since liberty is inalienable, no one can reasonably consent to give away his liberty to a government. Here arises the "right of the people to representation in the legislature" (Declaration), recognized in *Federalist* 54's admission, just referred to, that blacks by the right of nature deserve such representation. The point is that the people should retain the exercise of as much of their natural liberty as is consistent with the purpose of government.

What is that purpose? Here is a second criterion of just government in addition to that of consent. The Declaration says that government is instituted "to secure these rights," that is, the rights to "life, liberty, and the pursuit of happiness." It also says that when the people change their government, they must institute new government "to effect their safety and happiness." *The Federalist* follows the Declaration. Most comprehensively, "the object of government [is] the happiness of the people." Elsewhere Publius speaks of "the safety and happiness of society," "the public good," "the common good of the society," "the welfare and prosperity of the co˙ ı-munity," and "private rights and public happiness."[2] This last expr˙ssıon parallels the two formulations of the Declaration, "securing righ˙s" and "safety and happiness." We understand then that the public happiness includes more than securing the inalienable rights of man. Securing those rights is indeed the most urgent purpose of government, but not the only purpose. Where do its other ends come from? Since men are rational animals, they are reasonable creatures whose reason is often overcome by the foolish and self-interested passions characteristic of irrational animals. As man's common share in a rational nature makes no man another's slave, so that same rational nature points the way to natural moral obligation: to act in accordance with reason, not passion. So although men are naturally equal in the sense that no one has a natural right to rule, they need government to help them to rule their passions. "Why has government been instituted at all? Because the passions of men will not conform to the dictates of reason and justice without constraint" (*Federalist* 15, p. 110). "What is government itself but the greatest of all reflections on human nature? If men were angels [i.e., reasonable without passion], no government would be necessary" (*Federalist* 51, p. 322).

The principles of the Revolution therefore require government by officials who act under laws passed by popularly elected legislatures, intending the public good, and these legislatures are to be responsible to the people by periodic reelection. But why must the people's representatives rule through laws? What *is* a law? Laws are "rules for the regulation of society" (*Federalist* 75, p. 450). A rule is a standard that is publicly stated and stable enough to be known by the society. Being rules, laws apply to classes of people, not individuals. "[W]hat are many of the most important acts of legislation but so many judicial determinations, not indeed concerning the rights of single persons, but concerning the rights of large bodies of citizens?" (*Federalist* 10, p. 79). A tax law, to take one example, classifies citizens (e.g., by income) and lays down what classes pay what amount of taxes. Further, "A LAW . . . is a rule which those to whom it is prescribed are bound to observe" (*Federalist* 33, p. 204). It has coercive restraint by prescribing punishments for those who disobey.

"Law is called a rule, in order to distinguish it from a sudden, a transient, or a particular order: uniformity, permanency, stability, characterize a law."[3] In this way James Wilson, who along with Hamilton and Madison was the most thoughtful of the Constitution's framers, distinguished a law from an ad hoc decision made regarding a particular case. A lawless despot may decide whom to send to prison by judging each case according to criteria he applies in that case only, in the absence of established rules. In the 1780s, some state legislatures acted lawlessly by condemning or rewarding particular individuals outside of or contrary to the written laws.[4] This kind of lawless conduct can perhaps be warranted in a particular case where the strict application of the rule might lead to injustice or injury to the public good. But more typically, without rules publicly agreed upon that apply equally to all persons similarly situated, nothing prevents the whims and passions of the rulers from prevailing in government. Without laws that have a fair degree of stability, no one would know in advance what was forbidden or permitted. "Law is defined to be a rule of action; but how can that be a rule, which is little known and less fixed?" (*Federalist* 62, p. 381).

In addition, rule by laws insures responsibility, for publicly announced rules can be known and judged by the people better than thousands of particular actions. Above all, standing rules insure a certain rationality in government. An assembly may sense that debts ought to be forgiven in unusual circumstances, but formulating a general rule requires thought about the *reason* why such an exception ought to be made, and the slowness introduced by the need for this discussion can help prevent the legislature from acting precipitately. The government ought to reflect the sense of the people, but preferably their "cool and deliberate sense" (*Federalist* 63, p. 384). At its best the rule of law will embody the reason of the public, which will control their passions by compelling them to submit under threat of penalty, thereby fostering habits of sobriety and self-control. "[I]t is the reason, alone, of the public, that ought to control and regulate the government. The passions ought to be controlled and regulated by the government" (*Federalist* 49, p. 317).

The rule of law, in sum, is a governmental practice designed to make as likely as possible the coincidence of the two requirements of just government: that it be by the consent of the people, and that it secure the safety and happiness of society. The law aims to embody the public's reason by requiring the men who govern to act in conformity, at least in principle, to reasoned discussion and a rule of universal application.[5]

SEPARATION OF POWERS AND THE NEED FOR A WRITTEN CONSTITUTION

The commitment to the rule of law meant that there would be a difference between making laws, enforcing them, and judging particular violations of laws. Thus arises the idea of the distinct legislative, executive, and judicial powers of government. The French philosopher Montesquieu, the "oracle who is always consulted and cited on this subject" (*Federalist* 47, p. 301), recommended a separation of these governmental powers, especially of the legislative from the executive: "When the legislative and executive powers are united in the same person or body . . . there can be no liberty, because apprehensions may arise lest *the same* monarch or senate should *enact* tyrannical laws to *execute* them in a tyrannical manner" (p. 303, quoting Montesquieu's *Spirit of the Laws*). But mere separation of these powers is not enough: no part of the government should be able to transcend its legal limits "without being effectually checked and restrained by the others."[6]

These theories especially appealed to Americans because their experience with British government seemed to confirm them. In Britain the king, Parliament, and judiciary performed (more or less) the three functions, and in the colonies the locally elected legislatures and royally appointed governors were obvious analogues.

Montesquieu's exposition of the separation of powers idea looked to the British government as its model. But that government was popular or republican only in one part, the House of Commons. The House of Lords was filled by a hereditary aristocracy, and the executive was a hereditary monarch. So as long as Britain remained the exemplar for the separation of powers, the idea was bound to be confused with the old mixed-regime theory of Aristotle and Polybius. These authors had proposed a government in which the democratic many controlled one part and the wealthy few another part, with the possible addition of a monarch as a third element.[7] The intention was to prevent any one group in society—the many poor or the few rich—from gaining power or advantage at the expense of the other. Unjust laws were to be prevented by making sure that the two major classes in society each controlled at least one part of the government. As long as the British model prevailed, the separation of powers would mean the mixture of democracy, aristocracy, and monarchy.

But Britain was not to be America's example. The Americans were the first to understand with clarity that the separation of powers idea is compatible with a wholly popular government. Separate parts of government would still keep each other in line, but each part would be based on the people at large, not on separate classes in the society. With the expulsion of British power in 1776 the United States became entirely republican. By trial and error, and some sensible reflections along the way, the Americans achieved the beautiful solution that was given its best expression in the federal Constitution.

The Americans tried to keep the powers of government separate when they wrote their first state constitutions after independence in 1776, but they did not succeed. Instead, "The legislative department is everywhere extending the sphere of its activity and drawing all power into its impetuous vortex." By 1787 it was better understood why this had happened. In 1776 the Americans' enemy was British monarchy and aristocracy, represented in America in the persons of royal governors and their executive and judicial appointments. These were the principal objects of fear and suspicion. So the new constitutions generally established weak state executives and judiciaries and powerful legislatures, in their desire to create governments wholly republican (*Federalist* 48, p. 309). The consequence: "All the powers of government, legislative, executive, and judiciary, result to the legislative body. The concentrating of these in the same hands is precisely the definition of despotic government. It will be no alleviation that these powers will be exercised by a plurality of hands, and not by a single one. One hundred and seventy-three despots would surely be as oppressive as one."[8]

Fortunately, the Americans began to break with both the theory and the practice of legislative supremacy immediately after independence. The change in the understanding of constitutionalism was gradual, but it was completed by the time of the national Constitution of 1787.[9] The practical basis of the break was an American tradition of having written fundamental laws for their colonies, sometimes drawn up within the colonies themselves. This *practice* implied that there could and should be fundamental laws paramount to the ordinary statutes passed by the legislature. The Revolution's *theory* made this practice intelligible and showed the way for its future exercise. If the people are "the pure, original fountain of all legitimate authority" (*Federalist* 22, p. 152), the structure of the government ought to be determined by them or by men to whom they specifically delegate this power. Yet the first state constitutions were written by ordinary state legislatures and were generally changeable by ordinary legislative act. As early as 1776, several Massachusetts towns objected to their state legislature's proposal to write the state constitution. In order to distinguish the constitution-making legislative authority from the ordinary legislature, they proposed that a special convention be chosen by the people for the sole purpose of writing the state constitution.[10] The convention idea, which came to be adopted in other states, made it clear that the ordinary legislature was subordinated to the supreme law of the constitution no less than were the executive and the judiciary. The legislature was not a supreme power free to set down or change the form of the executive or judiciary at pleasure, as Locke and Blackstone, British theorists highly admired by the Americans, had maintained.[11] By 1788 *The Federalist* could say, with justice and native pride, "The important distinction so well understood in America between a Constitution established by the people and unalterable by the government, and a law established by the government and alterable by the government, seems to have been little understood and less observed in any other country" (*Federalist* 53, p. 331).

The idea of written constitutional law paramount to all branches of government embodies the two great themes of the Declaration, popular sovereignty and securing men's safety and happiness. The people's own constitutional law would govern the legislature and other branches even after the government was established. And the fact that this paramount law would take the form of a written document changeable only in rare circumstances reflected the conviction that government's duties were guided and limited by a permanent standard of natural right. Thus the higher law of the Constitution, limiting the government from without (by the restrictive provisions of the document), and from within (by the separation of powers), would be the people's effectual Bill of Rights (*Federalist* 84, p. 515), far more significant than the mere pious pronouncements that graced the very state constitutions whose legislatures ruled as despots.

Written *constitutionalism* is so familiar to us that we rarely consider how unique we are in this respect. Other countries (e.g., Britain) either have no written constitution, or, if they do have one, they either ignore or repudiate it within a few years. The following story is typical of most of the world's experience with written constitutions. A bookseller in Paris, upon receiving a request for a copy of the most recent French Constitution, sent the reply: "We do not deal in periodical literature." And this was in 1861, long before the French passion for numbering their republics really got going![12] The durability of our Constitution testifies not only to the good sense with which it was constructed but also to the enlightened reverence which the American people have accorded the document and its principles.

THE MEANING OF "LEGISLATIVE BALANCES AND CHECKS"

The problem faced by our 1776 founders was: on what principle may we justify revolt from Britain? Differently stated, on what principle is just government to be grounded? Their answer was: the principle of equality, which requires republican government (if prudence concurs that the circumstances are right)[13] under laws passed by representative legislatures, the purpose of which is to secure the rights of man and the people's safety and happiness.

The framers of the Constitution (and therefore also the authors of *The Federalist*) faced a somewhat different problem. They had observed a dozen years of state governments that were republican yet manifestly did not secure the equal rights of all citizens or the public safety and happiness. Trials were frequently conducted without due regard for proper judicial procedure. The rights of property were violated, sometimes whimsically, more often systematically, by legislatures who favored debtors over creditors (*Federalist* 10). Moreover, the national government, having nearly lost the Revolutionary War because of its weakness, was moribund and almost universally ignored. The moral state of the nation was in decline, and instead of the glory and greatness promised by the Revolution, America had "reached almost the last stage of national humiliation" (*Federalist* 15, p. 106). The framers' task, then, was to find "a republican remedy for the diseases most incident to republican government" (*Federalist* 10, p. 84). And, if such a remedy could not be found, "to abandon the cause of that species of government as indefensible" (*Federalist* 9, p. 72).

Surprisingly, the list of five "improvement[s]" in "the science of politics" that appears in *Federalist* 9 does not include "constitutionalism." One improvement that *is* mentioned is the principle of "legislative balances and checks." Readers of *The Federalist* often overlook this item, generally because they have heard the phrase "checks and balances" used so often in connection with the separation of powers idea that they do not notice that the expression refers here only to the legislative part of government. If we think for a moment about it, "legislative balances and checks" obviously refers to the division of the legislature into two parts, the House and the Senate. It probably also refers to the participation of the President in lawmaking through his veto power, whether exercised or merely threatened (*Federalist* 73, pp. 443–446). And Publius may well have meant to extend the idea of "legislative balances and checks" to the separation of ordinary lawmaking from the extraordinary lawmaking of constitution writing and amending. At any rate this split, effected by the founders, between constitution making and ordinary statute making is crucial to the success of republicanism in America.

There were other weighty reasons for the separation of fundamental from ordinary lawmaking. *The Federalist* speaks carefully but firmly about the imprudence of frequent revisions of fundamental law. The happy, perhaps even providential, conjunction of passion and reason during the Revolution and Constitutional Convention is very unlikely to recur again. Experience even speaks against the likelihood of successful founding by deliberative bodies; the great successes of the past were typically one-man jobs (*Federalist* 37, p. 230; No. 49, p. 315; No. 38, p. 231). The fact that the people are the ultimate "fountain of authority" does not make it prudent to recur frequently to that authority. Quite the contrary: the people, and the assemblies elected by them, are typically moved by passion and not reason, so if the people once consent to a rational constitution it would be folly ever to raise the question again except in case of dire necessity (*Federalist* 49, pp. 314–315; No. 58, p. 360; No. 62, p. 379).

The overwhelming structural cause of bad government in America under the state constitutions was the despotic dominance of the legislatures. A due separation of constitution making from ordinary lawmaking would properly reduce the legislature to a part of government under the Constitution; it would no longer be the legal repository of the supreme political power. But constitutionalism in this sense was not enough. Other "legislative balances and checks" had to be devised in order to prevent the legislature from becoming the de facto or illegal sovereign.

These additional checks would have to be discoveries of prudence, working within institutions the Americans had become accustomed to. As we saw, the theory of free government helped point out the way to constitutionalism, but theory was of little help beyond this. Republican theory is indifferent to whether the legislature is divided into two houses, or whether the executive should have a veto, or what role the judiciary could play in keeping the legislature in its proper place. In all these instances the colonial and British past furnished examples that provided material for these "inventions of prudence" (*Federalist* 51, p. 322), although the framers adapted them with the necessary changes to serve the "checking" purpose.

The assumption governing the founders' prudence here was that although the legislature should be kept in its proper bounds, it was still to be the most powerful branch. "In republican government, the legislative authority necessarily predominates" (*Federalist* 51, p. 322). The main reason for this predominance is that the power to make laws is constitutionally the broadest and the least capable of precise definition.[14] Besides the division between ordinary and constitutional lawmaking discussed above, ordinary lawmaking is further subdivided into three or more parts. Congress is to consist of a House of Representatives and a Senate, and while both houses are to be representative of the people, the character of the two bodies is kept as dissimilar as possible. There are different modes of election (popular for House, by state legislatures for Senate), different terms of office (two and six years), different composition (Senate has fewer members from populous states than the House), different size (Senate is small, House is large), and different activities (Senate shares in some executive powers, e.g., making treaties and appointing officials). The third part of the statute-lawmaking power is held by the President through the veto power.

The rest of the lawmaking power is that retained by the states, where the separation of powers within each state government complements the complex scheme (*Federalist* 51, pp. 322–323). The states had general authority over "all the objects which, in the ordinary course of affairs, concern the lives, liberties, and properties of the people, and the internal order, improvement, and prosperity of the State" (*Federalist* 45, p. 293).[15] The power of the national government was to be exercised only on matters of truly national scope, such as foreign policy and national security, general regulation of commerce, and other "great and national objects." Thus "the great and aggregate interests [are] referred [by the federal Constitution] to the national, the local and particular to the State legislatures" (*Federalist* 10, p. 83).

The American Constitution—and the thought and statesmanship that made it—was a great native achievement. Products of a distinctively American political science and political prudence were its purely republican separation of powers; its written constitutional law, approved by the people, and superior to the ordinary lawmaking power; the extent of the elaborate scheme of checks and balances within the legislative power, including the constitutional check, the House-Senate check, the Presidential veto check, the state-national check, and the ultimate check in the people's legal right to amend their Constitution. We may also add the daring expansion of the sphere of republican government over a large territory and population, discussed elsewhere in this volume. Publius boasts with some justice when, anticipating the ratification of the Constitution, he says: "Happy will it be for ourselves, and most honorable to human nature, if we have wisdom and virtue enough to set so glorious an example to mankind!" (*Federalist* 36, p. 224).

REPRESENTATION AND EXCELLENCE

It is generally understood that "balances and checks" are a central feature of the Constitution, even if their nature and scope are not often appreciated. Less well understood is how *The Federalist* expected the Constitution not merely to check legislative and popular excesses but to make possible a government informed by and fostering intelligence, virtue, and a dedication to greatness.[16]

The most urgent purpose of government is to secure the right to life—to "insure domestic tranquillity" and "provide for the common defense," in the words of the Constitution's Preamble. The largeness of America, combined with representation, makes for a national legislature less likely to engage in factious behavior. The multiplicity of interests in a large country should help keep the Congress from being dominated by a single majority faction bent upon its private interest at the expense of the public good or of the rights of the minority. Thus, "domestic tranquillity" is to be secured (*Federalist* 10; *Federalist* 51, pp. 324–325).

But the mere absence of factious government is not enough. Good government requires judgment, intelligence, information, and far-sightedness in its officials. Representation, whether by popular or indirect election, cannot accomplish this by itself. The selection of representatives must be arranged so as to make superior men more likely to seek out positions in government and to be chosen.

In 1776 Americans tended to think of "representatives" as the members of the popularly elected legislatures. Closeness to local communities, or reflecting the people in their diversity, seems to have been the criterion of representativeness. It was not expected that excellence and popularity would conflict.[17] This understanding is preserved in the name "House of Representatives," as though no one else in government were a representative. But during the period leading up to 1787 it became clear to some that this view was inadequate. On the one hand, the more popular branch of the legislature was *not* representative in the sense of acting on behalf of the whole people (as opposed to a factious majority). On the other hand, in a government wholly popular, it did not make sense to say that the executive is not a representative; in every state he (or they) was chosen directly or indirectly by the people. And it became evident in practice that the supposedly nonrepresentative executive acted more consistently in accord with the cool and deliberate sense of the people than the supposedly more representative legislature.[18] (Consequently the movement for a strong national government that led up the Convention was strongly supported by the people in all parts of the Union.[19])

The confusion over the representative character of the state executives and Senates arose in part because of the analogue of these branches in the old mixed-regime constitution of Britain. There the Senate was the hereditary House of Lords, and the executive the unelected king. Even in America some persisted in conceiving the Senate as the body representing property or, as John Adams thought, a body that should represent an aristocracy of the rich, the well-born, and the able.[20] Certainly the Convention intended the U.S. Senate to be an *upper* house, the higher-toned of the two legislative branches.[21] But that tone was to be gotten by the filtering effect of the election of senators by state legislatures, which were themselves popularly elected.

Thus as the Senate and the executive began to be seen more clearly for what they were—representatives of a different kind—they could be entrusted with extensive powers. The House would be firmly checked by other bodies, but even more important, the deliberations of the government would be improved by involving representatives of a different and perhaps better sort. The crucial changes made by the federal Constitution were six-year terms for Senators (no state had terms so long) and the major influence of the President on lawmaking through the veto power (only New York granted its governor this power; most states also hemmed in their governors with councils not appointed by the governor and whose consent was needed for the executive to act).

The Federalist occasionally indicates that the Senate and the President are "representatives" too, although that term is usually reserved for the members of the House. The broader conception is reflected in Publius's discussion of Senatorial and Presidential responsibility to the people. The Senators' longer terms allow the people to judge them better in one respect by observing the consequences of the policies they promoted or opposed during their years in office (*Federalist* 63, p. 383). The same point also applies to the President, with the additional aid to responsibility made possible by the fact that he is one man rather than a numerous group like the House and the Senate (*Federalist* 70, pp. 427–429).[22]

The aim of every form of government, republican or otherwise, is, or ought to be, "first, to obtain for rulers men who possess most wisdom to discern, and most virtue to pursue, the common good of the society; and in the next place, to take the most effectual precautions for keeping them virtuous whilst they continue to hold their public trust" (*Federalist* 57, p. 350). In republican government the "most effectual precaution" for keeping the rulers virtuous is "such a limitation of the term of appointment as will maintain a proper responsibility to the people" (p. 351). This is particularly true of the House of Representatives, with its short two-year terms.[23] If the members hope to be reelected, they must try to please their electors. Self-interest will therefore generally prevent them from betraying the people's trust in them. Furthermore, the electoral process at its best will tend to elevate to public office those most deserving of the office. And in large districts, as those for the House are, more fit characters are likely to be found. Well-qualified officials can "refine and enlarge the public views." But Publius is also aware of "the vicious arts, by which elections are too often carried" (*Federalist* 10, p. 82), and he places his ultimate trust, as he must, in a form of government that presupposes the capacity of the people to choose their own rulers—in "the vigilant and manly spirit which actuates the people of America—a spirit which nourishes freedom, and in return is nourished by it" (*Federalist* 57, p. 353). In the end, only the people can throw the rascals out.

Still, although it is a mistake to underrate the people's capacity for virtue, it is a graver error to count on it too much. Therefore, although the President and Senate are also controlled by frequent elections, their longer terms of office and perhaps firmer characters may enable them to oppose the "temporary errors and delusions" of the people that might be too quickly and accurately reflected in the House of Representatives (*Federalist* 62, p. 384; No. 71, p. 432).

The Senate's long term of office will contribute to the end of obtaining virtuous rulers in two further ways: knowledge and stability. Being in office for several years, Senators will be able to learn "the laws, the affairs, and the comprehensive interests of their country" better than the short-termed representatives. Second, their long duration in office will keep the Senate from changing its membership and its laws and policies too frequently. The indirect election of Senators by state legislatures will, Publius expects, lead to a more "select appointment" than election by the people at large. And finally, the character of the Senatorial body—the "upper house," named for its great Roman precursor, the visible emblem of deliberative wisdom in the national government—will engage the Senators' passion of pride on behalf of that body's dignity and America's respectability in the eyes of other nations (*Federalist* 63, p. 383).

Publius's expectations from the Senate are modest compared to what he hopes for from the President. Of the Presidency he asserts what he never does of the Senate, that it will be typically "filled by characters pre-eminent for ability and virtue" (*Federalist* 68, p. 414). Like the Senators, the President will be indirectly elected, and his spirited passions—his ambition, pride, and love of glory—will be even more fully enlisted in an office where success or failure is his alone.

Publius speaks of *deliberation* as the quality especially to be desired of the House and Senate, in contrast to the President. Deliberation is the thoughtful consideration of alternative courses of conduct with a view to a decision, and it is distinguished from mere bargaining and "horse-trading" by its concern for the common good. When Publius agrees in *Federalist* 10 that a multiplicity of factions may contribute to good government by preventing a majority faction, he does not mean that sound policy emerges out of the sum total of "opposite and rival interests." Rather, Publius hopes that the difficulty of conducting politics as a coalition of interest groups will make the legislature more likely to act on the principles of "justice and the general good" (*Federalist* 51, p. 325). Large bodies, Publius says, make their decisions slowly, but such slowness often promotes "deliberation and circumspection" (*Federalist* 70, p. 427). In a large body there will be fuller discussion of questions before they are acted upon.

For deliberation to be best encouraged, the body should be large enough that its members are well acquainted with and sympathetic toward the local circumstances of the different parts of the union (*Federalist* 56, p. 348), but small enough that it is not easily manipulated by clever but unscrupulous demagogues. For "the more numerous any assembly may be, of whatever character composed, the greater is known to be the ascendancy of passion over reason" (*Federalist* 58, p. 360). The Senate having but twenty-six members, and the House less than one hundred (in 1787 and for some years afterward), both bodies are of an appropriate size for due deliberation. But amplitude of discussion is not enough. It must also be well informed and intelligent if the public good is to be truly served. The House best embodies local information; the Senate, a due acquaintance with national and international affairs.

The President, on the other hand, may sometimes be a better deliberator than the Congress. It is true that executive energy, left to itself, might not pause long enough to think through the reasons for and against a choice. But as a partner in the lawmaking power by virtue of his veto, the President might lessen "the danger of those errors which flow from want of due deliberation, or of those missteps which proceed from the contagion of some common passion or interest" (*Federalist* 73, p. 443). This will be because, as Publius says in another connection, "The sole and undivided responsibility of one man will naturally beget a livelier sense of duty and a more exact regard to reputation" (*Federalist* 76, p. 455). We might also add that the President, as sole representative of the whole people, might be able to take a more comprehensive view of the public good and be less likely to sacrifice it to some local or partial consideration.

THE ENDS OF LEGISLATION: SAFETY AND HAPPINESS

The Federalist's concern for wisdom and virtue in the rulers serves the cause of liberty in two senses. It is obvious to Publius that free government will not survive if its laws and actions are constantly incompetent and unjust (*Federalist* 51, p. 325). "Justice is the end of government. It is the end of civil society. It ever has been and ever will be pursued until it be obtained, or until liberty be lost in the pursuit" (p. 324). The story of the state legislatures and the Confederation government brings out this danger. But there is a deeper sense in which liberty is threatened by bad government. For the founders never thought liberty meant the right to live in any way one pleases. They never hesitated to distinguish liberty from license, and *The Federalist* abounds with references to the difference in rank between passion and reason. Publius says, for example, that "it is the reason alone, of the public, that ought to control the government. The passions ought to be controlled and regulated by the government" (*Federalist* 49, p. 317). In the immediate instance he means that the reason embodied in a sound Constitution ought to control the passions of the legislature. But he also means that the responsible laws of the government ought to control the irrational passions of the people. Popular greed is to be checked by laws protecting the rights of property. Or, to use an example that was completely uncontroversial in Publius's day and which is therefore not even alluded to in *The Federalist*, the governments of the states everywhere forbid the printing and distribution of pornography and the practice of homosexuality. A people enslaved to "the tyranny of their own passions" is free in name only (quoted from *Federalist* 63, p. 384). Such a people, incapable of governing themselves as individuals, will also be incapable of free government. Tyrannized within, they must also be tyrannized from without. For at that point "nothing less than the chains of despotism can restrain them from destroying and devouring one another" (*Federalist* 55, p. 346).

The end of government is justice, but justice in a comprehensive sense. For Publius also frequently says that the end of government is "the happiness of the people" and "the common good of the society" (*Federalist* 62, p. 380; No. 57, p. 350). That common good consists in part of national prosperity (*Federalist* 12, p. 91). But it also involves a fostering of the public morality whenever that is appropriately accomplished by the national government. One such instance, mentioned in passing by *The Federalist*, would be to discourage the excessive use of alcohol by means of an excise tax (*Federalist* 12, pp. 95–96). Similarly, one purpose of the constitutional prohibition of ex post facto laws and laws impairing the obligation of contract is to "inspire a general prudence and industry, and give a regular course to the business of society" (*Federalist* 44, p. 283). In the same number Publius deplores "the pestilent effects of paper money [issued by factious state governments] . . . on the industry and morals of the people" (p. 281). And at the very end of *The Federalist*, Publius refers to "practices on the part of the State governments which . . . have occasioned an almost universal prostration of morals" (*Federalist* 85, pp. 521–522). This refers to the routine state abuses of property rights, which had evidently encouraged the vices of greed, faithlessness, and laziness at the expense of frugality, industry, and honesty. Federal constitutional law and statute law would promote the public morality by correcting these abuses.

Normally, of course, the state governments were to continue to play the primary role, at least on a day-to-day basis, in regulating the public morals. But regarding the federal territories, over which Congress was given exclusive jurisdiction by the Constitution, the Northwest Ordinance of 1787, renewed by the First Congress, had this to say: "Religion, morality, and knowledge, being necessary to good government and the happiness of mankind, schools and the means of education shall forever be encouraged." This act is an obvious sign of the founders' universal agreement that fostering morality was one of government's main concerns, and that where the states could not take care of it, as in the territories where state governments did not yet exist, the federal government should do so.

Some scholars today doubt that the Constitution's framers were serious about the moral formation of American citizens. They argue that *The Federalist* anticipates with approval a self-interested citizenry who would be purposely encouraged to pursue a commercial life of gain. The Constitution, in this view, not only tolerates but deliberately fosters the relentless pursuit of money and success. Private rights, then, exist so that each man can indulge his private passions and interests, and the public good is merely the aggregate of individuals' collective self-interest. Liberals (and some conservatives, such as George Will) are aghast at such a scheme, and denounce the "public purposelessness" of the founders' America.[24] Other observers are quite satisfied with this pluralistic free-for-all of factions unleashed, as they see it, by the Constitution, and they praise the system of mutually checking selfish interests for its success in channeling the explosive passions of religious and moral fanaticism into the gentler courses of comfortable self-preservation.[25] A different but related thesis has been advanced by Gordon Wood and other historians: that the political science of *The Federalist*, relying on institutional devices and self-interest, represents a break with the "classical republicanism" of 1776, which had placed its trust in virtuous, public-spirited citizens who were expected to care more for the public good than individual rights.[26]

It is true that Publius expected and wanted America to be a commercial republic. "The prosperity of commerce is now perceived and acknowledged by all enlightened statesmen to be the most useful as well as the most productive source of national wealth, and has accordingly become a primary object of their political cares." When commerce is prosperous, "The assiduous merchant, the laborious husbandman, the active mechanic, and the industrious manufacturer—all orders of men look forward with eager expectation and growing alacrity to this pleasing reward of their toils [i.e., money]" (*Federalist* 12, p. 91). But commerce and profit are never ends in themselves for Publius; they are in the service of national strength and greatness, wealth being necessary for defense and the fighting of war (*Federalist* 11 and 12). Publius also wrote that some future President's "love of fame, the ruling passion of the noblest minds" would prompt him "to plan and undertake extensive and arduous enterprises for the public good" (*Federalist* 72, p. 437). Could Hamilton and Madison have thought that such greatness would be in the service of "an innumerable multitude of men, alike and equal, constantly circling around in pursuit of the petty and banal pleasures with which they glut their souls"?[27] Far from it. Indeed, their concern for the nation's character and honor animates the entire *Federalist*. The founders' notion of virtue follows that of the classics, which included both the self-restraint of the lower passions and the noble aspiration to great deeds.

But it is not enough to say that forming the moral character of the citizens is in some respect the end of government. The founders had to ask what virtues are appropriate to life in democratic America. The intense brotherhood cultivated in the citizen-soldiers of the small cities of the ancient world is absent from America, as is the elegance of wealthy aristocracy. Section 15 of the Virginia Bill of Rights (1776) reads: "That no free government, or the blessings of liberty, can be preserved to any people, but by a firm adherence to justice, moderation, temperance, frugality, and virtue, and by frequent recurrence to fundamental principles."[28] Virginia recalls here the classical virtues of justice and moderation but adds the characteristically republican *frugality*, suitable for a hardworking people who mean to be self-reliant. The Massachusetts Constitution (1780) adds piety and wisdom, other traditional virtues, and calls on the public schools particularly "to countenance and inculcate the principles of humanity and general benevolence, public and private charity, industry and frugality, honesty and punctuality in their dealings, sincerity, good humor, and all social affections and generous sentiments among the people."[29] This mouthful—John Adams wrote it—gives us a picture of the qualities of friendly and honest industriousness that were expected to characterize ordinary Americans at their best. America was never intended to be a new Rome, harshly high-strung in its internal rivalries and grandiose foreign-policy ambitions. Even Hamilton, that lover of honor and military glory, recognized that American life would be for the most part private life, and that "The industrious habits of the people of the present day, absorbed in the pursuits of gain and devoted to the improvements of agriculture and commerce, are incompatible with the condition of a nation of soldiers, which was the true condition of the people of those [ancient] republics" (*Federalist* 8, p. 69). The founders understood that the business of most Americans was going to be business. They had no snobbish disdain for such activity, but neither did they overlook the need to foster those decencies that would make business an honorable and pleasant if unexalted manner of life. The founders' list of virtues that were to be promoted through education bespeaks a profound political awareness of the needs of our republican citizenry and of the moral adjustments appropriate to a more private, more family-oriented, more Christian world.[30]

Still, these qualities, important as they are for "good government and the happiness of mankind" (Northwest Ordinance), are not the highest virtues of human nature. The founders also looked to the more austere classical ideal of gentlemanship, not indeed for ordinary citizens, but as a model for the most outstanding men among us. *The Federalist* in particular speaks of the rarer excellences of prudence, wisdom, courage, and magnanimity in connection with those who are expected to fill government office, especially the President. Nor was this an empty dream, for they had constantly before their eyes the remarkable example of George Washington, a man of proud and austere rectitude. For the founding generation, and for most Americans throughout our history, George Washington embodied the noblest virtues best.

I add one further remark on morality, to answer a common misunderstanding. It has sometimes been said that although the founders believed that government has a legitimate interest in citizen character, that belief was qualified by their view of morality as a mere means to political liberty, not as something intrinsically necessary to human happiness. This conception reduces morality to a device employed by the statesman's prudence for political purposes, unrelated to individual well-being. As if self-restraint were in the service of self-indulgence, of the liberty of the individual to live however he pleases! *The Federalist* never discusses the question, since the purpose of morality was hardly an issue during the ratification campaign. I have already quoted the remarkable education passage from the Northwest Ordinance of 1787, which endorses the promotion of religion and morality not only for "good government" but also for "the *happiness* of mankind" (my emphasis). This same theme was an important part of Washington's Farewell Address (co-authored by Hamilton): "Of all the dispositions and habits which lead to political prosperity, religion and morality are indispensible supports. In vain would that man claim the tribute of patriotism who should labor to subvert these great pillars of *human happiness*—these firmest props of the duties *of men* and citizens. The mere politician, equally with the pious man, ought to respect and cherish them. A volume could not trace all their connections with *private* and public felicity. . . . Promote, then, as an object of primary importance, institutions for the general diffusion of knowledge" (my emphasis). These quotations, with their emphasis on morality as an ingredient of human happiness, and affirming a federal role in its promotion through educational institutions, testify eloquently to the founders' convictions.

This moral concern was in fact *the* overarching theme of Washington's Presidency from its very beginning. In the First Inaugural he says: "there exists in the economy and course of nature an indissoluble union between virtue and happiness; between duty and advantage; between the genuine maxims of an honest and magnanimous policy and the solid rewards of public prosperity and felicity; since we ought to be no less persuaded that the propitious smiles of Heaven can never be expected on a nation that disregards the eternal rules of order and right which Heaven itself has ordained. . . ." In the reply of the Senate to Washington's Inaugural, they said: "We feel, sir, the force and acknowledge the justness of the observation that the foundations of our national policy should be laid in private morality. If individuals be not influenced by moral principles, it is in vain to look for public virtue. It is therefore the duty of legislators to enforce, both by precept and example, the utility as well as the necessity of a strict adherence to the rules of distributive justice."[31]

Such were to be the ends of the rule of law in America.

8

Republicanizing the Executive

HARVEY C. MANSFIELD, JR.

When we come to the executive power in government, we see what government can produce—not its promises or wishes, but the result, the outcome, the accomplished fact. In the course of the eleven papers Alexander Hamilton (as Publius) wrote in *The Federalist* on the executive (Nos. 67–77), he says briskly that "a government ill executed, whatever it may be in theory, must be, in practice, a bad government" (*Federalist* 70).[1] The executive, it seems, is sovereign in the realm where practice is not subject to theory—where, if strength is not always good, feebleness is bad. The best modern commentator on the executive—Richard Neustadt—has also located it in a region far removed from what he calls the "literary theory" of the Constitution.[2]

Yet it was precisely in regard to the executive that the Constitution was most in need of the theorizing of political science, and most indebted to it. Publius implies that in theory, government might have a feeble executive. The theory he had in mind was republican theory, ever hostile to anything smacking of monarchy and never stronger than among Americans who had just fought themselves to independence from a king. As Charles Thach and Gordon S. Wood have shown, Americans had come to recognize during the course of the Revolutionary War that the executives they had instituted in the states in 1776 were too weak,[3] but American republicanism seemed to offer no remedy and left Americans bewildered at the claim of fact against their notions of legitimacy. The task of political science in *The Federalist* was to show that an energetic executive could be republicanized. That we take the completion of this task for granted today is a sign that it was well done, not that it was superfluous.

THE AVERSION TO MONARCHY

Earlier in *The Federalist* (Nos. 6, 9, 10, 14), Publius had scathingly criticized all previous republics, including the celebrated ancient ones, for the alternating anarchy and tyranny of their popular majorities. In *Federalist* 10 he formulated this sorry experience as the problem of majority faction and proposed, as the basis for a solution, to "extend the sphere" of the republic, and thus to overthrow the republican prejudice in favor of a close, homogeneous people and against imperial size. An extended sphere, however, requires an energetic government at the center to "preserve the Union of so large an empire" (*Federalist* 23); so the republican prejudice against energetic government must be abandoned together with the republican prejudice against diversity and size. And what is energetic government but an energetic *executive*?

Publius does not at first make it clear that the American people must give up their instinctive hostility not only to the imperial size that often goes with monarchy but also to the very idea, to the actual person, of one-man rule. He says that the "great and radical vice" of the Articles of Confederation is the principle of legislating for states in their collective capacities rather than for the individuals within them (*Federalist* 15). He explains patiently that a law is not a law without a sanction, and concludes that we have a choice between coercion by the magistracy ("the courts and ministers of justice") and coercion by the military—thus presenting civil sanctions, while not mentioning "executive power," as the alternative to "military execution." Since coercion is necessary, be glad, he seems to say to republicans, that it is civil coercion.

The necessity of union having been shown, Publius considers in the series *Federalist* 23–36 how much power is necessary to the union and upon whom that power should be exercised. But he saves the consideration, which is almost the disclosure, of *by* whom that power should be exercised, to the later series of papers on the executive. In this early section he appeals to the necessity of the case and to the recent history of the union under the Articles—an experience of necessity—against the "idea of governing at all times by the simple force of law" (*Federalist* 28). This idea, which Publius identifies as republican, "has no place but in the reveries of those political doctors whose sagacity disdains the admonitions of experimental instruction." Again, Publius draws no pointed conclusion recommending an energetic executive; he only prepares the way by reminding his readers of the force of necessity.

It seems to be characteristic of republican sagacity in particular to be impervious to the instruction of necessity.[4] The long, sad, horrifying experience of republics has taught republican theorists nothing, it appears; and their influence readily confirms the partisan prejudices of republican peoples who are hostile to monarchy and heedless of all experience but the recent cause of that hostility. It sometimes seems that for *The Federalist*, republican theory causes nothing but trouble for republics, and that nothing else causes more trouble. At the least, it must be clear that its impervious sagacity cannot be refuted by experience alone, that it must be met on its own level as theory, and that executive power in the American Constitution, though mainly preoccupied with the demands of necessity, did not arise simply in response to practical necessity.[5] Peoples generally, and especially those instructed by republican "doctors," do not respond automatically to what seems necessary to later generations gifted with hindsight. But the creation of executive power was made possible, indeed it was created, by a recognition, new to republican theory and contrary to previous republican theorists, of the power of necessity. As we shall see, this recognition did not become an excuse for doing ill but an incentive for doing better than necessary.

When Publius does reach the matter of *by* whom necessary power was to be exercised, he admits that he has to face the "aversion of the people to monarchy" (*Federalist* 67). Hardly any part of the Constitution ("the system") was more difficult to arrange than the executive, he says, and perhaps none has been criticized with less judgment. Then he denounces the misrepresentation of the critics and exposes one flagrant, but typical, example of it.[6] Neither the section of *The Federalist* on the legislature nor that on the judiciary begins with a comparable blast at the critics of the Constitution, and we are easily led to suppose that the difficulty in arranging the executive arose principally from the same source as the criticism of the result: "that maxim of republican jealousy which considers power as safer in the hands of a number of men than of a single man" (*Federalist* 70). Publius could and did appeal to politicians and statesmen most celebrated for their sound principles and just views, who have "declared in favor of a single executive and a numerous legislature" (*Federalist* 70). But these are identified neither as republican nor, though they may consist of such as Locke, Hume, and Montesquieu, as theorists.

A quick look at the Anti-Federalist critics of the new executive reveals the obstacle Publius had in his way. At the Constitutional Convention Edmund Randolph had pronounced a single executive to be "the foetus of monarchy,"[7] and Luther Martin, another nonsigning framer of the Constitution, declared that the president could, when he pleased, become King in name as well as substance.[8] During the ratification debates comparison of the American president to the British King became an Anti-Federalist theme. Cato, whom Publius attacked in *Federalist* 67, asked wherein the president, with his powers and prerogatives, essentially differed from the King of Great Britain; and Tamony, the target of a footnote in *Federalist* 69, asserted that the president will "possess more supreme power than Great

Britain allows her hereditary monarchs."[9] Some recognition of the need for
an executive of such power could be found, in the lesser-known Cato of
South Carolina, but with the requirement that it be held for a short term
without reelection.[10] The Federal Farmer, praised in *Federalist* 68 as the
most plausible of the Constitution's opponents, conceded that "in every
large collection of people there must be a visible point serving as a common
centre in the government, toward which to draw their eyes and attachments," but—or therefore—insisted on ineligibility of the president for
reelection.[11] Thus, when the Anti-Federalists were not railing against monarchy, they were reluctantly bowing to it.[12] They had no way to justify it as
republican.

REFLECTION AND CHOICE

Nonetheless, despite these loud fears (and quiet concessions), bullheaded
(or bewildered) republicanism was not merely an obstacle to the framing and
the ratification of the Constitution. *The Federalist*, after all, is preoccupied
with the diseases of republicanism because it has chosen republicanism.[13]
On the first page of *The Federalist*, Publius adopts an opinion frequently
heard, he says, that it is up to Americans to decide, by their conduct and
example, whether mankind is capable of establishing good government from
reflection and choice, or must always depend on accident and force. Good
government by reflection and choice cannot but be republican, though not
in the traditional sense of a government ruled directly by the people. The
Constitution differs from traditional republicanism by being wholly representative or wholly elective. This means that although all parts of government are derived from the people, they are also *withdrawn* from them. No
part of the government, such as a popular assembly, *is* the people (*Federalist*
63). By choosing representative government, the people choose to limit
themselves; they choose not to govern directly themselves. They choose to
have a government whose working is determined by its internal structure as
much as, or more than, by its dependence on the people—thus, they choose
to have a constitution. For representative government without a constitution
would merely be an awkward delegation from direct democracy, liable on
any difficult occasion to descend to the evils of direct democracy.

    Yet the Constitution remains definitely republican because it is "wholly
popular" (*Federalist* 14 and 39). *All* its branches are derived from the people,
not only the "lower" house of the legislature. All branches reflect the people's choice through elections; no favored class with more sense of honor or a
greater faculty of reasoning than the people's is postulated and endowed
with power to check the people's choice. The American Constitution is not a
mixed constitution giving different classes separate powers, nor does it make
any concessions to the idea of a mixed constitution (as did John Locke) by
accepting, while modifying, traditional institutions not based on consent

such as the monarchy and the House of Lords. Nor was the American Constitution government by a single act of consent, as in the theory of Thomas Hobbes, in which the people's "choice" is made once and for good, without any possibility of change or specification. The Constitution is republican because it rests on the capacity of *mankind*, not any particular class or race, for self-government.

Yet the people would not choose to limit themselves in a constitution if there were no difficulties in their choosing. Traditional or primitive republicanism, with its dependence on a small territory, a homogeneous people, and cultivated virtues, exaggerates the extent of human choice. The task of "reflection" (in Publius's phrase "reflection and choice") is to take account of things in nature and by chance that cannot be chosen and to match them with things that can be chosen. A republic might prefer to live by itself, under a homogeneous majority, and with virtues to keep it moderate. But a regard to the necessities of international relations and of human nature will reveal that these desirable things are beyond the power of human choice. Reflection, then, in the form of political science, will teach a republic not to choose what is, abstractly, most choiceworthy, but to be content with, or indeed make the best of, a large territory, a diverse people, and a spirit of interest and ambition.

It is characteristic of the American Constitution, by contrast with republican tradition, to *constitutionalize* necessities.[14] Those necessities limiting our choice, which we would like to wish away, are brought into the Constitution so that the people, through their government, can choose how to deal with them after having anticipated the necessity of dealing with them. That is how reflection enables choice to contend with "accident and force," which cannot in fact be removed from human affairs. Traditional republicanism might admit this, but still choose to keep its republican faith intact and take its chances with events even if its faith were frequently frustrated. This choice would account for the strength of republican faith despite the disasters of republican experience. But the Constitution constitutionalizes the necessities of republican experience—and in no respect more obviously than in the executive. The executive, in its quickness (its "energy" understood as quickness), deals more than any other branch with the accidents and force that come to thwart or disturb republican choice. By dealing with such necessities the executive represents them within the Constitution; it reflects a realistic recognition by the people, when they ratify the Constitution and as they elect the president, that emergencies will arise to confound their choices.

The essential distinction, then, in *The Federalist* is the one in *Federalist* 9, 10, and 14 between a democracy and a republic. A democracy is "pure" democracy (or it could be a mixed republic) which is small, homogeneous, and (it hopes) virtuous; a republic is large, diverse, and ambitious. A republic represents the necessities of being large, diverse, and ambitious in its constitution; or it *constitutionalizes* them. *The Federalist* appropriates the name "republic" from the republican tradition, leaving it with the less re-spectable name of "democracies" dominated by "demagogues." This delib-erate theft can perhaps be justified if *The Federalist* can show that by con-stitutionalizing the limits to republican choice, it has improved republican choice and would thus be entitled to sole possession of the name.[15] It does this by arguing that the virtuous majorities in which traditional republican-ism puts its faith are in fact often factious and always potentially so; thus the people's choice in such republics amounts only to the people's will or pas-sions. The purpose of the Constitution is to transform the people's will both by settling it into a determined intent (a "cool and deliberate sense" [*Federalist* 63]) and by elevating it from whim to deliberate choice. This is the work of reason, and it is "the reason, alone, of the public that ought to control and regulate the government. The passions ought to be controlled and regulated by the government" (*Federalist* 49). Madison specifies the reason of the *public*, not of philosopher kings, as what ought to prevail. He remains a republican, but a better, more sophisticated one than the primi-tive republicans or democrats who invite anarchy and tyranny with their reliance on popular will or with their trust in virtue that is too weak to restrain popular will.

Republican choice is improved by the same forms in the Constitution that represent, or constitutionalize, necessities. Through elections of the people's representatives, the legislature not only puts a distance between itself and the people's momentary inclinations but also draws the virtue out of the people (for virtue does exist there) and sets it to work (*Federalist* 55 and 57). Similarly, the judiciary uses its independence not only to take partisan choice out of criminal justice but also to ensure, through judicial review, that the legislature—and even the people themselves—keep to the fundamental law they have chosen (*Federalist* 78). But it is especially in the executive that republican choice is given a new capability. For the executive not only provides decisions in emergencies as one ingredient of "energy" but also, as another ingredient, the duration in administration that makes possi-ble "extensive and arduous enterprises" (*Federalist* 72). Such enterprises are familiar to us today as the long-term programs of legislation and administra-tion—the New Deal, the Reagan Revolution—which always have their ori-gin in the executive branch. Precisely the branch that most recognizes the limits to human choice arising from emergencies best extends human choice in the capability to set a general direction for policy now and in the future.[16] An able executive will improve upon the occasions of his decisions. He will make his quick reactions consistent with his general program, so that his quickness is not merely willful but somehow connects to his lasting intent.

The Federalist, then, constitutionalizes the republican tradition. By finding a place for the necessities of government within the constitution of government it corrects the foolish optimism of republicanism which thinks, in essence, that men can live by the laws they choose and never have to bow to the necessities they do not choose or learn from their experience of such necessities. But in teaching republicans to bow to the necessities represented especially in the need for executive power, *The Federalist* also shows them how to choose better, because more lastingly, while not departing from the republican principle that all government should be derived from the people. Thus it teaches republicans to be better republicans.

THE CONSTITUTIONAL TRADITION

To do this in regard to executive power, the framers had to borrow from the constitutional tradition of Locke and Montesquieu. But in that tradition, executive power was still held by a hereditary monarch (though perhaps advised, in Britain, by ministers selected from the House of Commons); it was not "strictly republican." If the Constitution was to borrow the British monarchy as understood in the constitutional tradition for its executive, it was necessary not only to limit monarchy but also to republicanize it. In *The Federalist* we see the republican tradition constitutionalized and the constitutional tradition republicanized. A brief comparison with John Locke, the founder (because he was the conceiver) of the modern executive power, will make this clear. Just as *The Federalist* makes better republicans by constitutionalizing republicanism, so it makes a better constitution by republicanizing it.

In his *Second Treatise* Locke shows how government is rightly instituted by consent, first, to a legislative power that he says is the "Supreme Power."[17] An executive power is needed, it seems at first, only in a subordinate capacity for the execution of the laws passed by the legislature. But as Locke's exposition of rightly constituted government proceeds, he becomes more and more doubtful that government can be directed merely by laws. Foreign affairs cannot be directed by "antecedent, standing, positive Laws" and require the use of prudence; and even domestic matters, it turns out, must be left in good part to the "discretion" of the executive, soon called the "Supream Executor."[18] Locke calls this power by its traditional name, prerogative, and, after all he had said against arbitrary power when he was presenting the case for laws and for the legislature,[19] he actually admits prerogative to be "an Arbitrary Power in some things left in the Prince's hand to do good, not harm to the People."[20] So in Locke's constitution we have two supreme powers, one representing law, the other representing extralegal, even illegal, discretion. The two powers are left in open, unresolved discord, and since the legislative appeals to Whig republican sentiment and the executive to Tory regard for prerogative, one can see that Locke has imported a moderated but still lively version of the English Civil War into his constitution. Indeed, as the party of discretionary prerogative, the executive is not properly within the constitution. For in Locke's conception, the constitution goes only so far as law extends; there is no fundamental or constitutional law above ordinary law, and the prerogative power of the executive goes as much against the constitution when necessary as against the law. It is limited only by the end for which it is entrusted by the people, which is the public good as interpreted by the people.[21]

Such an arrangement can be criticized from the standpoint of *The Federalist*. To allow a prerogative power so defined is to set the public good as a standard *against* the constitution, so as to imply that the constitution is a mere means to the public good, not a part of it. Locke thereby encourages an instrumental attitude toward the constitution in the public hardly compatible with the "veneration" that even a republican constitution cannot do without (*Federalist* 49).[22] Moreover, he leaves no place in the constitution for the executive's program, a combination of law and discretion in which the choice of legislation is guided by a more long-term choice of policy. No doubt there will be parties, and sometimes two of them gathered around the executive and the legislative powers as they conflict;[23] but it does not seem wise to permit one of them, the party of prerogative, to continue as an extraconstitutional party and the other, the republican, to regard the constitution as its own. For *The Federalist*, the political situation was different because America had no Tory party defending prerogative. But, as we have seen, it was necessary to face the truth in the argument for prerogative (which Locke saw to be the need for extralegal discretion as distinguished from divine right). To do so by setting law and prerogative against one another would have the further disadvantage, in the view of *The Federalist*, of not overcoming but actually aggravating republican distrust of the executive. It would confirm their conviction, shared ironically with their Tory opponents, that energy in the executive is inconsistent with the genius of republican government.[24] The strategy adopted by *The Federalist* of republicanizing the executive through election brings the dispute between law and prerogative into the Constitution: it does not end that dispute, but it makes both parties to it republican. The consequence is to improve the constitutionalism of Locke's constitution. Without denying the need for something like a prerogative power, that need is not to be satisfied outside the Constitution.[25] This does not mean that the Constitution will not be an issue in the conflict between the executive and the legislative powers, but it does ensure that both sides can cite the Constitution on their behalf.

THE ELECTORAL COLLEGE AND AMERICAN REPUBLICANISM

We see, then, that after attacking the misrepresentations of the Anti-Federalists, Publius begins his treatment of the executive power in the Constitution[26] with a discussion of its mode of election, which is its republican character (*Federalist* 68). Publius describes the mode of election in a beautiful distinction as "if not perfect, at least excellent." It has not been criticized, he notes; however, we cannot but be aware that it has not lasted either and soon had to be revised in the Twelfth Amendment, because parties took over the designation of presidential candidates and mounted "campaigns" to elect them. Nonetheless, it is worth considering what and how much was expected from the mode of election.

Avoiding any mention of what might be necessary, Publius speaks only of what was "desirable" in the choice of the president. It was "desirable that the sense of the people should operate in the choice": no more than the *sense* of the people (which is ambiguous—their good sense or their general sentiment?) and no more than *operate*. So much for the sovereignty of the people; this is a republican government unlike all previous republics—one in which the people choose not to be sovereign. But the realistic alternative to the Electoral College in 1787 was not direct election of the president; direct election had been proposed in the Constitutional Convention by Gouverneur Morris but was voted down after receiving little support.[27] The realistic alternative was election by the Congress, designed to render the executive subordinate to the legislature. This dependency was required by classical republican theory, and it was a feature of both the Virginia and the New Jersey plans in the Constitutional Convention. In Publius's satisfaction with the new Constitution's mode of election, no trace remains of the long and difficult persuasion in the Convention by which delegates were brought to see the necessity of a president made independent of the Congress by his own connection with the people.[28] For 1787 (and for us today) it was significant not so much that the president's election was indirect as that the indirect election was not by Congress, but rather by the president's own Electoral College. The Constitution does provide that the House of Representatives (voting by states) will choose a president among candidates who have failed to receive a majority in the Electoral College, and opponents of a strong, independent executive in 1787 may have believed that this provision would operate frequently;[29] but if so, they were deluded and in any case the process of election would prevent domination of the president by Congress.

It was equally desirable, Publius continues, that the immediate election of the president be made by capable men in circumstances favorable to deliberation; it should not be made by the people either dispersed or gathered in assemblies. This mode of election is a "process" of two stages; the people choose the choosers who meet once for that purpose only. Election by this process has the negative virtue of preventing or combating the tumult and corruption typical in the histories of republics when they have had, finally, to admit their need for one-man rule. The American Constitution anticipates this need by a regular process which also has the positive virtue of providing a better choice. It affords a "moral certainty" that a president will have more than "talents for low intrigue and the little arts of popularity"; these might gain him the election in a single state, that is, in a small republic, but not in the whole union. We today speak of the need for a candidate to appear "presidential," or somehow of a size to fit the office, the reverse of petty and small-minded.

Publius goes on to say that there will be a "constant probability" of seeing the office filled by "characters preeminent for ability and virtue." Such characters are important not, or not merely, because they serve well in emergencies but because they make the difference between a good and a bad administration. "The true test of a government is its aptitude and tendency to produce a good administration." Here Publius allows that the executive will have an undefined share in administration; later he asserts that administration in the most usual and precise sense is peculiarly executive (*Federalist* 72 and 76). Thus, even though the genius of republican government is in the legislature, the test of whether the republican form produces good government is entrusted to, and performed by, the executive. Republican government needs preeminent characters, and as we shall see, needs to give them sufficient powers, in order not merely to pass this test at a minimum, but to excel in it. This necessity, chosen or honorably determined (*Federalist* 39) by the American people when they decided to make their Constitution an experiment of the capacity of mankind for self-government, is very different from the necessity of survival in emergencies, though it may comprehend that more immediate justification for executive power. To excel as good government, the American republic must remain limited, constitutional government, but this does not mean passive or minimal government that governs best by governing least. It is government that uses and engages the virtue and ability of preeminent characters. Contrary to the republican spirit hostile to such characters, republics not only need them to survive but depend on them to excel. Yet in keeping with republicanism, the Constitution does not directly designate these characters as if they were a class requiring or deserving political recognition as a class; instead, it sets the people to the task of seeking them out. By the "process of election" the people identify those whom they choose, not merely for being preeminent, and not as their superiors, but as preeminent characters capable of making a superior and indispensable contribution to the public good.

Hamilton does not mention the right to vote in his discussion of electing the president. Obviously he takes it for granted as guaranteed by the states, though he does not believe it includes the right to vote on the final choice of candidates—the right to vote *for president*—as we assume today. The Electoral College as originally intended results in a president whom the individual voter cannot regard as his own, because he has not voted directly for that person. This distance between the voters and the president is a republican remedy against the influence of image and charisma, a remedy that we today have decided to do without. We complain about the manipulation of voters, but we forget that the right we insist on—to have voters make the final choice—makes manipulation easier. The process of election and Publius's presentation of it are meant to shift attention from the right to vote as an individual expression ("having one's say") to the exercise of that right toward an end. In any case, the right to vote for president presupposes that an energetic executive should exist; but Publius could not presuppose that point, and had to establish it.

THE ENERGETIC EXECUTIVE

In *Federalist* 70 Publius states the problem of republican aversion to executive power, and takes the bull by the horns. He proclaims that "energy in the executive is a leading character in the definition of good government" and remarks sardonically that "enlightened well-wishers" to republican government had better hope that a vigorous executive is consistent with the republican genius because if not, their principles are condemned.[30] Publius will show them how to save their principles, but to do so he must reinterpret both the principles and the object of their aversion.

What is energy in the executive? Energy is not something good in itself; it is not virtue. In the thematic discussion of *Federalist* 37, energy and stability appear as the two modes of political power in the definition of good government, but stability comes first because energy seems to be needed for the sake of stability rather than the reverse, and also because the people appreciate stability more.[31] "Energy" and "stability" are terms in physics, only just entering into political science and political discourse with *The Federalist*. They represent qualities in government that are neutral as to regime, and clearly it was an advantage to Publius's argument for the consistency of a vigorous executive and republicanism that executive power could be described with a term that abstracts from its origin in monarchy.[32] "Energy" also abstracts from the virtue that a monarch claims to rule by. It is merely a mode of power that may be used for good or ill, and a subordinate mode too, rather than a ruling principle.

Yet if energy is not virtue, in the American Constitution it leads to virtue. In Publius's argument we see a progression from the neutrality of energy as it answers the necessities that any government must face to the indispensable contribution energy makes to the goodness of republican government. In *Federalist* 70 he discusses unity, the first ingredient of energy because it ensures unanimity in the "most critical emergencies" when a decision—any decision—is "most necessary." In these circumstances differences of opinion can be fatal. Whereas dissensions may often promote deliberate choice in a legislature by bringing every consideration into view, they cannot be tolerated in the executive. A plural executive, therefore, is a misplaced legislature. We see that the partisan dispute Publius wants to avoid between monarchy and republic has been transformed into a separation of functions (or a separation of powers arising from a separation of functions) within a republic between the executive and the legislative powers. The most delicate aspect of executive power, the unity in which it most resembles monarchy, is justified at the lowest, but most universal, level as what is necessary—especially to a republic—when there is not time for choice. A plural executive, Publius continues, not only cannot act but also destroys responsibility by concealing faults, as the several executives accuse one another. A single executive, however, can both keep secrets and maintain open and public responsibility, for when one person has to shoulder the blame, it does not matter who advised him and one does not have to inquire into the "secret springs of the transactions" in order to find the culprit. One man with responsibility can be more narrowly watched than a numerous body whose members have no individual responsibility, and he will be.[33] Publius therefore directly denies the "maxim of republican jealousy which considers power as safer in the hands of a number of men than of a single man" (*Federalist* 70) as it applies to executive power, that is, in emergencies. The neutrality of energy at its most exigent forces a change in the maxim of republican jealousy, but a beneficial one in the interest of republics that teaches republicans how to be more effectually jealous.

Even in emergencies, where necessity is paramount, there may be time for a quick choice following on quick thinking, as when the executive seizes on an opportunity, one of the "tides" in the "affairs of men" (*Federalist* 64), to make a treaty or to exercise his pardoning power.[34] To be quick on such occasions it is not enough simply to decide, but the executive must decide well and have the virtue to do this. But when Publius comes to the second ingredient of energy, duration, the virtue as distinct from mere univocity in the executive comes to the fore. Duration is of course connected to unity, because what is meant is the duration of a single executive, of *his* personal firmness (the topic of *Federalist* 71) and of *his* system of administration (*Federalist* 72). Publius could have argued for unity in duration from the first, instead of presenting the case for unity separately from the case for duration. This would have pleased political scientists today, who take executive power for granted and want to see more discussion of the president's program than Publius supplies; but it would not have pleased republicans in Publius's day, to whom such a program smacks of monarchy. So Publius first proves the necessity of unity in quick response to emergencies, then shows the advantage of duration for the unity we have accepted for the opposite reason.

"Personal firmness" will be the result of extended duration in office because "it is a general principle of human nature that a man will be interested in whatever he possesses, in proportion to the firmness or precariousness of the tenure by which he holds it" (*Federalist* 71). Thus an executive with long tenure will act with more firmness than one whose tenure is kept short by republican jealousy. The long-term executive will not be tempted into "servile pliancy" to a prevailing current of opinion either in the people or in the legislature. Publius endorses the "republican principle" that the "deliberate sense of the community" should prevail in its government, but this republican principle requires a firm executive, precisely contrary to the maxim of republican jealousy, to see to it that the people's deliberate sense is defended against their "temporary delusion." This is his duty, Publius says. Personal firmness is needed in standing up to the legislature, which is most likely to reflect popular delusions and in republican governments tends to absorb the executive and the judiciary. Separation of powers requires independence in the powers, and above all, in practice, firmness in the executive, since the usual danger in republics is legislative domination and usurpation of the executive and judicial powers. Publius makes the executive the guarantor of separation of powers as well as the defender of the republican principle. All this is in the executive's "interest" if he is such a person as to be willing, or eager, to take risks in public affairs. If he is not, then his interest is likely to be "servile pliancy" so as to have an easy time in office no matter how long it lasts. Publius understates the virtue required of the executive by calling it "interest." If it is a man's interest to procure the "lasting monuments" of popular gratitude reserved to those who had "courage and magnanimity enough to serve the people at the peril of their displeasure," then one might as well call interest "duty," as Publius does.[35]

In *Federalist* 72, the subject lengthens from a four-year term for the president to his indefinite reeligibility for election, and the argument moves forward again. Those who believe their interest lies in taking risks are brought out into the open; they are called the "noblest minds," whose ruling passion is love of fame.[36] Instead of cautiously advancing the advantages of including them in the Constitution, Publius speaks of the disadvantages of *excluding* them (as if a one-term presidency were equivalent to ostracism). In doing so he sums up the reasons for constitutionalizing executive power. To try to keep the executive weak, like the republicans, or to allow a strong executive to escape the constitution, as did Locke, is to *exclude* the noblest minds from the Constitution. From their point of view—and Publius now looks at politics from their point of view—exclusion from reelection would diminish the inducements to "good behavior," by which he means not correct deportment but planning and undertaking "extensive and arduous enterprises for the public benefit"; and negatively it would tempt the risk seekers to "sordid views, to peculation, and, in some instances, to usurpation." The community would be deprived of experience, a quality that is more desirable, even essential, in governors than any other. Such exclusion would banish from office men who might be absolutely necessary at that time; and it would establish a constitutional prohibition of stability in administration. In this impressive passage republics are not merely told of the uses of ambition, but also warned of the dangers of thwarting it. It appears that consideration of the noblest minds introduces us to necessities to which only they have, or are, the answer. With all due respect for virtue in ordinary citizens, not they but these men will make or break the republic. And "make or break" refers not to mere survival or mediocrity, but to greatness. When the necessity that the republic can survive in emergencies only with the aid of such men is put into the Constitution, it is transformed into the necessity that republics employ these men's preeminent virtue and abilities to become great.

VIRTUE AND RESPONSIBLE GOVERNMENT

Yet republics do not thereby become mere vehicles for the noblest minds and their would-be imitators. At the end of his survey of energy in the executive (*Federalist* 77), Publius says he has shown how the executive combines energy and republican safety. The first topic included the second because, despite his first statement that "energy in the executive is a leading character in the definition of good government," Publius argued the case for energy within republican government—not as if republican government were identical with good government but as if good government must be *some* form of government. He had said that "republican safety," which is something less than the "genius of republican government," consisted in two things: a due dependence on the people and a due responsibility (*Federalist* 70). But in the event, due dependence is reduced, or rather elevated, to due responsibility.

"Responsibility" is a term apparently coined by Madison (see his use of it in regard to the Senate, *Federalist* 63) to mean, not only "accountable" or "responsive," to the people, but also to take responsibility out of their hands on their behalf: responsible politicians in this sense do for the people what they cannot do for themselves but can form a judgment about.[37] To republicans, responsible government had always meant many citizens governing for short terms, since this government is closer to the people. But when one considers what government has to do, especially to get energy from the executive, it appears that one man with a long term can be more reasonably responsible for both quick responses and systematic administration. He can *do* the job more capably, and he can be *seen* to have done it, or not, more readily. When many govern for short terms, "due dependence" on the people is a delusion because responsibility cannot be fixed; any individual in the government can always excuse himself because of the shortness of his term and the number of his collaborators. When one looks to the end of government, even to the end of *republican* government, some adjustments to the republican form and some resistance to the republican genius become necessary. Precisely for the sake of republican safety, or a secure liberty, or stability, republican government must leave space for an energetic executive (and, one must add, an independent judiciary). A republican people must conceive the republican form as a method not only for finding the culprit and fixing blame but also for giving the rewards of reelection, esteem, and lasting fame to those who appear to deserve them. Fame would go most fittingly to those who had "courage and magnanimity enough to serve the people at the peril of their displeasure," but it is the American Constitution that makes such fame possible by making it republican, and makes it republican by making it constitutional.

After discussing the ruling passion of the noblest minds in *Federalist* 72, Publius returns to the mundane in *Federalist* 73 with the third ingredient of energy in the executive, an adequate salary. "Stern virtue is the growth of few soils"; so most presidents will need a salary guaranteed against legislative manipulation if they are to maintain independence of will. This thought introduces the last ingredient of energy, "competent powers." Six constitutional powers of the president are considered; none of them is what one might consider the primary executive function, executing the laws. The first and most important, the president's (qualified) veto, is not, by a dictionary definition, an executive power at all. The executive's veto is perhaps the most apparently antirepublican feature in the Constitution, originating in the British King's power to thwart the will of the legislature. But Publius treats it primarily as necessary for the separation of powers, a republican invention in politics designed to keep the legislature from executing its own laws. Again he takes the opportunity to teach republicans a lesson in republicanism, or to reiterate a previous lesson. Publius (as Madison) had established in *Federalist* 51 that separate powers must be independent if they are to remain separate, and to be independent they must have constitutional means of defense, especially against the legislature, which is likely to dominate a republican government. He particularly mentioned the need for a "fortified" executive. Now Hamilton shows that the executive is to be fortified with a power so far from strictly executive as to be legislative. The veto, moreover, as Epstein has pointed out, is an item of "energy" designed to slow down the government,[38] contrary to the necessity of emergency action that first justifies a strong executive. That the veto is qualified by the possibility of being overriden by two-thirds of Congress, Hamilton remarks, only makes it stronger, because it will be used oftener than the British King's absolute veto.

Yet the veto has a further use, not only as a "shield to the executive" but as "additional security against the enaction of improper laws."[39] Publius calls this use "secondary" to the primary one of enabling the executive to defend himself, and he denies that it turns upon the "supposition of superior wisdom or virtue in the executive." But he finds a reason in the excess of lawmaking typical of republican legislatures to suggest why the executive might often show more "due deliberation" than the legislature. His office, situated and fortified as it is, calls for a certain virtuous behavior from the officeholder which is, as it were, accidental to the virtue or lack of it in his person. At a lower level, as in the "primary" use of the veto power, the officeholder's "fortitude would be stimulated by his immediate interest in the power of his office" (*Federalist* 73), which might be quite different from his personal interest. Even Neustadt, who makes a theme of the difference between the formal office and the actual behavior of the president, says that "no one else sits where he sits."[40] In other words, how you act partly depends on where you sit. Characteristically and for good reason, *The Federalist* puts forward the lower interest as "primary" and leaves the higher virtue to be "secondary." To do the reverse would imply the need to identify a class of men of higher virtue instead of allowing them to emerge as individuals through the process of republican choice.

When men of such virtue emerge as individuals in offices, safeguards remain against a president who "might sometimes be under temptations to sacrifice his duty to his interest, which it would require superlative virtue to withstand" (*Federalist* 75). Publius speaks of this possibility in his discussion of the treaty-making power shared between the president and the Senate. The president, he says, does not have sufficient interest in a four-year office, as might an hereditary monarch in his lifetime office, to warrant being trusted with the entire power of making treaties. That power, since it deals with contracts between sovereigns, is neither executive nor legislative in nature, though if anything, more legislative. Yet it requires executive "qualities," which are fittest for foreign negotiations. Still, because the trust is so great (and less visible than in domestic matters), and because treaties operate as laws, participation of the legislature, or a part of it, is called for. Thus, again, virtue is seen through interest in the office, while the checking function is described as a positive contribution.[41]

Constitutional republicanism is based on self-interest, but, one is irresistibly tempted to say, on self-interest properly understood. It relies on the interest of the people rather than their cultivated virtue, because their interest can tell them that it is better to confine themselves to choosing or electing their governors, whereas their virtue might lead them to want to rule on their own in accordance with primitive, preconstitutional republicanism. *The Federalist* makes frequent and crucial reference to the interests deriving directly from "human nature" as opposed to virtues cultivated artificially and undependably by particular regimes.[42] This has led some to say that the Constitution, according to *The Federalist*, is based on self-interest in the sense of what is lowest in human nature. But one must not mistake lessons in political necessity intended particularly for primitive or "classical" republicans for the whole of political science.[43] As a system of self-government the Constitution presupposes that men can rise above what is lowest in them. The Constitution, says *Federalist* 39, is based on an "honorable determination . . . to rest all our political experiments on the capacity of mankind for self-government." How may this be done?

What is lowest in human nature includes not only the love of gain and the need for security, but also the desire for liberty (*Federalist* 10). To lift this low desire (for liberty can mean no more than having your way) to the level of self-government requires honorable determination because success is not certain and one must therefore risk one's honor in the attempt to succeed. But the republican form made constitutional can make success possible, if not guarantee it. It can construct or "model"[44] an office of executive that has a "constant probability" (*Federalist* 68) or "bids fair" to be filled by capable men. This probability arises from the qualities associated with the quantities of the office—its unity in one person as opposed to the character of "any numerous body whatever" (*Federalist* 73–77), and its length of tenure which appeals to those ambitious of fame as well as power (*Federalist* 72). In the Constitution virtue appears not in its own name but under the qualifications for office. The people, whose interest is to elect rather than rule, must have the virtue to appreciate virtue and the judgment to trust it. But when they elect the constitutional officers, their virtue is not, or does not appear to them as, virtue deferring to greater virtue. They find virtue in their fellow citizens by looking for those who are qualified for the office[45]— originally, in presidential elections, for those qualified to be electors; now, for qualified presidential candidates. Candidates who run for office, for their part, claim to have not superior virtue but the necessary qualifications. These qualifications are not stated formally in the Constitution, nor could they be. They have to be inferred semiofficially by the authors of *The Federalist* from bare quantities and by reference to the plan of the whole. Whether men with these qualifications can be found is in some part up to us; whether they will succeed is in some part up to them. By republicanizing the executive, the framers tried to ensure that no one was overqualified for the job.

9

Bureaucratic Idealism and Executive Power: A Perspective on *The Federalist*'s View of Public Administration

JEREMY RABKIN

The term "bureaucracy" had not yet entered the English language when *The Federalist* set out to defend the new Constitution of the United States. Not only the term, but the notions now associated with it seem remote from the analyses offered in *The Federalist*. In nothing more than this, perhaps, does *The Federalist* seem so removed from the perspective of modern political science and the preoccupations of contemporary politics.

Today, commentators speak respectfully of "the bureaucracy" as "the fourth branch" of government.[1] *The Federalist*, like the Constitution it defends, seems to recognize only the legislative, executive, and judicial branches. Today, it is common to think of "bureaucracy" as the essential substratum in all modern governments, so that the development of any country's state bureaucracy can be regarded as the touchstone of its modernization.[2] From this perspective, the difference between parliamentary and presidential systems—even the difference between free countries and communist tyrannies—can seem altogether secondary.[3] *The Federalist* presents an improved "science of politics" which seems to regard the organization of "administration"—in the modern sense—as an altogether secondary matter.

The Federalist is most anxious to show that the American executive is "re-publican," rather than modern. It is most concerned to show why the executive must be "energetic" rather than efficient, or expert, or impartial.

The seeming naïveté of *The Federalist* nonetheless has much to teach us. For if *The Federalist* appears naïve in comparison to modern theorists of administration and bureaucracy, perhaps that is because *The Federalist* possesses more sophistication about politics: Publius sees clearly many things which modern theorists have done their best to forget.

BUREAUCRACY BY ANY OTHER NAME

If the term "bureaucracy" was unknown to *The Federalist*, the term "administration" appears often enough. The latter term had already acquired its predominant contemporary meaning of managing details in accord with the will or aim of another. Thus on the eve of the American Revolution, Blackstone's *Commentaries* relied on established usage in discussing the "administration" of estates or business concerns by court-appointed "administrators."[4] The "administrator" was charged with managing and maintaining property until bankruptcy claims could be satisfied or inheritances properly distributed. The "administrator" was not an owner and was certainly not free to dispose of property or business in his care as if he were the owner.

The Federalist plays on this usage but plainly conceives governmental administration in wider terms. Thus, in a famous dictum, Publius proclaims that "administration of government in its largest sense, comprehends all the operations of the body politic, whether legislative, executive or judicial" and only in "its most usual and perhaps most precise signification" is it "limited to executive details fall[ing] peculiarly within the province of the executive departments."[5] In itself, "administration" suggests implementation rather than intention, means rather than ends. *The Federalist*'s appeal to "administration in its largest sense" only makes sense on the understanding that "all the operations of the body politic" are a trust from the people, necessarily limited in their ends. In other words, all government can be conceived as "administration" only if government is first conceived as limited government. But within the bounds of limited government, *The Federalist* suggests that ends and means, policy and implementation, are not so readily separated.

The modern term "bureaucracy" has different roots and different implications, which make the concept—as much as the phenomenon—very hard to assimilate to limited government. The term derives not only from the French word for desk or office but also from the Greek word for political rule. In its "most precise signification," then, "bureaucracy" is an alternative to democracy or aristocracy or autocracy.

The term was first employed in France in the last years of the *ancien régime* and was already well established in French when Publius offered his definition of "administration in its largest sense." Unlike Publius's use of "administration," the original French usage of *bureaucratie* was satirical. The more important difference was that the French term was not premised on liberal notions of limited government but was rather, from the outset, seen as implying a repudiation of limited government.

The original satirical connotations of "bureaucracy" are easy to appreciate. To a large extent they remain evident in contemporary American associations of the term "bureaucracy" with wheelspinning and red tape. The term had more of an edge in the eighteenth century, however, when educated men were more imbued with classical learning and more receptive to the Aristotelian teaching that every type of ruler—whether the common people (the *demos*) in a democracy or the few best (the *aristoi*) in an aristocracy—tries to shape the whole city in its own image and in accord with its own interests. When the notion of "ruling" was taken more seriously, there was something particularly comical and incongruous in the suggestion that a great nation might be ruled in accord with the outlook and interests of deskbound clerks.

It was the very scale of the French monarchy's governing ambitions that made this joke seem half plausible, however. During the course of the seventeenth and eighteenth centuries, French kings had greatly strengthened their control over the provinces through a network of purely administrative officials, men who owed their authority to direct royal appointment rather than inherited estates, purchased titles, or local status. But the range of local matters under the control (and the detailed control) of these officials made them difficult to direct from the center. The term *bureaucratie* thus seems to have been coined by a royal minister of commerce, evidently intending to express with this term his frustration in trying to get trade liberalization measures implemented by royal officials in the provinces.[6]

In the course of the nineteenth century, the term lost much of its satiric edge, just as the prestige of liberal or limited government began to decline in continental Europe. It was particularly among German writers, never renowned for their light wit and rarely satisfied with liberal principles, that *Bürokratie* came to be employed in a neutral, often indeed in a respectful sense. As the claims of government to order and direct on a large scale became more accepted, the institutional machinery for accomplishing these larger ends could no longer be regarded as a subject for ridicule. New conceptions of government—and a more radical "science of politics" than that espoused by Publius—made the notion of "bureaucracy" seem both plausible and necessary.

To place the thought of *The Federalist* in proper perspective, then, it is appropriate here to undertake a brief digression to trace the connection between German idealism and contemporary conceptions of "bureaucracy." For it was largely under the influence of German theorists that contemporary notions of bureaucracy entered American discourse in this century and helped obscure and corrupt the constitutional legacy of *The Federalist*.

THE GERMAN PROBLEM

The modern usage of "bureaucracy"as a neutral descriptive term of social analysis is usually credited—with much reason—to the work of Max Weber. Weber is often described as the founder of modern social science because of his insistence that "scientific" analyses of social phenomena must focus on observable effects, without obtruding the assessments or concerns of the "scientist." More generally, Weber insisted on the necessity of sharply distinguishing "facts" from "values" in social science inquiries[7] and his analysis of "bureaucracy" does indeed have a curiously abstract, disembodied character.

Weber presents the growth of bureaucracy in the modern world as one of the principle manifestations of the increasing "rationalization" of social institutions in modern life. He does not say that modern forms of social organization are more reasonable—that would be expressing a "value" judgment. He simply claims that bureaucratic organization is the most rational means of securing any given goal or standard—however arbitrary or unreasonable the given standard may be. Weber himself draws a sharp distinction between "formal rationality" and "substantive rationality," parallelling his larger distinction between rational calculation about means, and judgments (or in his case, nonjudgments) about the reasonableness of ends.[8] But his own account of bureaucracy tends to obscure this distinction by focusing all attention on the "rationality" and "efficiency" of bureaucracy in achieving its official goals.

Thus Weber presents bureaucracy as the most developed form of authority grounded in "rational-legal norms." He contrasts this with "traditional" authority (where people accept a certain ordering of affairs because they have always been ordered that way) and with "charismatic" authority (where people uncritically accept the directives of a particular leader because of their mystical faith in his superhuman power and wisdom).[9] Distinctions between ends and means are readily lost in this peculiar framework, which inevitably suggests that bureaucracy bears the same relation to alternative governing forms as modern chemistry bears to medieval alchemy or modern medicine to ritual folk remedies. In fact, Weber explicitly compares bureaucracy with "precision machinery" which yields a "particularly high degree of calculability of results."[10] These characterizations derive from Weber's vision of bureaucracy as the systematic, hierarchical organization of specialists, each governed by rules and professional norms appropriate to his own delimited sphere of competence or authority.

Weber portrays the specialized expertise of officials as again a matter of pure technical capacity, with no necessary connection to particular ends or goals. The hierarchical organization of such specialists yields a bureaucratic machine which is highly resistant to "arbitrary" or irrational deflections from its given goals. Thus even "the tendency of officials" to adopt "a utilitarian point of view in the interest of those under their authority" is tempered by the compulsion to proceed through "measures which themselves have a formal character and tend to be treated in a formalistic spirit. . . . Otherwise the door would be opened to arbitrariness."[11] For similar reasons, control of bureaucracy "is possible only in a very limited degree to persons who are not technical specialists. Generally speaking, the trained permanent official is more likely to get his way in the long run than his nominal superior, the cabinet minister who is not a specialist."[12] But this is hardly an objection, for "the purely bureaucratic type of administrative organization . . . is, from a purely technical point of view, capable of attaining the highest degree of efficiency and is in this sense formally the most rational known means of carrying out imperative control over human beings."[13]

Some critics have suggested that Weber's account of bureaucracy betrays an excessive credulity for the particular conceits of the Prussian state bureaucracy in the decades before the First World War, when Weber did most of his writing.[14] But Weber was not, in fact, an uncritical enthusiast of bureaucracy. He wrote eloquently of the spiritually deadening effects of expert administration and warned that the impersonal, legalistic ethos of bureaucracy would encourage a world of "specialists without vision and voluptuaries without heart."[15] It is scarcely an exaggeration to say that he viewed as somewhat regrettable his own finding that the "dominance of a spirit of formalistic impersonality . . . without hatred or passion and hence without affection or enthusiasm" is most conducive to administrative "efficiency."[16]

Regrettable or not, Weber's claims about the superior efficiency of bureaucracy are not actually very persuasive as factual descriptions. Armies do not win victories and business corporations do not win profits by following fixed rules in a "spirit of formalistic impersonality." Even governmental bureaucracies usually depend on much more flexibility and inspiration than Weber allows—as is suggested by the phenomenon of the "rule book slowdown," where public employees, rather than going out on strike, paralyze government operations by fastidiously observing every official rule to the letter. In Weber's account of bureaucracy, questions of motivation, morale, or initiative simply disappear. Managers face no awkward trade-offs between inspiration and control, between creativity and reliability, between flexibility and predictability. All these considerations seem to disappear because the actual goals to be served are always out of view. In Weber's account, the most orderly administrative scheme always seems to be the most efficient and the most rational.

Weber's claims to this effect surely did not derive from empirical observation, then, any more than from patriotic enthusiasm for the government of Wilhelmine Germany. He seems to have felt compelled to assert the superior rationality of bureaucratic organization, first, because of his peculiar— though by now rather prevalent—conception of "values." Insisting on the complete disjunction between "values" or goals, on the one hand, and "facts" or consequences, on the other, Weber conceived of "values" as occupying a realm beyond reason or argument. This conception frees "rationality" to focus entirely on instrumental calculations, while disallowing a whole range of objections (regarding side effects or excessive social costs, for example) as mere "value" judgments.[17] Technical expertise is powerful for Weber precisely because it is so single-minded.

One might object that the citizenry, or the legislature, or the sovereign—the authority that provides ultimate goals for the state bureaucracy—is rarely so single-minded in its expectations. But Weber's account of bureaucracy does not simply depict impersonal devotion to rules and professional norms as a guarantee of superior effectiveness. It continually slides between this notion and the rather different notion that devotion to impersonal rules and norms is an essential attribute of legitimate authority in modern society.[18] But the latter claim, after all, is only another way of saying that bureaucracies must blind themselves to certain consequences of their decisions, just as courts must, to a large extent, blind themselves to the peculiarities of particular cases to lend an artificial clarity and an artificial air of absolute correctness to legal decisions. In Weber's idealized conception of "bureaucracy," as in ordinary law courts, prudence—the careful balancing of competing goals and concerns with an eye to particular circumstances— seems excluded almost entirely by the demand for fixed, impersonal formulas.

Weber's larger outlook has been described as "Kantian" for its insistence that "values" must be treated as ends in themselves, not susceptible to modification or adjustment in the light of instrumental calculations.[19] In truth, Weber's account of bureaucracy is marked throughout by the spirit of Kant. Where Weber's sociology merges power and legality in the impersonal forms of bureaucracy, Kant's political philosophy merges freedom and legality in the impersonal norms of morality.

Kant's moral teaching revived the ancient notion that man is not truly free if he allows himself to be compelled by physical appetite or blind passion. But in his determination to make freedom the absolute end of human conduct, Kant demanded a morality cleansed of any taint of personal feeling or calculation of advantage. He thought this could be achieved by defining morality as adherence to impersonal, universal rules, rules that can be followed in every case without exception. This uncompromising moralism is premised on the assertion that true morality must be indifferent to circumstances and consequences in particular cases, no matter how awkward or tragic.[20] Kant's moral teaching is, in other words, already an explicit celebration of the "spirit of formalistic impersonality." It seems to cast the conscientious bureaucrat as the archetype of human perfection. It was, in fact, well received in the higher reaches of the Prussian state bureaucracy in the late eighteenth century.[21]

Kant himself did not hesitate to apply his moral teachings to politics and to the proper conduct of public officials. Two examples from Kant's legal writings may be useful in illustrating their spirit. On the one hand, Kant's uncompromising moralism leads him to insist that the laws must always be fully enforced, punishment fully exacted "and woe to him who rummages around in the winding paths of a theory of happiness looking for some advantage to be gained in releasing the criminal from punishment or in reducing the amount of it. . . . If legal justice perishes, it is no longer worthwhile for men to remain alive on this earth."[22] On the other hand, Kant's legalism leads him to assert that the state may not properly punish the murder of an illegitimate baby: "A child born into the world outside marriage is outside of the law (for this is [implied by the concept of] marriage) and consequently it is also outside the protection of the law. The child has crept surreptitiously into the commonwealth (much like prohibited wares) so that its existence as well as its destruction can be ignored (because by right it ought not to have come into existence in this way)."[23]

Kant's obsession with adherence to impersonal norms suggests, on the plane of politics, that the laws and those charged with enforcing the laws must uphold obligations transcending the interests and opinions of the citizens—just as, on the plane of morality, moral laws must transcend the selfish interests and personal feelings of the individual who adheres to them. Kant indeed warns that "the well-being of the state must not be confused with the welfare or happiness of the citizens of the state."[24]

In the course of the nineteenth century, a succession of German theorists, beginning with Hegel, drew out the potential implications of this thought. If the state has a higher object than the welfare or happiness of the citizens, then the servants of the state—the professional administrators—must have higher and more disinterested motives than do ordinary citizens.[25] Weber's account of bureaucracy retains strong elements of this mode of thought in its repeated suggestions that legality and impersonal formalism—rather than public approval—underlie the legitimacy of governmental bureaucracy. At the same time, Weber reverts to the comprehensive spirit of Kant's moralism by suggesting that the rationality or impersonality of government bureaucracy is simply the most prominent feature of a larger trend toward rationalization—and consequent bureaucratization—of all aspects of social life. But perhaps it was true by Weber's time that great masses of Germans had imbibed the notion that discipline and obedience to rules were somehow good in themselves.

It is always dangerous to judge thinkers by their followers, and thought—or rather the mental habits and slogans derived from serious thought—by its consequences. Still, it may not be altogether out of place to recall that Weber's conception of bureaucracy did, after all, find its most hideous fulfillment in Germany. Eichmann, who greatly disapproved of spontaneous or unauthorized violence against Jews, pursued his program of mass murder in a "spirit of formalistic impersonality . . . without hatred or passion. . . ." He claimed to have had no personal ill will toward Jews and invoked Kant's teachings by name in explaining why he felt a moral obligation to follow out his monstrous official orders in a conscientious and devoted manner.[26] However bizarre and demented it may seem, this plea is a chilling reminder that the mechanical spirit of bureaucracy has roots, after all, in a peculiar, compulsive moralism.

POLITICS AND HUMAN NATURE

Impersonal norms do not loom so large in the world of classical liberalism. The American founders felt no compulsion to invest law—at least human law—with a high moral dignity. Regarding government as properly founded in consent—the consent of actual human beings—they saw no need to elevate the dignity of "the state" above the private concerns of ordinary citizens. Law can be limited in its moral authority for the founders because government is limited in its moral ambitions. It is almost sufficient for the laws to protect private property and personal liberty.

In a curious way, the limitation of government proves a liberation for politics in the liberalism of the founders. Only the judiciary, the special guardian of private property and private rights under the law, must be above or outside of politics. Kant, while acknowledging in theory the classic three-fold separation of powers, insists that executive officials must, like the judges, have life tenure in office and must follow the law unswervingly. The legislature is reduced to highly abstract generalities.[27] Weber's sociology, while purporting to describe rationalizing tendencies rather than pronounce moral imperatives, similarly depicts bureaucracy as resistant to control by political officials or parliamentary bodies—just as the logic of courts is opposed to political interference. In the logic of German idealism, more and more of government tends to be judicialized in spirit.[28]

By contrast, the American founders were more accepting of politics in government because more accepting of human nature. They did not think it possible or desirable to exclude all selfish passions from government, except in the very limited confines of judgment in individual lawsuits. They were, in consequence, less hostile to politics. This is perhaps only another way of saying that the American founders had limited expectations for law. "Parchment barriers" might be sufficient to shield individuals from particular intrusions, because judges might be detached and impartial in contemplating individual cases.[29] But "parchment barriers" could not be relied upon to stop political designs backed by the passion and interest of many.

By their own standards, looking to the natural rights of men, the founders were quite aware that justice could be threatened by every part of government. As *The Federalist* puts it: ". . . what are many of the most important acts of legislation but so many judicial determinations, not indeed concerning the rights of single persons, but concerning the rights of large bodies of citizens? And what are the different classes of legislators but advocates and parties to the causes which they determine?"[30]

Still, it did not occur to the American founders to try to solve the problem of factional self-dealing in government with an autonomous bureaucracy. In the same decade that Kant published his celebration of impartial legalism in Prussia, *The Federalist* dismissed the notion out of hand: "creating a will in the community independent of the majority—that is, of the society itself " would be "but a precarious security" for minority rights because "a power independent of the society may as well espouse the unjust views of the major as the rightful interests of the minor party and may possibly be turned against both."[31] Nor did it occur to the founders to claim that impersonal detachment—the protection for rights in lawsuits—could be a standard for good performance in government by itself. They assumed that a government dedicated to protecting rights would have to be responsive to the personal concerns—one might even say, selfish concerns—that rights in turn protect.

The Federalist thus praises the continental scale of the federal government for embracing such a variety of competing interests that no one faction will be able to impose its selfish designs. The multiplicity of interests does not make legislators indifferent to particular interests or particular constituencies, but it can provide a check on extreme partiality. Similarly, *The Federalist* praises the arrangement of powers in the federal Constitution precisely because it does not depend on "better motives" but rather summons personal "ambition" or "the interest of the man" to animate the duties of the official.

LOCKE ON THE EXECUTIVE POWER

The institutional implications of this perspective are already apparent in Locke's *Second Treatise*, which deserves a brief glance here for the way it prefigures the argument of *The Federalist*. Locke stresses the importance of "settled, standing laws" so that individuals may be secured against arbitrary assaults on their persons or property.[32] The law must be general to ensure that it does not become an instrument of oppression. And the legislative power should be separated from the executive to ensure that those who make the laws cannot place themselves above the law.[33] But the enforcement or execution of laws is not simply governed by impersonal norms in Locke's account. It is not even governed by single-minded devotion to the particular standards proclaimed in the laws. Rather, inasmuch as laws are designed for the protection of personal rights, the executive has an independent claim to act for the same end.

In the state of nature, according to Locke, each person already has rights to protect his own life and property and the duty to respect the rights of others. Consequently, each person has a power to demand compensation for wrongs against him and also a distinct power to punish those who do wrong to others. In civil society, the laws must protect the right to seek personal redress by establishing impartial judges to hear such claims. But Locke never suggests that each man has an *obligation* to seek redress for wrongs

against himself—as a German jurist argued, quite seriously, in the nineteenth century[34]—because, in Locke's scheme, rights serve the end of allowing each person to judge his own interest for himself. And it is not always
in one's own interest to insist on full redress and bear the cost of obtaining it.
In the same way, Locke argues that the civil magistrate, who inherits the
original power of each man to inflict punishment for wrongs against others,
need not insist on punishment in every case. Where Kant questions the
propriety of any sort of pardon power, Locke takes it for granted that the
executive must have the power to remit penalties where punishment is not
necessary to deter future wrongdoing.[35]

More generally, it does not occur to Locke to demand, as Kant would
later do, that officials must blind themselves to the tragic consequences of
full adherence to the law in particular cases. Where the ultimate purpose of
the law—"the preservation of [the life, liberty and property of] all as much
as may be"[36]—is better served by leniency or by departing from the letter of
the law, it is obvious, for Locke, that the executive must follow his own best
judgment about "the publick good."

In practice, of course, it is rarely obvious *when* "the publick good" will
be better served by departures from the law. Locke almost always refers to
the executive in the singular, as if it were one person. Even in Locke's day,
no king or minister could personally direct every aspect of law enforcement.
But Locke's personification of the executive—where judges, by contrast, are
often described in the plural[37]—draws attention to the element of personal
choice and personal responsibility in executive actions. Locke is not interested in the logic of institutions. He is, on the other hand, quite voluble
about the necessity for the executive to exercise discretion—that is, to make
choices.

The chapter in the *Second Treatise* on executive "prerogative" is indeed
remarkable for the extent to which it collapses the distance between ordinary and extraordinary occasions and obscures all the distinctions a legalist
might offer between routine discretion within the law, acts technically unauthorized by law, and acts clearly contrary to law. Everything seems to come
under Locke's definition of prerogative as a "power to act according to
discretion for the publick good, without the prescription of law and sometimes even against it." And Locke's enumeration of the justifications for such
power has a comparable sweep:

> . . . since in some governments the Lawmaking Power is not always in
> being and is usually too numerous and so too slow for the dispatch requisite
> to execution: and because also it is impossible to foresee and so by laws to
> provide for, all accidents and necessities that may concern the publick; or to
> make such laws as will do no harm if they are executed with an inflexible
> rigour on all occasions, on all persons that may come in their way, there-
> fore, there is a latitude left to the Executive power, to do many things of
> choice, which the Laws do not prescribe.[38]

This generous view of executive authority might seem rather difficult to reconcile with Locke's claim, earlier in the *Second Treatise*, that the executive has "no Will, no Power but that of law."[39] But Locke's point in this claim is that the executive has "no right to obedience"—no coercive authority over the liberty and property of private citizens—"otherwise than as the publick person vested with the Power of the Law." It is only in this capacity that the executive has "no Will, no Power but that of Law." Similarly, Locke warns that "Wherever Law ends Tyranny begins," but immediately adds the qualification, "if the law be transgressed to another's harm"[40]—in a context where "harm" refers to immediate threats to life and property.

While these qualifications take care of the problem of leniency or executive actions not directly affecting private rights, they do not, of course, fully solve the problem of reconciling forceful emergency actions with "law." Nor can there be much reassurance from Locke's acknowledgment that the legislature may have open-ended prerogatives "defined by positive law":[41] these cannot be much constraint while there continues to be a residual prerogative to "act for the publick Good . . . even against . . . the presciption of law." Locke seems to place ultimate reliance, then, not on legal norms but on the authority of the legislature to replace the holder of executive power and "to punish for any mal-administration against the laws."[42] And beyond this, he points to the inherent right of individuals to revolt against tyrannical government—"this operates not, till the inconvenience is so great, that the majority feel it" and "this the Executive Power or wise princes never need come in danger of . . . [as] 'tis the thing of all others, they have most need to avoid. . . ."[43]

The ultimate check on the executive, then, is political rather than legal and Locke seems equally comfortable with the resulting implication: the executive must act with discretion to retain political support—for himself and perhaps ultimately for the whole government. The occasions for emergency action outside the law may be rare, but in pointing to them Locke reminds us why there must be executive discretion regarding smaller matters within the law: "the publick good"—and the rights of individuals standing behind it—cannot always be secured by fixed rules.

GOOD ADMINISTRATION AND THE EXECUTIVE

The Federalist follows very much in the spirit of Locke. It does not begin with a philosophic discussion of the state of nature and the rights men may claim from nature. But five of the first ten papers of *The Federalist* (Nos. 5, 6, 7, 8, and 9) dwell on the dangers of disunion and civil strife, among the states and even within them. And the moral is clear: government is artificial and governing is, therefore, always a challenge. People will never entirely agree on what is right for government to do, for "as long as the reason of man continues fallible and he is at liberty to exercise it, different opinions will be formed. . . . The diversity in the faculties of men, from which the rights of property originate, is not less an insuperable obstacle to a uniformity of interests."[44] A government devoted to protecting liberty and property must therefore be strong enough to contend with faction and division—but also nimble enough to retain support.

The duties of the executive, as *The Federalist* presents them, thus go beyond—and sometimes even beneath—the conscientious application of existing laws. The famous celebration of "energy in the executive" in *Federalist* 70 is strikingly reminiscent of Locke's account of prerogative. Like Locke, *The Federalist* is eager to associate emergency interventions with routine discretion, dramatic political stands with narrow administrative decisions:

> Energy in the executive is . . . essential to the protection of the community against foreign attacks; *it is not less essential to the steady administration of the laws;* to the protection of the community against those irregular combinations which sometimes interrupt the ordinary course of justice; to the security of liberty against the enterprise and assaults of ambition, of faction and of anarchy.[45] [emphasis added]

In the same spirit, *The Federalist* praises the Constitution's provision for an unlimited presidential pardon power on the seemingly modest ground that "without an easy access to exceptions in favor of unfortunate guilt, justice would wear a countenance too sanguinary and cruel. . . ." But the same passage then moves quickly forward to the more momentous consideration that "in seasons of insurrection or rebellion . . . a well-timed offer of pardon to the insurgents may restore the tranquillity of the commonwealth. . . ."[46]

The Federalist offers no systematic distinction between executive power and administration. So, for example, a paper on the presidency asserts that all executive officials "ought to be considered as the assistants and deputies of the Chief Magistrate and on this account they ought to be subject to his superintendence."[47] Like Locke, *The Federalist* generally refers to "the executive" as if it were one person and is still more explicit about the basic rationale for unity in the executive: there must be clear responsibility because executive operations demand continual choices.

But the responsibility of the president, as *The Federalist* presents it, extends beyond executive details and this also turns out to be true of "administration." In an early paper, Publius observes that "as a general rule . . . confidence in and obedience to government will commonly be proportioned to the goodness or badness of its administration."[48] The observation would be wildly implausible if "administration" referred only to the small details of executive implementation: people do not, "as a general rule," develop feelings of confidence and obligation toward governments that execute absurd or onerous laws with meticulous care. And indeed *The Federalist* stipulates in a subsequent paper that "administration of govern-

ment in its largest sense, comprehends all the operations of the body politic"
and only "in its most usual and perhaps most precise signification" is it
"limited to executive details. . . ."[49] The Constitution's chief executive,
with his veto power assuring him an official role in legislative action, is
plainly not "limited to executive details." The "administration" subject to
the president's "superintendence" seems no more readily confined.

The linking of administration "in its most precise signification" with
administration "in its largest sense" not only extends the reach of the former,
however, but makes it, in some ways, hostage to the latter. Administration
"in its largest sense" must be political because it rests, in the end, on
consent. Thus the president will be unlikely to exercise his veto power over
legislation unless "stimulated . . . by the probability of the sanction of his
constituents" or "encouraged by . . . a very respectable proportion of the
legislative body whose influence would be united with his in supporting the
propriety of his conduct in the public opinion."[50] And this is so, notwithstanding that "the mischiefs of . . . inconstancy and mutability in the
laws . . . form the greatest blemish in the character and genius of our
[republican] governments."[51] It seems equally clear that in "executive details," too, the "energy" of administration must be tempered by "great
caution" for the sake of good administration "in its largest sense." In other
words, the fact that confidence and obedience "will commonly be proportioned to the goodness or badness of administration" means that administration must sometimes be adjusted to maintain confidence and obedience.

The Federalist thus calls attention to the fact that even "steady administration" requires an "energetic executive": methodical administrators are
not enough. But to sustain its energy the executive must also be cagey and
politic. It must cajole and seduce, as well as threaten. And *The Federalist* is
quite candid about the benefits of an enlarged federal administration in
providing more resources to win support: "The more [federal administra-
tion] circulates through those channels and currents in which the passions of
mankind naturally flow, the less will it require the aid of the violent and
perilous expedients of compulsion."[52]

In sum, *The Federalist* suggests at least three reasons why impersonal
norms cannot be the basis of "good administration." First, because government is established to secure definite ends—"private rights" and "the publick good"—the executive will be held responsible for results and not merely
for selfless intentions. Second, given human nature and the natural diversity
of interests in a free country, opinions about satisfactory results or attainable
results are bound to differ. Third, in a free country what the executive can
achieve is, in any case, much dependent on the cooperation of others, both
within the government and outside: the executive cannot simply order and
threaten to realize its objectives. All of these reasons reduce to this: "administration in its largest sense" cannot be fully separated from administration of
"executive details" because politics cannot be separated from government.
In accounts of bureaucracy inspired by German idealism, political strife and

political calculation do indeed seem to disappear. But neither the subjects, nor the beneficiaries, nor the participants in administration are any longer recognizable as full human beings in these accounts.

ADMINISTRATION AND THE PARTY SYSTEM

The large view of administration in *The Federalist* suggests a role for the executive as a kind of central balance wheel in American government. Alexander Hamilton, who wrote the largest share of essays in *The Federalist* (and all the papers specifically devoted to the presidency) did indeed try to implement this vision as President Washington's treasury secretary. It is necessary to recall, however, that Hamilton's conduct soon aroused much alarm and condemnation among leading figures of the founding era. And a prominent place in this opposition was occupied by James Madison, who had earlier collaborated extensively with Hamilton on the essays collected in *The Federalist*.[53]

Hamilton's opponents organized themselves as the "republican" party—using the name to stress their opposition to the allegedly "monarchist" tendencies of Hamilton and his followers. The Republicans charged that Hamilton was systematically manipulating treasury policy—that is, "executive details"—to win the favor of commercial interests in the cities and mobilizing this political constituency in turn to shape a compliant "administration party" in Congress. While no clearcut abuses were ever proved against Hamilton, the Republicans did arouse sufficient suspicion and concern to mobilize a powerful opposition party across the country—and in Congress—and their efforts finally drove Hamilton himself to resign from office.

In particular, the Republicans organized a system of congressional committees that kept a watchful eye on "executive details" and allowed Congress to make careful, independent assessments of the otherwise intimidatingly well-"digested" budgetary and legislative recommendations of the treasury secretary and other executive officials.

By 1800 the Republicans had gathered enough popular support to place their own candidate in the presidency and a succession of Republican presidents thereafter helped to enshrine the Republican view of the Constitution: Congress is the ultimate guardian of the public good and the whole duty of executive officials is simply to enforce the will of Congress. Yet it did not occur to the Republicans to establish or encourage an autonomous professional bureaucracy. They did not seek to extend judicial controls over administrative activity or encourage a judicialized spirit in administrators. This would have run contrary to their own populist outlook, their demands for a government closely accountable to the people. On the contrary, therefore, the Republicans demanded that executive officials pay close heed to the promptings and preferences of congressional committees—committees that were anything but nonpartisan and professional. At the height of their power in 1820, the Republicans even passed a law imposing fixed limits on tenure in all administrative posts, ensuring a continual turnover of patronage and a check on the authority and ambition of experienced officials.[54]

In a number of ways, however, the Republican vision of administration—which has long outlasted the original Republicans—has proved curiously complementary to the Hamiltonian vision of *The Federalist*. In some ways, the Republican outlook has even helped to sustain the alternative Hamiltonian outlook through all the ups and downs of our constitutional history. For in practice, the Republicans, like *The Federalist*, could not be satisfied with administration carried on by impersonal norms in total isolation from larger political currents. Even in the nineteenth century, therefore, "energetic" presidents like Jackson and Lincoln built support for their larger policies in Congress by systematically catering to party factions in patronage and smaller administrative decisions. On the other hand, presidents could, even in the nineteenth century, enhance their authority by posing as the champions of administrative honesty and efficiency against the partisan or factional promptings of congressional committees.[55] Republican rhetoric about administrative fidelity to law, though usually trumpeted in the halls of Congress, could easily be turned against Congress—a fact the founders certainly anticipated and one of the principal reasons they went to such lengths to devise a mode of selection for the president that would make him independent of Congress.[56]

The administrative system that has come down to us indeed still bears the impress of the founders' handiwork and still in many ways follows the expectations of *The Federalist*. The movement for civil service reform in the decades after the Civil War did—as intended—eventually remove the mass of lower-level federal jobs from the patronage coffers of party politicians.[57] Compared to the leaders of almost any other Western democracy, however, a new American president appoints an enormous number of new administrative officials, implanting his personal or partisan followers rather deeply into the permanent departments and agencies.[58] Conversely, whereas parliamentary majorities must support "their" cabinets in Western Europe, the American Congress can scrutinize, criticize, prompt, and pressure executive agencies with abandon—and it usually does. The system may not often allow for the sort of masterful presidential coordination sometimes suggested in *The Federalist*'s papers on the executive. But it does display the logic which *The Federalist* itself has made famous—the logic of a system where power is widely distributed, where "ambition" is "made to check ambition" so there is less need to rely on "enlightened statesmen" and "higher motives."

POLITICS AND ADMINISTRATION

Yet there has plainly been a good deal of foreign influence on our thinking in this century that has also marked our current patterns of governmental administration. For several decades after the turn of the century, the new academic discipline of "public administration"—many of whose founding figures studied in German universities in their formative years—continually preached the need to separate "politics" from "administration."[59] The predictable and very much intended effect of this division was to narrow the range of political debate and limit the opportunities for political compromise, while elevating the authority of the ostensibly impartial, administrative expert.

This ideological program was most influential in municipal politics, where the abuses of low-level patronage politics were often quite flagrant in the early decades of this century.[60] But it has left some important legacies in federal administration, as well. Among the most notable are the independent regulatory commissions, most of which were established in the 1930s, amidst the great expansion of federal controls associated with the New Deal.

The commissions are "independent" in the sense that the president cannot remove commissioners at will, as he can with all policy-level officials in executive agencies and departments. When the Interstate Commerce Commission, the prototype of the other commissions, was established in the late nineteenth century to regulate interstate railroad rates, nothing was said about the president's power to remove the commissioners.[61] The "independence" of the commissions was not fully established, in fact, until the 1930s, when President Roosevelt tried to remove a Republican appointee to the Federal Trade Commission over disagreements on basic commission policy.

In an ensuing court challenge to this action by the deposed commissioner, the Supreme Court ruled against the president. The FTC commissioner, it held, was "an officer who exercises no part of the executive power vested by the Constitution in the president" because the commissioners were "charged with no policy except the policy of the law."[62] Since "the policy" of the Federal Trade Commission Act was little more than a vague prohibition on "unfair methods of competition," this ruling expressed remarkable confidence in the ability of commissioners to discern the true nature of unfairness and adhere to their own insights unswervingly. In the same year, in fact, the Supreme Court struck down a prominent New Deal statute authorizing the president to promulgate binding regulations defining standards of "fair competition" in large sectors of the economy. This, the Court held, was an unconstitutional delegation of legislative power to the executive, because the legal standard for executive action was so vague and open-ended.[63] Plainly the Court's willingness to accept an almost equally open-ended power in the Federal Trade Commission reflected its hope that the commission could be insulated from politically motivated "policy."

As a matter of fact, the commissions were no better insulated than most executive agencies from the pressures and promptings of congressional committees. If anything, they may have been (and continue to be) more exposed. Celebrations of administrative expertise, so prominent a theme in New Deal rhetoric,[64] did not greatly intimidate congressional committees intent on gaining accommodations for particular constituencies.[65] But they may have eased some misgivings about extending federal administrative controls into more and more new fields. By the 1960s, appeals to "expertise" did not even go far in soothing consciences. Educated people were more likely to smile with knowing condescension at the notion that officials could be trusted to determine sound policy by impersonal, expert norms. By the late 1960s, liberal opinion had embraced many of the charges popularized by anti-New Deal conservatives, who had characterized "bureaucracy" as sluggish, self-serving, and overly attentive to powerful "special interests."

Liberal opinion in the 1960s and 1970s was still entranced, however, with the notion that politics could be removed from government. Ralph Nader and other champions of the new "public interest" movement denounced the influence of "special interests" and appealed for aid to what they viewed as a more reliably impartial institution—the federal judiciary. Thus courts began, for the first time, to allow suits charging—on behalf of "the public"— that regulatory agencies had not enforced their mandates vigorously or comprehensively enough.[66] When Congress enacted sweeping new controls on air and water pollution in the early 1970s, it included remarkable provisions authorizing "any citizen" to sue administrative officials to compel full enforcement or proper implementation of these measures.[67] This legislative sanction naturally did nothing to deter the courts from allowing such suits against a wide variety of programs where they had not been explicitly authorized by statute.

It is notable, however, that suits demanding more vigorous enforcement of the criminal law have continued to be rejected by the courts without exception.[68] Perhaps old doctrines of executive discretion have been too firmly attached to this core executive function. But it may also be that criminal law enforcement is too vividly associated with force and coercion for contemporary Americans to think of it as a process that can be governed by entirely impersonal, expert norms. In many regulatory fields, like pollution control, enthusiasts can suppose that higher "values" are at stake, which should properly exempt administrative programs from pressures for political compromise, from recognition of awkward policy trade-offs in the real world. Thus the purpose of judicial intervention in contemporary "public interest" cases, says a prominent professor of law, is "no longer primarily to protect private rights but instead to facilitate identification and implementation of the values at stake in regulation."[69]

The longing to separate politics from administration is, then, still very powerful. And the current appeal to "values" is not, after all, so removed in its theoretical roots from an earlier generation's appeal to "expertise." None of this is altogether surprising. As our expectations for federal administration have expanded, we find it hard to know how to judge its performance. We grasp for authoritative standards—though the expansion of federal administration in this century has plainly been driven forward by the denial that there are any authoritative limits on government.

Our contemporary confusions would probably not have surprised the authors of *The Federalist*. They understood that "the latent causes of faction are sown in the nature of man."[70] The most that could be done to remove division, without ending liberty, would be to remove the most dangerous sources of division—like "a zeal for different opinions concerning religion"[71]—from the responsibility of government altogether. They might not have been surprised that, as we ask more of government than we used to, we have come to think that "politics" should concern itself with "values" or "ideals" that soar far beyond the details of administration. Still, they would probably have been astonished by the contemporary notion that the "goodness or badness" of our "administration" can be settled by impersonal, nonpolitical standards.

10

Constitutionalism and Judging in *The Federalist*

JAMES STONER

One can scarcely read Numbers 78 through 83 of *The Federalist*, on the judiciary, without thinking that these papers do not quite fit. David Epstein comments in his recent book that Publius's treatment of the judiciary "stands somewhat apart from the rest of the book, just as the judiciary stands somewhat apart from politics."[1] The publication history of the text bears out this observation. Unlike all preceding numbers, the papers on the federal courts did not first appear in the newspapers but in the second volume of the bound collection, which was published in May 1788;[2] perhaps this explains why Hamilton writes several essays of unusual length, including the longest single paper in the whole series. Despite their unusual appearance, these pieces serve practically to conclude *The Federalist*. Only two numbers follow the sequence on the judiciary, and one of them treats a matter of no small consequence to the question of the courts' form and function, the question of a bill of rights.

Of course, as Epstein remarks, the distinctiveness of the text describing the judiciary only mirrors the uniqueness of the institution itself, or rather, its uniqueness in a republican government. In the first place, judges, alone among officers of the federal government, hold their positions on tenure of good behavior.[3] Likewise, the judiciary is the only one of the major branches that owes its selection to the process of appointment rather than election[4] and in which membership depends—albeit by general understanding, not constitutional command—upon certain professional qualifications. Moreover, its structure is the least defined in the Constitution itself; only the Supreme Court is mandated, Congress being left discretion over whether and how to establish inferior courts, and even the size of the Supreme Court being left to legislative discretion.[5] And of course, what in Hamilton's account (and subsequent history) quickly appears as this branch's most remarkable authority—the power to declare legislative acts unconstitutional—receives no mention in the very document this authority is designed to uphold.

But it is not the peculiarities of the text or of the institution alone that distinguish Publius's account of the judicial power. Rather, implicit in his treatment of the courts is the recognition of a constitutionalism that cuts against or goes beyond the political theory that permeates *The Federalist*. While the papers are written in defense of a proposed constitutional document, the guiding spirit of most of *The Federalist* is a distrust of "parchment barriers" and "constitutional shackles."[6] Publius holds a firm conviction of the necessity of lodging certain "objects" of politics in a central government whose means are adequate to its purposes; he pays respect to republican forms, but insists that we ought to be ready to subordinate form to substance, at least once the basic authority of the people is secured. But the authority of courts rests on taking the forms, the means, the shackles, and the parchment seriously. Hamilton's account of the judiciary surely seeks at many points to integrate that institution into the overall political theory of Publius, but he is only partially successful. The partiality of his success reveals something of the limits of that political theory. It also points ahead toward the substantial modification of the Constitution made soon after its ratification, despite the objections of Publius, though with the blessing of at least one of his creators: the addition of the Bill of Rights.

The Judiciary and the Constitution

However eccentric the account of the judiciary may seem to the theory of politics that pervades the papers, it is important at the outset to make it clear that the establishment of a federal judiciary was essential to the whole project of constitutional reform. The "radical vice" of the Articles of Confederation, Publius writes in *Federalist* 15, "is in the principle of LEGISLATION for STATES or GOVERNMENTS, in their CORPORATE or COLLECTIVE CAPACITIES, and as contradistinguished from the INDIVIDUALS of whom they consist" (p. 108). Such a legislature must either hope that, against "the true springs by which human conduct is actuated," the subordinate governments will obey federal law without a sanction, or it must be prepared to raise a military force against the offending government—or simply suffer the humiliation of seeing its law ignored. The corrective— granting the federal government authority to operate directly on individuals—involves in part an expansion of Congress's legislative powers to include the power to tax and to raise an army, rather than rely on requisitions of men and money from the states, as well as the power to regulate interstate commerce. But part of the corrective must be the establishment of a federal executive and judiciary charged with enforcing the law against the recalcitrant. Publius writes in *Federalist* 23 that "there is an absolute necessity for an entire change in the first principles of the system; . . . we must extend the laws of the federal government to the individual citizens of America . . . ."[7] This change in principles entails a change not only in formal powers but in institutions. Congress remains, though substantially changed in form; the feeble executive committee must become a strong, individual executive; and a federal judiciary, altogether new, must be added. Indeed, Hamilton writes in Number 22 that "the want of a judiciary" is "a circumstance which crowns the defects of the Confederation" (p. 150).

Though Publius, especially Hamilton, defends the direct operation of the federal government upon individuals as a new but necessary means of fulfilling the ends of common defense and regulation of interstate commerce—ends established in or generally conceded to the federal government under the Articles, but without the powers needed to meet them—frequent passages in *The Federalist* suggest that not only the means but the ends themselves must be expanded. The Preamble to the Constitution mentions first, after the general need to perfect the Union, the purpose "to establish justice," and in *Federalist* 51, a paper that in many respects stands at the crux of the argument, Madison asserts categorically that

> Justice is the end of government. It is the end of civil society. It has been and ever will be pursued until it be obtained, or until liberty be lost in the pursuit. [*Federalist* 51, p. 324]

A passage in Number 10 helps to explain what he has in mind: "The protection of these faculties [i.e., the diversity of the faculties from which the rights of property originate] is the first object of government" (No. 10, p. 78). Throughout *The Federalist* the authors decry actions of the state governments that have "impaired the obligations of contract," released debtors from their debts, and undermined public confidence. While infringement of property rights appears as the foremost complaint, Publius often defines justice to include individual rights generally speaking. And of justice so defined, the immediate guarantor must be the courts, since it is in court that individuals' obligations are determined and their rights vindicated.

Thus, whether one considers the proposed reform to apply to the means or to the ends of the general government, the judiciary appears at the heart of the project. It is, then, no surprise to find that the courts are involved in both of the principles that give the new government its form: federalism and the separation of powers.

FEDERALISM AND THE FEDERAL COURTS

In one respect the involvement of the judiciary in questions of the relation of the national and the state governments is clear from what has already been said, since the judiciary is an indispensable tool by which the federal government can act directly on individual citizens and, as sanctions cannot be avoided, can "substitute [for] the violent and sanguinary influence of the sword . . . the mild influence of the magistracy" (No. 15, p. 108). But this involvement remains ambiguous, for it is not clear from the constitutional text whether the enforcement of federal law is to be effected by a separate federal judiciary or entrusted principally to the state courts. Article VI explicitly binds state judges to the Constitution and the laws "made in Pursuance thereof," but as I noted above, Congress is left discretion as to whether and how far to constitute "inferior courts," and Publius in *Federalist* 81 and 82 interprets this to leave open the possibility that Congress will choose to assign to state courts many matters of federal jurisdiction.

The ambiguity in the text of the Constitution may reflect in part the reluctance of the Convention to settle upon one scheme or another, but it is also, Publius suggests, due to the nature of judicial power. While separate sovereignties must clearly possess separate legislative powers—even in a complex scheme of concurrent and unequal sovereignty, such as that proposed by the Constitution—judicial power is less rigidly aligned. Publius writes:

> The judiciary power of every government looks beyond its own local or municipal laws, and in civil cases lays hold of all subjects of litigation between parties within its jurisdiction, though the causes of dispute are relative to the laws of the most distant parts of the globe. Those of Japan, not less than those of New York, may furnish the objects of legal discussion to our courts. [No. 82, p. 493]

The judiciary, in other words, takes its orientation first from the parties to the dispute before it, and then looks to see what law must be consulted to settle the dispute. Its jurisdiction is defined in the first place by who may sue before it and concerning what sort of dispute; then whatever law is needed must be applied. This characteristic of judicial power raises specific problems for the federal judiciary, since if that judiciary is to be limited so as not to subsume the state courts, it must be limited in terms of what law it can apply, at least when the parties to a dispute are from the same state. Where there is federal law, state courts will be bound to apply it, and thus will have authority to interpret it. If there are federal courts, they must do the same with regard to the states. The potential for confusion and conflict here stems not only from the complexity of federalism, but from the nature of judicial power in contrast to legislative power. The prudence of leaving the establishment of ordinary federal courts and the definition of their jurisdiction to legislative adjustment rather than constitutional principle thus becomes apparent.

One point, however, is incontestable, according to Publius: there must be a Supreme Court established as part of the national government to ensure, through its appellate jurisdiction, uniformity in the interpretation of federal law throughout the land. This argument appears as early as *Federalist* 22, in the course of explaining why the lack of a judiciary power is a chief defect of the Confederation (p. 150), and it is repeated in Number 80 (p. 476). That the judicial power of the federal government must be "coextensive with its legislative" authority is a "political axiom," "if there are such things." "Thirteen independent courts of final jurisdiction over the same causes, arising upon the same laws, is a hydra in government from which nothing but contradiction and confusion can proceed" (No. 80, p. 476). Likewise, in disputes involving foreign powers, or between states, or between citizens of several states, the need for federal authority is plain. Though it may be in the nature of the judicial power for any court to spread its scope as wide as law itself, the fallibility of human reason and the feebleness of human impartiality recommend a single court of last appeal in matters of national concern.

But the place of the federal judiciary in general, and of the Supreme Court in particular, within the scheme of federalism is still more complicated than appears so far, for their task to enforce federal laws upon individuals entails the responsibility of ensuring that federal law is not impeded by the laws of the states. Once again, the judicial power's need to see the law as a whole runs up against the tendency of men to be partial. The impossibility of distinguishing with certainty the bounds of federal and state authority ensures that conflicts between federal and state law will arise (No. 37, p. 227ff.), and while both state and federal judges must resolve these difficulties whenever they arise in a dispute before them, the need for uniformity— and for protection of federal authority—dictates that decisions of this sort be reviewable in the Supreme Court (No. 39, pp. 245–246). Though it is impossible to ensure that no one is judge in his own cause in such disputes—since every court is constituted as an agency of one of the governments whose laws are in question—Publius seems to argue that the very generality of the national government is a guarantee, or at least the best available guarantee, of impartiality.

The structure of the judiciary in the federal system designed by the Constitution and defended in *The Federalist* is thus at the very least complex and perhaps more deeply problematic. The need for a single Supreme Court with appellate jurisdiction over disputes involving federal laws or conflicts between federal and state authority might be clear, but the organization of the courts of original jurisdiction is more difficult. Because the task of the federal courts—applying the laws to particular disputes—is "wholly national" in character, and because the applicability of law in a case depends on the nature of the case, not the nature of the court, it seems impossible to develop a rule to distinguish the jurisdictions of federal and state courts with even that degree of clarity achieved by the distinction between federal and state legislative powers.

But while pointing out the complexity of the question of jurisdiction and justifying its determination by Congress, Publius is not unaware that much rides on the decision of what the federal courts will be able to do. He writes in Number 17 that "the ordinary administration of criminal and civil justice" is the "great cement of society,"

> the most powerful, most universal, and most attractive source of popular obedience and attachment. It is this which, being the immediate and visible guardian of life and property, having its benefits and its terrors in constant activity before the public eye, regulating all those personal interests and familiar concerns to which the individual is more immediately awake, contributes more than any other circumstance to impressing upon the minds of the people affection, esteem, and reverence toward the government. [*Federalist* 17, p. 120]

Publius often notes that popular favor will fall upon the government that is best administered, but this passage makes plain that not only the quality of the administration but also its objects count. "Reverence for the laws" may depend in part upon the stability of the Constitution over time, but the success of the federal government must also rest, at least in part, upon the activities of its courts.

THE JUDICIARY AND THE SEPARATION OF POWERS

If the place of the federal judiciary in the federal system is complex and problematic, its place within the general government in the scheme of separation of powers is no less so. This assertion might seem odd, for one thing that distinguishes the judiciary proposed by the Constitution is its independence as a department of government, apparently equal in status to the legislative and executive branches. As is well known, not every version of the separation of powers includes coequal status for the judiciary. In Locke's *Second Treatise*, the judiciary is treated as part of the executive, and even Montesquieu, who formulated the threefold distinction the framers adopted, speaks not of a judicial power but of a "power of judging," apparently having in mind the English jury and ignoring the English judge.[8] Blackstone, meanwhile, commenting on judicial independence in England, clearly subsumes judges under the executive.[9] *The Federalist* is not without remnants of the British view. In his early papers commenting on the need for the direct operation of federal laws upon individuals, Publius repeatedly makes mention of the role of "magistrates," and while the term seems usually to apply to judges, it is worth keeping in mind that Publius routinely refers to the President as the "Chief Magistrate."[10]

The difficulty in assimilating the judiciary into the account of the separation of powers is only suggested by this ambiguity in drawing lines between the executive and judicial powers, however. It is more fully revealed if one compares the account of the separation of powers in Number 51 with the account of judicial review in Number 78. Of course judicial review—the power of courts to set aside as unconstitutional the acts of the other branches of government, most particularly the legislature—presupposes the separation of the branches of government. Indeed, as W. B. Gwyn has argued, one of the original purposes of the theory of the separation of powers was to ensure the rule of law—more precisely, to transform the king into an executive who carries out a rule previously legislated by a separate body.[11] But the account of the separation of powers in *The Federalist* goes beyond the "rule of law" version of the doctrine; and the understanding of law implicit in judicial review goes beyond the positivistic doctrine of "rule of law," in which the question of the accord between previous legislative will and subsequent executive act takes precedence over the question of the justice of the rule itself, not to mention the soundness of its results.

Though Publius often distinguishes the powers of government as if they involved different functions and displayed different characters—consider, for example, his contrast of the "vigor and expedition" needed by the executive with the "deliberation and circumspection" characteristic of the legislature (No. 70, p. 427)—his series on the separation of powers typically treats the branches as interchangeable. Whatever else they may be, the three branches are powers, particular institutions into which a "mass of power is distributed." Power itself "is of an encroaching nature," against which "parchment barriers between branches provide no security" (No. 47, p. 301; No. 48, p. 308). Publius's famous solution to the problem of making the separation of encroaching powers work is the mechanism by which "ambition [is] made to conteract ambition" (No. 51, p. 322); through institutional devices or "inventions of prudence" by which the partisans of separate kinds of power are distributed among dissimilar branches, the whole of each of the powers is kept distinct and free government ensured. As the mechanism of the extended sphere uses the plurality of factions to obviate the danger of faction, so the separation of powers turns ambition against the dangers it poses.

Now to say of this account that it abstracts entirely from the distinctiveness of each power would distort Publius's meaning. As he makes clear in Number 48 and in later papers, in a republican government the power most likely to encroach is the legislative, "inspired by a supposed influence over the people with an intrepid confidence in its own strength" (p. 309). Still he claims that legislative overreaching "must lead to the same tyranny as is threatened by executive usurpation." In Number 51, the example of a device to ensure separation is the presidential veto, a power legislative in kind but given to the executive to help fortify him against legislative predominance—though given in qualified form, lest he become a full branch of the legislature. In all of this the judiciary is noticeably absent.[12] Its only mention in Number 51 is in the context of an argument that each branch should derive its appointment independent of the others, directly from "the same fountain of authority, the people"; the judiciary is of course excused from the requirement, "peculiar qualifications being essential in the members," and the judges' dependence on the other branches for their mode of appointment is quickly erased by their permanent tenure (p. 321). To the naïve reader familiar with the modern Court, Publius might seem to have the judiciary in mind when he speaks later in the paper of "creating a will in the community independent of the majority" as a means of "guard[ing] one part of the society against the injustice of the other part," but actually he is referring to "an hereditary or self-appointed authority," a monarch or an aristocracy. He has, naturally, no place for such an independent will, as it would be

> at best . . . but a precarious security; because a power independent of the society may as well espouse the unjust views of the major as the rightful interests of the minor party, and may possibly be turned against both parties. [*Federalist* 51, pp. 323–324]

When Publius turns to discussion of the judiciary in Number 78, he speaks in the same spirit of institutional engineering that he had adopted some thirty numbers before. He sets out to discuss the permanent tenure granted the judiciary by the proposed Constitution and to explain its necessity in terms of strength and independence. The judiciary, he remarks in a much celebrated phrase, is the branch "least dangerous to the political rights of the Constitution," lacking as it does "influence over either the sword or the purse," and "ultimately depend[ent] upon the aid of the executive arm even for the efficacy of its judgments" (p. 465). It is the power least able, and thus least likely, to encroach upon the others, and so the attention of the science of politics must be toward shoring it up, not keeping it down. But it quickly appears that while its strength is slight, its claims are bold, for in the context of discussing the need for judicial independence Publius grants the courts power to declare statutes to be in violation of the Constitution and even to limit statutes which, though not infringing the document itself, nonetheless threaten justice or constrict rights. This disproportion between claim and strength appears to suggest to Publius a guarantee of balance in the exercise of the judicial function; certainly the distinction between paper claim and practical power runs throughout *The Federalist*. But in the case of the courts the distinction is misleading, for judicial power rests upon the respect courts receive both from the governed and from the other branches. The political theory of *The Federalist* is eloquent in explaining the judiciary's weakness, but is rather inarticulate in accounting for its strength.

THE COMMON LAW BACKGROUND OF JUDICIAL REVIEW

What I would like to suggest is that the strength of the judiciary, and its peculiar character, must be understood in light of the common law background of the institution. This background was in some respects taken for granted in *The Federalist*, and it comes to the forefront only incidentally. For example, at the end of Number 78, Publius adds, as a reason of "far inferior" importance for permanent judicial tenure, the need to recruit men of "long and laborious study" whose knowledge of "strict rules and precedents which serve to define and point out their duty in every particular case that comes before them" will allow us "to avoid an arbitrary discretion in the courts." This need, he says, will be hard to meet, as it will involve enticing fine lawyers into "quitting a lucrative line of practice to accept a seat on the bench" (p. 471). Though the federal courts will combine jurisdiction over law and equity and will in other respects differ from their English forebears, they nevertheless assume their basic structure from the forms of the old common law courts: respecting precedents as well as legislation, and staffed not by specially trained civil servants but by lawyers called to the bench.[13] While in an early paper he includes judicial tenure on good behavior among the "great improvement[s]" in the science of politics generally (No. 9, p. 72), by Number 78 he pays full tribute to its origin, commenting that "[t]he experience of Great Britain affords an illustrious comment on the excellence of the institution" (p. 472). American law in the early years of the republic was to modify many particulars of the inherited common law, and federal law, with its limited objects, never adopted and hardly developed a common law, but the basic forms of common law adjudication were sustained.[14] The English judge in America may have lost his wig, but he kept his robe.[15]

What do I mean by common law background? For most contemporary American legal scholars, living still in the shadow of Justice Holmes, common law is understood to be judge-made law.[16] This is, I submit, a simplistic and distorted concept of common law, which begins with the positivist notion that all law is the product of legislation, and then, finding certain areas of law—for instance, torts—well-developed in the absence of statutes, presumes them the creation of subtle judges. It would be better to drop these assumptions and begin with the simple observation that common law is first of all the law of precedent. A common law judiciary, then as now, is one in which precedent as well as statute has the force of law, and it has such force not to encourage stubbornness, but because justice demands that similar cases be similarly disposed of. Common law differs from statutory law not merely in its source or its grounding, but, more essentially, in its perspective. It is law seen from the point of view of a judge faced with a controversy, not a sovereign faced with an unmanageable people or a people faced with civil war. To the judge, law does not begin with a statute, which in turn began with a sovereign authority, which began in consent; consent, after all, is given for a reason. Statutes are law to a judge when statutes are there, but new cases come up which statutes do not cover, and, of course, what statutes themselves mean for a case often requires interpretation. Precedent law fills the gaps between statutes, though new gaps open as circumstances change. But common law judging seeks to reconcile the new to the old, indeed to do this almost imperceptibly, always leaving open the possibility that truly new situations may need a statutory cure. Its guide is reason, but not deductive reason that begins from first principles and demonstrates particular consequences; rather it is reason that moves from particular case to particular case through the discovery of a rule implicit in the first and applicable to the second.[17] Common law is thus unwritten law, and unwritten law is perfectible. A precedent found to be against reason can be abandoned or restricted, but the characteristic bent of the common law mind is to assimilate, not to sweep fresh.

With the establishment of a judiciary on the federal level that was more or less traditional in its form, the Constitution brought along certain ideas inherent in the institution—in particular the common law understanding of the nature of law—and this understanding was not in every way compatible with the political theory that informed the other institutions of government, much less the interpretation given that theory in *The Federalist*. I alluded above to positivist elements in the rule of law as generally understood in American constitutionalism; and other authors in this volume explain how the rule of law is secured by the separation of constitutive from ordinary legislation, and then by the separation of legislation and execution—even where execution means not the mere slavish carrying out of orders but the exercise, within constitutional forms, of discretion.[18] But to add courts of the common law mode to a government with a strong legislature and an energetic executive alters the equation. Both the legislative and executive powers see their task as acting to achieve certain objects of government, and laws are means, perhaps *the* means, by which such objects can be achieved in a free government. From this perspective, the judiciary appears as a last check upon the government, allowing, as Epstein puts it, "private men to dispute with the executive's decision about their case," with the consequence that "the executive cannot be quite so energetic" as he might otherwise have been, though since the disputes are undertaken individually and not collectively they pose no immediate political danger.[19]

But the perspective of a court is, as I noted, quite the reverse. It begins not with a policy to enact and enforce but with a dispute brought before it for judgment; its task is to resolve that dispute by expounding applicable law. Judicial reasoning, then, starts from a particular instance and explores law for a purpose that is neither abstract nor political but meant to resolve a dispute. On this account, to a court law is something not to be made but to be found, though moving from the case to the law and back to the case is something of an art. In a common law environment, the task of the judge is governed by the doctrine of precedent, according to which, as similar cases are to be decided similarly, prior cases are law to subsequent ones. Still, deciding under what precedent a new case falls is not much easier than deciding under what statute it falls—indeed, it is often more controversial. And in some areas of law statutes do not even form the starting point of inquiry; in others, they are, like the statue of Glaucus in antiquity, so covered with the barnacles of precedent that they have assumed a new form.[20]

Now, the authors of *The Federalist* were lawyers or had studied law, and their common law orientation appears when they discuss the judiciary. In several passages Publius tempers his apparent positivism with a comment on the incompleteness of law and the need for judicial interpretation. After his remarkable account in Number 37 of the imperfection and imprecision in all human science, especially in politics and law, Publius continues:

> All new laws, though penned with the greatest technical skill and passed on the fullest and most mature deliberation, are considered as more or less obscure and equivocal, until their meaning be liquidated and ascertained by a series of particular discussions and adjudications. [*Federalist* 37, p. 229]

He later restates this claim, in the context of discussing the judiciary but with less emphasis on the judicial role:

> The erection of a new government, whatever care or wisdom may distinguish the work, cannot fail to originate questions of intricacy and nicety; and these may, in a particular manner, be expected to flow from the establishment of a constitution founded upon the total or partial incorporation of a number of distinct sovereignties. 'Tis time only that can mature and perfect so compound a system, can liquidate the meaning of all the parts, and can adjust them to each other in a harmonious and consistent WHOLE. [*Federalist* 82, p. 491]

Though both of these statements suggest that no written constitution can of itself settle all the questions to which it will give rise, neither answers unambiguously the question of what body will serve to fill in the gaps that remain in the original. The latter remark in particular, especially as restated in a quotation from Hume in the final paper (No. 85, p. 526), appears to leave the matter to the political judgment of subsequent generations, or perhaps to the workings of what we would today call a self-correcting mechanism.

The most striking instance of common law reasoning in *The Federalist* is, significantly, the argument establishing judicial review. To refer judicial review to common law may seem preposterous at first sight, since, as noted above, English courts at the time the Constitution was written were abandoning any notion that they could lay to rest an act of Parliament. But this outrageousness disappears when one considers, first, that scholarship has not closed the debate over whether something like judicial review existed in England from Sir Edward Coke's opinion in *Doctor Bonham's Case* in 1610 down to the early eighteenth century;[21] and second, that a written constitution changes the issue altogether. The first consideration deserves fuller treatment at another time; the second appears as one examines Publius's argument.

The case for judicial review in *Federalist* 78 is simpler than it appears. From the premises that "[t]he interpretation of the laws is the proper and peculiar province of the courts" and that a "constitution is, in fact, and must be regarded by the judges as a Fundamental law," Publius concludes that when a constitution and a statute conflict in a particular case, the courts must declare the latter void (p. 467). The common law character of the reasoning becomes apparent when he compares the judicial scrutiny of an act alleged to violate the Constitution with what judges do when two statutes clash. Not only are statute and Constitution treated as analogous, but the character of the rules for what to do in case of a conflict correspond. If two statutes of the same legislative authority clash, the more recent prevails by "a mere rule of construction, not derived from any positive law but from the nature and reason of the thing"; by the same way of thinking, even if to apparently opposite results, "the nature and reason of the thing" command preference for a constitutional rule over a statute should they conflict (p. 468). Here then is common law thinking, not only as the object of the appeal but in the appeal itself. Judicial review, after all, rests on the need to enforce the limits of a written constitution, but the power is inferred from, not expressed in, the document.[22] Consistent with this toleration of unwrittenness, Publius assigns to the courts the power of "mitigating the severity and confining the operation of [unjust and impartial] laws," even in the absence of a constitutional provision (p. 470).

Now the legal argument against judicial review must begin by denying one or both of the premises. In fact, the weak link seems to be the assertion that the Constitution is law and thus subject to a judicial reading. Publius himself opens the door to such an objection several pages later when he claims that constitutions must be construed differently from technical rules (No. 83, p. 497).[23] The claim that a constitution is different in kind from law depends upon the claim that the constituent power of the people is unique; the object of the narrower legal argument is thus to prepare the way for the republican argument, the claim that the striking down by unelected judges of acts of the people's representatives violates the principle that the authority of the government derives entirely from the people.[24] This argument was advanced with much prescience by the Anti-Federalist "Brutus" in a series of essays that appeared in the New York press shortly before Publius (Hamilton) wrote the papers on the courts.[25] Brutus argued that the meaning of tenure on good behavior is entirely transformed when transplanted from English monarchy to American republics; whereas English judges need protection from the Crown while acknowledging parliamentary supremacy, American judges will be independent of the legislature as well as of the executive. Having the power to declare void any acts "inconsistent with the sense judges put upon the constitution," they will often prove superior to the legislature.[26] Instead, he advocated leaving constitutional construction with the legislature, who "would have explained it at their peril," as "an appeal will lie to the people at the period when the rulers are to be elected."[27]

Publius's defense of judicial review in Number 78 aims to refute Brutus's charge of judicial superiority—but without taking what I have called a common law perspective, the refutation remains unconvincing. Indeed, if one accepts Publius's claims that the courts are "an intermediate body between the people and the legislature" and that "the power of the people" is superior to both representatives and judges (p. 467), it seems logically necessary to place the courts above Congress. He goes on in fact to defend the power of the courts to frustrate not only congressional will but even the will of the majority of the people should it run against constitutional command. A "momentary inclination" of the people is no substitute for "some solemn and authoritative act" to change "the established form" (pp. 469–470). It is no argument against granting the courts such a power that they might abuse it:

> if they should be disposed to exercise WILL instead of JUDGMENT, the consequence would equally be the substitution of their pleasure to that of the legislative body. The observation, if it proved anything, would prove that there ought to be no judges distinct from that body. [*Federalist* 78, p. 469]

Where does the argument for judicial review leave Publius's account of the separation of powers and his defense of the republican principle? As for the first, the preceding quotation hardly seems to square with the spirit of counteracting ambitions. On the contrary, if it is not to be dismissed as rhetorical excess it must be understood as a comment on the integrity of the judicial function—the impossibility of chopping it up and distributing it among various institutions, as one can to some extent with the legislative— or of calling it to task, as one can with the executive. Rather, Hamilton appears to rely upon what he calls the "comparative weakness" of the judiciary, "its total incapacity to support its usurpations by force"; besides, the power of impeachment in Congress "is alone a complete security" (No. 81, p. 485). But both his underestimation of what judicial power would become and his exaggeration of the ease with which it could be curbed seem due to an inadequate confidence in the power of law, at least in the long run.[28] As he intimated in Number 17 and makes even more explicit in Number 27, a well-administered federal judiciary is bound to win public confidence, and this in turn might tempt it to usurpation. At the same time, if usurpation begins in small steps as misinterpretations of the law,[29] the power of impeachment is worthless to stop it precisely to the extent that there remains virtue in the legislature, for impeachment is, after all, a judicial proceeding, and when responsibly wielded goes against malconduct only, not mistake or even inability. In short, the ethic of competing ambitions does not belong to impartiality, to judgment, and is thus relatively useless with regard to the judicial branch.

Publius's response to the republican objection is that in voiding unconstitutional acts the courts serve as the people's champion. Yet one need not be a cynic to note that an appointed body also charged with disciplining popular will to its solemn and authoritative acts is not everyone's idea of a champion. The requirement that the people act by constitutional forms surely limits the claim of the people to absolute sovereignty. And it would be out of step with the spirit of *The Federalist* to insist on formal limitations while denying substantive ones. It is indeed true that no court is strong enough to resist sustained popular resentment, but that is only an argument for prudence in the exercise of judicial power, not an argument of principle against the power itself. Publius is clear that, however much judges are "the bulwarks of a limited Constitution" and "faithful guardians of the Constitution" (No. 78, pp. 469, 470), the people are its "natural guardians" (No. 16, p. 117), and "the general spirit of the people and of the government" is "the only solid basis of all our rights" (No. 84, p. 515). Far from contradicting the common law interpretation of judicial review here presented, these statements complete it, for it is of the essence of the common law and its unwrittenness that no particular statute nor the judgment of any court is the final word on what is just.[30] To be a guardian is not the same as to be a sovereign. The republican principle may, as Epstein argues, reflect an "honorable determination" on the part of the people to choose their government and order their lives.[31] But only the Machiavellian republican would deny the propriety of complementing the honor of choice with the humility that comes from recognizing the limits of human choice and the need for the guidance of law.

The Common Law and American Constitutionalism

Let me try to collect my argument, then add a brief coda. The judicial power and Publius's discussion of it bring to light an aspect of American government that often remains hidden in practice and certainly only lingers in the background in the bulk of *The Federalist*. Epstein notes in *The Federalist* a commitment to, and tension between, republican government and good government, but my suggestion is that there exists as well a commitment to justice that is not reducible to public or private right, or in Epstein's account, public or private selfishness.[32] The maintenance of what I have somewhat loosely called a common law judiciary embodies this dedication, for such a judiciary is committed by its forms of proceeding to serious attention to the concrete disputes of individuals and to the discovery of law through consideration of "the nature and reason of the thing." The judiciary and what it stands for hardly give the American regime its whole character. American government is enormously diverse, not only in its structures but in the principles that inform them. But without the temper given to the regime by its judicial power, our constitutionalism would oscillate between the heirs of republicanism and those of "good government," between self-assertive populism and utilitarian realism.[33] Nor is the faculty of judgment, which Publius treats as specific to the judiciary, without appearance elsewhere in the regime: he also uses the term in regard to legislators (No. 53, p. 332) and to the people's evaluation of the proposed Constitution itself (No. 1, p. 35; No. 85, p. 522). Indeed, one is tempted to add that in the faculty of judgment and the institutions that promote it, the reflection and choice invoked by Publius at the outset intertwine.

Still, Publius seems more explicitly bent on quieting republican jealousy and rallying the partisans of good government than on cultivating a general judiciousness, and though the form of *The Federalist* may contribute to this end,[34] his ambiguity on the judicial power suggests the limits either of his attention or his theory. This is confirmed by his treatment of juries and a bill of rights. With respect to both he admits the principle but balks at the complaints of his opponents, hoping to preserve for the new government full flexibility. The issue of the right to trial by jury, which deserves fuller treatment than it can here receive, had achieved, according to Publius, the most success of any objection to the Constitution (No. 83, p. 495). Whatever the merits of the Anti-Federalists' particular complaints, one should hardly be surprised at the controversy: after all, what is at issue is the reverse side of the direct operation of the government on its citizens, namely, their direct participation in the federal government, and while schemes of representation in an extended sphere can help ensure a national spirit in the federal government, a federal jury will be in its composition as local as a jury of the state. Likewise, Publius's objections to a bill of rights—contradictory though they are in first claiming that protection of particular rights is written into the Constitution and then arguing that to protect such rights in writing would be dangerous—reflect his tilt toward the importance of governmental power and away from judicially protected rights. Indeed, except obliquely through citing Blackstone on habeas corpus, he makes no mention of the judiciary in his entire discussion of a bill of rights, despite having just concluded his examination of the judicial power.[35]

I quoted above Publius's comment recognizing the necessary imperfection of the Constitution and perhaps, by extension, the imperfection of the account of politics provided by *The Federalist* or possible in any political theory. Though in many respects the maturing of the whole he speaks of was to take generations—and at least one terrible shock—in one sense the whole was quickly altered through the addition, of course, of the Bill of Rights. Herbert Storing may be correct in saying that the passage of the amendments that did pass in the form in which they passed was a Federalist victory of sorts;[36] after all, they were initiated and guided through the House by an author of *The Federalist*. Still, it is worth noting that half of the ten amendments had to do with judicial matters, bringing the protections of the common law to bear upon citizens in their relations with the central government.[37] Nor, from the perspective of our century, and in the wake of further amendments—especially the Fourteenth, made in the spirit of the first ten—can we ignore the extent to which the amendments have defined the preponderance of our constitutional law. *The Federalist* may be in some respects the authoritative commentary on the Constitution, but we ought to keep in mind that the document on which it comments was incomplete in a very real sense: especially with regard to the judiciary, and hence with regard to constitutionalism itself.

11

The Federalist's Understanding of the Constitution as a Bill of Rights

RALPH A. ROSSUM

Among the most frequently quoted passages from *The Federalist* is the following: "In framing a government which is to be administered by men over men, the great difficulty lies in this: You must first enable the government to control the governed; and in the next place oblige it to control itself."[1] When these words from *Federalist* 51 are read today, there is a tendency among most students of constitutional law to understand the resolution of this "great difficulty" in a peculiar way. The original Constitution is understood as providing the government with the power necessary to control the governed, and the Bill of Rights is seen as securing civil liberties and thereby as obliging the government to control itself.

That, surely, is how the legal professoriate approaches the matter. Gerald Gunther's *Constitutional Law* is illustrative. After introducing the judicial function, Gunther divides the recently published eleventh edition of his widely used and respected casebook into two parts: "The Structure of Government: Nation and States in the Federal System," which focuses exclusively on the way powers are allocated and distributed by the original Constitution; and "Individual Rights," which addresses only its amendments.[2] That also is how the political science profession has come to understand the relationship of the Constitution to the Bill of Rights. For decades, graduate students have prepared for their qualifying examinations in constitutional law by studying C. Herman Pritchett's *The American Constitution*. In this influential and popular treatise, Pritchett includes a chapter entitled "The Constitutional Basis for Protection of Individual Rights." The reader quickly learns that the basis of individual rights is not the Constitution itself but the Bill of Rights and the Fourteenth Amendment.[3] The implication in Pritchett as well as in Gunther is clear: the original Constitution affords no protection to individual rights and is, in fact, deficient in this respect, inasmuch as amendments have been necessary to secure these rights.

This contemporary understanding would surprise the authors of *The Federalist*. *Federalist* 51 antedated the drafting and ratification of the Bill of Rights, and the passage quoted above referred simply to the Constitution, a document that *The Federalist* proudly proclaimed a "republican remedy for the diseases most incident to republican government."[4] These diseases, which had inevitably proven fatal to all previous experiments with republican government, were the rival defects of democratic imbecility, on the one hand, and majority tyranny on the other. Any effort to correct the one served only to exacerbate the other. As republican governments vibrated between these opposite poles, they had invariably been "spectacles of turbulence and contention" and had acted in ways "incompatible with personal security, or the rights of property." They had proven to be "as short in their lives as they (were) violent in their deaths."[5] *The Federalist* fully recognized that these diseases had to be remedied before republican government could "be rescued from the opprobrium under which it has so long labored, and be recommended to the esteem and adoption of mankind."[6] Moreover, it believed that the delegates to the Federal Convention of 1787 had isolated a cure; the Constitution they had framed was designed in such a way that it would simultaneously avoid ineptitude—it gave the government power enough to control the governed—and tyranny—it so structured the institutions of the new government and extended the sphere of its influence that a majority could seldom act in a manner "adverse to the rights of other citizens, or to the permanent and aggregate interests of the community."[7] As a consequence, the Constitution itself was, in the words of *Federalist* 84, "in every rational sense, and to every useful purpose, A BILL OF RIGHTS."[8]

The Federalist believed that "bills of rights, in the sense and to the extent in which they are contended for," were, therefore, "unnecessary" in the new Constitution. It also viewed them as "dangerous. They would contain various exceptions to powers which are not granted; and on this very account, would afford a colorable pretext to claim more than were granted."[9] Further, it regarded them as ineffectual. They were merely "parchment barriers" that had been demonstrated by history to be unable to control the acts of overbearing majorities; as James Madison remarked, "experience proves the inefficacy of a bill of rights on those occasions when its control is most needed."[10] Nevertheless, in the First Congress, Madison served as principal sponsor of a series of amendments that, when ratified, became the Bill of Rights. In a letter to Jefferson, Madison noted that "[i]t is a melancholy reflection that liberty should be equally exposed to danger whether the Government have too much or too little power . . . ."[11] He believed that the Constitution struck the proper balance and that a bill of rights, if properly framed, would not jeopardize that balance but, in fact, could help preserve it. It could win the support of many who mistakenly thought a bill of rights was necessary for the protection of their liberties, and it could silence the Anti-Federalists' call for a general convention and thwart their attempts to revise the basic structure and powers of the new federal government. "We have in this way," he candidly confessed to his fellow members of the House of Representatives, "something to gain, and, if we proceed with caution, nothing to lose."[12] He saw the Constitution as the primary bulwark of liberty, and the Bill of Rights as a bulwark of the Constitution. A reconstruction of *The Federalist*'s understanding of the Constitution as a bill of rights and a systematic examination of Madison's understanding of the relationship of the Bill of Rights to the Constitution are, therefore, crucial. They are especially necessary at a time when most constitutional scholars see the Constitution and the powers it authorizes as a direct threat to liberty and assert that "the very foundation of America's free and democratic society"[13] is the Bill of Rights aggressively protected by an activist judiciary.

THE CONSTITUTION AS A BILL OF RIGHTS

As *The Federalist* described it, the overriding difficulty for the Constitutional Convention was to combine "the requisite stability and energy in Government, with the inviolable attention due to liberty, and to the republican form."[14] This was a problem that the framers believed Great Britain had largely remedied, but only by departing from purely republican principles and introducing into the government elements of a mixed regime: its monarchical element ensured energy and, together with its aristocratic element, restrained the tyrannical tendencies of the majority. This remedy, however, was ruled out by the framers, not only because America lacked a millennium's experience with monarchy and aristocracy but also because it was, as *Federalist* 39 noted, irreconcilable with the genius of the American people. A wholly popular remedy—one consistent with the republican form—had to be found and, *The Federalist* was confident, had been found. The framers recognized, and *The Federalist* was instrumental in persuading others to recognize, that power could not be limited by a set of constitutional prohibitions. The government had to possess all powers necessary to secure "the public good and private rights."[15] The framers knew that these powers could not be determined in advance and, therefore, they opposed any limitations of powers destined to effect purposes that were themselves incapable of limitation. In the words of *Federalist* 41: "It is in vain to oppose constitutional barriers to the impulse of self-preservation. It is worse than in vain; because it plants in the Constitution itself necessary usurpations of power, every precedent of which is a germ of unnecessary and multiplied repetitions."[16] The framers stressed that power could not be limited by "parchment barriers";[17] however, they insisted that it could be channeled and directed by a properly constructed constitution so that it could not be used to advance, in the words of *Federalist* 51, "any other principles than those of justice and the general good." They appreciated that human pride and the love of power are elemental forces that cannot be stifled or contained; thus they sought instead to harness and direct these forces through the process of mutual checking. Relying on what *The Federalist* termed the "policy of supplying by opposite and rival interests, the defect of better motives," they sought to enlist the "private interest of every individual" to check and restrain the tyrannical impulses of the majority and, by so doing, to serve as a "sentinel over the public rights."[18]

Federalist 9 remarked that recent improvements in the "science of politics" made it possible for the framers to devise a constitution "of a more perfect structure"[19]—one that was marked by a new understanding of separation of powers and federalism and that operated over an extended republic. That constitution, the framers believed, would be the means of securing the liberties of the people not only from the ravages of ineptitude and anarchy but also from the tyrannical tendencies of the majority. It was by virtue of this service to liberty that *The Federalist* could describe the Constitution as "in every rational sense, and to every useful purpose, a bill of rights."[20]

The Federalist saw the new understanding of separation of powers developed by the Constitutional Convention as helping to secure liberty from both democratic ineptitude and majority tyranny. This new understanding sought a government not of separated powers but rather, in Richard Neustadt's apt phrase, of "separated institutions sharing powers."[21] *The Federalist* acknowledged what the framers had come to understand: "The accumulation of all powers, legislative, executive, and judiciary, in the same hands, whether of one, a few, or many, and whether hereditary, self-appointed, or elective, may justly be pronounced the very definition of tyranny."[22] It followed from this understanding that "the preservation of liberty requires that the three great departments of government should be separate and distinct."[23] It did not follow, however, that the different kinds of governmental power had to remain separate. Quite the opposite; the powers of government had to be blended and balanced among the legislative, executive, and judicial departments.[24]

The framers rejected the two traditional understandings of separation of powers extant at the time of the Constitutional Convention. They rejected the British understanding in which each department of government represented a different principle of rule (with the Crown representing the principle of rule by the one, monarchy; the House of Lords representing the principle of rule by the few, aristocracy; and the House of Commons representing the principle of rule by the many, democracy) not only as impossible to duplicate in America, which lacked the social raw materials necessary to bring it into existence, but also as inconsistent with the American people's commitment to republican government. They also rejected the understanding of a rigid, functional separation of powers present in many of the state constitutions of the day as unable to check the will of tyrannical majorities expressed through a compliant or demogogic legislature. As Madison had observed in a letter to Jefferson, "Wherever the real power in a Government lies, there is the danger of oppression. In our Governments the real power lies in the majority of the community, and the invasion of private rights is chiefly to be apprehended, not from acts of Government contrary to the sense of its constituents, but from acts in which the Government is the mere instrument of the major number of the Constituents."[25] In a republican government, the greatest threat of tyranny came from the legislative branch, which was "everywhere extending the sphere of its activity and drawing all power into its impetuous vortex."[26] "Parchment barriers" could not be trusted to contain this "encroaching spirit of power."[27] The only effective solution to this threat of legislative tyranny was a separation of powers that established an independent executive and judiciary and provided them with the necessary constitutional means to resist these legislative encroachments.

Madison's contributions during the Constitutional Convention to this understanding of separation of powers are particularly significant and, paradoxically, are perhaps best reflected in his unsuccessful defense of a council of revision, which, as proposed, would have been composed of the president and selected members of the judiciary and authorized to exercise a conditional veto over "every act of the National Legislature before it shall operate."[28] Madison viewed the council as an additional means of providing the executive and judicial branches with the opportunity of defending themselves against "legislative usurpations." His fear was not that the council would "give too much strength either to the Executive or the Judiciary"; rather it was that "notwithstanding this cooperation of the two departments, the Legislature would still be an overmatch for them."[29] Many of his fellow delegates objected to such a council, believing it an "improper mixture" of the executive and judicial branches and, hence, a violation of the principle of separation of powers. Madison's response articulates well the new understanding of separation of powers that he was helping the Convention to develop:

> Mr. Madison could not discover in the proposed association of the Judges with the Executive in the Revisionary check on the Legislature any violation of the maxim which requires the great departments of power to be kept separate & distinct. On the contrary he thought it an auxiliary precaution in favor of the maxim. If a Constitutional discrimination of the departments on paper were a sufficient security to each agst. encroachments of the others, all further provisions would indeed be superfluous. But experience had taught us a distrust of that security; and it is necessary to introduce such a balance of powers and interests, as will guarantee the provisions on paper.

> Instead therefore of contenting ourselves with laying down the Theory in
> the Constitution that each department ought to be separate & distinct, it
> was proposed to add a defensive power to each which should maintain the
> Theory in practice. In so doing we did not blend the departments together.
> We erected effectual barriers for keeping them separate.[30]

While his fellow delegates rejected Madison's pleas for a council of revision, they ultimately accepted his understanding of separation of powers and his argument that the only way to solve the problem of "the encroaching spirit of power" was "by so contriving the interior structure of the government . . . that its several constituent parts . . . [are] by their mutual relations, the means of keeping each other in their proper places."[31] The result was a new model of separation of powers, with the government comprising three coordinate and equal branches, and with each performing a blend of functions, thereby balancing as opposed to strictly separating powers.[32]

Despite their rejection of the council of revision, the Convention worked steadfastly in other ways "to divide and arrange the several offices in such a manner as that each may be a check on the other."[33] Thus, while it gave most legislative power to the Congress, most executive power to the president, and most judicial power to the Supreme Court and such inferior courts as Congress might establish, it also set out to "divide and arrange" the remaining powers in such a manner that each branch could be "a check on the other." Bicameralism, the president's conditional veto power, judicial review, senatorial confirmation of executive appointees and judicial nominees, impeachment by Congress, congressional power to control the appellate jurisdiction of the Supreme Court, and staggered terms of office (two years for the House, four for the president, six for the Senate, and good behavior for the judges) are but a few of the most commonly recognized examples.

This separation and balancing of powers prohibited the majority from being tyrannized by any branch of government and, at the same time, prevented the majority from tyrannizing others. It served as a "defense to the people against their own temporary errors and delusions."[34] As *The Federalist* noted, the people, when "stimulated by some irregular passion, or some illicit advantage, or misled by the artful misrepresentations of interested men, may call for measures which they themselves will afterwards be the most ready to lament and condemn." The operation of separation of powers provided time and opportunity for "the cool and deliberate sense of the community" to prevail over this "tyranny of their own passions."[35] In addition to guarding against tyranny, however, separation of powers also minimized the prospects for that other defect of popular government, democratic ineptitude. Realizing that the democratic process of mutual deliberation and consent can paralyze the government when swift and decisive action is necessary, the framers reasoned that the government would be more efficient if its various functions were performed by separate and distinct agencies. A passage from James Wilson's law lectures is most instructive:

> In planning, forming, or arranging laws, deliberation is always becoming, and always useful. But in the active scenes of government, there are emergencies in which the man . . . who deliberates is lost. Secrecy may be equally necessary as dispatch. But, can either secrecy or dispatch be expected, when, to every enterprise, mutual communication, mutual consultation, and mutual agreement, among men of perhaps discordant views, of discordant tempers, and discordant interests are indispensably necessary? How much time will be consumed; and when it is consumed, how little business will be done. . . . If, on the other hand, the executive power of government is placed in the hands of one person, who is to direct all subordinate officers of that department, is there not reason to expect, in his plans and conduct, promptitude, activity, firmness, consistency, and energy.[36]

As the framers knew and *The Federalist* testified, separation of powers made possible the existence of an independent and powerful executive capable of supplying the "energy in government . . . essential to that security against external and internal danger, and to that prompt and salutary execution of the laws, which enter into the very definition of good government."[37] It made it possible to avoid the administrative irresolution and imbecility that had characterized the Articles of Confederation.[38] It made it possible to provide for that "vigor of government [which] is essential to the security of liberty."[39]

The new understanding of separation of powers present in the Constitution was one of the major reasons for *The Federalist's* confidence that liberty could be secured from both democratic ineptitude and majority tyranny and for its insistence that a bill of rights was unnecessary, inasmuch as the Constitution was itself a bill of rights. Another major reason for *The Federalist's* confidence and insistence was that a new kind of federalism was present in the Constitution. The framers worked not only to distribute and balance power among the three branches of the federal government but also to divide power between the federal government and the states. The result was a "compound government"[40] that was neither wholly federal nor wholly national.[41] This system, which has come to be known simply as federalism, is chiefly marked by a division of power between the federal government and the states. It is, however, also characterized by the presence of federal elements in the central government itself; these include the mode by which the Constitution itself was ratified, the amendment process, equal representation of the states in the Senate, and the electoral college.

The Convention initially considered a proposal, found in the Virginia Plan, to establish a national government, not a "compound" one. Only a national government, it was argued, would be "adequate to the exigencies of

Government and the preservation of the Union."[42] Most delegates, however, were reluctant to abolish the states altogether and concluded that, since the new Constitution was "in some respects [to] operate on the states, in others on the people,"[43] both ought to be represented in the new government. When it was clear that neither the Convention delegates nor the people would accept a completely national or unitary government, the framers labored instead to create "a more perfect Union" than the traditional federalism of the Articles of Confederation. In so doing, they mixed together in varying proportions both national and federal elements until they had created what was "in strictness neither a national nor a federal constitution, but a composition of both."[44]

This new federalism eliminated the weakness and imbecility that had so long disgraced the Articles of Confederation.[45] The power of the federal government was enhanced considerably by national elements that allowed it not only to operate directly on the citizenry but also to deal with matters of internal administration—for example, it could now regulate commerce among the several states, establish uniform rules of bankruptcy, coin money, establish a postal system, tax, and borrow money. The federal government was also made supreme over the states through the supremacy clause. This new federalism also helped to remedy the republican disease of majority tyranny. It preserved the presence of powerful states capable of checking and controlling not only the new federal government, but each other as well. Federalism granted the new federal government only those powers expressly or implicitly delegated to it in the Constitution and allowed the states to retain all powers not prohibited to them. Moreover, by blending federal elements into the structure and procedures of the central government itself, this new federalism dimmed in still other ways the prospects for majority tyranny. The presence in the Senate of the federal principle provides an instructive illustration; because of the equal representation of all states, the presence of a nationally distributed majority—with the moderating tendencies that provides—is virtually assured. The threat of tyranny from regionally concentrated factious majorities is, therefore, effectively removed.

The preservation of powerful states, in turn, provided yet another remedy for the ills of democratic ineptitude. With two levels of government at their disposal, the people are able to assign their sovereign power to whichever level they believe is more conducive to the common good. As James Wilson declared in the Pennsylvania ratifying convention: "They can distribute one portion of power to the more contracted circle called State governments; they can also furnish another proportion to the government of the United States."[46] Likewise, the federal system permits the states to serve, in Justice Harlan's words, as "experimental social laboratories,"[47] in which new policies and programs can be initiated. If these experiments are successful, they can be adopted elsewhere; if they fail, the damage can be confined to the states in question. Since the risks are lessened, experimentation is encouraged, and the chances of positive reform and innovative governance are increased. In a wholly national system where experimentation can only take place on a national scale, the risks are so high that social inertia predominates and the status quo is likely to prevail. Coming full circle, this enhanced efficiency itself dims the prospect for majority tyranny. As *Federalist* 20 observed: "Tyranny has perhaps oftener grown out of the assumptions of power, called for, on pressing exigencies, by a defective constitution, than by the full exercise of the largest constitutional authorities."[48]

The Federalist's confidence that the Constitution was itself a bill of rights was strengthened as well by the presence and operation of still a third remedy to the diseases of republican government, viz., the operation of a multiplicity of interests present in the extended republic established by the Constitution. In the Convention, Madison argued that "in all cases where a majority are united by a common interest or passion, the rights of the minority are in danger. What motives are to restrain them?" He then identified and discarded the only possible motives:

> A prudent regard to the maxim that honesty is the best policy is found by experience to be as little regarded by bodies of men as by individuals. Respect for character is always diminished in proportion to the number among whom the blame or praise is to be divided. Conscience, the only remaining tie, is known to be inadequate in individuals: In large numbers, little is to be expected from it. Besides, Religion itself may become a motive to persecution & oppression.[49]

For Madison, "the only remedy" was "to enlarge the sphere, & thereby divide the community into so great a number of interests & parties, that in the 1st. place a majority will not be likely at the same moment to have a common interest separate from that of the whole or of the minority; and in the 2d. place, that in case they shd. have such an interest, they may not be apt to unite in the pursuit of it." Madison insisted that it was incumbent upon his fellow delegates to try this remedy and, "with that view to frame a republican system on such a scale & in such a form as will controul all the evils wch. have been experienced."[50] They accepted his prescription which, in turn, made it possible for them to reject the traditional arguments of Montesquieu concerning the need for a confederate republic and allowed them instead to embrace the new understanding of federalism that they were simultaneously developing.

The advantages that Madison saw as flowing from framing an extended republic can best be seen by contrasting the defects of a small republic. As he noted in *Federalist* 10, the smaller the republic, "the fewer probably will be the distinct parties and interests composing it; the fewer the distinct parties and interests, the more frequently will a majority be found of the same party; and the smaller the number of individuals composing a majority, and the smaller the compass within which they are placed, the more easily will they concert and execute their plans of oppression." This leads to majority tyranny, which can be prevented only by rendering the government impotent and thereby fostering democratic imbecility. By contrast, by extending the sphere, "you take in a greater variety of parties and interests; you make it less probable that a majority of the whole will have a common motive to invade the rights of other citizens; or if such a common motive exists, it will be more difficult for all who feel it to discover their own strength, and to act in unison with each other." Because of the "greater variety" of economic, geographic, religious, political, cultural, and ethnic interests present in an extended republic—especially a vibrant commerical one—rule by the majority is effectively replaced by rule by ever-changing coalitions of minorities that come together to act as a majority on one particular issue but that break up on the next. The coalition of various minority interests that acts as a majority on one issue is unlikely to remain intact on another, and the fact that allies in one coalition may well be opponents in the next encourages a certain moderation in politics, in terms of both the political objectives sought and the political tactics employed. Political interests are reluctant to raise the political stakes too high, for by scoring too decisive a political victory on one issue, these interests may find that they have only weakened themselves by devastating future allies and by thus rendering themselves more vulnerable to similar treatment by others. Accordingly, politics is moderated, not through appeals to conscience and fair play but through the inclination of individuals to look after their own self-interest. The multiplicity of interests present in the extended republic renders "an unjust combination of a majority of the whole very improbable."[51] It makes it possible for the the Constitution to give the national government sufficient power to prevent democratic ineptitude without raising the specter of majority tyranny.

Madison's Understanding of the Relationship of the Bill of Rights to the Constitution

Madison believed that the Constitution, marked by a new understanding of separation of powers and federalism and operating over a large, differentiated, commercial republic, was the complete remedy for the diseases of republican government. It was the means of "secur[ing] the public good, and private rights, against the danger of a [tyrannical majority], and, at the same time, [of] preserv[ing] the spirit and form of popular government."[52] He saw no need for a bill of rights, as the Constitution was itself a full defense of liberty. Neither, apparently, did most of his fellow delegates. Over three months passed before it even occurred to anyone to include a bill of rights, and, when George Mason proposed on September 12 (just five days before the Convention adjourned) that the Constitution be prefaced by a bill of rights, his motion was defeated by a vote of ten states to none.[53] During the ratification struggle, however, pressure mounted to add a bill of rights. Massachusetts, South Carolina, New Hampshire, New York, and Virginia all ratified the Constitution on the understanding that a series of widely desired amendments to the Constitution would be proposed by the First Congress and submitted to the states for ratification. Madison argued against these amendments so long as the Constitution remained unratified. As he wrote to George Eve in January of 1789: "I freely own that I have never seen in the Constitution as it now stands those dangers which have alarmed many respectable Citizens. Accordingly, whilst it remained un- ratified, and it was necessary to unite the States in some one plan, I opposed all previous alterations as calculated to throw the States into dangerous contentions, and to furnish the secret enemies of the Union with an oppor- tunity of promoting its dissolution."[54] Once the Constitution was ratified, however, Madison became the principal sponsor of the Bill of Rights. The explanation of his apparent change of heart can be found in a letter he wrote to Thomas Jefferson: "I have never thought the omission [of a bill of rights] a material defect, nor been anxious to supply it even by *subsequent* amend- ment, for any other reason than that it is anxiously desired by others. I have favored it because I supposed it might be of use, and, if properly executed, could not be of disservice."[55]

Madison labored persistently on behalf of the Bill of Rights not because *he* thought it essential but because *others* did. In much the same way that the Constitution he helped to design channels and directs the self-interest and passions of the citizenry in directions that serve the public good and happiness, so, too, Madison channeled the public's desire for a bill of rights into a set of amendments that gave "satisfaction to the doubting part of our fellow-citizens"[56] without "endangering any part of the Constitution, which is considered as essential to the existence of the Government by those who promoted its adoption."[57] On June 8, 1789, Madison addressed the House of Representatives and introduced a series of amendments, most of which were ultimately ratified as the Bill of Rights. It is significant that in this crucial speech, Madison never argued on behalf of these amendments in his own name. He proposed these amendments, he said, so that "those who had been friendly to the adoption of this Constitution may have the opportunity of proving to those who were opposed to it that they were as sincerely devoted to liberty and a Republican Government, as those who charged them with wishing the adoption of this Constitution in order to lay the foundation of an aristocracy or despotism."[58] Those who believed that the Constitution was deficient because it lacked a bill of rights were "mistaken," but, he continued, "there is a great body of the people falling under this description, who at present feel much inclined to join their support to the cause of Federalism, if they were satisfied on this one point." Accordingly, he urged the Congress "not to disregard their inclination, but, on principles of amity and moderation, conform to their wishes, and *expressly declare the great rights of mankind secured under this Constitution*."[59] These words have particular significance as they clearly indicate that Madison saw the Bill of Rights as declaring rights already secured under the Constitution, not protecting rights that the Constitution had somehow placed in jeopardy. A bill of rights would, he continued, reassure "a great number of our fellow-citizens who think these securities necessary."[60] It would "satisfy the public mind that their liberties will be perpetual."[61]

The people wanted a bill of rights, and even though there was no need for it, Madison was prepared to give it to them—but only if it was "properly executed." Only then could there be "something to gain" and "nothing to lose." Thus, Madison proposed amendments that were "of such a nature as will not injure the Constitution."[62] He did not seek to alter the structure of the federal government (by imposing, for example, a council on the president, as many Anti-Federalists wanted). Neither did he seek to restrict its powers (by prohibiting standing armies, the granting of monopolies, or suspension of the writ of habeas corpus, as Jefferson had urged).[63] These measures would have undermined the constitutional scheme and sapped the vigor and capacity of the government. Rather, he sought measures that relied on the principles of, and restated the rights secured by, the Constitution. Thus the words comprising what became the first eight amendments merely made explicit the rights that Madison believed were secured by separation of powers, federalism, and the operation of a multiplicity of interests in an extensive commercial republic. The Ninth Amendment merely stated that other rights, in addition to those already enumerated, were protected by these same institutional arrangements. The Tenth Amendment met the objection that *The Federalist* itself had raised to a bill of rights—that its presence would suggest that the federal government was one of reserved rather than of delegated powers—and, again, was wholly consistent with the original constitutional scheme.

Even the amendments proposed by Madison that failed to win congressional approval or subsequent ratification by the states were of the same nature. Thus, he proposed to add language that

> The powers delegated by this Constitution are appropriated to the departments to which they are respectively distributed: so that the Legislative Department shall never exercise the powers vested in the Executive or Judicial, nor the Executive exercise the powers vested in the Legislative or Judicial, nor the Judicial exercise the powers vested in the Legislative or Executive Departments.[64]

Madison went on in the same speech to concede that "perhaps the best way of securing this . . . dogmatic maxim . . . in practice is, to provide such checks as will prevent the encroachment of the one upon the other."[65] As Madison so skillfully demonstrated in *The Federalist*, however, this very security is provided by the Constitution. His proposals to increase rapidly the size of the House of Representatives and to prohibit members of Congress from voting themselves pay increases until an election intervened were consistent with the Constitution's reliance on the extended republic argument and with the framers' understanding of the need to check self-interest. Even his proposal to preface the Constitution with a declaration of rights sought no more than an elaboration of the words already present in the Preamble—language that *Federalist* 84 had described as "a better recognition of popular rights than volumes of those aphorisms which make the principal figure in several of our state bills of rights, and which would sound much better in a treatise of ethics than in a constitution of government."[66]

Only one of Madison's proposals represented an attempt to improve substantially the original constitutional design; interestingly, however, it was directed against the states. Madison proposed that "No State shall violate the equal rights of conscience, or the freedom of the press, or the trial by jury in criminal cases."[67] Madison described this amendment as "the most valuable amendment in the whole list."[68] It was rejected by the Senate, but it reflected his and *The Federalist's* recognition that the principal threat to liberty was not the new federal government but the tyrannical excesses and incapacity of the state governments—governments not yet improved by the framers' science of politics, and that, given their smaller size, would never be able to duplicate fully the federal Constitution's "more perfect structure."[69]

Madison saw nothing in these amendments that could "endanger the beauty of the Government in any one important feature, even in the eyes of its most sanguine admirers." Thus, he appealed to the members of Congress, declaring that "*if we can make the Constitution better in the opinion of those who are opposed to it,* without weakening its frame, or abridging its usefulness in the judgment of those who are attached to it, we act the part of wise and liberal men to make such alterations as shall produce that effect."[70]

He also proposed that these amendments be incorporated into the body of the Constitution itself. He declared that "there is a neatness and propriety in incorporating the amendments into the Constitution itself; in that case the system will remain uniform and entire; it will certainly be more simple, when the amendments are interwoven into those parts to which they naturally belong."[71] He saw no tension between the original Constitution and these amendments. The Constitution and the Bill of Rights had, for him, the same objective, and he saw no need to introduce a distinction between them, which he believed placing the amendments elsewhere would do. On this point, however, Madison did not prevail.[72] Roger Sherman, who generally opposed any bill of rights as unnecessary and dangerous, argued that the amendments should be added at the end of the Constitution, as any attempt to "interweave" these amendments into the Constitution itself would "be destructive of the whole fabric. We might as well endeavor to mix brass, iron, and clay . . . ."[73] George Clymer agreed; he argued that the amendments should be kept separate so that the Constitution "would remain a monument to justify those who made it; by a comparison, the world would discover the perfection of the original, and the superfluity of the amendments."[74]

The Congress ultimately agreed with Sherman and Clymer, but the results have not been what Clymer predicted. By placing the amendments at the tail of the Constitution, a significance has been given to the Bill of Rights that neither Madison nor the other members of Congress intended. Moreover, the unity of purpose and commitment to rights in both the Constitution and Bill of Rights has been obscured. Madison regarded the Constitution as the fundamental protector of the public's rights and liberties—securing them from both the threats of too much governmental power (tyranny) and too little (ineptitude and anarchy). In contemporary constitutional law, however, the Bill of Rights tail has come to wag the constitutional dog. Clymer's reason for appending the amendments at the end of the Constitution has been turned on its head, with the original Constitution now regarded as a "superfluity" (when not an actual threat) to the protection of rights and with "perfection" now ascribed to the Bill of Rights—or more specifically, to activist judges interpreting (or, better still, noninterpreting) its provisions.[75] The unity of purpose of the Constitution and the Bill of Rights is denied, and the Constitution, when it is not being denigrated, is ignored.

Contemporary constitutional law's denial of the unity of the Constitution and the Bill of Rights places us, unfortunately, in a kind of double jeopardy. First, it increases the prospects that the Bill of Rights will be reduced to a vulnerable and easily punctured "parchment barrier." As *The Federalist* was well aware, any bill of rights—any set of "thou shalt nots"—has the potential to be a mere parchment barrier, unable to prevent assaults on the very liberties it was drafted to secure. What spared the Bill of Rights Madison sponsored from this fate was that it was "properly executed"—its provisions protected rights that were already secured by the Constitution. Behind the parchment barrier of the "thou shalt nots" of the Bill of Rights were the institutional barriers of separation of powers, federalism, and the extended republic. Today, however, the Bill of Rights is being construed to prohibit acts (or, increasingly, to require acts) in respect to rights that have nothing to secure them save judicial declarations. Nothing stands behind these paper rights but the power of the judiciary. That power can, of course, be great, but only because, as Tocqueville has sagaciously noted, "it is the power of public opinion." The judges, Tocqueville observed, "are all-powerful as long as the people respect the law; but they would be impotent against popular neglect or contempt of the law." Given the vast fund of public support that an activist judiciary has recently drawn down, the barriers protecting the new rights that the courts continue to identify in the Bill of Rights have become exceedingly thin and brittle. This jeopardizes not only these newly created rights but the rights secured by the Constitution itself, for, as Tocqueville goes on to observe, failure on the part of judges to "discern the signs of the times" can "sweep them off, and the supremacy of the Union and the obedience due to the laws along with them."[76]

Second, by focusing on the Bill of Rights and ignoring the Constitution, contemporary constitutional law ignores what was seen by Madison and the other principal framers as *the* remedy for the diseases of republican government. At the time of the Constitutional Convention, republican government was understood to be inherently problematic. In fact, until the Constitution, a stable and free republican government had never been established. The framers were able to rescue republican government from the "opprobrium" under which it had previously labored, and to design institutions that recommended republican government to the esteem and adoption of mankind. They succeeded so admirably that, today, the problematic nature of republican government is all but forgotten. By ignoring the Constitution, contemporary constitutional law ignores as well the questions and problematics of republican government for which the Constitution was an answer. It treats republican government as nonproblematic, and treats with contempt the very Constitution that makes it so.

Federalist 1 noted that it seems to have been reserved to the United States "to decide the important question, whether societies of men are really capable or not, of establishing good government from reflection and choice, or whether they are forever destined to depend, for their political constitutions, on accident and force."[77] It remains to be seen whether contemporary constitutional law may not unleash the problematical nature of government that by "reflection and choice" the framers of the Constitution have kept in check, and place the American public once again in jeopardy of living under political institutions shaped by "accident and force."

12

Early Uses of
The Federalist

JACK N. RAKOVE

As often as modern scholars disagree in their readings of Publius, the overall value of his eighty-five essays seems beyond dispute. *The Federalist* stands as the single most comprehensive, enlightened, and authoritative original commentary on the Constitution whose ratification it was designed to promote. Its analyses of individual clauses are typically more sustained, systematic, and levelheaded than those provided by its contemporary competitors, and its judgments deserve greater attention because of the preeminent role that its principal authors, James Madison and Alexander Hamilton, played in the movement that led to the adoption of the Constitution. But the value of *The Federalist* also transcends what it reveals about the original understanding of the constitutional text or the politics of ratification. Its greatest passages are taken to embody and express the founding generation's conception of the first principles of republican government, and thus to speak to us, across two centuries, of the *res publica* with which we should still be concerned.

The reputation of *The Federalist* has never stood higher than it does at present; the passage of time has enhanced rather than diminished our appreciation of its merits. True, some of its early readers can be found offering the kinds of enthusiastic endorsements that modern authors customarily ask friends to provide for dust-jacket copy. And a healthy share in the market for *Federalist* commentary is still held by dissenters skeptical of its teachings. Even so, modern appreciation of *The Federalist* is, on balance, far more profound, complex. and even (in some circles) reverential than was ever the case before the middle of the twentieth century. Partial credit for this must go to Charles Beard, whose interpretation of the tenth *Federalist*, however flawed, nevertheless encouraged other scholars to begin to come to grips with Madison's argument. Of these the most important was, of course, Douglass Adair, whose seminal essays have inspired and made possible a seemingly inexhaustible stream of Publian analyses. [1]

How *The Federalist* acquired its current preeminence has itself become a legitimate subject of intellectual history[2]—and at the close of this chapter I shall offer some ironic reflections on this subject. But there is a prior issue that is also worth considering. How was *The Federalist* regarded *before* Beard, Adair, and other scholars initiated the recovery of its teaching? Or to put the question another way: what was there about the previous uses to which *The Federalist* had been put that delayed full appreciation of its merits until well after the centennial of the Constitution? For no period of our history are these questions of greater interest than the early decades of the republic, when disagreement over the essential nature of the federal union helped make possible its attempted dissolution in 1861.

A REPUTATION IS BORN

The first occasion (after ratification) on which the authority of Publius was invoked to interpret a disputed clause of the Constitution occurred, appropriately enough, during the first great constitutional debate in the First Federal Congress. In mid-June 1789, the House of Representatives took up the bill organizing the Department of State. The question immediately arose whether the President possessed unilateral power to remove subordinate officials by virtue of the constitutional grant of the executive power; whether the same senatorial consent that was required for the appointment of officers was not also necessary for their removal; whether the power of removal should be vested in the President legislatively, rather than constitutionally; or whether such officials could be displaced only through impeachment. Among those opposing the idea of an inherent presidential power of removal was William Loughton Smith of South Carolina, and when his turn came to address the House, Smith read the opening sentences of *Federalist* 77 to his colleagues. "[O]ne of the advantages to be expected from the cooperation of the Senate, in the business of appointments," Publius had there written, was

> that it would contribute to the stability of the administration. The consent of
> that body would be necessary to displace as well as to appoint. A change of
> the Chief Magistrate, therefore, would not occasion so violent or so general
> a revolution in the officers of the government as might be expected, if he
> were the sole disposer of offices.

If Smith hoped this evidence would clearly prove that the President did not possess the sole power of removal, however, he soon received a rude shock. As he informed Edward Rutledge shortly thereafter:

the next day [Egbert] Benson [of New York] sent me a note across the house
to this effect: that *Publius* had informed him since the preceding day's
debate, that upon mature reflection he *had changed his opinion* & was now
convinced that the President alone should have the power of removal at
pleasure; He is a Candidate for the office of Secretary of Finance!

The candidate was, of course, Alexander Hamilton; and it is more than likely
that Smith knew that his fellow congressman, James Madison, was the other
of the "two gentlemen of great information" rumored to have written that
"publication of no inconsiderable eminence."[3] Yet if Smith hoped that an
appeal to Publius could sway Madison, who stood on the opposite side of the
question, he was disappointed again. For in his own reply to Smith, Madison
simply ignored *Federalist* 77, arguing instead that the right to remove officials was constitutionally delegated by the opening words of Article II, which
declared that "The executive power shall be vested in a president."[4]

Four years later, it was Hamilton (writing as Pacificus) who invoked the
same words from Article II to argue that President Washington could uni-
laterally issue a proclamation of American neutrality toward the conflict that
had just erupted between Britain and France, notwithstanding the Franco-
American alliance of 1778 and the constitutional allocation of the treaty
power to the President and Senate jointly. When Madison took up the pen
to reply, it was probably a curious mixture of relish and embarrassment that
led him to close his first Helvidius essay with a lengthy quotation from
Federalist 75. There Hamilton, perhaps following Locke, had argued that
the treaty power was not inherently executive in nature, but would instead
"be found to partake more of the legislative than of the executive character,
though it does not seem strictly to fall within the definition of either of
them." For Madison, this was a convenient conclusion. If executive power
was not understood to embrace anything more than the conduct of routine
correspondence with American diplomats and foreign emissaries, the President had acted improperly by failing to consult the Senate on a matter with
far-reaching implications for foreign policy.[5]

Taken together, these two episodes nicely anticipate the difficulties and
ironies that often accompanied early attempts to use *The Federalist* to resolve constitutional disputes. They may also help to explain why both Hamilton and Madison tended to treat their joint effort with a certain studied
coolness.[6] In the preface he composed in March 1788 for the first bound
volume of the essays, Hamilton struck a distinctly apologetic note in observing the "violations of method and repetitions of ideas which cannot but
displease a critical reader."[7] When Madison belatedly informed Jefferson of
his own share in the work, he took care to point out that "the writers are not
mutually answerable for all the ideas of each other." Madison attributed this
to the pressure of time under which they had been forced to work, but he
had known Hamilton long enough to realize that their collaboration could
not disguise some significant differences of opinion. Neither man appears to

have allowed the passage of time to soften his judgment or enhance his attachment. When Jefferson proposed including *The Federalist* in the legal curriculum for the University of Virginia, Madison agreed that it could "fairly enough be regarded as the most authentic exposition of the text of the federal Constitution," but he quickly added that "it did not foresee all the misconstructions which have occurred; nor prevent some that it did foresee. And what equally deserves remark," he continued, was that "neither of the great rival Parties have acquiesced in all its comments."[8] What is perhaps more revealing is that Madison seemingly made little use of *The Federalist* in fielding the numerous constitutional queries that he received during the eighteen intellectually vigorous years of his retirement.

The reserve that the two principal authors apparently felt about their work was not, however, shared by the general public. The original McLean edition of 1788 had been advertised as "the cheapest as well as the most valuable publication ever offered to the American public" and during the 1790s readers responded to this dual appeal by purchasing a reported 25,000 copies. A second edition appeared in 1799, to be followed by seventeen further reprintings over the next half century.[9] From an early stage references to *The Federalist* became almost ritualistic in their praise, and it was the rare speaker or writer who failed to preface a quotation from Publius with a hearty encomium. A grudging John Adams could only praise it obliquely by noting that the essays "were all written after the publication" of his own *Defence of the Constitutions of Government of the United States,* but his son John Quincy represented the prevailing opinion more accurately and his family more generously when he called it "a classical work in the English language, and a commentary upon the Constitution . . . of scarcely less authority than the Constitution itself."[10] After a French translation of 1792 identified "MM. Hamilton, Madisson et Gay" as the authors, their prestige complemented the essays' intrinsic appeal. After 1800, the party conflicts between Federalists and Republicans led a few of Hamilton's and Madison's partisan biographers to denigrate the importance of the other man's contributions to *The Federalist*[11]—but even these claims stopped well short of implying that the work as a whole amounted to an unhappy fusion of two rival philosophies.

THE FEDERALIST IN CONGRESS

Recourse to the authority of Publius was made most frequently by congressmen contesting the constitutionality of specific pieces of legislation. As one might expect, such occasions turned *The Federalist* into a kind of debater's handbook, which congressmen searched for particularly apt and pointed quotations that could be brought to bear on the matter in question. Occasionally, as in William L. Smith's initial invocation, Publius seemed to speak unequivocally. But more often, his counsel appeared divided, and those who appealed to his authority managed to demonstrate that *The Federalist* was marked, if not by outright inconsistency, than at least by an unwieldy diversity in its opinions. *The Federalist* proved no less demanding of interpretation than the Constitution itself.

Sometimes congressmen could not agree what a given passage in *The Federalist* meant. When, for example, the House of Representatives took up the bill to charter the national bank in 1791, two members offered conflicting interpretations of the explanation of the "necessary and proper" clause set forth in *Federalist* 44, while a third, Elbridge Gerry, saw only duplicity in its narrow description of federal power.

> *The Federalist* is quoted on this occasion, but although the author of it discovered great ingenuity, this part of his performance I consider as a political heresy. His doctrine, indeed, was calculated to lull the consciences of those who differed in opinion with him at that time; and having accomplished his object, he is probably desirous that it may die with the opposition itself.[12]

On other occasions, the emphasis of one essay seemed to contradict the plain meaning of another. When the House attempted to determine what role, if any, it might play in the ratification of the controversial Jay's Treaty, two Republican members cited *Federalist* 53, which asserted that the House would retain a vital interest in foreign affairs. But Uriah Tracy of Connecticut promptly found two other passages that clearly stressed the Senate's unique role in treaty ratification.[13]

Variations on these themes recurred in later debates. Take the issue of internal improvements. Did the power to establish post roads extend to the use of federal resources for the construction of a network of interstate turnpikes? When congressmen marshaled their quotations for and against the constitutionality of such acts, the two concluding sentences of *Federalist* 42 seemed particularly illuminating—but to both sides.

> The power of establishing post-roads must, in every view, be a harmless power [Madison had written] and may, perhaps, by judicious management, become productive of great public conveniency. Nothing which tends to facilitate the intercourse between the States can be deemed unworthy of the public care.

Supporters of internal improvements, like Henry Clay in 1818, implied that the noble goal espoused in these sentences warranted a broad reading of the constitutional text.[14] But would Publius really have considered this power "'a harmless one,' unworthy of discussion," one congressman asked in 1824, "if [he] had supposed that it conveyed such powers as are now claimed for it?"[15] The expansive interpretation of this passage seemed more difficult to sustain when it was set against another sentence in *Federalist* 45, where Madison had even used the magic words. "The powers reserved to the several States will extend to all the objects which, in the ordinary course of affairs, concern the lives, liberties, and properties of the people; and the internal order, improvement, and prosperity of the state." On balance, the tactical advantage in quoting from Publius fell to the opponents of improvements, for on several occasions they forced their protagonists to challenge his authority. *The Federalist* was "the exposition of zealous advocates," declared William Lowndes of South Carolina; "is it to be believed, that they never represented a power less extensive, a limitation as somewhat more strict, than an impartial judge would have pronounced it?" Its authors, Lowndes conceded, were "able advocates whose speculations may be admitted to illustrate any question of Constitutional laws"; but because they were also "zealous advocates," their "opinions should never be permitted to decide it."[16]

Lowndes had hit upon an important point which remains relevant even today. Like Gerry in 1791, Lowndes recognized that the emphases in *The Federalist* had to be weighed in the context of its composition. Because one of its principal purposes had been to demonstrate that the Constitution had not established the leviathan its worst detractors imagined, many of its arguments were framed to emphasize apparent limitations on the scope of federal power. Whether those limitations would prove effective when ambiguous or "open-textured" clauses became the subject of operational decisions was something Publius could only predict but hardly guarantee. Indeed (as Hamilton's change of mind over the removal power suggests) it is a fair question how well the cautionary readings of *The Federalist* accorded not only with the private preferences of its authors but also with their expectations of what would prove possible once the Constitution was adopted.

It is, in any event, clear that Publius had shaded his language to stress safeguards against loose construction of the Constitution rather than possibilities for broad interpretation of national power. For that reason those who opposed the extension of federal authority in suspect areas tended to find *The Federalist* more useful than those who favored a latitudinarian approach to the Constitution. During the debate over the admission to the union of Maine and Missouri, eight out of nine speakers who cited *The Federalist* did so while justifying the right of the states to determine the propriety of slavery.[17] Again, during the tariff debate of 1832 four of the five speakers who quoted Publius did so to argue that federal power to levy duties on imports had been intended only for the purpose of raising revenue and not for the protection of domestic manufactures.[18] And when Congress turned its attention the next year to the Revenue Collection Bill that was designed to compel South Carolina to comply with that tariff, three senators cited *The Federalist* as being opposed to the coercion of a state, while only two found its arguments on national supremacy worth citing (Daniel Webster in a passing reference, and William Rives at greater length).[19]

From these and other references it would be difficult indeed to conclude that *The Federalist* exerted anything resembling influence over congressional interpretations of the Constitution. But, it might be objected, what more could be expected of members of Congress than a sophistical ransacking of quotations to be used and discarded as the needs of debate dictated? Arguably a more informed and deliberate consideration of the teachings of Publius could take place only in a different forum, one safely removed from the kinds of pressures to which congressmen were exposed. The most likely place in which a more balanced and subtle use of *The Federalist* would be expected to occur would be in the courts, as questions about the meaning and intent of the Constitution came to be addressed systematically.[20]

PUBLIUS AND THE JUDICIARY

Certainly there is good evidence that both state and federal judges regarded Hamilton's defense of judicial review in *Federalist* 78 as authoritative, as three cases heard outside the Supreme Court over a period of twenty-five years attest. Two eminent jurists—St. George Tucker in *Kamper* v. *Hawkins* (Virginia, 1793)[21] and Levi Woodbury in *Merrill* v. *Sherburne* (New Hampshire, 1818)[22]—both quoted Publius while invalidating acts of their respective state legislatures. In the third case, *United States* v. *The William*, federal judge John Davis was asked to determine the constitutionality of the Embargo Acts. Relying heavily on Hamilton's essays, Davis agreed that the question was cognizable before the court, and then carefully proceeded to uphold the law, using criteria set forth by Hamilton twenty years earlier.[23]

The Federalist was also quoted during the course of the most famous of all cases of judicial review, *Marbury* v. *Madison*—but not, curiously enough, by Chief Justice John Marshall. Charles Lee, counsel for William Marbury and a former Attorney General, twice called the court's attention to *The Federalist*, thereby providing Marshall with a convenient opportunity to buttress what he knew would be a much disputed decision with an appeal to authority. But Marshall made no mention of Publius in his decision. Doubtless he knew the argument of *Federalist* 78 well; and it is equally apparent that he had concurred with Hamilton on a host of other points. Perhaps it is this very concurrence that suggests why Marshall felt no need to appeal to *The Federalist*; his jurisprudence and its Hamiltonian strains were independent expressions of a set of principles and beliefs that both men had long shared.[24] A decade and a half had passed since Marshall had spoken of judicial review in the Virginia ratification convention; and if he had then been impressed, like other early Federalists, with the writings of Publius, the years since could only have made those views more persuasively his own.

In fact, Marshall rarely made use of *The Federalist* in his opinions.[25] He ignored it again in *Fletcher* v. *Peck*, although Justice Johnson, in a concurring opinion, found it an appropriate authority on the sanctity of contract.[26] In *McCulloch* v. *Maryland*, he was forced to discuss it when counsel for Maryland made it a mainstay for their argument that the state had a right to impose a tax on a federal bank. Only in *Cohens* v. *Virginia* did Marshall find it useful to invoke *The Federalist* in support of the right of appeal from state to federal courts. After first observing that the opinions of Publius "are entitled to the more consideration where they frankly avow that the power objected to is given, and defend it," Marshall quoted *Federalist* 82, which had dealt with precisely this question and come down decisively in favor of federal appellate jurisdiction.[27] *Cohens* was perhaps the single case in which it could be argued that any essay of *The Federalist* made a significant contribution to enlarging either the jurisdiction of the Court or the scope of federal power in general.

Even before 1800, however, *The Federalist* was being used to assert the concurrent or residual powers of the states against claims of federal jurisdiction.[28] But it was the great case of *McCulloch* v. *Maryland* that revealed the most important and striking use to which *The Federalist* would be put. Each of the three eminent counsels for Maryland found seemingly unequivocal support for the constitutionality of the state tax on the Bank of the United States in the words of its original architect, "the great champion of the Constitution," Alexander Hamilton. With no small irony they bombarded the Court with quotations from Hamilton's essays on taxation. Most dramatic of these was the opening paragraph of *Federalist* 32, where Hamilton had sought to dispel fears that Congress would sap the power of the states by appropriating to itself all possible sources of revenue. Joseph Hopkinson read the entire paragraph, including Hamilton's blunt conclusion:

> I am willing here to allow, in its fullest extent, the justness of the reasoning which requires that the individual States should possess an independent and uncontrollable authority to raise their own revenues for the supply of their own wants. And making this concession, I affirm that (with the sole exception of duties on imports and exports) they would, under the plan of the convention, retain that authority in the most absolute and unqualified sense; and that an attempt on the part of the national government to abridge them in the exercise of it, would be a violent assumption of power, unwarranted by any article or clause of the Constitution.

Hopkinson went on to cite the taxation essays (Numbers 30–36) *en bloc*, and then pointedly noted that "under such assurances from those who made, who recommended, and carried, the constitution, and who were supposed best to understand it, was it received and adopted by the people." *The Federalist* thus provided the basis for the Maryland argument that the states had an irreducible right to levy a tax on anything save imports and exports.[29]

It was the defendants' use of Hamilton that forced Marshall to take notice of an authority he would otherwise have ignored. The Chief Justice prefaced his response with words of praise for the essays—"No tribute can be paid to them which exceeds their merit"—but he was quick to note that "in applying their opinions" to specific cases "a right to judge of their correctness must be retained." Rather than dispute the blunt force of Hamilton's language, however, Marshall sought to make it consistent with the doctrine of implied power he had developed earlier in his opinion. *The Federalist*, Marshall wrote, had sought to answer objections "to the undefined power of the government to tax, not to the incidental privilege of exempting its own measures from State taxation." Its defense of the concurrent powers of the states had thus been designed to demonstrate that the union would not "absorb all the objects of taxation to the exclusion and destruction of the state governments; not to prove that the government was incapable of executing any of its powers, without exposing the means it employed to the embarrassment of state taxation." Marshall rightly concluded that the authors of *The Federalist* would have rejected Maryland's interpretation. Alexander Hamilton would certainly have agreed. Even so, the Chief Justice's logic could not entirely blunt the direct force of the language Hamilton had used.[30]

In 1819, the language of *Federalist* 32 was hardly enough to steer Marshall and his brethren away from the ideas of implied power and national supremacy that *McCulloch* did so much to establish. But from then until the Civil War, the Court's principal use of *The Federalist* tended to follow the argument that counsel for Maryland had developed. Only Justice Joseph Story managed to make *The Federalist* serve nationalist purposes. When other justices invoked its authority, they typically did so in support of the emerging doctrine of dual federalism,[31] whose appeal gathered force as Congress acquiesced in state efforts to regulate both internal and interstate commerce. As early as 1820, Justice Bushrod Washington cited *Federalist* 82 to support the finding that where neither the Constitution nor Congress had prohibited the exercise of a concurrent jurisdiction, the states were free to act in areas that had fallen under their purview before 1789.[32] In argument for *Gibbons* v. *Ogden*—the great steamboat monopoly case—counsel for New York buttressed the state's claim to an exclusive privilege of regulation with a dozen references to Publius, while it was the United States Attorney General who found himself dismissing *The Federalist* as a "polemic."[33] Two justices cited *The Federalist* in concurring opinions in *Ogden* v. *Saunders*, while upholding the validity of state bankruptcy legislation. Perhaps most important, in the various cases in which the Supreme Court somewhat confusedly applied notions of dual federalism to the regulation of commerce, the primary use of Publius—and especially *Federalist* 32—was on behalf of concurrent state authority rather than preemptive federal power.[34]

By the late 1830s, of course, the Supreme Court was retreating from the high ground of nationalist jurisprudence to which Marshall and Story had led it in *Martin* v. *Hunter's Lessee*, *McCulloch*, and *Cohens*. In practice the broad theoretical implications of economic nationalism were severely constrained by the realities of application. As the legal historian Harry Scheiber has noted, Supreme Court decisions cannot be "read as an accurate map of how power is actually exercised and limited." In point of fact, a combination of federal abstention and state activism created a situation in which the exercise of national authority was limited to tariffs, fiscal policy, and the disposal of public lands, while the states played a far more enterprising role in distributing various forms of "public largesse" and by making "direct capital investment" in canals, turnpikes, and railroads.[35] The doctrine of dual federalism helped to legitimate this devolution of power, but its sources lay far deeper than the ideas either of Marshall or his successor, Roger Taney.

THE SOUTHERN VIEW

But the damage had been done long before Marshall's death in 1835. The implications of the nationalist decisions in *Martin* and *McCulloch* were still being sifted when the Missouri crisis broke upon the country in 1819. The connection between the notions of national sovereignty implicit in the Court's decisions and the future status of slavery was impossible to ignore. As southern spokesmen and polemicists began to develop a new theory of state sovereignty, they read Publius with a certain ambivalence. Reluctant to attack either the Constitution or its framers directly, they preferred to use *The Federalist* to prove that the original design of 1787 was to create a national government vested with limited powers for narrowly specified ends. Yet they could not overlook those passages that seemed to portend an expanding national sovereignty; and some southern commentators came to believe that Publius himself had taken the first step in fomenting the heresies from which that renegade priest, John Marshall, was now fashioning a dangerous orthodoxy. States' rights adherents quoted *The Federalist* freely but praised it sparingly.

St. George Tucker of Virginia was the first southern commentator to use *The Federalist* in behalf of state sovereignty. The Appendix to his 1803 edition of *Blackstone's Commentaries* marked the first significant exposition of the Constitution to be published since *The Federalist* itself. An early and firm believer in judicial review, Tucker filled eight pages of his "Note on the Constitution of Virginia" with excerpts from the discussion in *Federalist* 78 of the virtues of an independent judiciary and its role as constitutional guardian. But Tucker made more interesting use of Publius when he shifted his attention to the federal Constitution. Arguing that it was a compact voluntarily entered into by sovereign states, Tucker drew upon various passages to illustrate the essentially federal nature of the union. He found it noteworthy, for example, that Publius had described the proposed union as confederal rather than consolidated. Tucker also called attention, as one might expect, to key passages in *Federalist* 39, where Madison had argued that in the "extent" of its powers the union was "federal, not national," and *Federalist* 45, where he suggested that the change effectuated by the Constitution "consists much less in the addition of new powers to the Union, than in the invigoration of its original powers." Perhaps most important, Tucker pointed to the carefully delimited exposition of the "necessary and proper" clause given in *Federalist* 33 and 44, which, when taken with the Twelfth Amendment, provided a "remarkable security against misconstruction." Publius himself had not contributed, therefore, to the plan "to destroy the effect of the particular enumeration of powers" that Tucker found manifest in such measures as the Alien and Sedition Acts and the Bank. He wished only that "the defects of the Constitution had been treated with equal candour, as the authors have manifested abilities in the development of its eminent advantages."[36]

Such moderation proved more difficult to sustain once the opinions of the Marshall Court revealed how broadly the Constitution could be construed. Beginning with Spencer Roane—Tucker's colleague on the Virginia Court of Appeals, and Marshall's staunchest critic—southern use of *The Federalist* bifurcated. All those passages that defended the supremacy of the federal judiciary and the appellate jurisdiction of the Supreme Court came in for heavy criticism. When, for example, the Virginia Court of Appeals refused to enforce the Supreme Court's instructions in *Martin* v. *Hunter's Lessee*, Roane's concurring opinion criticized counsel who had appealed to Publius to support federal jurisdiction. Without denying the "general ability" of *The Federalist*, Roane reminded his readers that it was "a mere newspaper publication, written in the heat and hurry of battle," whose "principal reputed author" was "a supposed favourer of a consolidated government."[37] But when Roane and his colleague, William Brockenbrough, wrote a series of essays against Marshall's opinions in *McCulloch* and *Cohens*, they followed the lead of the counsel for Maryland by turning again to the numerous occasions on which Publius had taken pains to defend the idea of concurrent powers remaining with the states.[38]

Southern writers remained divided as to whether *The Federalist* was better regarded as a problem in its own right or as an authority to be brought to bear against loose construction of the Constitution. In his posthumously published *New Views of the Constitution* (1823), the agrarian apostle and Jeffersonian philosopher John Taylor of Carolina expended over a hundred pages of his tortured prose in an effort to blame Hamilton and Madison, individually and together, for attempting to deny that the states and the union had in fact been meant to act as "coequal" departments, each supreme within its own proper sphere. Like Roane, Taylor emphasized the particular evil of allowing the Supreme Court to exercise appellate jurisdiction over the states. But Taylor went one step further by asserting that the authors of *The Federalist* had attempted to endow the national government with a supremacy that the other framers had never contemplated. The idea of a national supremacy, Taylor alleged, had been rejected by the Federal Convention, but both the pregnant word "national" and its supremacist "progeny were resumed in the Federalist, and have since supplied a foundation for the project of a consolidated supreme government to stand upon."[39]

Later writers—if they managed to wade through his work—may have concluded that Taylor had gone too far. During the nullification crisis of 1828–33, spokesmen for South Carolina revived the tactic of quoting statements such as the one Hamilton had made in *Federalist* 28, when he predicted that "the State governments will in all possible contingencies, afford complete security against invasion of the public liberty by the national authority."[40] But as the theorists of state sovereignty developed greater confidence in their arguments, it became possible to treat *The Federalist* both more neutrally and less seriously. The point, after all, as the Virginia jurist Abel Parker Upshur observed in 1840, was that "The Constitution is much better understood at this day than it was at the time of its adoption." This was "emphatically true of some of its provisions, which were considered at the time as comparatively unimportant, or so plain as not to be misunderstood," but which since had proven "pregnant with the greatest difficulties, and to exert the most important influence upon the whole character of the government."[41] A like opinion was expressed the same year by John C. Calhoun (who would later succeed Upshur as Secretary of State when the Virginian was killed by the explosion of the cannon "Peacemaker" aboard the *Princeton*). Calhoun described *The Federalist* as "the fullest and, in many respects, the best" work on the American system of government, but was quick to add that "it takes many false views and by no means goes to the bottom of the system."[42] By the close of his life, Calhoun seemed to adopt Taylor's view of *The Federalist*, arguing that its "radical and dangerous" errors had "contributed, more than all others combined, to cast a mist over our system of government, and to confound and lead astray the minds of the community as to a true conception of its real character." The motives of its authors, Calhoun conceded, were "above suspicion; but it is a great error to suppose that they could better understand the system they had constructed, and the dangers incident to its operation, than those who came after them."[43]

THE NORTHERN VIEW: JOSEPH STORY

From Tucker to Calhoun, southern commentators were consistently selective and pragmatic in their use of *The Federalist*. The limited number of key passages that could be made to serve the cause of state sovereignty were repeatedly invoked as candid admissions of the modest aims of the framers; but when Publius spoke in terms of national supremacy, his authority was immediately challenged and dismissed. Entirely different was the use made of *The Federalist* by the northern writers whose constitutional commentaries began to appear during the decade after 1825. Their attitude toward the authority of Publius was utterly deferential. Less polemical than their southern counterparts, they took upon themselves the task of expounding both the original text and the growing body of law with which it had been annotated. Their approach to constitutional law was in certain essential ways historical. Unlike Tucker, Roane, and their successors, the northern commentators accepted the decisions of the Marshall Court as valid exercises of judicial power and legitimate efforts either to extend the principles of the Constitution or at least give meaning to its ambiguities and silences.

The role that *The Federalist* played in their work is easy to describe. At one level—the less important—it served as a repository of information about the concerns underlying particular provisions of the Constitution. In this sense Publius could be used as a sourcebook for a careful, clause-by-clause survey of the Constitution, a reliable guide to be quoted when he seemed instructive and ignored when he did not.

But the deeper purpose *The Federalist* could serve became especially apparent in the one work which dominated the field of constitutional law throughout the nineteenth century and arguably into the twentieth as well: Joseph Story's *Commentaries on the Constitution*, first published in three volumes in 1833. Readers of the *Commentaries* have long recognized Story's extensive reliance on Publius, but only when one compares the two texts patiently and systematically does it become possible to confirm that Story had been telling the literal truth when, in June 1831, he informed Chancellor Kent that "I mean to embody in them the *whole substance* of the Federalist."[44] It would barely stretch the point to suggest that Story's *Commentaries* amounted almost to a updated revision of *The Federalist*. Time and again, Story took as his point of departure not only the arguments but the very language—sometimes mildly paraphrased, but more often simply regurgitated—with which Publius had defended the various clauses of the Constitution.

The whole was, however, more than the sum of its parts. Story meant his massive incorporation of *The Federalist* to serve a deeper polemical purpose, which was quite simply to refute the radical notions of state sovereignty that now informed the emerging southern position on the nature of the union—especially as it was being espoused by the nullifiers of South Carolina. Story was prepared to concede that the states had possessed certain (but limited) aspects of sovereignty prior to the Constitution. Such a concession, indeed, had its advantages, for it served to remind his readers of the chaotic conditions that the Constitution had been designed to check. Here was where the massive appeal to *The Federalist* fit his scheme. However many layers of meaning modern readers can unpeel in its essays, its one overriding theme has always been manifest: the necessity of adopting a Constitution superior in every respect to the "imbecility" of the Confederation it had been framed to replace. The condition to which the union would devolve if the arguments of South Carolina were not decisively rejected was precisely the *status quo ante* the adoption of the Constitution.

Story's use of *The Federalist* thus had a purpose exactly opposite to that which had been sought by the advocates of state sovereignty. Whatever concessions Publius had made to true federalism, his argument had always stressed the creation of a new government which, without threatening popular liberty or the rights of the states, would accomplish the purposes for which it had been conceived. By using *The Federalist* to illuminate the diverse considerations that had shaped the careful construction of a new instrument of government, Story persistently emphasized the character of the Constitution as a point of departure and not, as strict constructionists would have it, a confirmation of the paramount and preexisting sovereignty of the states. Against an ahistorical conception of unchanging state sovereignty, Story used *The Federalist* to carry his readers back to the 1780s, using its vivid criticism of the Articles of Confederation to justify the Constitution as a novel, creative act. Readers could hardly ignore the message. As one early reviewer of the *Commentaries* who was sensitive to Story's debt to Publius observed,

> In reading this [that is, *The Federalist*] we are carried back to the anxious days of the confederation, when the whole government was aptly represented in one of the pasquinades of the time, as a sinking edifice, with loosened rafters, which left its inmates open to the rude visitings of every wind of heaven.[45]

As it was in the beginning, so it had become again: for Story, as for Publius, the preservation of a vigorous federal union remained the preeminent goal.

Yet even here the reasoning of *The Federalist* proved susceptible to unexpected uses. It was, of all things, to the tenth *Federalist* that one impassioned delegate felt impelled to turn for support when he spoke in favor of secession before the Virginia state convention of 1861. To a modern reader, the words that James Holcombe quoted seem all too familiar. "The influence of factious leaders may kindle a flame within their particular States," Madison had written, "but will be unable to spead a general conflagration through the other states." "For a long time," Holcombe observed, "the experience of the country attested the justice and sagacity of these anticipations." But now the case was altered: the geographic barriers to factious politics had crumbled; and when the national government was demonstrably controlled by a faction, disunion was justified.[46] This is, perhaps, one of the few interpretations of Madison's essay that remains beyond the pale of modern commentary.

THE LEGACY OF *THE FEDERALIST*

A catalogue of the uses to which *The Federalist* was put during the early decades of the republic can be said to produce results that are at once desultory and predictable—yet also not entirely unrevealing of larger processes. A good case could be made that Joseph Story alone was faithful to the spirit that had informed the entire work of Publius. But the rhetorical uses to which Story's southern antagonists attempted to put particular passages of

The Federalist cannot be dismissed as disingenuous. These writers did not have to strain overmuch to place Publius in opposition to John Marshall and the claims for sweeping national supremacy. A great deal of what might be called authentic federalism was indeed to be found in *The Federalist*. It was there in the letters on taxation, in the emphasis on the enumeration of specific powers, in the predictions that the states would act as barriers against federal usurpation. What made *The Federalist* so valuable to men like Roane and Upshur was simply the fact that to some extent it had been written for men like Roane and Upshur. It was precisely because *The Federalist* had sought to demonstrate that the new national government would not overwhelm the states that it could prove so attractive to theorists of state sovereignty when the progress of broad construction and the rise of antislavery evoked new fears of the dangers of national supremacy.

Though it had been written originally as a partisan tract, and had first found favor among those it had no need of convincing, *The Federalist* had been directed not toward the avowed supporters of the Constitution but toward those who either required persuasion or whose doubts could only be overcome by sustained argument. It should not be surprising, then, that *The Federalist* retained its basic popularity during an era when the meaning of the Constitution it expounded was becoming more controversial and less settled. For in different ways Publius appealed to the two major schools of interpretation. To those who sought to deny or repudiate the history of the Constitution after its adoption, *The Federalist* offered the major concessions of two men known for their nationalism in 1787–88. To their opponents, Publius provided a vivid reminder of the advantages and necessity of union, a reminder no less relevant to the political realities of the 1830s than to those of the 1780s.

Evidence of use is not proof of influence, however. One would be hard pressed to demonstrate that *The Federalist* played anything more than a peripheral role in the constitutional disputes that figured so largely in American politics during the decades leading up to the Civil War. Publius may not have been quite as divided in his mind as Alpheus Mason suggested thirty years ago, but he was sufficiently ambivalent to allow his later readers to attach divergent meanings to his pronouncements. Or perhaps the problem was simply that the tensions in *The Federalist* mirrored ambiguities in the Constitution itself. Thus its use tended to reinforce rather than resolve the original sources of disagreement.

One further irony can be noted. When set against the subtle and detailed level of analyses that characterize contemporary writings on *The Federalist*, the nineteenth-century commentaries seem facile and undiscriminating. (What more can we say, after all, of their failure to appreciate the novelty and significance of *Federalist* 10?) In a curious way, however, our absorption in the teachings of Publius reveals something important about the way in which we now view the period of "the founding." Notwithstanding the peculiar importance that appeals to the original nature of the union had in the political disputes of the antebellum decades, our interest in the original meaning of the Constitution, the original intentions of its framers, and the original understandings of their contemporaries—and thus in *The Federalist*, which touches upon all three—seems in many ways to run far deeper than that felt by the early commentators with whom this essay has been concerned. History, to be sure, had its uses for the antebellum disputants, but they were limited at best. Perhaps because questions about the nature of the federal union had so great an urgency, and perhaps because they had arisen so quickly, the early commentators could not afford to take such limited evidence as they had too seriously. Had Madison's notes of the debates at the Federal Convention been published *before* the alternative positions had hardened, a different pattern of use might have evolved. In their absence, *The Federalist* remained the best source for an "originalist" approach to the Constitution. But the stakes had already been set too high to allow it to be used dispassionately and comprehensively. Under the circumstances of partisan debate, the only use that could be made of it was partial and expedient.

If our appreciation of *The Federalist* is thus richer today than it has been at any point in the past, it is because our distance from the world of the framers has made it both easier and more necessary to reconstruct the assumptions and concerns that shaped their actions. We are used to thinking that the passage of time erodes the importance of the original intentions of lawgivers, but in some ways it may also enable later generations to approach the work of their predecessors with greater intelligence and even empathy. So it has been with *The Federalist*.

13

A Newer Science of Politics: *The Federalist* and American Political Science in the Progressive Era

DENNIS J. MAHONEY

Its third half-century was not a propitious time for *The Federalist*. Between the end of Reconstruction and the beginning of World War II, Publius's work all but disappeared from the discourse of American law, history, and politics.

In the fifty years (1888–1938) between publication of the centennial and sesquicentennial editions of *The Federalist*—when only four other complete American editions were produced, the same number published in 1961 alone—the Supreme Court did not look upon *The Federalist* as the authoritative commentary on the original intention of the framers and ratifiers of the Constitution; nor did the justices turn to it for guidance on controverted questions of constitutional interpretation. According to Charles Pierson's list, published with the 1923 edition, *The Federalist* was cited in only eleven Supreme Court cases between its centennial and the publication of his list, fewer cases than cite *The Federalist* in a typical term as we approach the bicentennial.[1]

In legal commentaries there was a similar void. In Thomas McIntyre Cooley's *The General Principles of Constitutional Law*, first published in 1880 and revised in 1891 and 1898, there are only three references to *The Federalist*.[2] And one of those was made to point out what seemed to Cooley to be an error in Publius's exposition of the veto power.

250

Historians treated *The Federalist* no better. Woodrow Wilson, in his five-volume *History of the American People*, published in 1902, devoted only two paragraphs to *The Federalist*: it was a "masterpiece of letters in the sober kind bred by revolution"; it was destined to become "the chief manual of all students and historians of the constitution"; it comprised "the utterances of statesmen . . . drawn for the nonce out upon the general field of the theory and practice of government." Of its content, Wilson had nothing to say. Andrew C. McLaughlin, in his Pulitzer Prize–winning *Constitutional History of the United States*, published in 1935, allowed one paragraph of text plus three footnotes to *The Federalist*. McLaughlin accounted *The Federalist* "among the few great treatises on government ever published" (largely because it was less "vague, distant, (and) theoretical" than most treatises), but concluded that it probably did not have a great deal of "immediate practical effect" on the outcome of the ratification controversy. Indeed, *The Federalist* had its most important effect "in the days of uncertainty when the fate of the Union seemed to hang in the balance," for, during those days, it was "influential in solving the practical problems of law and government."[3]

Even foreign visitors and commentators were affected. Alexis de Tocqueville, whose *Democracy in America* had been published just before the fiftieth anniversary of *The Federalist*, relied on Publius as an authoritative guide to the American constitutional system, and often quoted from the essays. But James Bryce, whose *American Commonwealth* was published on the centennial of *The Federalist*, referred to the work in only four places.

The problem is to account for the absence of *The Federalist* from the counsels of historians, political scientists, courts, and legal scholars during a period extending roughly from its centennial until its sesquicentennial. I believe that a significant factor in this account is the emergence of a newer science of politics in America, namely professional academic political science. A second problem seems to be to account for the revival of interest in Publius just before the sesquicentennial of *The Federalist*. Of that revival we are the beneficiaries; in the aftermath of that revival we are even now the participants. It seems that the responsibility for reviving interest in *The Federalist* must be laid at what may seem to be an unlikely door.

The Newer Science

Publius claimed that the new federal Constitution of 1787, and therefore the political teaching of *The Federalist*, was based on a new or at least improved science of politics that could achieve the benefits while mitigating the disadvantages of popular government.[4] This improved political science was founded on the political theory of the Declaration of Independence, according to which government is established by the consent of the governed for the security of their equal natural rights; and it relied in the first instance upon institutional arrangements to achieve the ends of government without permitting the government to become oppressive.

Between the centennial and the sesquicentennial of *The Federalist*, a newer political science made its appearance in America, and ultimately came to dominate both the academic study and the practice of politics. The newer science of politics was founded on the political theory of German historicism—according to which, government is the expression of the state, the organic representation of the racial genius of a particular ethnic group—and did not recognize either in theory or in practice any permanent ends of government.

In form the newer science was academic and professional. But the essential difference between the older American tradition of political science and the new academic political science was that the former was based on an understanding of immutable principles—self-evident truths—about the nature of man and of political things, while the latter was based on a notion of evolutionary progress which denied the existence of such principles. Frank J. Goodnow, the founding president of the American Political Science Association (A.P.S.A.), made that clear in the opening paragraph of a book published in 1911:

> The tremendous changes in political and social conditions due to the adoption of improved means of transportation and to the establishment of the factory system have brought with them problems whose solution seems to be impossible under the principles of law which were regarded as both axiomatic and permanently enduring at the end of the nineteenth century. That law was permeated by the theories of social compact and natural right, which in their turn were based upon the conception that society was static rather than dynamic or progressive in character.[5]

The new political science, of which the A.P.S.A. was the organizational embodiment and within which Goodnow was an acknowledged leader, was based upon the conception that society was dynamic *and* progressive.

It would be difficult to understand how the newer science of politics displaced the political science of *The Federalist* without knowing something of its history and character. American academic political science began with one individual, John W. Burgess, America's first real professor of political science. Looking back on his career when he was about ninety years old, Burgess claimed to have formed the resolution to study political science on a dark night of sentry duty during the Civil War:

> I found myself murmuring to myself: is it not possible for man, a being of reason, created in the image of God, to solve the problems of his existence without recourse to the destructive means of physical violence? And then I registered a vow in heaven that if a kind providence would deliver me alive from the perils of the existing war, I would devote my life to teaching men how to live by reason and compromise instead of by bloodshed and destruction.[6]

And then, according to his own account, Burgess set out to discover the science of peace. He enrolled at Amherst College, but the science was not taught there; he then went to Columbia Law School, but the science was not taught there either.

At Columbia, he encountered Francis Lieber, who advised him to go to Europe to continue his quest. Burgess finally discovered political science at the University of Berlin, where the professors were also the officers and advisors of the Prussian government. And he witnessed the efficacy of their political science when he watched the victory parade of the Kaiser and the armies of the newly united German Reich at the end of the Franco-Prussian War.

Burgess—and within a few years a number of other young Americans—brought back to the United States the political science of the German university: the science of identifying the great movements of history as they were revealed in the institutions of the most progressive nation states and of adapting and introducing those institutions in less progressive countries. Progressive nations and institutions were to be identified by the historical-comparative method. It was this orientation and this method that American scholars introduced into American classrooms in the last two decades of the nineteenth century.

In 1880 Burgess established America's first graduate school of political science at Columbia.[7] From that program, and from the program at Johns Hopkins University presided over by Herbert Baxter Adams, came the first professors of political science at dozens of American colleges and universities. From Columbia also came the first organization of American political scientists, the American Academy of Political Science and the first American political science journal, the *Political Science Quarterly*. Under Burgess's direction and sponsorship the young professors produced the first series of textbooks for use in college political science courses. Once political science had become an accepted part of the professional academic establishment, it inevitably became organized. The founding of a national association was the next step. The American Political Science Association was officially organized on December 28, 1904. The rapid acceptance of political science as a separate and legitimate discipline, and the common experience of most of the active members of the profession, gave to the membership of the fledgling association a remarkable homogeneity of viewpoint about what their discipline ought to be and how it ought to proceed.

Like Publius, but unlike most contemporary political scientists, most members of the founding generation of the American political science profession did not regard practical politics as "extrascientific activity"[8] but as the source of direction for their scientific activity and the field upon which that activity was ultimately played out. That attitude was one product of the "revolt" within the discipline against its first parents, which revolt occurred so early and was so thorough that it must be regarded as part of the founding process itself. It is for this reason that Burgess's influence over the discipline, though great, was primarily as a "negative reference."[9] Burgess and Adams had taught their students, in part, to look to local institutions to find the character of the nation. When the students looked at American local institutions, and especially at urban institutions, however, what they saw was corruption, boss rule, and inefficiency. A large number of these students consequently turned their attention to developing methods for reform, and from that orientation emerged the study of public administration.

Throughout the whole period, political science was dominated by an ideology of progress borrowed from German historicism. Human society was envisaged as capable of permanent and perpetual improvement, and the state was the chosen instrument for accomplishing that improvement. This ideology was never challenged within the discipline, and, in fact, continues to dominate the discipline even into its second century. Humanity, culture, economics, and politics are all, according to this doctrine, constantly evolving. Society becomes constantly more complex; and complexity is therefore itself a guarantee of progress. The more complex society becomes, the more government regulation is needed. Regulation is therefore also a guarantee that progress has occurred.

Three forms of the doctrine of progress have exerted influence on and been reflected in the new political science. The first version was imported with academic political science itself from the nineteenth-century German university. Following Hegel, it united absolute faith in inexorable progress with a nearly equal faith in the state. A second version was carried over from the school of philosophy called pragmatism, which relied on human thought and institutionalized planning to supplement and hasten the inevitable course of progress. The third version of the doctrine of progress was that of the Progressive movement in politics, which recognized progress in the eradication of poverty and political oppression and relied on a humane, but interventionist, state to accomplish that eradication.

The common element of the various forms of the doctrine of progress is the notion that there is no good or bad, only new and old. The idea of continuous advance implies that what is most advanced is most preferable, and is therefore to be sought. Political science must therefore consist of the identification of the direction of historical development. To know what is to be sought in politics, one must ask not "how ought we to be governed?" or "what end is to be served by politics?" but "what is the next step in the process of development?" or "what is the next stage of political evolution?"

The most notable practitioner of the newer science of politics was Woodrow Wilson. Wilson treated the state exclusively in historical terms. His treatise, *The State: Elements of Historical and Practical Politics*,[10] bears the subtitle: "A Sketch of Institutional History and Administration." Institutional history provided Wilson with the answers to questions that political philosophers had previously and unavailingly wrestled with:

> This, then, is the sum of the whole matter: the end of government is the facilitation of the objects of society. The rule of governmental action is

necessary cooperation; the method of political development is conservative adaptation, shaping old habits into new ones, modifying old means to accomplish new ends.[11]

In Wilson's analysis, the ends of government were to be discerned from what governments actually did. He began his treatment of the question, "What are the functions of government?" by discoursing on the "nature" of the question.[12] That discourse was an assertion of the "fact-value" distinction:

> It is important to notice at the outset a single general point touching the nature of this question. It is in one aspect obviously a simple *question of fact;* and yet there is another phase of it, in which it becomes as evidently a question of opinion.
> The distinction is important because over and over again the question of fact has been confounded with that widely different question, *"What ought the functions of government to be?"* The two questions should be kept entirely separate in treatment.[13]

Wilson proposed to answer the fact question merely by discovering what functions existing governments actually performed: "When asked, therefore, What are the functions of government? we must ask in return, Of what government? Different states have different conceptions of their duty, and so undertake different things."[14]

Moreover, the different states did not come to have different conceptions of their duty through some process of reflection and choice. Duty and function, like everything else, are the products of history and circumstance. The different states "have had their own peculiar origins, their own characteristic histories; circumstance has moulded them; necessity, interest, or caprice has variously guided them."[15] One searches in vain for a theoretical discussion of the functions of the state or of government in Wilson's writings as a political scientist.

While *The Federalist* purports to put the new science of politics in the service of the purposes of government as explained in the Declaration of Independence, rejection of the Declaration, of its teachings, and of its applicability to our own times, was a necessary part of the foundation of a new American political science. To say as much is neither a naked assertion nor a bold act of interpretation. The founders of the new political science recognized the necessity of freeing American politics from the eighteenth-century conceptions embodied in the Declaration. Hence, W. W. Willoughby declared (quoting approvingly from sociologist Lester Frank Ward):

> Our Declaration of Independence, which recites that Government derives its just powers from the consent of the governed, has already been outgrown. It is no longer the consent, but the positively known will of the governed, from which the government now derives its powers.[16]

And John W. Burgess assessed the significance of the Declaration in this way:

> A nation and a state did not spring into existence through that declaration, as dramatic publicists are wont to express it. . . . The significance of the proclamation was this: a people testified thereby the consciousness of the fact that they had become, in the progressive development of history, one whole, separate, and adult nation, and a national state. . . .[17]

The rejection of the Declaration of Independence took explicit form in the writings of Burgess, Willoughby, Wilson, and others, who dismissed the natural rights thesis and the doctrine of social contract out of hand, and who described the Declaration, if they bothered with it at all, as a tract for its times, a rhetorical incident of the Revolution. The political philosophy of natural rights and social contract, authoritative because of the "laws of Nature and of nature's God," justified the existence of government on the ground that the existence of government made men secure in the enjoyment of what was theirs by nature. For Willoughby, that was nonsense: "The State is justified by its manifest potency as an agent for the progress of mankind."[18]

Wilson did acknowledge that "there are natural and imperative limits to state action."[19] Those limits are the limits of necessity: the objects of government are those for which action on the part of society as a whole is necessary and not merely convenient. This stance Wilson took in opposition to socialist opinions about what government ought to do. Wilson had distinguished the "objects of government" from the "functions of government," the former being matters of opinion, the latter matters of fact to be ascertained by the historical and comparative method.[20] Henry Jones Ford, whom Wilson added to the faculty at Princeton, included among the conclusions of his *Natural History of the State*: "Rights are not innate but are derivative. They exist in the State but not apart from the State." Therefore, contrary to the principles of the Declaration of Independence, wherein it is asserted that governments are instituted among men to secure the enjoyment of natural rights, "the end to which a state, at any given time, should chiefly direct its efforts depends, of course, upon the point that has been reached in its development."[21]

How, then, does the newer science of politics relate to the earlier "new science of politics," the political science of *The Federalist?* Publius's political science was calculated to make government strong enough to protect the citizen in the enjoyment of his life, liberty, and property, and yet not so strong as itself to become a threat to the citizen. Fortunately, the science of politics, like most sciences, had received vast improvement since the days of the ancient republics, and various principles had been discovered that tended to make such a government possible:

> The regular distribution of power into distinct departments; the introduction of legislative balances and checks; the institution of courts composed of judges holding their offices during good behavior; the representation of the people in the legislature by deputies of their own election . . . are means,

and powerful means, by which the excellencies of republican government may be retained and its imperfections lessened or avoided.[22]

To this catalog, of course, Publius adds the device of federation to enlarge the orbit of the government. The political science of *The Federalist* was aimed in part at breaking the violence of factional politics and was intended to thwart factional rule even if the faction comprised a majority of the citizens. The Constitution envisions democratic government in which the majority accepts certain checks upon the exercise of its power: "A dependence on the people is, no doubt, the primary control of the government; but experience has taught mankind the necessity of auxiliary precautions."[23]

It is perhaps an indication of the success of Publius's political science that the founders of the newer American political science did not perceive the problem of majority faction as a major threat to free government. The constitutional limits of majority rule—Publius's "auxiliary precautions"—were perceived as limiting majority rule and, therefore, as curtailing democracy.

The vanguard of the attack on the Constitution was led by J. Allen Smith and Charles A. Beard. The former asserted[24] and the latter affected to demonstrate[25] that the Constitution was written with the object of protecting the economic interests of a particular class. According to Smith and Beard, the Constitution was framed for the purpose of frustrating just such attempts at political reform and economic regulation as were frustrated on constitutional grounds during the early years of the Progressive era. The effect of their critique of the Constitution was described, in somewhat extravagant terms, by the liberal intellectual historian V. L. Parrington:

> With the flood of light thrown upon the fundamental law by the historians, the movement of liberalism passed quickly through successive phases of thought. After the first startled surprise it set about the necessary business of acquainting the American people with its findings in the confident belief that a democratic electorate would speedily democratize the instrument. Of this first stage the late Professor J. Allen Smith's *The Spirit of American Government* (1907) was the most adequate expression, a work that greatly influenced the program of the rising Progressive Party. But changes came swiftly and within half a dozen years the movement had passed from political programs to economic, concerned not so greatly with political democracy as with economic democracy. Of this second phase Professor Beard's *An Economic Interpretation of the Constitution* (1913) was the greatest intellectual achievement.[26]

Parrington attributed to Smith and Beard "the discovery that the drift toward plutocracy was not a drift away from the spirit of the Constitution, but an inevitable unfolding from its premises."[27]

But crude economic determinism was not the preferred mode of analysis in the new political science. From the point of view of the politics of progress, the crucial defect of the Constitution, and therefore of *The Federalist*'s science of politics, was not economic, but chronological. It was simply impossible for eighteenth-century man to address the needs of twentieth-century man. (The same argument is familiar in our time in the vulgar form: "Madison did not have the atomic bomb to worry about.")

One of the imperatives for the new political science, as its practitioners understood it, was to replace eighteenth-century superstition with twentieth-century knowledge about political things. The superior understanding available to the twentieth century would render unnecessary the precautions of the founders. Despite the efforts of Smith, Beard, and their followers, it was not thought necessary to assume that the authors of the Constitution had other than the purest motives, for it was not their motives, but their science, which was ultimately to blame. Acceptance of the Smith–Beard critique would, seemingly, require restructuring the American government to remove the class bias inherent in the Constitution. But the newer science of politics offered an alternative: reform according to a scientific understanding of politics and administration.

Woodrow Wilson, writing in 1885, already understood that the attitude of the new political science represented a radical change in the self-understanding of the American regime:

> We are the first Americans to hear our own countrymen ask whether the Constitution is still adapted to serve the purposes for which it was intended; the first to entertain any serious doubts about the superiority of our own institutions as compared with the systems of Europe; the first to think of reorganizing the administrative machinery of the federal government . . . .[28]

Indeed, the whole of Wilson's book answers the description just provided, and it ends with a ringing appeal to replace the "political witchcraft" of the Constitution with the "expedients necessary to make self-government among us a straight-forward thing of simple method, single, unstinted power, and clear responsibility."[29] Wilson's reference to "political witchcraft" may seem a bit flippant, but it was meant to indicate the relationship that the prescientific politics of the framers of the Constitution had to the political science of the Progressive era.

The critique of the Constitution was by no means limited to the radicals and Progressives; it permeated the whole of the new political science. John W. Burgess, for example, in suggesting that the amending process be simplified to make it more responsive to national majorities, wrote that "development is as much a law of state life as existence. Prohibit the former, and the latter is the existence of the body after the spirit has departed."[30] He declared himself in sympathy with those jurists and publicists (i.e., writers on public law) who were "beginning to feel, and rightly too, that present considerations, relations and requirements should be the chief consideration."[31]

The younger generation of political scientists, caught up as they were in the Progressive movement, criticized the Constitution more directly as being outmoded by the progress of society and technology. The Constitution had been written by and for men who were innocent of technological progress, of urbanization and industrialization, and could not have foreseen, let alone provided for, life under the conditions that would prevail at the beginning of the twentieth century.

Goodnow challenged the various auxiliary precautions of American constitutional government severally as incompatible with the exigencies of the modern era. Regarding the separation of powers:

> The force of the principle as a rule of law is also being weakened. With the development of the more complex conditions characteristic of modern life, it has been felt imperitive [sic] to depart at any rate from the strict application of the principle.[32]

Goodnow referred here primarily to the creation of administrative offices and agencies that are vested with the legislative power to make ordinances with the force of law, or with the judicial power to decide individual cases applying statutes or ordinances, or with both.

Nothing so much characterizes Goodnow's political science as his rejection of the doctrine of separation of powers in favor of a separation of politics from administration. The great mistake of the Founding Fathers, he maintained, was their acceptance of Montesquieu's teaching that executive, legislative, and judicial functions should be carried out by different officers or bodies in the government. But this mistake was one to which the founders were impelled by the times in which they lived.

> At the time our early constitutions, including the national Constitution, were framed, this principle of the separation of powers with its corollary, the separation of authorities, was universally accepted in this country.[33]

Goodnow's general position in *Social Reform and the Constitution* was optimistic with respect to judicial review. Although many, perhaps most, of the reforms he thought desirable or necessary ran counter to his understanding of the intention of the framers of the Constitution, he believed that the judiciary, and especially the Supreme Court of the United States, would so interpret the Constitution as to find those reforms constitutional. For Goodnow accepted what is now termed the notion of a "living Constitution," that is, the Constitution understood as a malleable mass of general good intentions available to be shaped by the courts to provide authority for desired measures. However, Goodnow was disappointed that the courts did not, as of 1911, understand the nation's predicament to be as grave as he did.

A constant ally of Goodnow's was Woodrow Wilson. Throughout Wilson's career, at least as a political scientist, he sought the twin goals of democracy and efficiency. In 1901, he published an article under the title

"Democracy and Efficiency"[34] in which he argued that if a country's legislative authority were democratic it had no reason to fear efficiency in its administrative authority. In that article, Wilson criticized the framers of the American Constitution for being overly cautious in making dispersion of authority the rule of the government: "We printed the *SELF* large and the *government* small in almost every administrative arrangement we made."[35]

In *Constitutional Government*, Wilson wrote that "governments have their natural evolution and are one thing in one age, another in another."[36] It is clear that he believed that the United States had passed into an age much different from that in which the Constitution was framed, and one in which the ideas and intentions of the framers had been superseded:

> The makers of the Constitution constructed the federal government upon a theory of checks and balances which was meant to limit the operation of each part and allow to no single part or organ of it a dominating force; but no government can be successfully conducted upon so mechanical a theory.[37]

The problem that the framers had was that they were saddled, however unconsciously, with an obsolete world view:

> The government of the United States was constructed upon the Whig theory of political dynamics, which was an unconscious copy of the Newtonian theory of the universe. In our own day, whenever we discuss the structure or development of a thing, whether in nature or in society, we consciously or unconsciously follow Mr. Darwin; but before Mr. Darwin they followed Newton.[38]

To say this, however, is no different, in Wilson's view, from simply saying (consciously or unconsciously following Darwin) that America has a form of constitutional government. The end of constitutional government, in Wilson's "Darwinian" understanding, is to have no end:

> The object of constitutional government is to bring the active, planning will of each part of the government into accord with the prevailing popular thought and need, and thus make it an impartial instrument of symmetrical national development; and to give to the operation of the government thus shaped under the influence of opinion and adjusted to the general interest both stability and an incorruptible efficiency. Whatever institutions, whatever practices serve these ends [sic!], are necessary to such a system; those which do not, or which serve it [sic] imperfectly, should be dispensed with or bettered.[39]

There is perhaps no better statement of the difference between *The Federalist*'s political science and the newer science of politics concerning the significance of constitutional government than this.

If it is so that constitutionalism is nothing other than stability and efficiency in carrying out the national will and expediting the national development, then the task of political science is to determine the necessary conditions for stability and efficiency. The first step toward success in that new political science is the task of organization. The next step is the determination, individually or, better, collectively, of the method best calculated to produce practical results. Finally, the organization and the methodology must be put to work in the solution of the problem of constitutional government, that is, the problem of stability and efficiency. To that end, the science of politics must produce its corollary, the science of administration. And production of a science of administration was the major objective of Wilson's career as a political scientist.

Wilson was one of the few practitioners of the new political science who actually named *The Federalist* as his adversary. For example, in 1885, in complaining about the perverse hold of *The Federalist* on the study of government:

> [T]hose incomparable papers of the "Federalist," . . . though they were written to influence only the voters of 1788, still, with a strange, persistent longevity of power, shape the constitutional criticism of the present day, obscuring much of that development of constitutional practice which has since taken place. The Constitution in operation is manifestly a very different thing from the Constitution of the books.[40]

And, sixteen years later, with respect to the theory of government:

> The admirable expositions of the *Federalist* read like thoughtful applications of Montesquieu to the political needs and circumstances of America. They are full of the theory of checks and balances. . . . Politics is turned into mechanics under his touch. The theory of gravitation is supreme. . . . The trouble with the theory is that government is not a machine but a living thing. It falls, not under the theory of the universe, but under the theory of organic life. It is accountable to Darwin, not to Newton.[41]

Although Wilson called *The Federalist* "incomparable,"[42] "most striking,"[43] "most notable,"[44] "admirable,"[45] "thoughtful,"[46] etc., he thought its political science fatally flawed by a complete misunderstanding of the nature of political life.

REVIVAL

From the point of view of one interested in the influence of *The Federalist* on the theory and practice of American government in the last part of the nineteenth and first part of the twentieth centuries, surely the most important event was the publication of Charles Beard's *An Economic Interpretation of the Constitution of the United States* in 1913, and the second most important event was the republication of the same book in 1935. In a perverse way, Beard was probably more responsible than anyone else for the revival of interest in *The Federalist* in the twentieth century. Moreover,

Beard must be given at least partial credit for the revivification of Publius-Madison. Henry Cabot Lodge and others had not only stolen, as Douglass Adair wrote, fifteen of Madison's essays and attributed them to Hamilton, they had even tried to steal the very personality of Publius for their hero. In Lodge's words:

> In this great work [Hamilton] was much assisted by Madison and slightly by Jay, both of whom brought ability, training, and sound sense to the task. There has been some controversy as to the proportionate share of these eminent men in this undertaking, but the discussion is of little moment. The original conception was Hamilton's, he wrote considerably more than half the numbers, and to posterity "Publius" will always be Hamilton.[47]

Beard snatched back from Lodge and from posterity at least an equal share in Publius's personality and restored it to Madison by treating Madison's Number 10 as the epitome of *The Federalist* and as "the most philosophical examination of the foundations of political science."[48]

The idea of an economic interpretation of the Constitution did not originate with Beard. It did not originate with J. Allen Smith, either, but Smith first gave the economic interpretation currency during the Progressive era, and Beard gave Smith credit for exposing "the underlying political science of the Constitution."[49] But Smith did not trust *The Federalist* to reveal that underlying political science. Quoting from Number 85, he showed that Publius admitted that the Anti-Federalists had charged the "wealthy (and) well-born" with "unwarrantable concealments and misrepresentations."[50] Smith agreed: "The advocates of the new form of government did not propose to defeat their own plans by declaring their real purpose—by explaining the Constitution to the people as they themselves understood it."[51]

Beard, of course, was to claim that that is just what they did. The key sixth chapter of the *Economic Interpretation* in fact relies on *The Federalist*'s explanation of the Constitution. Smith had argued that *The Federalist* was untrustworthy as a guide to the meaning of the Constitution or the intentions of its framers, but Beard treated *The Federalist* as definitive of that meaning and of those intentions. The sixth chapter of the *Economic Interpretation* represents the longest sustained treatment of *The Federalist* to have been published up to its day.

According to Beard, *The Federalist* "presents in a relatively brief and systematic form an economic interpretation of the Constitution by the men best fitted . . . to expound the political science of the new government."[52] The rhetoric of *The Federalist* consisted of appeals to the economic interests of the various groups that would be represented at the state ratifying conventions. "Indeed," wrote Beard, "every appeal in it is to some material and substantial interest."[53] Beard found the explanation of this rhetoric in *Federalist* 10, which he took to be a complete statement of the underlying political science not only of *The Federalist* but also of the Constitution itself. The discussion of faction, and of the different and unequal distribution of property as the chief cause of faction, he treats as a frank admission of the class-based politics of the framers.

Although Beard professed to find the principles of Publius's political science in *Federalist* 10, he did not accept the proposition that the extended republic was *The Federalist*'s solution to the problem of faction. Beard could not accept the idea that there could be so great a multiplicity of interests that a majority faction would be difficult, if not impossible, to assemble. Indeed, Beard seems to have regarded the propertyless many as a homogeneous class—a ready-made and permanent majority faction—and the real object of Publius's and the framers' concern. The political science of *The Federalist*, in Beard's interpretation, was designed to keep that permanent majority faction from exercising real political power.

The device by which this goal was to be achieved was not extension of the sphere but the separation of powers. "The structure of the government as devised at Philadelphia . . . makes improbable any danger to the minority from the majority,"[54] and so provides "propertied interests" an "immunity from control by parliamentary majorities."[55] Beard credited the framers with a marvelous ingenuity:

> If we examine carefully the delicate instrument by which the framers sought to check certain kinds of positive action that might be advocated to the detriment of established and acquired rights, we cannot help marvelling at their skill. Their leading idea was to break up the attacking forces at the starting point: the source of political authority for the several branches of government.[56]

For the economic interpretation of the separation of powers, Beard's ostensible source was *Federalist* 51. But, although he quoted Publius to the effect that society itself will be divided into many parts, interests, and classes, so that majority combinations will afford little danger, Beard himself concluded that the institutions of government were being divided so as to prevent the majority combination that must exist from exercising power.

Curiously, though, it is not even the separation of powers, but rather judicial review that is the "keystone" of the constitutional system in Beard's view. "Certainly," he wrote, "the authors of *The Federalist* entertained no doubts on the point,"[57] and, with that introduction, he quoted a full page from *Federalist* 78. The efficacy of judicial review was tied, in Beard's reading of *The Federalist*, to the contract clause of Article I, Section 10. That clause, along with the clause prohibiting the states from issuing paper money as legal tender, "appealed to every money lender, to every holder of public paper, to every man who had any personalty at stake."[58] Beard asserted that "the authors of *The Federalist* advance in support of these two clauses very substantial arguments which bear out" the view he expressed, and he cited, in particular, *Federalist* 44.[59]

The prohibitions on the states were but one part of the scheme for government by the commercial class; the other part was the conferral of power on the new national government. According to Beard, only a few important powers were granted the new government, and all of those were intended to secure class interests:

> These are the great powers conferred on the new government: taxation, war, commercial control, and disposition of western lands. Through them public creditors might be paid in full, domestic peace maintained, advantages obtained in dealing with foreign nations, manufactures protected, and the development of territories go forward with full swing. The remaining powers are minor . . . .[60]

For the economic interpretation of this aspect of the Constitution, Beard again relied upon *The Federalist*. The advantages of indirect taxation were found in *Federalist* 12, the uses of military power for the protection and expansion of commerce in *Federalist* 4 and 11, the corresponding use of military power to suppress "class war" at home in *Federalist* 21, and the authority of Congress under the commerce clause to "institute protective and discriminatory laws in favor of American interests, and to create a wide sweep for free trade throughout the whole American empire" in *Federalist* 34 and 43.[61]

Alone among the political scientists and historians of the Progressive era, Beard turned to *The Federalist* for guidance about the principles of political science underlying the arrangement of institutions in the American government. To answer Beard, it was necessary for would-be defenders of the American regime to read *The Federalist* and to try to understand anew the science of politics improved and applied by Publius. This process of recovering the real *Federalist* was the work of Douglass Adair and Martin Diamond.

14

Was the Founding an Accident?

EDWARD C. BANFIELD

> To balance a large state or society, whether monarchical or republican, on general laws, is a work of so great difficulty that no human genius, however comprehensive, is able, by the mere dint of reason and reflection, to effect it.
>
> David Hume, quoted in the final
> paragraph of *The Federalist*

"It has been frequently remarked," Publius observes in the first paragraph of *Federalist* 1, "that it seems to have been reserved to the people of this country, by their conduct and example, to decide the important question, whether societies of men are really capable or not of establishing good government from reflection and choice, or whether they are forever destined to depend for their political constitutions on accident and force." In another essay (*Federalist* 38) he recalls that among the ancients government (perhaps not *good* government?) had sometimes been established with deliberation and consent. In all of these cases, however, he remarks, the framing of the government was done by some one citizen of recognized wisdom and integrity. In the United States, the draft constitution was made by a convention; it was the product of a political process. The political process would continue in each of the states to decide, by reflection or otherwise, whether or not to ratify the proposed constitution.

Accidents of history—"as if it was the design of Providence," Publius says in *Federalist* 2—gave some grounds for thinking that the American people might do what no people had ever done. The Americans, Publius writes, were

> one united people—a people descended from the same ancestors, speaking the same language, professing the same religion, attached to the same principles of government, very similar in their manners and customs, and who, by their joint counsels, arms, and efforts, fighting side by side throughout a long and bloody war, have nobly established their general liberty and independence. [*Federalist* 2, p. 38]

But for these and other accidents of history one might well have said of the American outlook for government what John Adams said of Condorcet's scheme to establish democracy in France: ". . . as absurd as similar plans would be to establish democracies among the birds, beasts, and fishes."[1] Even with so many favoring circumstances the outcome was highly uncertain.

THE NATURE OF MAN

Publius did not expect a good government to be created by reflection even in America. "Happy will it be," he goes on in *Federalist* 1,

> if our choice should be directed by a judicious estimate of our true interests, unperplexed and unbiased by considerations not connected with the public good. *But this is a thing more ardently to be wished than seriously to be expected.* [*Federalist* 1, p. 33]

The words I have emphasized he repeats in *Federalist* 2.

The proposed constitution, Publius explains, "affects too many particular interests, innovates upon too many local institutions, not to involve in its discussion a variety of objects foreign to its merits, and of views, passions, and prejudices little favorable to the discovery of truth." In the following paragraphs, and, indeed, throughout *The Federalist*, he explains why it cannot be expected that a good government will be established by reflection and choice: it is the nature of men to have divergent opinions and interests, and to subordinate the common good to their private and particular interests. Providence may have designed this country as an inheritance to a band of brothers. But the harsh fact is that American society—any society— is not a band of brothers but a set of competitors. Man is a creature more of passion than of reason; he is vain, avaricious, shortsighted. "The history of almost all the great councils and consultations," he writes in *Federalist* 37,

> held among mankind for reconciling their discordant opinions, assuaging their mutual jealousies, and adjusting their respective interests, is a history of factions, contentions, and disappointments, and may be classed among the most dark and degrading pictures which display the infirmities and

depravities of the human character. If in a few scattered instances a brighter aspect is presented, they serve only as exceptions to admonish us of the general truth; and by their luster to darken the gloom of the adverse prospect to which they are contrasted.[2]

Among British philosophers and statesmen this had long been the predominant view of the nature of man and society. It had never been that of the Calvinists who settled New England, however. They were Old Testament people, in covenant with God and, as saints, with each other.[3] Long before 1776 the covenant idea had become secularized; a political society was seen as an entity with respect to which the individuals had a covenantal relationship; it possessed a collective interest to which the interests of individuals were subordinate: it was a moral person, endowed with a will of its own, a will which should prevail over the wills of persons. That the collective will often did *not* prevail became an increasingly conspicuous fact of life. Nevertheless, that the common good *ought* to prevail was the almost universally accepted ideal. As Gordon S. Wood has written, "The sacrifice of individual interests to the greater good of the whole formed the essence of republicanism and comprehended for Americans the idealistic goal of their Revolution."[4]

During and, especially, after the Revolution the state legislatures passed legal tender, paper money, debt installment, and other laws serving special interests—debtors, creditors, merchants, religious sects—with little or no regard to the rights of individuals or the promotion of the common good.[5] "Everyone knows," Publius writes in *Federalist* 46, "that a great proportion of the errors committed by the State legislatures proceeds from the disposition of the members to sacrifice the comprehensive and permanent interest of the State to the particular and separate views of the counties or districts in which they reside" (p. 296). Can it be imagined, he asks, that members of the legislatures will be any more attached to national objects?

Publius consistently deplores faction, which he defines (*Federalist* 10) as action "adverse to the rights of other citizens, or to the *permanent and aggregate interests of the community*" (emphasis added). Except in his final essay, however, where he says that disregarding particular interests is a duty from which nothing can give a man dispensation, he does not call upon men to act contrary to their interests. To do so he would have thought a waste of words, for the causes of faction are (*Federalist* 10) "sown in the nature of man," the diversity of whose faculties is "an insuperable obstacle to a uniformity of interests."[6] One might show men where their real interests lie and one might sometimes contrive matters to make their interest coincide with their duty (*Federalist* 72). But with the exception of the few men of "superlative virtue" (*Federalist* 75), it had to be expected that interest would prevail.

In Publius's view, there existed a common good, and no action could properly be called rational that did not at least aim at securing it. But the nature of man being what it was—"much more disposed to vex and oppress each other than to cooperate for their common good"—factional struggle was inevitable. Conceivably such struggle might yield an outcome that left every particular interest fully satisfied. From the standpoint of the common good, which no one had intended, that would be an accident—a very happy one, of course, but nonetheless an accident.[7]

THE PHILADELPHIA CONVENTION

Providence favored the efforts of the people of the United States to form a more perfect union by, among other things, favoring the Convention that gathered in Philadelphia to—as it turned out—draft a constitution. The number of delegates was neither too large nor too small (of the seventy-four chosen, fifty-five came, of these some serving briefly or intermittently); most were young men (four were under thirty, and more than one-third were in their thirties); most were politically experienced (thirty-nine had served or were serving in Congress); two carried immense national prestige (Washington and Franklin); and about a dozen others were men of extraordinary intellectual gifts (most notably Madison, Hamilton, and Wilson). It was an accident that certain others did *not* serve as delegates. Adams and Jefferson, whose presence would surely have overloaded the Convention, were abroad. (Jefferson would not have stood for the secrecy rule, and it is hard to believe that without it any sort of agreement could have been reached.) Eight or nine Anti-Federalists who had been appointed delegates refused to serve (it was "pretty clear," Richard Henry Lee, one of them, later wrote, that if they had been present the draft Constitution would not have had its "consolidating effect").[8] Of the delegates who did attend, some were back-benchers, willing to let the leaders decide (judging from Madison's notes, half a dozen said not a single word before the final session), while two delegates—Washington and Franklin—were national figures. Washington's prestige was immense: it was generally assumed that he would be the first President, and this had its effects in Philadelphia and in the ratifying conventions that followed.[9]

Two other delegates—Lansing and Yates of New York—seem to have come to Philadelphia in the hope of preventing the formation of a stronger government. The other delegates doubtless desired to create a more perfect union, but for some this meant a government that would have special advantages for their states. It was unrealistic—utopian—to expect agreement upon the concrete meaning of the common good.[10] As Publius later remarked (*Federalist* 26), "the spirit of party in different degrees must be expected to infect all political bodies. . . ."

For several weeks it seemed that agreement would be reached on the essentials of the Virginia Plan, which would, in effect, supplant the states. Ending their power was a principal, perhaps *the* principal, object of Madison and certain other leading figures of the Convention, among them Washington, James Wilson, and Gouverneur Morris.[11]

This, however, was not to be. The Convention soon gave Wilson occasion to recall that in the first Congress the sentiment at first was that the states were no more: "We are now one nation of brethren. We must bury all local interests and distinctions. This language continued for some time. The tables at length began to turn. No sooner were the state governments formed than their jealousy and ambition began to display themselves. Each endeavored to cut a slice from the common loaf, to add to its own morsel, til at length the confederation became frittered down to the impotent condition in which it now stands."[12] Franklin too was disappointed. "I must own," he told the Convention, "that I was originally of opinion it would be better if every member of Congress, or our national Council, were to consider himself rather as a representative of the whole, than as an Agent for the interests of a particular state; . . . But as I find this is not be be expected. . . ."[13] A month later Gouverneur Morris found that the states had many representatives on the floor but few were to be deemed representatives of America.[14]

The state governments were political realities that could not be brushed aside for the sake of any common interest. Publius, describing in *Federalist* 1 the obstacles in the way of ratification of a draft constitution, gave an *ex post* account of forces at work within the Convention: "the obvious interest of a class of men in every State to resist all changes which may hazard a diminution of the power, emolument and consequence of the offices they hold under the State establishments; and the perverted ambition of another class of men, who will either hope to aggrandize themselves by the confusions of their country, or will flatter themselves with fairer prospects of elevation from the subdivision of the empire into several partial confederacies than from its union under one government."

The Convention appeared about to founder on the issue of state representation in the national legislature. Madison would compromise, he said, if he could do it on "correct principles." But this was impossible, for "if the old fabric of the confederation must be the ground-work of the new, we must fail."[15] The next day the celebrated Franklin intervened to say that the proceedings were "a melancholy proof of the imperfection of Human Understanding" and to call (unsuccessfully) for daily prayer. Without the aid of God, he warned, "We shall be divided by our little partial local interests" with the result that "mankind may hereafter from this unfortunate instance, despair of establishing Governments by Human Wisdom and leave it to chance, war and conquest."[16]

Everything, then, hung on a motion to give the states equal representation in the second house. The result of that vote, the late Herbert J. Storing has written, "seems to suggest that Franklin's prayer for Divine Providence was not altogether fruitless, though human reason also played its part." The Maryland delegation was divided. "Providentially," Storing writes, one of that delegation was late in taking his seat; because of this the state's vote went in favor of the motion. This made the count five states for and five against when the rollcall reached Georgia, which was expected to vote against. "By chance or Providence," as Storing puts it, two Georgia delegates were absent, making it possible for a third, one who by chance or Providence was a native of Connecticut, to divide the state's vote, thus maintaining the tie and the possibility of compromise.[17]

Compromise, however, did not seem at all likely. Lansing and Yates chose this moment to walk out of the Convention, presumably in the hope that others would follow. Washington, writing to Hamilton, declared that he "*almost*" despaired of a favorable outcome "and do therefore repent of having had any agency in the business."[18]

A few days later another vote was taken. To the surprise of all but a few insiders, this time the compromise was accepted. Rutledge of South Carolina and Sherman of Connecticut had privately struck a deal: South Carolina would help Connecticut protect its large land claims in the Ohio country if Connecticut would support it on the issues of slave trade and exports. "And thus," writes Forrest McDonald, "*almost by accident*, was created the magnificent system of checks and balances of the United States Constitution" (emphasis added).[19]

Madison, who had come to Philadelphia intending to all but kill the states, was bitterly disappointed that they were left very much alive. Curiously, neither he nor his opponents realized that the supremacy clause, the necessary-and-proper clause, and judicial review, operating together, must insure the supremacy of the national government.[20] Their failure to see that what they had done they had also undone must be counted an accident of even greater consequence than the Connecticut Compromise.

Madison suffered another disappointment when, under threat that South Carolina and Georgia would not join the Union, the Convention denied Congress the power for twenty years to prohibit the importation of slaves. "Twenty years," Madison protested, "will produce all the mischief that can be apprehended from the liberty to import slaves. So long a term will be more dishonorable to the national character than to say nothing about it in the Constitution."[21] But the vote went against him, seven states to four.

That the Convention did not break up without producing any plan was (in McDonald's words) almost by accident. Moreover the plan produced was itself an accident, an outcome no one intended, one derived not from principles held in common but from the ability of one side to force the other to accept its terms. Madison and Hamilton both believed that the Convention had failed to produce a good government or even one capable of governing. "I hazard an opinion," Madison wrote Jefferson, "that the plan, *should it be adopted*, will neither effectually *answer* its *national object*, nor prevent the local *mischiefs* which everywhere *excite disgusts* agst. the *State Governments*."[22] Hamilton told the Convention that no man's ideas were more remote from the plan proposed than his.[23]

THE STRUGGLE FOR RATIFICATION

Madison and Hamilton preferred the draft constitution to its alternative, which Hamilton said was "anarchy and Convulsion."[24] Publius, however, while acknowledging (in *Federalist* 37) that the Convention ". . . must have been compelled to sacrifice theoretical propriety to the force of extraneous considerations," found it impossible for a pious man not to see in the fact of agreement "a finger of [the] Almighty hand. . . ." Madison, writing from New York at the end of October (using a phrase from *Federalist* 1, which had appeared just three days before), admitted that ". . . if any Constitution is to be established by deliberation and choice, it must be examined with many allowances. . . ."[25]

The draft constitution was to be sent to Congress with the suggestion that it be submitted to popularly elected conventions in the states. If nine states ratified it, it would become binding; other states might join the union later if they chose. Publius had good reason to believe that if the popular vote was heavy, there would be a large majority opposed to adoption. Even with a light vote, the Federalists (as nationalists now called themselves) were by no means sure of winning the required nine states. However it turned out, the process would not be one of reflection and choice. As Publius pointed out in *Federalist* 1, in all previous cases of great national discussion, "a torrent of angry and malignant passions" had been let loose. This would surely happen again; whatever the outcome it might be determined by these passions.

As it turned out, the popular vote was light: of the approximately 640,000 adult males eligible to vote, only about 30 percent did so, and this 30 percent were more favorable to the draft constitution than were the other 70 percent.[26] Here again chance and Providence were at work: a disproportionate share of the nonvoters were backwoodsmen who wanted little or no government, who saw no newspapers and were out of touch with affairs, and who could not get to the polls without great expense of time and trouble; whereas a disproportionate share of the voters lived in towns and were engaged in activities somehow related to commerce and trade. As Publius observed in *Federalist* 6, personal considerations sometimes play a part in the production of great national events. If Shays had not been "a *desperate* debtor," he said by way of illustration, "it is much to be doubted whether Massachusetts would have been plunged into a civil war." (Publius misses no opportunity to mention Shays, whose Rebellion had frightened the more prosperous elements of the electorate in several states.)

By the end of the second week of 1788 five states—Delaware, Pennsylvania, New Jersey, Georgia, and Connecticut—had ratified the draft constitution. Accident and force had played some part in two of these. In Pennsylvania, Anti-Federalists, in order to gain a delay that might have been decisive, absented themselves from the legislature to prevent a quorum: a band of Federalist searchers "forcibly dragged" two of the absentees back in the nick of time.[27] In Georgia an Indian uprising opportunely reminded voters of what they might gain from the existence of a national government.[28]

Massachusetts came next. The outlook there, Madison thought, was "very ominous." Convention delegates, chosen by special town meetings, were mostly uninstructed, which meant that the Convention would be wide open. Two very influential delegates—Samuel Adams and Governor John Hancock—were known to dislike the Constitution. The Federalist managers, however, were skillful politicians. First they tricked Adams with a staged "mass meeting" into supposing that his supporters among the ordinary people of Boston favored ratification. Then they flattered Hancock with the suggestion that, if Virginia failed to ratify, he might become the first President. Finally, they got him to present to the Convention as his own nine proposed amendments, all of them dear to Anti-Federalist hearts, with the promise that when the Constitution had been adopted they would soon be made part of it.[29] These maneuvers secured ratification by a vote of 187 to 168. Ten country rubes, unswayed by the histrionics of Hancock, McDonald writes, could have stopped the campaign for ratification dead in its tracks.[30]

Federalist worries deepened in March when elections in North Carolina returned delegates who opposed ratification by more than two to one and again in April when Rhode Islanders voted ten to one against ratification in a referendum.

The Federalists feared that Maryland, which also voted in April, might follow New Hampshire's example by postponing a decision; this, Washington wrote, would be seen as "tantamount to a rejection. . . ."[31] The Anti-Federalists proved ill-organized, however, and the Convention ratified the Constitution by a large majority. In South Carolina the Anti-Federalists failed by a single vote to prevent the calling of a convention; in the Convention, however, the Constitution was ratified by a two to one majority. When in June the New Hampshire convention reconvened, many towns, influenced perhaps by the example of Massachusetts and by the efforts of Federalist political missionaries, had changed their delegates' instructions. The vote was to ratify, fifty-seven to forty-seven.

The necessary nine states had now ratified. The Federalist victory was technical, however, inasmuch as two crucial states, Virginia and New York, had not yet voted. If Virginia were to vote against, Washington, not being a citizen of the United States, could not be President, a calamity which might end the Union before it began. Luckily, Richard Henry Lee, a formidable opponent of the draft, fell ill and could not attend the Convention. Patrick Henry, a no less formidable opponent, dominated the Convention with his oratory for twenty-three days, causing Madison to write Hamilton that, although the Federalists had a majority of three or four votes, he feared they might not prevail.[32] Eventually, they did prevail, eighty-nine to seventy-nine.

New York was hardly less important. There the Antis held a large majority of the delegates. They were shaken when Hamilton suggested that if New York State failed to ratify New York City would secede and ratify by itself, and they were thrown into confusion when news came that Virginia had ratified. Before they could rally, the Federalists had won by three votes.

While the New York convention was still under way, the North Carolina delegates met briefly to reject the Constitution by an overwhelming majority. The new government was a going concern before North Carolina and Rhode Island (the latter by a vote of thirty-four to thirty-two) finally voted to join the Union.

The success of the Federalists in securing ratification in the face of widespread opposition is to be accounted for not by the strength of their arguments, but by their organizational talents and, perhaps even more, by a timely movement of the business cycle. The Anti-Federalists, whose outlook tended to be local rather than cosmopolitan, showed themselves incapable of mounting a national—or, in some instances, even a statewide—campaign against ratification. By contrast, the Federalists, with Washington in the background and Madison in the foreground, made and carried out a national strategy. Publius's writings, although an element of that strategy, had little or no direct effect on the vote in any state.[33] This must not have surprised Publius, who believed (*Federalist* 6) that "general or remote considerations of policy, utility, or justice" invariably have less influence than do "momentary passions and immediate interests."

But perhaps the decisive factor affecting ratification was the business cycle. In 1788–89 there was an upturn in business, one widespread enough to bring prosperity to shippers, farmers, and merchants.[34] Perhaps it was the prospect of ratification that caused the upturn rather than the upturn that caused the ratification, but very likely the causal stream ran in both directions at once.

STATESMEN AND POLITICIANS

The founders congratulated each other—after giving due credit to the Almighty—on the making and adoption of a new Constitution without the use of force. But unless the word "force" is taken in its narrowest meaning, their self-congratulations were not justified. Allowing for some important exceptions, the "compromises" of the Constitution were not compromises at all: they were forced concessions. As Publius observes in *Federalist* 22, under unanimity rule a majority must conform to the wishes of a pertinacious minority if it wants to get anything done. On the two greatest issues the delegates confronted in Philadelphia—the scope of the national power and the future of slavery—pertinacious minorities required the majority to concede to them or else accept the perceived alternative, "anarchy and Confusion." One who thinks that this was compromise must think that a victim compromises if he hands over his money when presented with the alternatives: "Your money or your life."

It is going too far to say of the Convention that it was just another political struggle. Many delegates were indeed politicians acting on behalf of more or less opposed parochial interests. Some, however, were statesmen, guided by moral-political principles, having a wide perspective of present and future reality, and possessed of a conception of the common good. Left to themselves the statesmen could doubtless have reached agreement by reasonable discussion on the concrete implications of their shared ends; if this involved compromise, the compromise would have been a principled one. But the statesmen had to deal with the politicians, and these were trying to win out in a competitive struggle; for them a compromise was whatever distribution of spoils was entailed by the existing distribution of power.[35] In contests with statesmen, politicians have the advantage: their weapons—guile, deception, fraud, etc.—are highly effective and, having nothing at stake by way of principle, the politicians are under no constraint in their use. To cope with politicians a statesman must become one himself, and this of course is to lose as Madison did (or thought he did) when he finally accepted a "compromise" not on "correct principles."

THE LIMITATIONS OF REASON

Experience and time, Publius wrote in his final paper, must correct the errors of the founders and bring the Constitution to perfection.

That the government today is very different from the one put in place in 1789 is beyond dispute. It will suffice for present purposes to mention only some of the things that have happened: creation of the party system; acceptance of judicial review and the consequent elevation of the Supreme Court; establishment of the principle that a state may not secede from the Union; popular election of Senators; popular election of the President; assumption by the President of the role of chief legislator; and, finally, general agreement that the powers of the national government are not (as Publius asserted in *Federalist* 45) few and defined but the very opposite: many and undefined.

Whether these and other changes have brought the Constitution nearer to perfection need not be discussed. Here the question is whether they resulted from reflection and choice, or from accident and force.

The most fundamental of them was brought about by a war that cost a million lives. As Harry V. Jaffa has written, it was military conquest that kept at least one-third of the states in the Union.[36] That the Union is one and inseparable was established by force. With one exception the other changes listed did not result from any formal deliberative process (and therefore did not entail amendment of the Constitution). This is indicative: they were not "brought" about, they "came" about.

Publius seems to have expected this: it is what his phrase "experience and time," which contrasts so sharply with "deliberation and choice," suggests. What part, then, did reason play in the founding? What was the achievement of Madison, Hamilton, and the other great men among the founders?

My answer is that these great men displayed their wisdom by recognizing that what they judged to be the mistakes of the Convention would have to be corrected, as Publius (quoting Hume) said, by experience and time. Certainly they did not believe that in the future men would subordinate passion to reason or self-interest to the public good. They saw, I think, that eventually competition and struggle would produce outcomes—accidents, when viewed from a public standpoint—that, if Providence were kind, would not differ greatly from what they had tried to bring about from the beginning. The contribution of reason, in short, was to recognize its own limitations.

Notes

INTRODUCTION

1. Letter to Hamilton, August 28, 1788, in John C. Fitzpatrick, ed., *The Writings of George Washington*, 39 volumes (Washington, D.C.: U.S. Government Printing Office, 1931–44), vol. 30, p. 66.

2. Letter to Madison, November 18, 1788, in Andrew A. Lipscomb, ed., *The Writings of Thomas Jefferson*, 20 vols. (Washington, D.C.: The Thomas Jefferson Memorial Association, 1903), vol. 7, p. 183.

3. From the Minutes of the Board of Visitors of the University of Virginia, March 4, 1825, in *The Writings of Thomas Jefferson*, vol. 19, pp. 460–461. For an overview of the contemporaneous and later reaction to *The Federalist*, see Gottfried Dietze, *The Federalist: A Classic on Federalism and Free Government* (Baltimore: Johns Hopkins, 1960), pp. 3–31. The most up-to-date bibliography of editions of and writings on *The Federalist* is contained in Roy P. Fairfield's selected edition, *The Federalist Papers* (Baltimore: Johns Hopkins, 1981), pp. 307–324.

4. Willmoore Kendall makes a similar point in his cogent introduction (written with George W. Carey) to *The Federalist*. See "How to Read *The Federalist*," in Nellie D. Kendall, ed., *Willmoore Kendall Contra Mundum* (New Rochelle, N.Y.: Arlington House, 1971), pp. 403–417. But Kendall's interpretation is ultimately derailed by his refusal to connect the constitutionalism of *The Federalist* with the principles proclaimed in the Declaration of Independence. Cf. Willmoore Kendall and George W. Carey, *The Basic Symbols of the American Political Tradition* (Baton Rouge: Louisiana State University Press, 1970), chapters 5 and 6, with the powerful critique by Harry V. Jaffa, *How to Think About the American Revolution* (Durham: Carolina Academic Press, 1978), chapters 2 and 3.

5. See, e.g., Douglass Adair, "The Authorship of the Disputed *Federalist* Papers," in Trevor Colbourn, ed., *Fame and the Founding Fathers: Essays by Douglass Adair* (New York: W. W. Norton, 1974), pp. 27–74; and Alpheus T. Mason, "*The Federalist*—A Split Personality," *American Historical Review*, 57, no. 3 (April 1952), 625–643. For a trenchant rejoinder to Adair and Mason, see

George W. Carey, "Publius—A Split Personality?" *The Review of Politics*, 46, no. 1 (January 1984), 5–22.

1. FEDERALIST 10 AND AMERICAN REPUBLICANISM

1. *Federalist* 14, p. 104.
2. *Federalist* 14, pp. 104–105; No. 9, p. 72.
3. *Federalist* 9, pp. 72–73.
4. Diamond was not the first, however, to discover the significance of the extended republic. The credit for that seems to belong to Douglass Adair. See his "The Tenth Federalist Revisited," originally published in 1951, and "'That Politics May be Reduced to a Science': David Hume, James Madison, and the Tenth Federalist," originally published in 1957. Both essays are republished in Trevor Colbourn, ed., *Fame and the Founding Fathers: Essays by Douglass Adair* (New York: W. W. Norton, 1974), pp. 75–106. For Adair's earliest reflections on the argument of *Federalist* 10, see his unpublished Ph.D. dissertation, "The Intellectual Origins of Jeffersonian Democracy: Republicanism, the Class Struggle, and the Virtuous Farmer," Yale University, 1943, pp. 220–271. For Adair, the extended republic offered a way to stabilize and moderate the republican form without having recourse to the mixed regime. Unlike Diamond, however, Adair regarded this as a fulfillment rather than a repudiation of the republican tradition that stretched back, in his view, to the sixth book of Aristotle's *Politics*. Adair was not of course the first to draw attention to the novelty of Publius's argument. See, for example, Charles Merriam, *A History of American Political Theories* (New York: Macmillan, 1903), pp. 103–106; and much earlier, and with more attention to No. 14 than to No. 10, John Quincy Adams, "Life of James Madison," in *The Lives of James Madison and James Monroe* (Boston: Phillips, Sampson, 1850), pp. 41–44. Cf. *Fame and the Founding Fathers*, pp. 77–79 and 84.
5. Martin Diamond, "The Federalist," in Leo Strauss and Joseph Cropsey, eds., *History of Political Philosophy* (Chicago: Rand McNally, 1972; 2nd edition), pp. 631–651, at 635, 646.
6. Martin Diamond, "Democracy and The Federalist: A Reconsideration of the Farmers' Intent," *The American Political Science Review* 53 (March 1959): 52–68, reprinted in James Morton Smith, ed., *The Constitution* (New York: Harper & Row, 1971), pp. 171–191, at 183–184. See also Thomas L. Pangle, "Federalists and the Idea of Virtue," *This Constitution: A Bicentennial Chronicle* 5 (Winter 1984): 19–25, at 21.
7. Diamond, "The Federalist," pp. 647, 649; *Federalist* 10, p. 78; cf. Diamond, "Democracy and The Federalist," pp. 188–189.
8. Diamond, "Ethics and Politics: The American Way," in Robert H. Horwitz, ed., *The Moral Foundations of the American Republic* (Charlottesville: University Press of Virginia, 1977), pp. 39–72, at 58–59.
9. Ibid., pp. 56, 59, 65; Diamond, "Democracy and The Federalist," p. 186.
10. Diamond, "Ethics and Politics," pp. 52, 63–67, 70; "The Federalist," p. 650; "Democracy and The Federalist," p. 190. It is not simply that in America virtue

is subordinated to liberty, but that virtue is redefined in terms of liberty. Consider: "And Publius is aware that his scheme involves an enormous reliance on the ceaseless striving after immediate private gains; the commercial life must be made honorable and universally practiced." "The Federalist," p. 650.

11. See, for example, Walter Berns, *In Defense of Liberal Democracy* (Chicago: Gateway Editions, 1984); Irving Kristol, *On the Democratic Idea in America* (New York: Harper & Row, 1972); Herbert J. Storing, *What the Anti-Federalists Were FOR* (Chicago: University of Chicago Press, 1981); Frank M. Coleman, *Hobbes and America: Exploring the Constitutional Foundations* (Toronto: University of Toronto Press, 1977); James W. Ceaser et al., *American Government: Origins, Institutions, and Public Policy* (New York: McGraw-Hill, 1984). Mention should also be made of Diamond's influence on the writing of American history, where his and Adair's interpretations have tended to reinforce one another. See, in particular, Gordon S. Wood, *The Creation of the American Republic, 1776–1787* (Chapel Hill: University of North Carolina Press, 1969).

12. See Adair, "The Tenth Federalist Revisited," pp. 75–77, 82–88.

13. Charles Beard, *An Economic Interpretation of the Constitution of the United States* (New York: The Free Press, 1935; orig. ed., 1913), pp. 15, 156–158.

14. Ibid., pp. xi–xiii, xvi–xvii, 4–7, 13–18, 153–156.

15. Adair, "The Tenth Federalist Revisited," pp. 77, 86–88, 92; " 'That Politics May be Reduced to a Science,' " pp. 97–106.

16. Diamond, "The Revolution of Sober Expectations," in *America's Continuing Revolution* (Garden City, N.Y.: Anchor, 1976), pp. 23–40; and cf. Diamond, "The Problems of the Socialist Party after World War One," in John H. M. Laslett and Seymour Martin Lipset, eds., *Failure of a Dream? Essays in the History of American Socialism* (Garden City, N.Y.: Anchor, 1974), pp. 362–379. This essay was originally a chapter in Diamond's unpublished Ph.D. dissertation, "Socialism and the Decline of the American Socialist Party," University of Chicago, 1956.

17. For a critique of Diamond along these lines, see Harry V. Jaffa, *How to Think About the American Revolution* (Durham, N.C.: Carolina Academic Press, 1978), pp. 75–140. In fairness to Diamond, he was not unaware of the problem. See especially his "Ethics and Politics"; *The Electoral College and the American Idea of Democracy* (Washington, D.C.: American Enterprise Institute, 1977); and "Lincoln's Greatness," in *"With Firmness in the Right. . ."* (Claremont, Calif.: Claremont Men's College, n.d.).

18. Cf. Lincoln: "In this and like communities, public sentiment is everything. With public sentiment, nothing can fail; without it nothing can succeed. Consequently he who molds public sentiment, goes deeper than he who enacts statutes or pronounces decisions. He makes statutes and decisions possible or impossible to be executed." Roy P. Basler, ed., *The Collected Works of Abraham Lincoln* (New Brunswick: Rutgers University Press, 1953), vol. 3, p. 27.

19. Alexis de Tocqueville, *Democracy in America*, trans. George Lawrence (Garden City, N.Y.: Anchor, 1969), p. 12.

20. *Federalist* 9, pp. 72–73.

21. See Charles R. Kesler, "The Founders and the Classics," in James W. Muller, ed., *The Revival of Constitutionalism* (Lincoln: University of Nebraska Press,

1988); and Douglass Adair, "A Note on Certain of Hamilton's Pseudonyms," in *Fame and the Founding Fathers*, pp. 272–285.

22. *Federalist* 1, p. 36; Diamond, "The Federalist," pp. 633–634; David F. Epstein, *The Political Theory of The Federalist* (Chicago: University of Chicago Press, 1984), pp. 7–9.

23. *Federalist* 37, p. 224; No. 1, p. 36; cf. No. 39, p. 240.

24. *Federalist* 2, p. 37; No. 3, p. 42.

25. *Federalist* 8, pp. 67–68. See the fine discussion in Epstein, *Political Theory*, pp. 16–21, 26–28.

26. *Federalist* 36, p. 224; No. 37, pp. 224–225.

27. *Federalist* 1, p. 36; No. 37, p. 224; Epstein, *Political Theory*, pp. 61–63.

28. *Federalist* 9, pp. 71–73; No. 10, p. 77.

29. *Federalist* 9, p. 72. Cf. the ironical use of "enlightened" in Publius's later description of Thomas Jefferson's plan for securing the separation of powers in his draft constitution for Virginia. *Federalist* 49, p. 313.

30. *Federalist* 9, pp. 73, 76.

31. *Federalist* 9, pp. 72, 74; No. 39, p. 241; Epstein, *Political Theory*, pp. 15–16, 59–62, 110, 118–125, 195–197; William Kristol, "Liberty, Equality, Honor," *Social Philosophy and Policy* 2, no. 1 (Autumn 1984): 125–140.

32. *Federalist* 9, pp. 72–73.

33. *Federalist* 10, p. 77; No. 9, pp. 71, 75. The "firm" Union is in the end also the result of a firm opinion—an opinion confirmed by the Constitution. See No. 49, pp. 314–315.

34. *Federalist* No. 9, pp. 73–74.

35. *Federalist* 10, p. 77; No. 1, p. 36; 47, pp. 307–308; No. 48, p. 309; cf. No. 49, p. 315. See also Epstein, *Political Theory*, pp. 61–63, and Diamond, "The Federalist," pp. 639–640.

36. *Federalist* 10, p. 78, and cf. p. 81. The "zeal for different opinions concerning religion, concerning government, and many other points, as well of speculation as of practice," mentioned on page 79, is the more remarkable for its making no impression either on Publius's statement of the problem or his statement of the solution to the problem of faction.

37. *Federalist* 10, pp. 78 and 81.

38. *Federalist* 10, p. 78. I am indebted for this line of reasoning as well as many other elements of this interpretation to the splendid study by William Kristol, "The American Judicial Power and the American Regime," unpublished Ph.D. dissertation, Harvard University, 1979.

39. *Federalist* 10, p. 78.

40. *Federalist* 10, p. 78; No. 43, p. 279; No. 57, p. 350; No. 62, p. 380.

41. *Federalist* 10, p. 78; No. 23, p. 153; cf. Diamond, "Democracy and The Federalist," pp. 183–184.

42. *Federalist* 10, pp. 78–79.

43. *Federalist* 9, p. 73; No. 10, pp. 79, 81.

44. *Federalist* 10, pp. 79, 84; No. 51, p. 324; cf. Diamond, "Ethics and Politics," pp. 52–53. See the spirited discussion in Sanderson Schaub, "Justice and Honor, the Surest Foundation of Liberty: The Natural Law Doctrine in *Federalist* No. 10," a paper prepared for the first conference of the University of Dallas Bicentennial Project, "Constitutionalism in America," October 18–19, 1985.

45. *Federalist* 10, p. 79.

46. *Federalist* 6, pp. 56–57; No. 7, p. 63; No. 11, pp. 84–85; No. 12, pp. 91–92; cf. No. 8, p. 69.

47. *Federalist* 10, pp. 78–79; No. 11, p. 84; No. 12, p. 91.

48. *Federalist* 10, p. 79; No. 51, p. 324.

49. *Federalist* 10, p. 80; No. 51, p. 324; Diamond, "The Federalist," p. 649. Cf. the insightful account in Colleen A. Sheehan, "Madison's Empire of Reason," a paper presented at the Northeastern Political Science Association meeting in Philadelphia, November 14–16, 1985.

50. On the ambiguities of "interest," see Robert A. Rutland, ed., *The Papers of James Madison* (Chicago: University of Chicago Press, 1975), vol. 9, p. 141: "There is no maxim in my opinion which is more liable to be misapplied and which therefore needs more elucidation than the current one that the interest of the majority is the political standard of right and wrong. Taking the word 'interest' as synonymous with 'Ultimate happiness,' in which sense it is qualified with every necessary moral ingredient, the proposition is no doubt true. But taking it in the popular sense, as referring to immediate augmentation of wealth and property, nothing can be more false. In the latter sense it would be the interest of the majority in every community to despoil & enslave the minority of individuals; and in a federal community to make a similar sacrifice of the minority of the component States. In fact it is only reestablishing under another name and a more specious form, force as the measure of right. . . ." Letter to James Monroe, October 5, 1786. Cf. Harvey C. Mansfield, Jr., *The Spirit of Liberalism* (Cambridge, Mass.: Harvard University Press, 1978), pp. 23–24. See also Gerald Stourzh, *Alexander Hamilton and the Idea of Republican Government* (Stanford: Stanford University Press, 1970), pp. 80–87, 90–94.

51. *Federalist* 10, p. 80; cf. especially No. 68, p. 414: "This process of election affords a moral certainty that the office of President will seldom fall to the lot of any man who is not in an eminent degree endowed with the requisite qualifications. . . . It will not be too strong to say that there will be a constant probability of seeing the station filled by characters preeminent for ability and virtue." On the Roman Publius, see Plutarch, *Publicola*, X.1–6, in *Plutarch's Lives*, trans. Bernadotte Perrin (London: William Heinemann, 1928), vol. 1, pp. 527–531.

52. *Federalist* 10, p. 80; No. 43, p. 279; cf. No. 10, pp. 83–84 with No. 49, pp. 315–317; No. 51, pp. 323–325; No. 78, pp. 466–472; No. 84, pp. 514–515, 517–518; No. 85, pp. 522–523.

53. *Federalist* 10, pp. 80–81; No. 49, pp. 314–315; and consider No. 63, p. 384. See also Diamond, "The Federalist," pp. 645–646; and the excellent discussion in Harvey C. Mansfield, "The Constitution and Modern Social Science," *The Center Magazine* 19, no. 5 (September/October 1986): 42–59, at 42–46.

54. See *Federalist* 2, pp. 38–40; No. 37, pp. 229–231; No. 38, pp. 231–233; No. 40, pp. 252–254.

55. *Federalist* 9, p. 71; No. 10, p. 81; No. 14, p. 100; No. 63, pp. 385–387.
56. *Federalist* 10, p. 82; Epstein, *Political Theory*, pp. 124–125, 193–197. On the importance of numbers, cf. No. 31, p. 194 with No. 55, p. 342.
57. *Federalist* 10, pp. 82–83; No. 68, p. 414; cf. Epstein, *Political Theory*, pp. 95–99.
58. *Federalist* 10, p. 83.
59. *Federalist* 10, pp. 77, 83; No. 11, p. 87.
60. *Federalist* 10, pp. 77, 83; No. 51, p. 325.
61. Consider *Federalist* 15, p. 105 and No. 49, pp. 314–315.
62. *Federalist* 1, p. 36; No. 9, p. 71; No. 10, p. 84; No. 63, p. 385.

2. ANTI-FEDERALISM IN *THE FEDERALIST*: A FOUNDING
   DIALOGUE ON THE CONSTITUTION, REPUBLICAN GOVERNMENT,
   AND FEDERALISM

1. *Federalist* 1, p. 36. For a discussion of Publius's publication strategy and the importance of the form of *The Federalist*, see Albert Furtwangler, *The Authority of Publius: A Reading of the Federalist Papers* (Ithaca: Cornell University Press, 1984), chapter 2. For the publication history of the work, see Jacob Cooke's introduction to his edition of *The Federalist* (Cleveland and New York: Meridian Books, 1961).
2. *Federalist* 67, pp. 408, 411; No. 69, p. 418; No. 73, p. 446; No. 78, p. 469; No. 83, pp. 503, 506.
3. Herbert J. Storing, ed., *The Complete Anti-Federalist*, 7 vols. (Chicago: University of Chicago Press, 1981). Volume I of that work contains Storing's essay on the political thought of the Anti-Federalists, which has also been separately published in a paperback entitled *What the Anti-Federalists Were FOR* (Chicago: University of Chicago Press, 1981). The passage quoted above comes from page 3 of that edition. Storing's edition of the Anti-Federalists is also available in a one-volume abridgement entitled *The Anti-Federalist*, ed. Murray Dry (Chicago: University of Chicago Press, 1985). All citations to the Anti-Federalists will be to *The Complete Anti-Federalist*. In addition to citing the particular Anti-Federalist who is writing, and (where relevant) identifying the letter by its Roman numeral, a three-part number will be used to identify the volume, entry in the volume, and paragraph or group of paragraphs.
4. See Storing's introductory sketches and citations to both writings, at 2.8.intro and 2.9.intro.
5. The seventeen "Letters of Brutus" were published in the New York *Journal* from October 18, 1787 through April 10, 1788. The *Federalist* papers were published in different New York papers, mainly the New York *Independent Journal*, from October 27, 1787 through May 28, 1788. The "Letters of the Federal Farmer" were published and widely circulated in pamphlet form (a first series of five letters, followed by an additional thirteen), but they were also published in the (NY) *Poughkeepsie County Journal*. See Storing, introduction to Federal Farmer, 2.8.

6. 2.8.1; 2.9.2. For an example of the view that the "critical period" thesis was a fabrication, see Charles Beard, *An Economic Interpretation of the Constitution of the United States* (New York: The Free Press, 1935), p. 48, and Merrill Jensen, *The New Nation* (New York: Vintage, 1950), pp. xiii, 348–349. Each is a critique of John Fiske, *The Critical Period of American History, 1783–1789* (Boston: Houghton Mifflin, 1888).

7. Brutus, I, 2.9.3; Federal Farmer, I, 2.8.1.

8. Federal Farmer I, 2.8.4; see also Brutus, I, 2.9.4.

9. Federal Farmer, I, 2.8.3.

10. Federal Farmer, VII, 2.8.93.

11. Brutus, I, 2.9.3; Brutus, II, 2.9.24.

12. See Max Farrand, ed., *The Records of the Federal Convention of 1787*, 4 vols. (New Haven: Yale University Press, 1966), vol. 2, pp. 449–455 (August 29).

13. Brutus, III, 2.9.38.

14. For Publius's discussion of the language of the congressional authorization and his defense of the nine-state ratification requirement, see *Federalist* 40 and 43.

15. Federal Farmer, I, 2.8.8.

16. Brutus, I, 2.9.4.

17. Brutus, I, 2.9.11 quoting from Montesquieu's *Spirit of the Laws*, book VIII, chapter 16.

18. Brutus, I, 2.9.16.

19. Federal Farmer, III, 2.8.25–26.

20. Montesquieu discusses representation and separation of powers in connection with the English Constitution, whose principle is political liberty (book XI). Publius could have argued that Montesquieu regarded England as "a republic disguised under the form of monarchy" (book V, chapter 11), and that the proposed Constitution was a thoroughly republican, i.e., elective, version of English government. But that might have sounded like Publius was advocating an elective monarchy.

21. Federal Farmer, II, 2.8.15; III, 2.8.24.

22. Federal Farmer, XVI, 2.8.190.

23. David Epstein, *The Political Theory of the Federalist* (Chicago: University of Chicago Press, 1984), p. 120; from *Federalist* 37, p. 227.

24. See Epstein, *Political Theory*, pp. 193–197.

25. While Federal Farmer is responding to a Federalist objection that his earlier account was "chemerical," as Storing points out, it cannot be to *Federalist* 35, since that was published after Farmer's VIIth letter. See Federal Farmer, VII, 2.8.97, note 62.

26. Federal Farmer, VII, 2.8.97.

27. Federal Farmer, XI, 2.8.147.

28. Federal Farmer, XIV, 2.8.178–182.

29. Brutus, XI, 2.9.135–138; Brutus, XV, 2.9.187–193.

30. Storing, *What the Anti-Federalists Were FOR*, pp. 9–10.

31. See the statements of Gouverneur Morris and George Mason in the Convention, in Farrand, *Federal Convention*, vol. 1, pp. 33–34, 37.

32. See Smith, 6.12.5 and Impartial Examiner, 5.14.26.

33. In this discussion of federalism, I shall refer to Hamilton's and Madison's views individually, rather than to the collective "Publius." I do so because their approaches to the definition of federalism vary, and while each covers similar ground in the discussion of the powers of government, it is worth keeping the two men's views separate here, in light of their subsequent disagreement, in 1791, over the bank bill and the enumeration of powers generally.

34. *Federalist* 9, p. 75, quoting from Montesquieu, *Spirit of the Laws*, book IX, chapter 1.

35. Federal Farmer, I, 2.8.10.

36. Federal Farmer, I, 2.8.11,13.

37. Federal Farmer, VI, 2.8.72.

38. Federal Farmer, XVII, 2.8.205.

39. See Madison's speech of July 14, 1787, in Farrand, *Federal Convention*, vol. 2, pp. 8–9.

40. See Martin Diamond, "*The Federalist*'s View of Federalism," in George C. S. Benson, ed., *Essays in Federalism* (Claremont: Institute for Studies in Federalism, 1962), pp. 21–64.

41. See his speeches of June 5 and 19, in Farrand, *Federal Convention*, vol. 1, pp. 122–123; 317.

42. For Henry's argument about the preamble, see 5.16.1.

43. The dates are December 19, 1787, through January 9, 1788, for *The Federalist*, and December 13, 1787, through January 24, 1788, for Brutus.

44. Brutus, I, 2.9; see also Brutus, V, 2.9.57–58.

45. Brutus, XI, 2.9.130.

46. This describes the original debate over loose, or liberal, versus strict construction. It took place in 1791, first in the House, where Madison urged strict construction and lost, and then in the executive branch, where Jefferson urged strict construction and lost to Hamilton, who argued, to President Washington's satisfaction, for liberal construction. Chief Justice John Marshall later established liberal construction in our constitutional law, in *McCulloch* v. *Maryland* 4 Wheat. 316 (1819).

47. Brutus, V, 2.9.62.

48. Brutus, V, 2.9.63.

49. Brutus, V, 2.9.63.

50. See Jonathan Elliot, ed., *The Debates in the Several State Conventions on the Adoption of the Federal Constitution*, 5 vols. (Philadelphia: J. P. Lippincott, 1891), vol. 1, pp. 318–337.

51. Federal Farmer, XVII, 2.8.209.

52. Brutus, VI, 2.9.80.

53. Just before taking up the war power, Brutus suggests that the Constitution should have required a two-thirds vote of both Houses for the borrowing of money (VIII, 2.9.95). I find no explicit reply to this in *The Federalist*, although I assume Hamilton may be said to have covered it with the argument we just examined.

54. Brutus, VIII, 2.9.97; Federal Farmer III, 2.8.39. Black's Law Dictionary defines *posse commitatus* as a "group of people acting under authority of police or sheriff and engaged in searching for a criminal or in making an arrest."

55. Brutus, VIII, 2.9.98.

56. See *Federalist* 24, pp. 159–60, and Brutus, IX, 2.9.112–114.

57. Brutus, X, 2.9.124.

58. Brutus, X, 2.9.126.

59. Federal Farmer, III, 2.8.39.

60. See Storing, *What the Anti-Federalists Were FOR*, pp. 34–37.

61. See Elliot, *Debates on the Adoption of the Federal Constitution*, note 50.

62. See Michael Sandel's introduction to a collection which he edited, entitled *Liberalism and its Critics* (New York: New York University Press, 1984).

63. See *Federalist* 27.

64. See Chief Justice White's opinion of the court in the 1918 *Selective Services Cases* (245 U.S. 366), which identifies the Civil War Act of March 3, 1863 as a national draft (p. 386).

65. The most important tenth amendment cases are *National League of Cities* v. *Usery* 426 U.S. 833 (1976), which overturned the application of federal minimum wage and overtime regulations to state and local employees, and *Garcia* v. *San Antonio Metropolitan Transit Authority* 53 U.S. Law Week 4135 (1985), which overturned *Usery* and reinstated the extension of the federal law to state employees. Both were 5–4 decisions. The current minority position is closer to the Anti-Federalist position than the Federalist position. The Supreme Court has also interpreted the eleventh amendment to incorporate the doctrine of sovereign immunity for state governments in federal courts. See *Hans* v. *Louisiana* 134 U.S. 1 (1890) and, most recently, *Atascadero State Hospital* v. *Scanlon* 53 U.S. Law Week 4985 (1985).

3. Federalism and Political Life

1. Harry V. Jaffa, "The Political Theory of the Civil War," in Robert A. Goldwin, ed., *A Nation of States*, 2nd edition (Chicago: Rand McNally, 1974), pp. 129–152.

2. Martin Diamond, Winston Mills Fisk, and Herbert Garfinkel, *The Democratic Republic: An Introduction to American National Government*, 2nd edition (Chicago: Rand McNally, 1969), chapter 2, "The Formative Years."

3. Allen and Lloyd regard the "reservation of powers" as one of "two principles [which] formed the basis of the Antifederalist idea for the American republic." W. B. Allen and Gordon Lloyd, eds., with Margie Lloyd, associate ed., *The Essential Antifederalist* (New York: University Press of America, 1985), p. x. The Anti-Federalist fear found perfect expression in the Tenth Amendment to the Constitution, especially when it is read as a summary of the first nine amendments.

4. Herbert J. Storing, ed., *The Complete Anti-Federalist*, 7 vols. (Chicago: University of Chicago Press, 1981), vol. 1, p. 26.

5. See also Allen and Lloyd, *The Essential Antifederalist*, "Interpretative Essay."

6. Gerald M. Capers, *John C. Calhoun: Opportunist* (Gainesville: University of Florida Press, 1960), p. 252.

7. The quotation is from the Anti-Federalist writer, "A Georgian." See *Complete Anti-Federalist*, vol. 5, p. 129.

8. In saying this, we disagree profoundly with Storing, who says that Federalist and Anti-Federalist "disagreements were not based on different premises about the nature of man or the ends of political life." *Complete Anti-Federalist*, vol. 1, p. 5.

9. The rhetoric of *The Federalist* is aimed at combating an exhaustive (and often exhausting to the modern reader) array of errors produced by Anti-Federalist biases. But it also focuses on persuading the Anti-Federalists to *see* first principles *clearly*. See *Federalist* 31, pp. 193–195, for an example.

10. *Complete Anti-Federalist*, vol. 4, p. 83. Historians have tended to accept the Anti-Federalist claim that they had the common touch, and have concluded that the Constitution might not have been ratified had the yeoman farmer and frontiersman made it to the polls. There is not much evidence to support this assertion, however, beyond the logic of the Anti-Federalist self-understanding.

11. See Brutus in *Complete Anti-Federalist*, vol. 2, p. 369. Also see Melancton Smith, ibid., vol. 6, pp. 160–61.

12. See Maryland Farmer in *Complete Anti-Federalist*, vol. 5, pp. 57–58.

13. This is Publius's phrase. He protests repeatedly that the charge, which of course has echoed through American history, is insubstantial.

14. *Complete Anti-Federalist*, vol. 2, p. 178.

15. Alexis de Tocqueville, *Democracy in America*, ed. J. P. Mayer (Garden City, N.Y.: Doubleday, 1967), pp. 555–558.

16. *Complete Anti-Federalist*, vol. 5, pp. 57–58.

17. Martin Diamond, *The Founding of the Democratic Republic* (Itasca, Ill.: F. E. Peacock, 1981), p. 28.

18. *Complete Anti-Federalist*, vol. 4, p. 87.

19. *Complete Anti-Federalist*, vol. 1, p. 25.

20. *Complete Anti-Federalist*, vol. 5, p. 30.

21. *Complete Anti-Federalist*, vol. 1, p. 67.

22. *Complete Anti-Federalist*, vol. 1, p. 45. The phrase is used repeatedly by Storing to characterize a central tenet of the Anti-Federalist cause.

23. This conviction is implied in one of their most oft-repeated complaints about the Constitution. It was voiced by Centinel as follows: "The number of representatives . . . appears to be too few either to communicate the requisite information of the wants, local circumstances, and sentiments of so extensive an empire, or to prevent corruption and undue influence in the exercise of such great powers." See *Complete Anti-Federalist*, vol. 2, p. 142.

24. Diamond, Fisk, and Garfinkel, *The Democratic Republic*, pp. 40–42.

25. Publius's hostility to state governments is hardly distinguishable from his antagonism to legislative government. See *Federalist* 48, p. 309.

26. Harvey C. Mansfield, Jr., argues that the executive of modern republics acts more energetically when he pursues a limited purpose. See his "The Ambivalence of Executive Power" in J. Bessette and J. Tulis, eds., *The Presidency in the Constitutional Order* (Baton Rouge: Louisiana State University Press, 1981), p. 326.

Mansfield's modern executive does not encourage human nobility, however. The argument of this paper differs from Mansfield's in that American executive power is seen as part of a limited, and therefore more energetic, national government, which *is* able to shape lower government activities to the ends of human nobility.

27. Anti-federalism favors the continent man whereas federalism favors virtue and magnanimity. Cf. Aristotle, *Ethics* 4.3 and 7.1–6.

28. Such skill is encouraged more generally by *The Federalist's* insistence on including the "requisite stability and energy [and the requisite "character," also] in government" (No. 37, p. 226). It is spoken of by a contemporary of Publius as follows: "[Rulers] should be likewise men of great resolution and firmness of mind;—not easily dismayed and overcome by difficulties, or intimidated by threatened dangers:—Able to maintain a calmness of mind, and to guide with a steady hand, in tempestuous seasons:—Able to bear with the unpolished plainness of some honest men, and with the weakness and follies of others:—Not apt, in a pet, to desert the common cause, and to sacrifice the public happiness to their own passionate resentments." Quoted in Charles S. Hyneman and Donald S. Lutz, *American Political Writing during the Founding Era 1760–1805* (Indianapolis: Liberty Press, 1983) vol. 1, p. 167.

29. Cf. Leo Strauss's comment on *Federalist* 10 in his *Natural Right and History* (Chicago: University of Chicago Press, 1953), p. 245.

30. For a further elaboration of this viewpoint, see John Alvis, "The Slavery Provisions of the U.S. Constitution: Means For Emancipation," unpublished manuscript, The University of Dallas, p. 30ff.

31. Modern scholars notwithstanding, the Bill of Rights was not generally accepted as a limiting addition to the Constitution. On the contrary, as discussed above, it was thought of by the founders as *expanding* the national government.

32. It is important to notice in this connection, however, that Publius is not excessively sanguine. He expects the best side of voters to show itself only when they are put to the test. An important example of such putting to the test is mentioned in *Federalist* 10, where Publius expects distrust among conspirators to undermine the work of unjust factions. This distrust will grow because of communications difficulties that will be experienced in an extended republic (No. 10, p. 83). See Sanderson Schaub, "Justice and Honor, The Surest Foundation of Liberty: The Natural Law Doctrine in The Federalist No. 10," unpublished paper prepared for the Bicentennial Conference, University of Dallas, October 18–19, 1985. See especially p. 36ff.

33. See *Complete Anti-Federalist*, vol. 1, p. 17.

34. The continuing superiority of federal administration to state administration is often and well argued. For a recent repetition, see Gregg Easterbrook, "50 Miniature Washingtons: The Flaw in Reagan's New Federalism," *The Washington Monthly* (January 1982): 11–21.

35. Morris P. Fiorina, *Congress, Keystone of the Washington Establishment* (New Haven: Yale University Press, 1977), pp. 41–49 and passim.

36. See George Will, *Statecraft as Soulcraft: What Government Does* (New York: Simon and Schuster, 1983), chapter 2.

37. This is the view, for example, of David Epstein in his *The Political Theory of The Federalist* (Chicago: University of Chicago Press, 1984). Epstein does not argue,

as the Anti-Federalists tended to, that the Federalist love of honor was an instrumental passion, a means for them to achieve wealth and power. Instead, for him "love of fame" is an independent "political" passion. It is an extension of the love of power (pp. 6–7). It craves satisfaction for itself. Epstein's formulation is dictated by his allegiance to a post-Machiavellian, in fact Rousseauian, appreciation of honor, which denies to it any special character as distinguished from other passions. Epstein does not believe, as Plato teaches in *The Republic*, that honor may be fundamentally at odds with all other passions, denying them satisfaction as it serves what is sacred.

38. *Complete Anti-Federalist*, vol. 1, p. 40 and vol. 5, pp. 211–220.

39. According to some current texts, local governments are holdouts against the national liberal agenda. See Robert A. Dahl, *Democracy in the United States: Promise and Performance*, 4th edition (Boston: Houghton Mifflin, 1981), pp. 205 and 331. But the prevailing view is that grants-in-aid programs characterize the federal-state relationship well. A "marble cake" of interacting jurisdictions results. And so, states are said to have their value in that they "can be experimental, can keep in touch with popular sentiment, and can help government adapt to changing conditions." See Lewis Lipsitz, *American Democracy* (New York: St. Martin's Press, 1986), p. 100. Nowhere in this analysis do the authors differentiate national and state powers as the founders did.

40. It would seem that this scholarship owes much to Tocqueville. His understanding was contrary to that of the founders, who viewed man's equality as an equality of spirit. Tocqueville maintains that a different and dangerous kind of equality could be preserved in a regime where envy had grown to insist on an equality of income and material possessions. Local associations, he said, are the most important antidote to such a tendency. They are schools for "concrete" and therefore vivid experience of cooperation and public spiritedness. Such reasoning easily leads to the inference that healthy national politics is abstract and indifferent, and relies on local experiences to generate the proper spirit of democracy.

41. According to Herbert Storing's gloss on this struggle, it was between those who prefer government at the local level and those who prefer an American empire. Simple virtuous republicanism versus commercial grandeur—these were the rough alternatives. The Anti-Federalists, he says, thought that "in a republic, the manners, interests, and sentiments of the people ought to be similar" (*The Complete Anti-Federalist*, vol. 1, p. 45). On the other hand, "the Federalists [relied] on the many diverse gratifications available in the extended republic" (*The Complete Anti-Federalist*, vol. 1, p. 43). For a more extended criticism of this rehabilitation of Anti-Federalist sentiment in the work of Herbert Storing, see the author's "On Anti-Federalism: A Scholarly Polemic" and "Letters to the Editor" in *Claremont Review of Books* 1, no. 4 (May 1982).

42. Diamond, Fisk, and Garfinkel, *The Democratic Republic*, pp. 73–74, 77. Herbert Storing gives the Anti-Federalists the same favorable treatment when he cautions Paul Eidelberg to pay greater heed to the Anti-Federalist argument in Eidelberg's *The Philosophy of the American Constitution* (New York: The Free Press, 1968), p. xi.

43. Similarly, Herbert Storing states the reasons for the Anti-Federalists' capitulation as follows: "The basic problem of the Anti-Federalists was that they accept-

ed the need and desirability of the modern commercial world, while attempting to resist certain of its tendencies with rather half-hearted appeals to civic virtue." *ibid.*, p. 46. A current textbook statement of the same thesis is found in James Ceaser et al., *American Government: Origins, Institutions, & Public Policy* (New York: McGraw-Hill, 1984), p. 27. "The most important question that divided the nation in 1787," says Ceaser, "was whether to remain essentially a confederation of independent states or become a genuine union under a strong national government. This question, in the view of many founders, was a matter to be decided as much on the basis of necessity as on desirability."

44. Perhaps the best contemporary representative of this tradition is Professor M. E. Bradford of the University of Dallas. See his *Remembering Who We Are: Observations of a Southern Conservative* (Athens: University of Georgia Press, 1985).

45. The conservatives generally fail to note that Washington technocrats strengthen local government, although for reasons which they would deplore.

46. Dahl, *Democracy*, pp. 27ff.

4. FOREIGN POLICY AND *THE FEDERALIST*

1. Henry Kissinger, *White House Years* (Boston: Little, Brown, 1979), pp. 58–61, 65.

2. Ibid., p. 58.

3. Among the historians who have taken up the intellectual connection between American foreign policies of the twentieth century and those of the Founders are Felix Gilbert, *To the Farewell Address: Ideas of Early American Foreign Policy* (Princeton: Princeton University Press, 1961); Paul A. Varg, *Foreign Policies of the Founding Fathers* (East Lansing: Michigan State University Press, 1963); and James H. Hutson, "Intellectual Foundations of Early American Diplomacy," *Diplomatic History* 1 (Winter 1977): 1–19.

4. This would be the equivalent of allowing the Dutch to determine NATO nuclear policy.

5. *Federalist* 11, p. 91.

6. See especially *Federalist* 5–8 on this point.

7. *Federalist* 6, p. 59.

8. *Federalist* 7, p. 60.

9. *Federalist* 8, pp. 69–71. Of course, even an insular nation such as Britain must fear seaborne invasion—hence the traditional British concern that no power dominate the European continent, especially the Low Countries. But there is no single "natural" enemy that poses that threat; at the time of *The Federalist*, France represented the most immediate potential danger to Britain, but this role was earlier occupied by Spain and would later be assumed by Germany and the Soviet Union.

10. *Federalist* 5, p. 53.

11. *Federalist* 6, pp. 55, 57, and 59. *Federalist* 5 (p. 51) predicts that such motives would exist even among the smaller American confederacies if the Union were dissolved.

12. *Federalist* 34, p. 208.

13. *Federalist* 4, p. 46.

14. *Federalist* 6, pp. 56–58.

15. There is no explicit and full treatment of the European balance of power in *The Federalist*, but there is also no question that the founders had a sophisticated understanding of "realistic" international politics and that this informs the argument of *The Federalist* throughout. See, for example, Madison's remarks in the Constitutional Convention, June 28, 1787, in Robert A. Rutland et al., eds., *The Papers of James Madison* (Chicago and London: University of Chicago Press, 1962–), vol. 10, pp. 81–82. Hereinafter referred to as *Madison Papers*.

16. *Federalist* 6, pp. 56–59.

17. *Federalist* 34, p. 208.

18. *Federalist* 59, p. 366. In *Federalist* 11 (p. 85), Hamilton refers to three specific objectives of hostile European powers: "preventing our interference in their navigation, of monopolizing the profits of our trade, and of clipping the wings by which we might soar to dangerous greatness."

19. This was a particular theme of John Jay. In reference to the Barbary pirate problem, Jay wrote John Adams in October 1785: "The Algerines, it seems, have declared war against us. If we act properly, I shall not be very sorry for it. In my opinion it may lay the foundation for a navy, and tend to draw us more closely into a federal system." On the threats to American security in North America, Jay wrote to Lafayette that same month: "Good will come out of evil; these discontents nourish federal ideas. As trade diminishes, agriculture must suffer; and hence it will happen that our yeomen will be as desirous of increasing the powers of Congress as our merchants now are. All foreign restrictions, exclusions, and unneighborly ordinances will tend to press us together, and strengthen our bands of union." Henry P. Johnston, ed., *The Correspondence and Public Papers of John Jay* (New York: G. P. Putnam's Sons, 1891), pp. 161, 173.

20. See, for example, *Federalist* 4, pp. 46–47; *Federalist* 15, pp. 106–107. The threats to American national security during the 1780s are well described in Edward Marks, *Independence on Trial: Foreign Affairs and the Making of the Constitution* (Baton Rouge: Louisiana State University Press, 1973), especially pp. 3–51. Among the frequent references to these dangers by the authors of *The Federalist*, see also Hamilton, "Remarks on an Act Acknowledging the Independence of Vermont," New York Assembly, March 28, 1787, in Harold C. Syrett, ed., *The Papers of Alexander Hamilton* (New York and London: Columbia University Press, 1962–), vol. 5, pp. 135–136. Hereinafter cited as *Hamilton Papers*.

21. *Federalist* 5, p. 50. It was widely held that the British had a hand in the Vermont separatist movement and in Shay's rebellion. See, for example, William Grayson to Madison, November 23, 1786, in *Madison Papers*, vol. 9, p. 174, and Jay to Jefferson, December 14, 1786, in Julian P. Boyd et al., eds., *The Papers of Thomas Jefferson* (Princeton: Princeton University Press, 1950–), vol. 10, p. 596.

22. *Federalist* 11, p. 88. According to Forrest McDonald, however, Hamilton "rejected Montesquieu's widely-held proposition that the spirit of a people determined its government on the grounds that laws and institutions were more important that 'spirit,' and that a people received its 'manners' and morals and

'national character' from the example of 'people in authority,' anyway." *Alexander Hamilton: A Biography* (New York: W. W. Norton, 1979), pp. 96–97. In any event, *The Federalist* certainly did not neglect the institutional component of how the national interest should be politically conceived.

23. *Federalist* 2, p. 38. The authors of *The Federalist* were concerned about the strength of the American "genius" toward Union; Madison and Jay had been preoccupied with the sectional problems brought on by the negotiations with Spain over navigation of the Mississippi. At one point, Madison identified the "centrifigul problem" as being between North and South, which resulted "partly from climate, but principally from the effects of their having or not having slaves." On another occasion, however, Madison remarked that the human character could not be determined by the points of the compass. (Madison, "Remarks at the Constitutional Convention," June 30 and July 11, 1787, in *Madison Papers*, vol. 10, pp. 90, 98.)

24. *Federalist* 6, p. 59.

25. *Federalist* 9, pp. 70–71. See also Hamilton's remarks to the Constitutional Convention, June 29, 1787, in *Hamilton Papers*, vol. 4, pp. 220–221.

26. *Federalist* 11, pp. 87. 91. In the view of Samuel Flagg Bemis ("The Background of Washington's Foreign Policy," *Yale Review* 16 [January 1927]: 325): "During the period of confederation . . . there was not so much question about the United States being involved in European affairs as there was of keeping European powers out of American affairs and American territory."

27. See, most notably, Bemis, *Jay's Treaty: American's Advantage from Europe's Distress, 1783–1900*, rev. ed. (New Haven: Yale University Press, 1960), and *Jay's Treaty: A Study of Commerce and Diplomacy*, rev. ed. (New Haven: Yale University Press, 1962). Thus Madison's point to Horatio Gates (December 11, 1787): "A general war in Europe will open a new scene to this Country: a scene which might be contemplated with pleasure if our humanity could forget the calamities in which it must involve others; and if we were in a condition to maintain the rights and pursue the advantages of neutrality." *Madison Papers*, vol. 10, p. 315.

28. See *Federalist* 6, pp. 56–59.

29. *Federalist* 11, p. 85.

30. Ibid., pp. 85–86. These words were penned by Hamilton, who would later find fault with what was apparently a similar policy advocated by Madison in the 1790s.

31. *Federalist* 7, p. 63.

32. Of course, despite the apparent agreement between Hamilton and Madison that emphasis on commerce was a necessary component of Union and a sensible foreign policy, the two disagreed vehemently during the 1790s over precisely what the commercial policy should be.

33. See *Federalist* 3, pp. 42–43.

34. *Federalist* 25, pp. 166–167.

35. *Federalist* 11, p. 87.

36. Ibid., pp. 86–87.

37. *Federalist* 41, p. 258.

38. *Federalist* 4, p. 49. Hamilton makes a related argument in *Federalist* 11, p. 89.

39. *Federalist* 39, p. 240. The authors of *The Federalist* were very much concerned, however, with the propensity of republics to admit foreign influence.

40. Madison does not make this point lightly; he notes that, had the other nations of Europe failed to respond to Charles VII of France's peacetime establishment of military forces, "all Europe must long ago have worn the chains of a universal monarch. Were every nation except France to disband its peace establishment, the same event might follow." *Federalist* 41, p. 257.

41. *Federalist* 8, pp. 70–71.

42. *The Federalist* is even prescient enough to recognize the danger of surprise attack (No. 25, p. 165).

43. *Federalist* 41, p. 257.

44. Ibid., p. 258. Also *Federalist* 8, p. 67: "To be more safe, they at length become willing to run the risk of being less free." This point is well made in David F. Epstein, *The Political Theory of the Federalist* (Chicago: University of Chicago Press, 1984), pp. 14–21.

45. *Federalist* 41, p. 257.

46. Ibid., pp. 260–261.

47. *Federalist* 24, p. 162.

48. Admittedly, *The Federalist* is much less explicit on the question of the relationship between the liberty and welfare of the American people, and that of the peoples of other nations. Emphasis is placed on the importance of the American experiment succeeding (". . . it seems to be reserved to the people of this country, by their conduct and example, to decide the important question, whether societies of men are really capable or not of establishing good government from reflection and choice, or whether they are forever destined to depend for their political constitutions on accident and force." *Federalist* 1, p. 33) rather than on any speculation about how that example would be received by the rest of the world. Differences over this question have been, and they remain, probably the single most important obstacle to the articulation of the national interest (as it relates to foreign affairs) since the founding. This problem was a theoretical one for the founders until the French Revolution, at which time Hamilton and Madison, among many of the founding generation, parted philosophical company on this and several other critical issues.

49. Senator William E. Jenner, cited in Dean Acheson, *Present at the Creation* (New York: W. W. Norton, 1969), p. 365.

5. The Problem of the Separation of Powers: *Federalist* 47–51

1. Thus Publius begins Number 52, "From the more general enquiries pursued in the four last papers. . . ."

2. Indeed, by at least one possible division of the work, Numbers 47–51 would be the central of the thirteen sections of *The Federalist* (plus Introduction and Conclusion).

3. Baron de Montesquieu, *Spirit of the Laws*, in *Oeuvres complètes*, Vol. II (Paris: Pléiade, 1966), Book XII, chapter 2: "Philosophic liberty consists in the exercise

of the will, or at least (if we must speak agreeably to all systems) in the opinion one has that one exercises his will. Political liberty consists in security, or at least in the opinion that one has of his security." Consider also *Federalist* 37, pp. 227–229.

4. Montesquieu, *Spirit of the Laws*, Book XI, chapter 6, paragraph 46.

5. That the legislature, and especially the House of Representatives, is particularly popular, republican, or "representative" is also evident on the basis of *Federalist* 52, p. 327; No. 57, p. 350; No. 63, pp. 389–390; and No. 66, p. 403. It is appropriate that those who argue for the democratic character of the American regime, and for the lack of resemblance between the American separation of powers and the mixed regime, also argue that the American regime is one of legislative supremacy; see especially Ann Stuart Diamond, "The Zenith of Separation of Powers Theory; The Federal Convention of 1787," *Publius* 8, no. 3 (Summer 1978): 45–70.

6. In Number 49 the mode of appointment and tenure are taken for granted; by contrast, in Number 51 the mode of appointment is defended but the purpose of the judiciary is only alluded to, and permanent tenure is taken for granted; in Number 78 the mode of appointment is taken for granted, but the character and purpose of the judicial power are only discernible from the defense of the permanent tenure of the judges.

7. Cf. *Federalist* 52, pp. 327–328, with No. 57, pp. 350–351.

6. Justice and the General Good: *Federalist* 51

1. This paper is indebted to Colleen Sheehan, who brought James Madison's 1792 "Notes on the foundations of government" to my attention, and to David F. Epstein's *The Political Theory of the Federalist* (Chicago: University of Chicago Press, 1984). Epstein's work is not cited in the text only because it is largely an exegesis of *Federalist* 10, the centrality of which I mean to call into question here.

The following analysis assumes an orientation toward the founding that is not made explicit herein. The question of the character of the American regime, given its foundation in modern principles, constitutes an important point of difference among many profound interpreters of our past. I refer above all to the exchanges that have taken place for more than ten years now among Harry V. Jaffa, Martin Diamond, Paul Eidelberg, Irving Kristol, and others. This analysis reflects my understanding of those exchanges, as I expressed it even ten years ago. The central question in those exchanges has been the role of equality in the founding; that the discussion of *Federalist* 51 has been possible without a special consideration of equality does not imply its insignificance.

As I understand Jaffa, the differences stem precisely from the necessity of discovering philosophy in an understanding of this regime. The thought of studying philosophy *instead* of American government, in Jaffa's terms, is a non sequitur. His chief criticism—or mine read into his intentions—is that a studied indifference to kinds of regimes and a pretense of a universal standard of judgment that transcends modern regimes in particular is no more than an uninformed parroting of a regnant morality. They who assume such a posture are intellectuals. Only by coming to terms with the quasi-philosophic demands of this regime can one fully judge of the requirements of philosophy. This runs the risk of nihilism.

Harry Neumann's essays on *Madame Bovary* and *Salambo* describe the necessity of a cosmopolitan horizon to judge both prephilosophic piety and cosmopolitan humanitarianism. But that transcendent cosmopolitanism shows both the impossibility of prephilosophic piety and the evil of *all* cosmopolitan horizons. Hence its nihilism. Only prudent intellectuals escape this nihilism, because, in fact, their cosmopolitanism, their philosophy, is nothing more than the ascetic application of a regnant morality. They judge of prephilosophic men as examples of mankind; they judge of universalistic moralities as examples of mankind: they maintain that there exist irreconcilable differences; and yet they say that we must examine—nay, insist on the existence of—diverse forms of regime as a counter to the modern project. Yet, what is their entire study but *the* manifestation of the intent of the modern project? Studied indifference is not, itself, indifferent.

The other alternative is to resist—i.e., refute—both studied indifference and an eros for philosophy independent of the love of justice. That is, one may immerse—not lose—himself even in this regime. The key: to know and perhaps love it not for its quasi-philosophic demands but for itself. And what do we find behind the door? A particular regime which dedicates itself to the relief of man's estate. But is there no difference between a particular regime so dedicated and the *idea* of such a project? According to Aristotle there must be. Hence, it is not the idea—the modern project—that compels Jaffa's attention. That is but an intellectual pretense. It is rather the fact of the regime and those things required for its health.

Diamond and Kristol argue in effect that the moderns deny that (1) moral virtue is the proper purpose of a well-constructed regime, and (2) that it is even—whether laudable or not—necessary for it. If this is so, then the regime is essentially hostile to virtue, which means that those who are not must take their bearings from non-American sources. I would caution us, however, not to take our bearings from a form of speculative positivism: "As the moderns say, so shall it be." Giving due allowance for the weight of a regnant morality, once created, it remains the task of philosophy to consider the human end not as man decrees it but as nature decrees it—or to put an end once for all to the notion of nature. This latter alternative we recognize from the "second wave" of modernity, and therefore we can more fully appreciate the distinction between ancients and moderns in the context of the American regime by grasping this impulsive "transcendence" on the part of modernity itself. The real thrust of the "second wave"—the antirational modernity—is to reject the possibility of utopia and thereby to consider the modern project in its rational bearings as superseded. This is the manner in which the intelligible question, "Is man essentially hostile to virtue?" comes to be replaced by the unintelligible question, "Is modernity essentially hostile to virtue?"

To question what bearing we should take in this context is a problem indeed. We take "non-American" to mean non-modern, in the context. Thus, it would follow that we cannot become conversant with the demands of virtue save through our acknowledgment of the demands of ancient, particularistic piety. Nevertheless, the only access we have to ancient, particularistic piety in the nature of things is through the radical attack on that particularity. To rephrase: If we can discover virtue's demands only by means either of birth in an ancient regime or the universalizing inquiry that destroys the basis of that virtue, we are forever barred from appreciating virtue. There can be none of us who is not hostile to virtue! It is at this point that we seem forced to recall that the battle of the ancients and the moderns is a *Battle of the Books*, not a battle of cities and nations. And because we enter this battle of philosophers from the protective precincts of a nation, we are enabled to discover the ways of cities. Still, to forget the necessary condition of our discovery and seek bearings we cannot have is to foreclose prematurely the prospect of reaching an end.

That possibility remains open to us when we confront the fundamental demands of the American regime, which collapse into an argument about equality and speak in a manner wholly intelligible to ancient souls. That no one can decide (Locke says "judge") for another the means necessary to preservation does *not* suggest that no one can *know* better than another the means necessary to the other's preservation. Consequently, the question is still whether the wisdom (natural superiority) of the few confers upon the few a title to rule. The insistence on consent is the formal means of denying this. Thus, men never consent to be ruled by their superior as such; they consent rather to be ruled in accord with their own judgment of the necessities of preservation (however they arrive at that judgment). Within that horizon the rule of the naturally superior as such will always be an accident. The enlightenment that legitimizes consent is this radical understanding of a necessary equality—an equality that abstracts from the unequal faculties of men.

2. Victor Hugo Paltsits, *Washington's Farewell Address* (New York: New York Public Library, 1935), pp. 162–163.

3. "Notes for the National Gazette Essays," in Robert A. Rutland et al., eds., *The Papers of James Madison*, (Charlottesville: University of Virginia Press, 1983), vol. 14, pp. 157–169.

4. Ibid., pp. 160–161.

5. "Government of the United States," for the *National Gazette*, February 4, 1792, in *Madison Papers*, vol. 14, pp. 217–218.

6. December 20 [1792], in *Madison Papers*, vol. 14, pp. 426–427, emphasis added.

7. "Government," for the *National Gazette*, December 31, [1791], in ibid., vol. 14, pp. 178–179.

8. "Notes for the National Gazette Essays," pp. 163–64.

9. "Charters," in *Madison Papers*, vol. 14, pp. 191–192.

10. "Of Property," for the *National Gazette*, March 27, 1791, in *Madison Papers*, vol. 13, pp. 266–267.

11. "Who Are the Best Keepers of the People's Liberties?" for the *National Gazette*, December 20, [1792], in *Madison Papers*, vol. 14, pp. 426–427.

12. An uncomfortable hiatus intervenes between *Federalist* 39 and *Federalist* 40. Number 39 poses several questions about constitutional authority and the performance of the Constitutional Convention. That essay answers only one of those questions. Number 40 turns immediately to the "second point." Where is the hiatus? Number 40 establishes the purpose of the Convention after a summary of enabling documents and political necessity. The provisional form of its conclu-

sion is that the convention was to frame a *"national government . . . adequate to the exigencies of government and the preservation of the Union. . . ."* Number 39, however, had already *proved* that the Constitution was neither federal nor national! Apparently, Number 40 proves, in light of Number 39, that the Convention failed to achieve its goal. This only apparent paradox stems from the fact that the "second point" was in fact the original question, hence the first point in Number 39. Insofar as the latter does prove the government to be neither national nor federal, the Convention's task, as conceived in Numbers 40–44, remained unfulfilled. Insofar as that is not the case, Number 40 stands in the place of, rather than follows, Number 39.

I therefore dissent from Martin Diamond's judgment that *Federalist* 39 "is in a sense the central essay." See his essay "The Federalist," in Leo Strauss and Joseph Cropsey, eds., *History of Political Philosophy* (Chicago: Rand McNally, 1972), p. 651, n. 5. For the best account of the results of Number 39, consult Diamond's "What the Framers Meant by Federalism," in Robert A. Goldwin, ed., *A Nation of States* (Chicago: Rand McNally, 1962).

Madison's sleight of hand in Numbers 39–40 sets the stage for all the following essays, which purport to prove that the advice given by the Constitutional Convention is good—that is, for the public good. Not accidentally, Madison returns to strict Declaration of Independence language in order to answer his own questions. And not surprisingly, he dedicates papers 41–44 to a detailed discussion of the institutions of government with the intention of vindicating their faithfulness to the Declaration. Accordingly, the argument of Number 39, there said to be secondary to the question of the Convention's authority, *logically* follows rather than precedes the argument developed in Numbers 40–44. The national-federal dispute, in logical terms, is a mere sidelight to the question of the architectonic scope of the vision of the public good which animated the fathers. That, in turn, leads ineluctably to Number 51.

13. Madison offers a sixfold consideration of those capacities essential to realizing the public good of America. They are the following: (1) the capacity to secure the nation against foreign dangers; (2) the capacity to regulate relations with foreign nations; (3) the capacity to maintain "harmony and proper" relations among the states; (4) the capacity to provide "certain miscellaneous objects of general utility"; (5) the capacity to restrain "the states from certain injurious acts"; and (6) to provide that all these "powers" are efficacious. Number 41 discusses the first capacity, Number 42 the second and third. Number 43 treats the fourth, and Number 44 discusses the fifth and sixth.

Madison announces the "necessary and proper" clause as the last hurdle in this discussion. His analysis makes clear that there is no "pretext" for "drawing into question the essential powers of the Union." We note that what is actually accomplished in his discussion is to display the devices employed to avoid debilitating constitutional adjudications of the powers of government. This enabled the founders to focus on strict construction of the public good as opposed to strict construction of the Constitution. According to Madison, the "necessary and proper" clause restricts not the government but those factions that form the base of free government. That conclusion alone explains how a provision can be defended as a restriction on government after being introduced as an instrument "by which efficacy is given to all the rest" of the powers of government. The question of possible abuses of public authority is not allowed to undermine authority itself. Madison turns to the people, via the states, to reform officers of government who would corruptly wield these extensive powers. *Federalist* 51 explains how the people fulfill their assignment. Accordingly, Number 51 logically follows Number 44, as part of the scheme which is revealed in the analysis of the relation between Numbers 39 and 40.

14. Consult Edward Erler, "The Problem of the Public Good in *The Federalist*," *Polity* 13, no. 4 (Summer 1981): 649–667.

15. Madison describes the relation between the states and the nation thus in Number 51: "In the compound republic of America, the power surrendered by the people is *first* divided between two distinct governments, and then the portion allotted to each subdivided among distinct and separate departments" (emphasis added). By placing the line of division between the states and the nation on the same grounds as that among the departments of the government, Madison implies that both divisions are created in the same instant by the same authority. Accordingly, one may say the states are created anew in 1787–1788.

16. In Number 43 Madison had reflected that reality may contradict theory and place right on the opposite side of might even in republican governments. Accordingly, it was necessary to investigate the question of the legitimacy of the republican form in those cases in which the majority of citizens did not amount to the majority of persons. Far from vindicating an idea of the right of the stronger, however, this consideration led Madison to emphasize more strongly the inherent tendency of republicanism. In Number 51, therefore, he is able to make still clearer the inadequacy of might as a standard of legitimacy: "where the weaker individual is not secured against the violence of the stronger; and as, in the latter state, even the stronger individuals are prompted, by the uncertainty of their condition, to submit to a government which may protect the weak as well as themselves; so, in the former state, will the more powerful factions or parties be gradually induced, by a like motive, to wish for a government which will protect all parties, the weaker as well as the more powerful" (p. 324). In short, the popular form of government—and rights therefore—is secure only insofar as it is distanced from the idea of the right of the stronger.

17. *Federalist* 51, p. 320. Note that Madison implies by these words a continuation of the discussion in Papers 46–49.

18. Ibid., p. 322.

19. The fullest statement of this theme is in *Federalist* 43. It appeared before in the private note, "Vices of the Political System of the U. S.," in Marvin Meyers, *The Mind of the Founder* (Indianapolis: Bobbs-Merrill, 1973; reprinted Shelburne, VT.: The New England Press, 1985), and subsequently in the party press essay, "A Candid State of Parties," September 22, 1792, in *Madison Papers*, pp. 370–372.

20. James McGregor Burns, *The Deadlock of Democracy: Four-Party Politics in America* (Englewood Cliffs, N.J.: Prentice-Hall, 1963), is the celebrated progenitor of this view, which Gordon Lloyd has described as reading "the history of American democracy and the history of democracy backwards." Akin to Burns's theory that Madison's fear of majority faction produced a veto-ridden, ineffective political system is the work of Burns's spiritual ally, Robert Dahl, *A Preface to Democratic Theory* (Chicago: University of Chicago Press, 1966). Lloyd reviewed the recent performance of this theory for the Western Political Science

Association at its annual meeting in Sacramento, California, in 1984. His essay is titled, "The Burns Thesis Twenty Years Later: Has the Deadlock Interpretation Stood the Test of Time?"

21. Consider Thomas Hobbes's *Leviathan,* in which in chapter 13 Hobbes argues that the strong cannot be ever watchful in the state of nature and thus cannot escape fear of the weak.

22. Madison likened rule by the stronger party to the anarchy "in a state of nature." By this he seems to mean that it is less a form of rule than a condition of individual oppressions, "where the weaker individual is not secured against the violence of the stronger." When "a will independent of the society rules," individuals may yet be governed if only tyrannically. This is the way of "hereditary or self-appointed authority." In this discussion in Number 51 Madison drops the terms "elective" and "many," as they applied in an apparently similar case in Number 47: "The accumulation of all the powers, whether of one, a few, or many, and whether hereditary, self-appointed, or elective, may justly be pronounced the very definition of tyranny." When the passages from these two essays are compared a singular meaning emerges: not only is nontyrannical pure democracy impossible by definition (for how could the powers be separated at all in that situation?), but insofar as tyranny is rule by a will independent of the society, rule by a majority faction is better understood as anarchy—no rule— than any form of rule whether legitimate or illegitimate. The reason seems to be that although the majority faction may appear to express the will of the many or the society, it is in fact only a concurrence of individual wills. In this situation, every man is for himself. In other words, if there were the direct, nonfactious rule by the many, it would be tyrannical, while factious rule by the many would be anarchical. The only way for a majority to rule dependent on the will of society, then, is indirectly—the Hamiltonian argument. Hamilton's coining the term "representative democracy" in 1777 set the tone for these conclusions. We can see then that where, in the interest of republicanism, Madison elevates our notion of the conceptions of oligarchs, he also depreciates our expectations of democrats.

23. Consult W. B. Allen, "Federal Representation: The Design of the Thirty-Fifth *Federalist Paper," Publius* 6, no. 2 (1976): 61–71, where such qualification as this principle admits is discussed in terms of *Federalist* 63. Also, see Harry V. Jaffa's analysis of the causes of political parties, the second and central of which is "the partisanship of those animated by a knowledge of human nature, who would set up a regime of liberty and so dispose the competing interests of an emancipated human nature that they are permitted or compelled to co-operate for the common good." Jaffa, "The Nature and Origin of the American Party System," in his *Equality and Liberty* (New York: Oxford University Press, 1965), p. 20.

24. Max Farrand, ed., *The Records of the Federal Convention of 1787,* 4 vols., (New Haven: Yale University Press, 1966), vol. 2, p. 203; the debate of August 7.

25. See "Property and Suffrage: Second Thoughts on the Constitutional Convention," in Meyers, *The Mind of the Founder,* pp. 501–509.

26. Farrand, *Federal Convention,* note 17, p. 204.

27. Meyers, "Property and Suffrage," p. 502.

28. Ibid., p. 504.

29. Farrand, *Federal Convention,* vol. 1, June 26 debate, p. 422.

30. Meyers, "Property and Suffrage," p. 505.

31. After reviewing the possibilities Madison says that "three modifications present themselves." He went on to list five, however. The first was to confine "the right of suffrage to freeholders." The "objection to this regulation is obvious," namely, it "violates the vital principle of free Government" relative to non-freeholders. Secondly, he speaks of confining "the right of suffrage for one Branch to holders of property," while leaving the other to the propertyless. This would *seem* fair, for "the rights to be defended would be unequal, being on one side those of property as well as persons, and on the other those of persons only." Nevertheless, the frank class division would create Roman-like tensions. Thirdly, one could confine "the right of electing one Branch to freeholders" and admit all others in common with freeholders to elections for the other. The theory of this system is that non-freeholders would ultimately gain a majority and thus ultimate defensive power. "Experience alone can decide how far the practice in this case would correspond with the theory." Nor, it must be said, is it clear how in the eventuality foreseen, it would not simply become a special case of the second option. Madison says nothing further, but that is perhaps the reason he goes on to a fourth modification: namely, to grant "an equal and universal suffrage for each branch." In this case, however, we may protect the propertied by "an enlargement of the Election Districts for one Branch of the Legislature, and an extension of its period of service." Madison offers no objection to this back-door approximation of the remedy achieved by the Constitutional Convention, but he does propose a fifth modification. He offers it in case the fourth modification should "be deemed inadmissible, and universal suffrage and very short periods of elections within contracted spheres be required. . . ." In that case, the security for property holders must be "derived from the ordinary influence possessed by property, & the superior information incident to its holders; from the popular sense of justice enlightened and enlarged by a diffusive education; and from the difficulty of combining & effectuating unjust purposes throughout an extensive country. . . ." Meyers, "Property and Suffrage," pp. 506–508.

32. Meyers, "Property and Suffrage," p. 508.

33. See "Partnership of Power: The Virginia Convention of 1828–1830," in Meyers, *The Mind of the Founder,* p. 516.

34. Meyers, "Partnership of Power," p. 517.

35. Ibid., p. 519.

7. THE RULE OF LAW IN *THE FEDERALIST*

1. The quotations in this paragraph are from *Federalist* 54, pp. 337–338.

2. *Federalist* 62, p. 380; No. 43, p. 279; No. 71, p. 432; No. 57, p. 350; No. 26, p. 169; No. 14, p. 104.

3. James D. Andrews, ed., *The Works of James Wilson* (Chicago: Callaghan, 1896), vol. 1, p. 55.

4. According to a speaker at the Virginia ratifying convention, a man was arbitrarily deprived of his life without trial by the Virginia legislature during the 1780s. See Jonathan Elliot, ed., *The Debates in the Several State Conventions* (Philadelphia: J. P. Lippincott, 1836), vol. 3, p. 66.

5. Harry V. Jaffa has argued convincingly that the founders' conception of the rule of law was the same as that exhibited in Aristotle's aphorism that the law strives to be "reason without passion": "Equality, Liberty, Wisdom, Morality, and Consent in the Idea of Political Freedom," a paper prepared for presentation at the Center for the Study of Democratic Institutions, Santa Barbara, Calif., February 1986, mimeographed.

6. Jefferson, *Notes on the State of Virginia*, Query 13, quoted with approval in *Federalist* 48, p. 311.

7. Aristotle, *Politics*, IV; Polybius, *Histories*, VI, chapter 3–10. Cicero presents a similar argument in Book I of his *Republic*.

8. Jefferson, *Notes on Virginia*, Query 13, quoted in *Federalist* 48, pp. 310–311. Some particulars of these frequent state legislative violations and injustices are given in *Federalist* 48, pp. 311–312. For more detail, see Gordon Wood, *The Creation of the American Republic, 1776–1787* (New York: W. W. Norton, 1976), pp. 403–409.

9. Wood, *The Creation of the American Republic*, pp. 273–282, 306–343, shows how the theoretical understanding of constitutionalism changed (*The Federalist* and I would say improved) from 1776 to 1787.

10. Samuel E. Morison, ed., *Sources and Documents Illustrating the American Revolution*, 2nd ed. (London: Oxford University Press, 1929), p. 176.

11. John Locke, *Second Treatise*, in Peter Laslett, ed., *Two Treatises of Government* (New York: New American Library, 1965), chapter 11; William Blackstone, *Commentaries on the Laws of England* (Chicago: University of Chicago Press, 1979; orig. ed. 1765), vol. 1, p. 156 (book I, chapter 2). Locke is closer to the American position than Blackstone is, for Locke insists that only the people may change the legislative power once they have established it, and the legislative may not delegate any lawmaking power to other bodies or officials. To that extent Locke *is* a constitutionalist, although his constitutionalism is limited to the structure of the lawmaking body. Blackstone, on the other hand, goes so far as to say that the legislature "can change and create afresh even the constitution of the kingdom and of parliament themselves."

12. Harold A. Hyman, *A More Perfect Union* (New York: Knopf, 1973), p. 105.

13. Republican government may not be for everyone. In *Federalist* 39 Publius consults not only "the fundamental principles of the Revolution" but also "the genius of the American people," that is, the fact that the American character was well suited for, and insisted upon, free government due to its long habituation in local self-government under the colonial conditions preceding independence. Publius would probably agree with Solzhenitsyn that the attempt to institute a republican government in Russia in 1917 was a mistake, for it led almost by necessity to a new despotism far worse than the old regime of the tsars.

14. *Federalist* 48, p. 310. Other reasons are also given there.

15. This approaches a paraphrase of the original recommendation of the Congress on May 10, 1776 to the states to establish governments "for the preservation of

internal peace, virtue, and good order, as well as for the defense of their lives, liberties, and properties. . . ." John Adams was a co-author of this resolution. Morison, *Sources and Documents*, p. 148.

16. Paul Eidelberg has made a similar case, but he qualifies it more than he should by suggesting that the U.S. Constitution synthesizes the classical aspiration to excellence and the modern elevation of the passions. See *A Discourse on States- manship* (Urbana: University of Illinois Press, 1974), pp. 241–276. David F. Epstein, in *The Political Theory of the Federalist* (Chicago: University of Chi- cago Press, 1984), argues that *The Federalist* seeks excellence in the rulers, but believes (wrongly, I think) that this excellence is essentially in the service of private rights, peace, and prosperity, that is, of ends that do not include virtue or excellence for its own sake.

17. Consider John Adams's apparently contradictory criteria for representatives: (1) they are to be a mirror of the people; (2) they are to be those who are best and most virtuous, from his *Thoughts on Government* (1776), in Charles S. Hyneman and Donald S. Lutz, eds., *American Political Writing during the Founding Era* (Indianapolis: Liberty Press, 1983), vol. 1, p. 402. Section 7 of the 1776 Pennsylvania Constitution mandated (!) the election of the "persons most noted for wisdom and virtue" to the state House of Representatives: Mor- ison, *Sources and Documents*, p. 165.

18. Gordon Wood cites numerous examples of this change of sentiment: *The Cre- ation of the American Republic*, chapter 10 (pp. 393–429).

19. William W. Crosskey, *Politics and the Constitution in the History of the United States*, vol. 3 (Chicago: University of Chicago Press, 1980).

20. *A Defence of the Constitutions*, Preface, in Charles Francis Adams, ed., *Works of John Adams*, ed. (Boston: Little, Brown, 1865), vol. 4, p. 290. It should be understood that Adams wanted the aristocrats in the Senate so they could be isolated or "ostracized" there, out of the way of doing the society any harm.

21. See the Convention debates for June 25 and 26 in Adrienne Koch, ed., *Notes of Debates in the Federal Convention of 1787 Reported by James Madison* (New York: W. W. Norton, 1969), pp. 181–201.

22. James Wilson made the representative character of every branch of the federal government more of an explicit theme than did *The Federalist*: "The extension of the theory and practice of representation through all the different departments of the state is another very important acquisition made, by the Americans, in the science of jurisprudence and government." From his lectures on law, in *Works of James Wilson*, vol. 1, p. 387.

23. *Federalist* 52–61 deal with the House; Nos. 62–66 with the Senate; and Nos. 67– 77 with the President.

24. The most influential statement of the liberal view is Richard Hofstadter, "The Founding Fathers: An Age of Realism," in *The American Political Tradition* (New York: Vintage, 1954; orig. ed. 1948). More recent is Benjamin R. Barber, "The Compromised Republic: Public Purposelessness in America," in Robert H. Horwitz, ed., *The Moral Foundations of the American Republic*, 2nd ed. (Char- lottesville: University Press of Virginia, 1979). The Hofstadter essay is also re- printed in this volume. George Will's strictures on the founding may be found in his *Statecraft as Soulcraft: What Government Does* (New York: Simon and Schuster, 1983), chapters 1–2.

25. Martin Diamond maintained this thesis in his influential "Democracy and *The Federalist:* A Reconsideration of the Framers' Intent," *American Political Science Review* 53 (March 1959): 52–68. Reprinted as *"The Federalist,"* in Morton J. Frisch and Richard G. Stevens, ed., *American Political Thought,* 2nd ed. (Itasca, Ill.: F. E. Peacock, 1983).

26. Wood, *The Creation of the American Republic,* pp. 428–429.

27. Quoted from Alexis de Tocqueville's chapter on "What Sort of Despotism Democratic Nations Have to Fear," in *Democracy in America,* trans. George Lawrence (Garden City, N.Y.: Anchor, 1969), pp. 691–692.

28. Morison, *Sources and Documents,* p. 151.

29. Massachusetts Constitution, Part I, Article III; Chapter VI, Section II. In *Works of John Adams,* vol. 4, pp. 221, 259.

30. In their regard for government's role in the formation of the characters of the citizens, the founders departed once again from Locke, who had recommended that education and moral training be conducted entirely by private families.

31. James D. Richardson, ed., *Messages and Papers of the Presidents* (New York: Bureau of National Literature, 1897), vol. 1, pp. 45, 47.

8. REPUBLICANIZING THE EXECUTIVE

1. *Federalist* 70. See also Hamilton's comments in the Constitutional Convention: Max Farrand, ed., *The Records of the Federal Convention of 1787,* 4 vols., rev. ed. (New Haven: Yale University Press, 1966), vol. 1, pp. 289, 310; and Harold G. Syrett, ed., *The Papers of Alexander Hamilton,* 26 vols. (New York: Columbia University Press, 1962), vol. 4, p. 186.

2. The phrase "literary theory" is from Walter Bagehot, quoted by Woodrow Wilson in *Congressional Government* (New York: World Publishing, 1956), p. 30, and used in Richard Neustadt, *Presidential Power* (New York: John Wiley, 1962), p. 43. For the author's defense of literary theory on the executive, see Harvey C. Mansfield, Jr., "The Ambivalence of Executive Power," in Joseph M. Bessette and Jeffrey Tulis, *The Presidency in the Constitutional Order* (Baton Rouge: Louisiana State University Press, 1981), pp. 314–333.

3. Charles C. Thach, Jr., *The Creation of the Presidency, 1775–1789,* rev. ed. (Baltimore: The Johns Hopkins Press, 1969), chapters 1–3; Gordon S. Wood, *The Creation of the American Republic, 1776–1787* (Chapel Hill: University of North Carolina Press, 1969), pp. 134–143, 432–436.

4. Gerald Stourzh, *Alexander Hamilton and the Idea of Republican Government* (Stanford: Stanford University Press, 1970), p. 96; W. B. Gwyn, *The Meaning of the Separation of Powers* (New Orleans: Tulane University Press, 1965), p. 22.

5. Cf. Thach, *The Creation of the Presidency,* pp. 18, 27, 52–54, who ignores the effect of republican theory and American republicanism on that creation and thus, while stressing the uniquely American character of the process and result, underestimates it as an accomplishment.

6. By "Cato," in the *New York Journal.* See Herbert J. Storing, ed., *The Complete Anti-Federalist,* 7 vols. (Chicago: University of Chicago Press, 1981), V, 2.6.37.

7. Farrand, *Federal Convention*, vol. 1, p. 66; this was concurred in by Benjamin Franklin, vol. 1, p. 83, and by William Paterson, vol. 1, p. 287, but denied by James Wilson, vol. 1, p. 66.

8. Storing, *Complete Anti-Federalist*, 2.4.86.

9. Storing, *Complete Anti-Federalist*, Cato, IV, 2.6.31; Tamony, 5.11.6; see also Impartial Examiner, IV, 5.14.40; Cornelius, 4.10.21; Countryman, IV, 6.6.28. Wood, *The Creation of the American Republic*, pp. 521, 561.

10. Storing, *Complete Anti-Federalist*, II, 5.10.4.

11. Ibid., XIV, 2.8.178; see Storing's discussion at note 106 and in his preface to Thach, *The Creation of the Presidency*, pp. ix–x. Storing points to the similar language of Blackstone regarding the need for royal dignity, *Commentaries on the Laws of England*, 4 vols., 5th ed. (Oxford: Clarendon Press, 1773), vol. 1, p. 241. But Blackstone, unlike The Federal Farmer, was not a republican.

12. Thomas Paine did both in *Rights of Man*, Part II. "I leave to courtiers to explain what is meant by calling monarchy the executive power," he said; yet a few pages later gave his approval to the presidency in the American Constitution. *Rights of Man* (Baltimore: Penguin Books, 1969; orig. ed. 1792), pp. 221, 226.

13. That is why not "much anxiety [is] displayed over the dangers arising from minority tyranny" in *The Federalist*, pace Robert A. Dahl, *A Preface to Democratic Theory* (Chicago: University of Chicago Press, 1956), p. 9. Publius is occupied with "means . . . by which the excellencies of republican government may be retained and its imperfections lessened or avoided," *Federalist* 9, pp. 72–73.

14. For the notion of constitutionalizing I am indebted to Herbert J. Storing, and also to Gerald Stourzh; see the latter's "Fundamental Laws and Individual Rights in the Eighteenth Century Constitution," Bicentennial Essay No. 5 (Claremont, Calif.: The Claremont Institute for the Study of Statesmanship and Political Philosophy, 1984), pp. 12–14. While Stourzh uses the term to mean putting certain questions beyond the reach of ordinary legislative majorities, I use it more broadly and positively as empowerment of a government not controlled by a republican or popular majority.

15. In *Federalist* 39, Publius asks whether the new Constitution is "strictly republican" and then defines republican as government "derived from the people," rather than directly by the people—thus leaving the impression that "strictly republican" is minimally so. But upon consideration Publius shows that strictly republican is *fully* republican; the Constitution goes as far as republicanism can go, farther than traditional republicanism in establishing government by choice. Cf. Hamilton's use of "strictly republican" in Farrand, *Federal Convention*, vol. 1, p. 300 and vol. 3, pp. 397–398, also in the defensive sense.

16. If executive power projects republican choice into the future, judicial review keeps it consistent with the past.

17. Locke, *Second Treatise*, in Peter Laslett, ed., *Two Treatises of Government*, (New York: New American Library, 1965) ¶132.

18. Ibid., ¶147, 159, 151.

19. Ibid., ¶8, 22, 23, 90–92, 135–137, 139.

20. Ibid., ¶210.

21. Ibid., ¶131, 210.

22. Compare the levity of Locke's treatment of reverence in a people's resistance to tyranny and his apparent belief that reverence for a good constitution can be taken for granted; Ibid., ¶220, 223–226, 230, 235.

23. Montesquieu, *De l'esprit des lois*, book XIX, chapter 27.

24. Blackstone leaves executive power within the Constitution since, as he says, emergency imprisonments by the executive are authorized by Parliament's suspending the habeas corpus act: ". . . the happiness of our constitution is that it is not left to the executive power to determine when the danger to the state is so great as to render this measure expedient." *Commentaries*, vol. 1, p. 136. But Blackstone, no republican, believed that executive power had to be sustained by reverence for royal dignity rather than by popular election. Ibid., vol. 1, pp. 336–337.

25. The "necessary and proper" clause makes this clear. See David Epstein, *The Political Theory of The Federalist* (Chicago: University of Chicago Press, 1984), pp. 43–44. In the first Helvidius letter (August 24, 1793), Madison remarks that Locke's "chapter on prerogative shows, how much the reason of the philosopher was clouded by the royalism of the Englishman." I take this for an excuse of Locke, not blame of him.

26. Briefer studies of *Federalist* 67–77 can be found in Lynton K. Caldwell, *The Administrative Theories of Hamilton and Jefferson* (Chicago: University of Chicago Press, 1944), pp. 24–30; and Leonard D. White, *The Federalists* (New York: Macmillan, 1948), pp. 90–96. But the most authoritative treatment, to which this study is much indebted, is in Epstein, *Political Theory*, pp. 171–185.

27. Farrand, *Federal Convention*, vol. 2, pp. 52–58. See William H. Riker, "The Heresthetics of Constitution-Making," *American Political Science Review* 78, no. 1 (March 1984): 6–8.

28. Thach, *The Creation of the Presidency*, chapters 4–6; Richard M. Pious, *The American Presidency* (New York: Basic Books, 1979), chapter 1. Hamilton as Publius does not mention Hamilton's own proposal in September 1787 for a restrictive property qualification in presidential elections; *Hamilton Papers*, vol. 4, p. 259.

29. Riker, "The Heresthetics of Constitution-Making," p. 13.

30. Stourzh, *Alexander Hamilton*, pp. 46, 51–52.

31. Epstein, *Political Theory*, pp. 35–36, 113–114, 171.

32. Blackstone seems to use "energy" to describe a source of power from "influence" distinct from the king's prerogative; *Commentaries*, vol. 1, p. 336. See Epstein, *Political Theory*, p. 204, note 3.

33. As Epstein says, "The republican genius of short terms and many men makes each man invisible. . . ." *Political Theory*, p. 183; Stourzh, *Alexander Hamilton*, p. 185; James Wilson, *Lectures on Law* (1790–1791), in R. G. McCloskey, ed., *The Works of James Wilson*, 2 vols. (Cambridge, Mass.: Harvard University Press, 1967), vol. 1, p. 295.

34. See also *Federalist* 74; Epstein, *Political Theory*, pp. 174–175.

35. On this ambiguity of interest, see James Madison's letter of October 5, 1786, in Robert A. Rutland, ed., *The Papers of James Madison* (Chicago: University of

Chicago Press, 1975), vol. 9, p. 141, and Stourzh, *Alexander Hamilton*, pp. 80–87, 90–94.

36. Cf. Hamilton's phrase, "men of the first pretensions," in his letter on the "defects of our present system" of September 1780; *Hamilton Papers*, vol. 2, p. 405.

37. Trevor Colbourn, ed., *Fame and the Founding Fathers: Essays by Douglass Adair* (New York: W. W. Norton, 1974), p. 257; Stourzh, *Alexander Hamilton*, pp. 180–185; Epstein, *Political Theory*, pp. 179–184.

38. Epstein, *Political Theory*, p. 175.

39. Ibid., pp. 140–141, 175–178.

40. Neustadt, *Presidential Power*, pp. 7, 9, 179, 183.

41. See Jack N. Rakove, "Solving a Constitutional Puzzle: The Treatymaking Clause as a Case Study," *Perspectives in American History* I (1984): 254–255.

42. Most notably in *Federalist* 10 and 51; see the excellent book, T. S. Engeman, E. J. Erler, and T. B. Hofeller, eds., *The Federalist Concordance* (Middletown, Conn.: Wesleyan University Press, 1980).

43. Nor must one mistake *Federalist* 10 and 51 (and a partial view of them) for the whole of *The Federalist*. See Epstein, *Political Theory*, passim and pp. 118–125.

44. On the importance of a "modelled" Constitution (*Federalist* 23), see Epstein, *Political Theory*, p. 45.

45. "The institution of delegated power implies that there is a portion of virtue and honor among mankind, which may be a reasonable foundation of confidence," *Federalist* 76, p. 458. See Martin S. Diamond, "The Federalist," in L. Strauss and J. Cropsey, eds., *History of Political Philosophy*, 2nd edition (Chicago: Rand McNally, 1972), pp. 645–646.

9. Bureaucratic Idealism and Executive Power: A Perspective on *The Federalist*'s View of Public Administration

1. See, e.g., Peter Woll, *American Bureaucracy*, 2nd ed. (New York: W. W. Norton, 1979).

2. See, e.g., Gabriel A. Almond and G. Bingham Powell, Jr., *Comparative Politics: A Developmental Approach* (Boston: Little, Brown, 1966), p. 155 ("bureaucracy as the core of modern government") and p. 158 ("Other governmental structures, such as political executives, legislatures and courts, must be viewed in relation to the functioning of bureaucracy").

3. For a penetrating elaboration of this strangely myopic perspective, see Samuel H. Huntington, *Political Order in Changing Societies* (New Haven: Yale University Press, 1968).

4. William Blackstone, *Commentaries on the Laws of England*, 4 vols., facsimile of the first edition, 1765–1769 (Chicago: University of Chicago Press, 1979), vol. 2, p. 496.

5. *Federalist* 72, p. 435.

6. Fritz Morstein Marx, *The Administrative State: An Introduction to Bureaucracy* (Chicago: University of Chicago Press, 1957), p. 17.

7. Weber's fullest discussion of the need to separate "values" from social science analysis appears in a paper on scientific method, originally delivered in 1913, which can be found in translation as "Value-judgments in Social Science," in W. G. Runciman, ed., *Max Weber: Selections in Translation* (London: Cambridge University Press, 1978). The most celebrated critique of this position is in Leo Strauss, *Natural Right and History* (Chicago: University of Chicago Press, 1953), pp. 36–78, which however focuses on other examples in Weber's sociological work and does not pursue the consequences of this perspective for Weber's view of bureaucracy.

8. Talcott Parsons, ed. and trans., *The Theory of Social and Economic Organization* (New York: Oxford University Press, 1947), p. 339. The distinctions are not quite the same because Weber uses "formal rationality" to mean the achievement of given, subsidiary objectives or the satisfaction of given, subsidiary standards, as contrasted with the attainment of ultimate goals or standards (which he calls "substantive rationality"). But ultimate goals or "values" cannot, in Weber's view, be rational or irrational and this is what makes them ultimate: they do not serve some further or higher objective.

9. Ibid., pp. 328–329, 341–345, 358–363.

10. Ibid., pp. 339–340, 337.

11. Ibid., p. 340.

12. Ibid., p. 338.

13. Ibid., p. 337.

14. See, e.g., Carl Friedrich, "Some Observations on Weber's Analysis of Bureaucracy," in Robert K. Merton, ed., *Reader in Bureaucracy* (New York: Free Press, 1952).

15. Weber's personal and political reservations about the spirit of bureaucracy in general—and the state bureaucracy in his own Wilhelmine Germany, in particular—are reviewed in J. G. Merquior, *Rousseau and Weber: Two Studies in the Theory of Legitimacy* (London: Routledge & Kegan Paul, 1980), pp. 117–121.

16. Parsons, *The Theory of Social and Economic Organization*, p. 340.

17. By Weber's own terminology, objections regarding undesired side effects would not be "value" judgments unless they concerned ultimate goals. But once an ultimate goal or "value" is itself the goal, Weber's view implies that no objection can be admitted without compromising the ultimate status of "values." In other words, there is no rational basis in politics for preferring the statesman to the ideologue, the reasonable or prudent man to the fanatic. And Weber's entire discussion of bureaucratic "rationality" and "efficiency" abstracts from the question of what sort of men or what sort of government directs the bureaucracy at the top—as if this made no difference to the merits of bureaucratic organization.

18. Note that Weber's most extended discussion of bureaucracy, in *The Theory of Social and Political Organization*, occurs in the context of a larger exposition of "types of legitimate authority," where "bureaucracy" is presented as the characteristic manifestation of "rational-legal authority." Where unquestioned tradition or devotion to a mystically annointed leader are the only alternatives to the bureaucratic mode of authority, the claims of bureaucracy to "rationality" are bound to seem more than merely formal.

19. Strauss, *Natural Right and History*, p. 60, note 22.

20. The most notorious illustration is Kant's claim that it is wrong to lie even when necessary to save another's life ("On a Supposed Right to Lie from a Benevolent Motive").

21. Hans Rosenberg, *Bureaucracy, Aristocracy and Autocracy: The Prussian Experience 1660–1815* (Boston: Beacon Press, 1966), p. 189.

22. Kant, *The Metaphysical Elements of Justice*, trans. John Ladd (Indianapolis: Bobbs-Merrill, 1965), p. 100.

23. Ibid., p. 106.

24. Ibid., p. 83.

25. Hegel thus denounced the "vulgar presupposition" that representative assemblies were more to be trusted than the permanent civil service. This notion, "characteristic of the rabble," ignores the fact that representative assemblies "start from isolated individuals, from a private point of view, from particular interests" which they are inclined to pursue "at the expense of the general interests," while the civil servants "explicitly take up the standpoint of the state from the start and devote themselves to the general end." *Philosophy of Right*, trans. T. M. Knox (Oxford: Clarendon Press, 1952), p. 196.

26. Hannah Arendt, *Eichmann in Jerusalem* (New York: Viking Press, 1965), pp. 135–137.

27. See Kant, *The Metaphysical Elements of Justice*, p. 96.

28. Thus Hegel distinguishes "the monarchy" from "the executive" in order to separate the personal willfulness of the sovereign—as in exercising his power to pardon—from the duties of civil servants. He then does not hesitate to include the judiciary in "the executive"—an "executive" now sufficiently purified of personal willfulness to be a fit home for judges. See *Philosophy of Right*, p. 188. On the importance of "public law" training and thinking for German notions of administration in the century after Hegel, see Kenneth Dyson, *The State Tradition in Western Europe* (New York: Oxford University Press, 1980).

29. The phrase "parchment barriers" has become famous. But it is often forgotten that it first appears (in *Federalist* 48, p. 308) not in connection with guarantees of particular civil rights but in the context of a warning about the difficulty of separating the different powers of government from each other. Each power can only "be effectually restrained from passing the limits assigned to it [a]fter discriminating . . . in theory the several classes of power, as they may in their nature be legislative, executive or judiciary . . . ." The independence of the judiciary, therefore, can only be effectually defended against legislative encroachments when powers "in their nature" judicial have been distinguished in theory from the overall power of government. And these powers must be rather limited. Indeed in No. 51, where this discussion of the need to maintain each power in its place reaches its immediate culmination, *The Federalist* still concedes that in "republican governments, the legislative authority necessarily predominates" (p. 322). And the ultimate culmination of the argument, it might be said, comes in No. 84 where the omission of a bill of rights from the Constitution is defended on the grounds that the proper arrangement of powers within the Constitution is "in every rational sense and to every useful purpose a bill of rights" (p. 515). Where efficacy or usefulness is the standard of "every rational sense," "parchment barriers" and judicial devotion to parchment provisions can have only a limited role to play.

30. *Federalist* 10, p. 79.

31. No. 51, pp. 323–324.

32. John Locke, "An Essay Concerning the True Original Extent and End of Civil Government" *(Second Treatise)*, in Peter Laslett, ed., *Two Treatises of Government* (New York: New American Library, 1965), ¶137, p. 405; ¶136, p. 404; ¶131, p. 398; ¶124, p. 396.

33. Ibid., ¶143, p. 410.

34. This position was urged by Rudolf von Ihering in *Der Kampf um's Recht* (trans., John J. Lalor, *The Struggle for Law* [Chicago: Callaghan, 1879]). Ihering was a proponent of "interest jurisprudence," often regarded as the forerunner of "sociological jurisprudence" in America in the early decades of this century. Ihering held to the seemingly hard-headed, "realist" view that law could be understood as a reflection of the power of dominant groups in society, that is, that the law's assignment of rights and duties should be seen as part of a larger scheme for ordering society from the top down. But then with characteristic German earnestness, he held that every citizen, in his capacity as a bearer of rights, had an obligation to enforce his own rights in every case to see that this scheme was upheld.

35. Locke, *Second Treatise*, ¶11, p. 314.

36. Ibid., ¶159, p. 421.

37. E.g., Ibid., ¶136, p.404; ¶131, p. 399. The term "judge" is used in the singular in describing situations where there is no "common judge" or "no judge on earth"—where the singular reinforces the allusion to the One who renders ultimate judgment from above the earth; and the earthly counterpart here below does not seem to be the members of the judiciary but the legislative or supreme lawmaking power. See ¶89, p. 369; ¶181, p. 436; ¶240–241, p. 476.

38. Ibid., ¶160, p. 422.

39. Ibid., ¶156, p. 414.

40. Ibid., ¶202, p. 448.

41. Ibid., ¶163, p. 423.

42. Ibid., ¶153, p. 415.

43. Ibid., ¶168, p. 427.

44. *Federalist* 10, p. 78.

45. No. 70, p. 423.

46. No. 74, pp. 447, 449.

47. No. 72, p. 436.

48. No. 27, p. 174.

49. No. 72, p. 435.

50. No. 73, p. 445.

51. No. 73, p. 444.

52. No. 27, p. 176.

53. Two recent accounts, devoting close attention to party doctrine, are Richard Buel, *Securing the Revolution, Ideology in American Politics, 1789–1815* (Ithaca: Cornell University Press, 1972) and Lance Banning, *The Jeffersonian Persuasion* (Ithaca: Cornell University Press, 1978), but neither is entirely convincing in its explanation of Madison's apparent change of heart.

54. Leonard White, *The Jeffersonians: A Study in Administrative History, 1801–1829* (New York: Macmillan, 1956), pp. 348–357, 387–390. White notes that while Jefferson and his immediate successors preferred to appoint "gentlemen" of good social standing, they were under tremendous pressure from congressmen and party leaders to extend the circle of appointees more broadly.

55. See Wilfred Binkley, *President and Congress*, 3rd rev. ed. (New York: Vintage Books, 1962), pp. 180–204, describing popular reaction against the Senate "oligarchy" in the Grant administration and the authority this gave to Presidents Hayes, Arthur, and Cleveland in resisting senatorial patronage and clientalist service demands.

56. The founders' concern for executive independence as a safeguard of administrative order and integrity is emphasized in Charles Thach, *The Creation of the Presidency, 1775–1789*, Johns Hopkins University Studies in Historical and Political Science, vol. XL (Baltimore: Johns Hopkins University Press, 1922), esp. pp. 554–579.

57. The dominant concern of civil service reform advocates in the decades after the Civil War was not corruption but waste and expense in administration, as the patronage system provided continual incentives to expand the number of federal offices and fill them with untrained people. Even in later years, it was not so much the corruption of administration that troubled the reformers as the corruption of politics—as politicians, so it was charged, became preoccupied with thousands of low-level patronage appointments, nearly to the exclusion of basic policy concerns. See Leonard White, *The Republican Era: 1869–1901, A Study in Administrative History* (New York: Macmillan, 1958), pp. 295–301.

58. J. W. Macy, Bruce Adams, and J. Jackson Walters, eds., *America's Unelected Government* (Cambridge, Mass.: Bollinger, 1983) reports 4,000 direct presidential appointees in the federal administration, but this figure includes diplomatic and advisory posts. Hugh Heclo, *A Government of Strangers* (Washington, D.C.: Brookings Institution, 1977), p. 38, estimates 3,800 "political" appointees in the regular federal bureaucracy, though not all these appointments are made directly in the name of the president. For a suggestive survey of the differences in civil service career paths in the United States compared with Western Europe, see Edward C. Page, *Political Authority and Bureaucratic Power* (Knoxville: University of Tennessee Press, 1985), pp. 15–30.

59. Frank Goodnow, for example, often credited as the "father of public administration" as an academic discipline in the United States, was one of the earliest exponents of the need for a strict separation between "politics" and "administration." Goodnow studied administrative law in Germany in his youth and his turn-of-the-century text on comparative administrative law is particularly striking for its strange pairing of administrative patterns in Imperial Germany and the United States, which it sets in contrast to "parliamentary" systems like Britain and France. On the general influence and appeal of German patterns in American thinking about administration before the First World War, see Barry Karl, "Executive Reorganization and Presidential Power," in Philip Kurland, ed., *The Supreme Court Review: 1977* (Chicago: University of Chicago Press, 1978), pp. 1–37.

60. For a dismayed account of municipal corruption by an otherwise rather admiring foreign observer of the period, see James Bryce, *The American Commonwealth* (New York: Century, 1889), vol. 2, p. 111.

61. Robert Cushman, *The Independent Regulatory Commissions* (New York: Oxford University Press, 1941), p. 65.

62. *Humphrey's Executor* v. *U.S.*, 295 U.S. 602 (1935) at 628, 624.

63. *Schechter Poultry Corp.* v. *U.S.*, 295 U.S. 495 (1935).

64. See, e.g., James M. Landis, *The Administrative Process* (New Haven: Yale University Press, 1938), esp. pp. 23–26.

65. Marver P. Bernstein, *Regulating Business by Independent Commission* (Princeton: Princeton University Press, 1955), chapter 3.

66. The most important early cases were *Office of Communication of United Church of Christ* v. *FCC*, 359F.2d 994 (1966), demanding that the Federal Communications Commission withdraw a TV broadcasting license from a station charged by the appellant with poor service to the public, and *Scenic Hudson Preservation Conference* v. *FPC*, 354F.2d 608 (1966), demanding that the Federal Power Commission deny a license for constructing a power plant that appellants charged would disrupt the scenic splendor of the surrounding area.

67. See, e.g., §304 of the 1970 Clean Air Act Amendments, now codified at 42 U.S.C. §7604.

68. See *U.S.* v. *Nixon*, 418 U.S. 683 (1974) at 693; *Linda R.S.* v. *Richard D.*, 410 U.S. 614 (1973) at 619; and most recently, *Nathan* v. *Smith*, 737F.2d 1069 (1984) at 1079.

69. Cass Sunstein, "Deregulation and the Hard Look Doctrine," *Supreme Court Review* 177 (1983), at p. 178.

70. No. 10, p. 79.

71. No. 10, p. 79.

10. Constitutionalism and Judging in *The Federalist*

1. David Epstein, *The Political Theory of the Federalist* (Chicago: University of Chicago Press, 1984), p. 186.

2. See Albert Furtwangler, *The Authority of Publius: A Reading of the Federalist Papers* (Ithaca: Cornell University Press, 1984), p. 58.

3. Since the Pendleton Act a century ago, judges have been joined more or less by civil servants, but the latter can still be removed by procedures rather less formidable than impeachment, and besides, they are presumed to take their orders from political appointees.

4. This distinction was somewhat less pronounced at the time the Constitution was proposed than it is today, now that senators are elected directly by the people and the Electoral College has become little more than a mechanical device for tallying presidential votes by state.

5. The number and kind of the executive departments under the President were also left to legislative determination, but the choices involved in structuring the subordinate executives are less fundamental than those at issue in constituting lower courts. The question with regard to the former is which departments to establish, while regarding inferior federal courts the question is not only which but whether.

6. *Federalist* 48, p. 308, and *Federalist* 23, p. 153.

7. *Federalist* 23, p. 154. Cf. *Federalist* 39, where Madison admits, in the context of distinguishing national and federal features of the plan, that in its operation the government will be entirely national (p. 245).

8. *The Spirit of the Laws,* book XI, chapter 6; cf. book XIX, chapter 27, where English parties are shown to ally with the two political branches and no mention is made of the courts.

9. Blackstone, *Commentaries on the Laws of England* (Chicago: University of Chicago Press, 1979), vol. 3, chapter 3, pp. 23–24.

10. E.g., No. 77, p. 464.

11. W. B. Gwyn, *The Meaning of the Separation of Powers* (New Orleans: Tulane University Press, 1965), p. 35. See also M. J. C. Vile, *Constitutionalism and the Separation of Powers* (Oxford: Oxford University Press, 1967), chapter 2, and Francis Wormuth, *The Origins of Modern Constitutionalism* (New York: Harper and Brothers, 1949), chapter 20.

12. This is also noted by Epstein, *Political Theory*, p. 186. In the Convention, Madison, of course, had proposed a council of revision, which would join the President and "a convenient number of the National Judiciary" in exercising the veto over legislation. The debate that led to rejection of such a council provides some of the best evidence that the framers intended, or at least expected, judicial review. See Max Farrand, ed., *The Records of the Federal Convention of 1787* (New Haven: Yale University Press, 1911), vol. 1, pp. 21, 97–98.

13. On the combination of law and equity, as in Scotland but in contrast to England, see Gary McDowell, *Equity and the Constitution* (Chicago: University of Chicago Press, 1982), chapter 1.

14. See generally, William Nelson, *The Americanization of the Common Law* (Cambridge, Mass.: Harvard University Press, 1975).

15. See Nathan Glazer, "Towards an Imperial Judiciary," in Nathan Glazer and Irving Kristol, eds., *The American Commonwealth, 1976* (New York: Basic Books, 1976), p. 104, quoting Bryce.

16. Oliver Wendell Holmes, Jr., *The Common Law* (Boston: Little, Brown, 1881); see also his *Collected Legal Papers* (New York: Harcourt, Brace, and Howe, 1920).

17. See Edward H. Levi, *An Introduction to Legal Reasoning* (Chicago: University of Chicago Press, 1949). For a use of the term common law in a sense as untechnical as that here employed, see Richard Posner, *The Federal Courts: Crisis and Reform* (Cambridge, Mass.: Harvard University Press, 1985), especially chapter 1.

18. See Chapters 7 and 8 of this volume.

19. Epstein, *Political Theory*, p. 186.

20. In England, the common law began as unwritten law, and statutes were interpreted to be either declaratory of it or remedial to it, though it became settled by about the time of Blackstone (and hence Publius) that in case of a conflict between statutory law and common law, the statute was to prevail, though this rule is itself a rule of common law. On the subsequent development of a rigid doctrine of precedent in English law, in conjunction with the triumph of the doctrine of parliamentary sovereignty, see Rupert Cross, *Precedent in English*

Law (Oxford: Clarendon Press, 1961). In the United States, where the origins of government were within men's memories and usually inscribed in written documents, the legal status of the common law itself could depend on statutory provision, but since courts continued to do their work of construing laws and applying them in particular cases, a sort of common law would develop.

21. 8 *Reports* 118. Cf. Raoul Berger, "*Doctor Bonham's Case:* Statutory Construction or Constitutional Theory," *University of Pennsylvania Law Review* 117, no. 4 (1969): 521–545, and Charles M. Grey, "Bonham's Case Reviewed," *Proceedings of the American Philosophical Society* 116, no. 1 (1972): 35–58, two recent accounts that have reopened the argument once thought laid to rest by T. F. T. Plucknett, "Bonham's Case and Judicial Review," *Harvard Law Review*, vol. 40 (1926): 30–70, and Samuel Thorne, "Dr. Bonham's Case," *The Law Quarterly Review*, no. 216 (1938): 543–552.

22. Cf. *Federalist* 33, p. 205, where Hamilton cites the Supremacy Clause in a somewhat oblique reference to judicial review, an argument he does not repeat in Number 78.

23. Alexander Bickel notes the same conflict in the opinions of John Marshall: *Marbury* v. *Madison* depends upon the analogy of constitutional law to ordinary law, but in a famous passage in *McCulloch* v. *Maryland* Marshall draws a line between a constitution and a legal code. See *The Least Dangerous Branch: The Supreme Court at the Bar of Politics* (Indianapolis: Bobbs-Merrill, 1962).

24. For Publius's assertions of the wholly popular or republican character of the government proposed by the Constitution, see *Federalist* 14, p. 100, and No. 39, pp. 240–242; cf. No. 51, p. 321.

25. A complete text of Brutus's Letters can be found in Herbert Storing, ed., *The Anti-Federalist* (abridged by Murray Dry) (Chicago: University of Chicago Press, 1985), pp. 103–197. Ann Stuart Diamond argues that Hamilton's papers on the judiciary are a direct response to Brutus. "The Anti-Federalist 'Brutus'," *Political Science Reviewer* 6 (1976): 249–281. While this view somewhat underrates the systematic character of Hamilton's treatment of the judiciary, he surely does begin with a response to Brutus's central charge, and his comment at the beginning of *Federalist* 81 on the power of construing laws according to their spirit appears a direct reply to Brutus's Essay XI.

26. Storing and Dry, *The Anti-Federalist*, p. 185.

27. Ibid., p. 187.

28. Or perhaps what appears to be an underestimate is in fact a sly silence. Charles Kesler notes that of the four attributes of legislative and executive powers mentioned by Hamilton at the beginning of Number 78, only force and will are excluded, perhaps leaving to judges some power to dispense "honors" and to prescribe "rules by which the duties and rights of every citizen are to be regulated" (p. 465).

29. See Brutus, Essays XII and XV, for an account of how the judiciary can do its work quietly, in Storing and Dry, *The Anti-Federalist*, pp. 168–170, 186–187.

30. The most vivid illustration of this way of thinking that I know is the criticism of the Supreme Court's decision in *Dred Scott* by that great common lawyer, Abraham Lincoln. See Robert Johannsen, ed., *The Lincoln-Douglas Debates of 1858* (New York: Oxford University Press, 1965), passim.

31. Epstein, *Political Theory*, especially chapter 4.

32. Ibid., pp. 6–8.

33. For a characterization of constitutionalism in contrast to both legalism and realism, see Harvey C. Mansfield, Jr., "Constitutionalism and the Rule of Law," *Harvard Journal of Law and Public Policy* 8, no. 2 (1985): 323–326.

34. See Furtwangler, *The Authority of Publius*, chapters 2–3.

35. His contemporaries were not so reserved about the connection between a bill of rights and judicial review. Madison cites the possibility of judicial enforcement in introducing on the floor of the House the amendments that were to become the Bill of Rights, and Jefferson had spoken of this possibility in his letter to Madison of March 15, 1789.

36. Herbert Storing, "The Constitution and the Bill of Rights," in M. Judd Harmon, ed., *Essays on the Constitution of the United States* (Port Washington, N.Y.: Kennikat Press, 1978), pp. 32–48.

37. Consider Amendments IV–VIII, which have to do with judicial procedure and include among their provisions the privilege against self-incrimination, the guarantee of due process, and the right to a jury trial.

11. *The Federalist*'s Understanding of the Constitution as a Bill of Rights

1. *Federalist* 51, p. 322.

2. Gerald Gunther, *Constitutional Law*, 11th ed. (Mineola, N.Y.: The Foundation Press, 1985). See also the organization of Edward L. Barrett, Jr. and William Cohen, *Constitutional Law: Cases and Materials*, 7th ed. (Mineola, N.Y.: The Foundation Press, 1985).

3. C. Herman Pritchett, *The American Constitution*, 3rd ed. (New York: McGraw-Hill, 1977), chapter 18.

4. *Federalist* 10, p. 84.

5. Ibid., p. 81.

6. Ibid.

7. Ibid., p. 78.

8. No. 84, p. 515.

9. Ibid., p. 513.

10. Letter to Thomas Jefferson, October 17, 1788, in Gaillard Hunt, ed., *The Writings of James Madison*, 9 vols. (New York: Putnam, 1904), vol. 5, pp. 271–275.

11. Ibid. See also *Federalist* 63, p. 387: "Liberty may be endangered by the abuses of liberty, as well as by the abuses of power."

12. Speech in the House of Representatives, June 8, 1789, in *The Debates and Proceedings of the Congress of the United States* (Washington, D.C.: Gales and Seaton, 1834), vol. 1, p. 450.

13. *Citizens' Guide to Individual Rights Under the Constitution of the United States of America*, 96th Congress, 2d session, July 1980. See Walter Berns's critique of this position in Robert A. Goldwin and William Schambra, eds., "The Constitu-

tion as Bill of Rights," in *How Does the Constitution Secure Rights?* (Washington, D.C.: American Enterprise Institute, 1985).

14. *Federalist* 37, p. 226.

15. No. 10, p. 80.

16. No. 41, 257. See also Hamilton's comments in *Federalist* 25, p. 167, and David F. Epstein, *The Political Theory of The Federalist* (Chicago: University of Chicago Press, 1984), pp. 42, 49–50.

17. No. 48, p. 308.

18. No. 51, p. 322.

19. No. 9, p. 72.

20. No. 84, p. 515.

21. Richard E. Neustadt, *Presidential Power* (New York: John Wiley, 1960), p. 33.

22. *Federalist* 47, p. 301.

23. Ibid.

24. As James Wilson declared in the Constitutional Convention: "The separation of the departments does not require that they should have separate objects (i.e., functions) but that they should act separately though on the same objects." Max Farrand, ed., *The Records of the Federal Convention of 1787*, 4 vols., rev. ed. (New Haven: Yale University Press, 1937), vol. 2, p. 78.

25. Letter to Thomas Jefferson, October 17, 1788, in *Madison Writings*, vol. 5, pp. 271–275.

26. *Federalist* 48, p. 309. See also Farrand, *Federal Convention*, vol. 2, pp. 35, 74.

27. *Federalist* 48, p. 308.

28. Farrand, *Federal Convention*, vol. 1, pp. 21.

29. Ibid., vol. 2, p. 74. See also ibid., vol. 1, pp. 138–139.

30. Ibid., vol. 2, p. 77. See also Paul Peterson, "Separation of Powers and the American Constitution," in Paul Peterson, ed., *Readings in American Democracy* (Dubuque, Iowa: Kendall/Hunt, 1979).

31. *Federalist* 51, p. 320.

32. Ralph A. Rossum and Gary L. McDowell, eds., *The American Founding* (Port Washington, N.Y.: Kennikat Press, 1981), pp. 6–11.

33. *Federalist* 51, p. 320.

34. No. 63, p. 384.

35. Ibid.

36. Robert Green McCloskey, ed., *The Works of James Wilson* (Cambridge, Mass.: Harvard University Press, 1967), pp. 294, 296.

37. *Federalist* 37, p. 226.

38. *Federalist* 15, 16, and 22.

39. No. 1, p. 35.

40. James Madison, "Outline," in *Madison Writings*, vol. 9, p. 351.

41. *Federalist* 39, p. 246.

42. The words quoted in the text come from the Resolution of February 21, 1787, in which the Congress called for a Constitutional Convention. See Farrand,

Federal Convention, vol. 3, p. 13. See Madison's speech to the Constitutional Convention on June 19, in Farrand, *Federal Convention*, vol. 1, pp. 314–322. See also *Federalist* 40.

43. The words are those of William Richardson Davie, in Farrand, *Federal Convention*, vol. 1, p. 488.

44. *The Federalist* 39, p. 246. See Martin Diamond, "*The Federalist* on Federalism: Neither a National nor a Federal Constitution, But a Composition of Both," *Yale Law Journal* 86, no. 6 (May 1977): 1273–1285.

45. See *Federalist* 15, 16, and 22.

46. See John Bach McMaster and Frederick D. Stone, eds., *Pennsylvania and the Federal Constitution* (Philadelphia: The Historical Society of Pennsylvania, 1888), vol. 1, p. 302.

47. *Roth* v. *United States* 354 U.S. 476 (1957).

48. *Federalist* 20, pp. 136–137.

49. Farrand, *Federal Convention*, vol. 1, p. 135.

50. Ibid., p. 136.

51. *Federalist* 51, p. 324.

52. No. 10, p. 80.

53. Farrand, *Federal Convention*, vol. 2, pp. 587–588.

54. Letter to George Eve, January 2, 1789, in *Madison Writings*, vol. 5, p. 319.

55. Letter to Thomas Jefferson, October 17, 1788, in ibid., pp. 271–272. Emphasis in the original. The following analysis has benefited greatly from Herbert J. Storing's excellent "The Constitution and the Bill of Rights," in Ralph A. Rossum and Gary L. McDowell, eds., *The American Founding* (Port Washington, N.Y.: Kennikat Press, 1981), pp. 29–45.

56. Speech in the House of Representatives, June 8, 1789, in *Debates of the Congress of the United States*, vol. 1, p. 449.

57. Ibid., p. 450.

58. Ibid., p. 449.

59. Ibid. Emphasis added.

60. Ibid., p. 450.

61. Ibid.

62. Ibid., p. 449.

63. Letter to James Madison, December 20, 1787, in Julian Bond, ed., *The Papers of Thomas Jefferson*, 18 vols. (Princeton: Princeton University Press, 1955), vol. 12, p. 440.

64. Speech in the House of Representatives, June 8, 1789, in *Debates of the Congress of the United States*, vol. 1, p. 453.

65. Ibid., p. 454.

66. *Federalist* 84, p. 513.

67. Speech in the House of Representatives, June 8, 1789, in *Debates of the Congress of the United States*, vol. 1, p. 452.

68. Speech in the House of Representatives, August 17, 1789, in ibid., p. 784.

69. See Storing, "The Constitution and the Bill of Rights," pp. 29–45.

70. Speech in the House of Representatives, June 8, 1789, in *Debates of the Congress of the United States*, vol. 1, p. 459. Emphasis added.

71. Speech in the House of Representatives, August 13, 1789, in ibid., p. 736. See letter to Alexander White, August 24, 1789, in *Madison Writings*, vol. 5, p. 418: "It became an unavoidable sacrifice to a few who knew their concurrence to be necessary, to the dispatch if not the success of the business, to give up the form by which the amendts. when ratified would have fallen into the body of the Constitution, in favor of the project of adding them by way of appendix to it. It is already apparent I think that some ambiguities will be produced by this change, as the question will often arise and sometimes be not easily solved, how far the original text is or is not necessarily superceded, by the supplemental act."

72. Herbert J. Storing speculates on what the consequences might have been had Madison prevailed on this point: "It is interesting to consider what our constitutional law would be like today if there had been no Bill of Rights. Its focus would presumably be to a far greater extent than it is today on the powers of the government. We might expect a more searching examination by the Supreme Court of whether federal legislation that seems to conflict with cherished individual liberties is indeed 'necessary and proper' to the exercise of granted powers. We might expect a fuller articulation than we usually receive of whether, in Marshall's term, 'the end' aimed at by given legislation 'is legitimate.' Might this not foster a healthy concern with the problems of *governing*, a healthy sense of responsible self-government?" "The Constitution and the Bill of Rights," p. 37. Emphasis in the original.

73. Speech in the House of Representatives, August 13, 1789, in *Debates of the Congress of the United States*, vol. 1, pp. 734–735.

74. Ibid., p. 737.

75. See, for example, Michael J. Perry, *The Constitution, the Courts, and Human Rights* (New Haven: Yale University Press, 1982), and Arthur S. Miller, *Toward Increased Judicial Activism: The Political Role of the Supreme Court* (Westport, Conn.: Greenwood Press, 1982).

76. Alexis de Tocqueville, *Democracy in America*, 2 vols. (New York: Random House, 1945), vol. 1, p. 157.

77. *Federalist* 1, p. 33.

12. Early Uses of *The Federalist*

1. Adair's essays are gathered in Trevor Colbourn, ed., *Fame and the Founding Fathers: Essays by Douglass Adair* (New York: W. W. Norton, 1974). Mention should also be made of Alpheus Thomas Mason, "The Federalist—A Split Personality," *American Historical Review* 57 (1952): 625–643, which raised important questions about the theoretical coherence of the essays taken collectively.

2. See especially Paul Bourke, "The Pluralist Reading of James Madison's Tenth *Federalist*," *Perspectives in American History* 9 (1975): 271–295.

3. William L. Smith to Edward Rutledge, June 21, 1789, *South Carolina Historical Magazine* 69 (1968); *Annals of Congress*, 1st Congress, 1st Sess. (1789): 456. See

the discussion in Louis Fisher, *Constitutional Conflict between Congress and the President* (Princeton: Princeton University Press, 1985), pp. 60–66.

4. Speech of June 16, 1789, in Robert A. Rutland et al., eds., *The Papers of James Madison*, (Charlottesville: University Press of Virginia, 1979), vol. 12, p. 228.

5. The first Helvidius letter can be found in Gaillard Hunt, ed., *The Writings of James Madison*, 9 vols. (New York: Putnam, 1900–1910), vol. 6, pp. 138–151. In my view, Madison's position in 1793 was inconsistent neither with his speeches on the removal power in 1789 nor (more important) with the understanding of the nature of the power to conduct foreign relations that prevailed at the time of the framing of the Constitution. See the discussion in Jack N. Rakove, "Solving a Constitutional Puzzle: The Treatymaking Clause as a Case Study," *Perspectives in American History*, n.s., 1 (1984): 250–267.

6. On this point at least I agree with the observations in Albert Furtwangler, *The Authority of Publius: A Reading of the Federalist Papers* (Ithaca: Cornell University Press, 1984), pp. 32–39.

7. *The Federalist* (New York: McLean, 1788), vol. 1, pp. iii–iv.

8. Madison to Jefferson, August 10, 1788, *Madison Papers*, vol. 11, pp. 226–227; and Madison to Jefferson, February 8, 1825, *Madison Writings*, vol. 9, p. 219. For one example of Madison confirming a major opinion he had expressed in *Federalist* 39, see his letter to Jefferson of June 27, 1823, in *Madison Writings*, p. 142.

9. New York *Independent Journal*, March 22, 1788; early editions are listed in Paul L. Ford, *Bibliography and Reference List of the History and Literature Relating to the Adoption of the Constitution of the United States, 1787–1788* (Brooklyn: Historical Printing Club, 1888), pp. 14–23; the sales figure of 25,000 comes from William F. Swindler, "The Letters of Publius," *American Heritage* 12 (June 1961): 4.

10. L. H. Butterfield et al., eds., *Diary and Autobiography of John Adams* (Cambridge: Harvard University Press, 1961), vol. 3, p. 359. John Quincy Adams, *An Eulogy on the Life and Character of James Madison* (Boston: J. H. Eastburn, 1836), p. 31.

11. Thus the preface to the Hopkins edition of 1802, which was prepared with the reluctant cooperation of Hamilton, asserted that "The work is primarily the production of a man, whose talents and integrity render him the ornament and boast of this country; the name of *Hamilton* will be held in sacred respect, long after the malignant attempts which have been made to slander his fame shall have sunk, with their authors, into oblivion." *The Federalist* (New York: Hopkins, 1802), vol. 1, pp. iii–iv. Compare the respective claims in Samuel M. Schmucker, *The Life and Times of Alexander Hamilton* (Philadelphia: Keystone, 1856), pp. 257–258, and William Rives, *History of the Life and Times of James Madison* (Boston: Little, Brown, 1866), vol. 2, p. 302.

12. *Annals of Congress*, 1st Congress, 3d Sess. (1791), pp. 1891, 1926, 1950.

13. Ibid., 4th Congress, 1st Sess. (1796), pp. 451, 582, 619.

14. Ibid., 13th Congress, 1st Sess. (1818), pp. 1367.

15. Ibid., 18th Congress, 1st Sess. (1824), p. 1271.

16. Ibid., 13th Congress, 1st Sess. (1818), p. 1239.

17. Ibid., 16th Congress, 1st Sess. (1820), pp. 305, 308, 320, 322, 1025, 1151–1152, 1222, 1230, 1239, 1257–1258, 1275, 1357.

18. *Debates in Congress*, 22nd Congress, 1st Sess. (1832), pp. 199, 307, 441, 449–450, 581, 3538.

19. Ibid., 22nd Congress, 1st Sess. (1833), pp. 295–298, 499, 504, 569, 629, 653, 658, 660.

20. For a list of Supreme Court Cases in which *The Federalist* has been cited, see Charles W. Pierson, "The Federalist in the Supreme Court," *Yale Law Journal* 33 (1924): 728–735. Jacobus tenBroek, "Use by the United States Supreme Court of Extrinsic Aids in Constitutional Construction," *California Law Review* 27 (1939): 157–181, examines the basis on which the Court has justified its use of *The Federalist*, but not the specific applications to which the essays have been put.

21. 1 Virginia Cases 20 (1793).

22. 1 New Hampshire 199 (1818).

23. 25 Federal Cases of 614 (1808).

24. *Marbury* v. *Madison*, 1 Cranch 147–148, 151 (1803). On the relation between Marshall and Hamilton, see in general, Samuel Konefsky, *John Marshall and Alexander Hamilton* (New York: Macmillan, 1964).

25. Of all the justices who sat on the Court before the Civil War, only Joseph Story was inclined to make regular use of *The Federalist*. See his opinions in *Houston* v. *Moore*, 5 Wheaton 49 (1820); *Martin* v. *Mott*, 12 Wheaton 30 (1827); *Briscoe* v. *Bank of Commonwealth of Kentucky*, 11 Peters 332–333 (1837); and perhaps the most interesting and important, *Prigg* v. *Pennsylvania*, 16 Peters 616 (1842).

26. 6 Cranch 144 (1810).

27. 6 Wheaton 415, 418–420 (1821).

28. *Commonwealth* v. *Schaffer*, 4 Dallas (appendix) xxx (1797); *Respublica* v. *Cobbett*, 3 Dallas 472 (1798); and see *Worthington* v. *Masters*, 1 *Hall's Journal of Jurisprudence* 199, 204–205, 208–209 (1803).

29. *McCulloch* v. *Maryland*, 4 Wheaton 344–345, 348–351, 363, 369–370, 372 (1819).

30. 4 Wheaton 433–434.

31. This is the term that scholars have used to describe the conception of federal relations that gradually became dominant after 1820, and which modified the overt nationalism of many of the key decisions of the Marshall Court. "Dual federalism" reduced the presumption of national supremacy by regarding the states and the nation as coequal sovereignties; it placed greater emphasis both upon the limited extent of the enumerated powers the Constitution delegated to the nation and upon the rights of the states to act in all areas vital to their internal welfare. See especially Edward S. Corwin, "The Passing of Dual Federalism," in Robert G. McCloskey, ed., *Essays in Constitutional Law* (New York: Knopf, 1957), pp. 185–210.

32. *Houston* v. *Moore*, 5 Wheaton 8, 9, 25 (1820).

33. *Gibbons* v. *Ogden*, 9 Wheaton 37–38, 48, 61, 64, 86, 88, 109, 128–129, 141, 146, 163–164, 179 (1824). The opinion of the Court did not cite *The Federalist*.

34. *Brown* v. *Maryland*, 12 Wheaton 430, 432, 434–435, 456 (1827); *New York* v. *Miln*, 11 Peters 107, 123, 132–139, (1837); *License Cases*, 5 Howard 606–607 (1847); *Passenger Cases*, 7 Howard 288, 352, 369, 370, 374, 377, 396, 453, 471, 474, 479–480, 594, 511, 526, 533, 543, 545, 554 (1849); *Cooley* v. *Board of Wardens*, 12 Howard 318 (1851).

35. Harry N. Scheiber, "Federalism and the American Economic Order, 1789–1910," *Law and Society* 10 (1975–76): 68, 86–92

36. St. George Tucker, *Blackstone's Commentaries: with Notes of Reference to the Constitution and Laws, of the Federal Government of the United States, and the Commonwealth of Virginia* (Philadelphia: Birch and Small, 1803), vol. 1, pt. 1, pp. 141–143, 146–149, 286–287, 376.

37. The opinion is reprinted in "Spencer Roane—Reprints from the Richmond Enquirer," *John P. Branch Historical Papers of Randolph-Macon College* 1 (1904): 328–329.

38. Roane's and Brockenbrough's essays, along with two series of letters that John Marshall wrote in reply, are reprinted in Gerald Gunther, ed., *John Marshall's Defense of McCulloch v. Maryland* (Stanford: Stanford University Press, 1969). See pp. 59, 69, 74, 108, 113, 115, 122, 124, 129, 140, 144–147, for citations to Publius.

39. John Taylor, *New Views of the Constitution of the United States* (Washington: Way and Gideon, 1823), pp. 63–169.

40. *Journals of the Conventions of the People of South Carolina, Held in 1832, 1833, and 1852* (Columbia, S.C., 1860), 32; and see Robert J. Turnbull, *The Crisis: or, Essays on the Usurpations of the Federal Government* (Charleston, S.C.: 1827), 17, 30, 34, 59, 76, 83, 92, 95, 102, 107–108.

41. Abel Parker Upshur, *A Brief Enquiry into the True Nature and Character of Our Federal Government* (Petersburg, 1840), 6–7.

42. Calhoun to A. D. Wallace, December 17, 1840, *Annual Reports of the American Historical Association* 2 (1899): 468–469.

43. John C. Calhoun, *Disquisition on the Constitution and the Government of the United States*, in Richard K. Cralle, ed., *The Works of John C. Calhoun* (New York: D. Appleton, 1853), vol. 1, pp. 161, 343. Appropriately enough, Calhoun reinforced this remark by quoting *Federalist* 38: "Is it unreasonable to conjecture, that the errors which may be contained in the plan of the convention, are such as have resulted, rather from the defect of antecedent experience on this complicated and difficult subject, than from the want of accuracy or care in the investigation of it, and consequently, that they are such as will not be ascertained, until an actual trial will point them out?"

44. Story to Kent, June 24, 1831, Joseph Story Papers, Massachusetts Historical Society, quoted in R. Kent Newmyer, *Supreme Court Justice Joseph Story: Statesman of the Old Republic* (Chapel Hill: University of North Carolina Press, 1985), 421–422, n. 133.

45. "Story's Commentaries," *American Monthly Review* 4 (1833): 504.

46. George H. Reese, ed., *Proceedings of the Virginia State Convention of 1861* (Richmond, Va.: Virginia State Library, 1965), vol. 2, pp. 90–91; for other references, see vol. 1, pp. 478–480; vol. 3, p. 14.

13. A NEWER SCIENCE OF POLITICS: *THE FEDERALIST* AND AMERICAN POLITICAL SCIENCE IN THE PROGRESSIVE ERA

1. Pierson's list is found in *The Federalist*, ed. Henry Cabot Lodge (New York: G. P. Putnam's Sons, 1923); a search of the WestLaw computerized data base shows six citations to *The Federalist* in 1985, seven in 1984, four in 1983, nine in 1982, and eight in 1981.

2. Thomas McIntyre Cooley, *The General Principles of Constitutional Law* (Boston: Little, Brown, 1898).

3. On the "uses" to which *The Federalist* was put before the Civil War, see Chapter 12 of this volume.

4. *Federalist* 9, pp. 72–73.

5. Frank J. Goodnow, *Social Reform and the Constitution* (New York: Macmillan, 1911), p. 1.

6. John W. Burgess, *Reminiscences of an American Scholar* (Morningside Heights, N.Y.: Columbia University Press, 1934), p. 29.

7. Ibid., pp. 194–195; Anna Haddow, *Political Science in American Colleges and Universities, 1636–1900* (New York: D. Appleton-Century, 1939), pp. 178–182.

8. Albert Somit and Joseph Tanenhaus, *The Development of American Political Science* (Boston: Allyn and Bacon, 1967), pp. 42–48. 80–85.

9. Michael H. Frisch, "Urban Theorists, Urban Reform, and American Political Culture in the Progressive Period," *Political Science Quarterly* 97, no. 2 (Summer 1982): 299.

10. Woodrow Wilson, *The State: Elements of Historical and Practical Politics* (Boston: D. C. Heath, 1897; orig. ed. 1889).

11. Ibid., p. 668.

12. Ibid., p. 637.

13. Ibid., pp. 637–638.

14. Ibid., p. 637.

15. Ibid.

16. Westel Woodbury Willoughby, *An Examination of the Nature of the State: A Study in Political Philosophy* (Farmingdale, N.Y.: Dabor Social Science Publications, 1978), p. 141. This is a photographic reprint of the original edition published at New York by Macmillan, 1896.

17. John W. Burgess, *Political Science and Comparative Constitutional Law* (Boston: Ginn, 1890), vol. 1, p. 100.

18. Willoughby, *Examination of the Nature of the State*, p. 112.

19. Wilson, *The State*, p. 664.

20. Ibid., pp. 637–638.

21. Henry Jones Ford, *The Natural History of the State: An Introduction to Political Science* (Princeton: Princeton University Press, 1915).

22. *Federalist* 9, pp. 72–73.

23. No. 51, p. 322.

24. J. Allen Smith, *The Spirit of American Government: A Study of the Constitution: Its Origin, Influence and Relation to Democracy* (New York: Macmillan, 1907).

25. Charles A. Beard, *An Economic Interpretation of the Constitution of the United States* (New York: Macmillan, 1935; orig. ed. 1913).

26. Vernon L. Parrington, *The Beginnings of Critical Realism in America, 1860–1920*, vol. 3 of *Main Currents in American Thought* (New York: Harcourt, Brace & World, 1958), p. 406. This book, which Parrington left unfinished, was first published in 1930.

27. Ibid., p. 411.

28. Woodrow Wilson, *Congressional Government: A Study in American Politics* (New York: Meridian Books, 1956; orig. ed. 1885), p. 27.

29. Ibid., p. 215.

30. Burgess, *Political Science and Comparative Constitutional Law*, vol. 1, pp. 151–152.

31. Ibid., p. 153.

32. Goodnow, *Social Reform and the Constitution*, p. 214.

33. Frank J. Goodnow, *Politics and Administration: A Study in Government* (New York: Russell & Russell, 1967; orig. ed. 1900), p. 13.

34. Ray Stannard Baker and William E. Dodd, eds., *The Public Papers of Woodrow Wilson*, 6 vols. (New York: Harper, 1925–27) vol. 1, pp. 396–415. "Democracy and Efficiency" was originally published in *Atlantic Monthly* 87 (March 1901).

35. Ibid., p. 408.

36. Woodrow Wilson, *Constitutional Government in the United States* (New York: Columbia University Press, 1911), p. 54.

37. Ibid.

38. Ibid., pp. 54–55.

39. Ibid., p. 14.

40. Wilson, *Congressional Government*, p. 30.

41. Wilson, *Constitutional Government*, p. 56.

42. Wilson, *Congressional Government*, p. 30.

43. Ibid., p. 33.

44. Woodrow Wilson, *History of the American People*, 5 vols. (New York: Harper, 1902), vol. 3, p. 98.

45. Wilson, *Constitutional Government*, p. 56.

46. Ibid.

47. Henry Cabot Lodge, *Alexander Hamilton* (Boston: Houghton Mifflin, 1882), p. 66.

48. Beard, *Economic Interpretation*, p. 156.

49. Ibid., p. 156.

50. Smith, *Spirit of American Government*, p. 77.

51. Ibid., p. 78.

52. Beard, *Economic Interpretation*, p. 153.

53. Ibid., p. 154.

54. Ibid., p. 160.
55. Ibid., p. 161.
56. Ibid.
57. Ibid., p. 163.
58. Ibid., p. 179.
59. Ibid., pp. 177–178.
60. Ibid., p. 176.
61. Ibid., pp. 169–177.

14. WAS THE FOUNDING AN ACCIDENT?

1. *Works of John Adams* (Boston: Little, Brown, 1850–56), vol. 10, p. 145.
2. *Federalist* 37, p. 231. The Philadelphia Convention, he goes on to say, was one of the exceptions.
3. Donald S. Lutz, "From Covenant to Constitution in American Political Thought," *Publius* 10, no. 4 (1980): 101–133.
4. Gordon S. Wood, *The Creation of the American Republic, 1776–1787* (New York: W. W. Norton, 1972), p. 53.
5. Charles D. Hobson, "The Negative on State Laws: James Madison, the Constitution, and the Crisis of Republican Government," *William and Mary Quarterly*, third series, 36, no. 2 (April 1979): 222. See also Wood, *The Creation of the American Republic*, chapters 10–12.
6. Writing in 1782, Alexander Hamilton made the point in strong language:

   > We may preach until we are tired of the theme, the necessity of disinterested-ness in republics, without making a single proselyte. The virtuous declaimer will neither persuade himself nor any other person to be content with a double mess of porridge, instead of a reasonable stipend for his services. We might as soon reconcile ourselves to the Spartan community of goods and wives, to their iron coin, their long beards, or their black broth. There is a total dissimulation in the circumstances, as well as the manners, of society among us; and it is as ridiculous to seek for models in the simple ages of Greece and Rome, as it would be to go in quest of them among the Hottentots and Laplanders. (Quoted in Stanley N. Katz, "Thomas Jefferson and the Right to Property in Revolutionary America," Journal of Law and Economics, vol. 19, no. 3 [October 1976]: 485.)

7. Etymologically "accident" and "chance" have a common origin in the Latin "cadere," to fall. An accident is the "falling out" of an event; like a "chance" event, it proceeds from an unknown cause. See the *Oxford English Dictionary*.
8. Quoted in Alpheus Thomas Mason, *The States Rights Debate* (Englewood Cliffs, N.J.: Prentice-Hall, 1964), p. 30.
9. Ibid.
10. In the opinion of Forrest McDonald, twenty-four of the thirty-three delegates who were present when the Convention proceedings began were men "few would have listened to anytime, anywhere." Eventually, he says, there were twelve "possessed of an idea of a great nation, and possessed of the ruthlessness and the daring and the skill that make ideas into reality. . . ." *E Pluribus Unum* (Indianapolis: Liberty Press, 1979), p. 270. See also McDonald's more recent

book, *Novus Ordo Seclorum* (Lawrence: University Press of Kansas, 1985). On the delegates in general and Washington in particular, see Charles Warren, *The Making of the Constitution* (Cambridge, Mass.: Harvard University Press, 1928), chapter 2 and pp. 729–730. Jefferson was one of those who expected Washington to be the first President. He alone, Jefferson wrote in 1789, ". . . by the authority of his name and the confidence reposed in his perfect integrity is fully qualified to put the new government so under way as to secure it against the efforts of the opposition." Quoted in Warren, *The Making of the Constitution*, p. 177.

11. On Madison, see Max Farrand, *The Records of the Federal Convention of 1787*, 4 vols., rev. ed. (New Haven: Yale University Press, 1966), vol. 1, p. 471. On Washington, vol. 3, p. 51. See also John Roche, "The Founding Fathers: A Reform Caucus in Action," *The American Political Science Review* 55 (October 1961): 799–816.

12. Farrand, *Federal Convention*, vol. 1, p. 166.

13. Ibid., p. 197.

14. Ibid., pp. 451–452.

15. Ibid., p. 476.

16. Ibid., p. 567.

17. Herbert J. Storing, "The Federal Convention of 1787," in Ralph A. Rossum and Gary L. McDowell, eds., *The American Founding* (Port Washington, N.Y.: Kennikat Press, 1981), p. 26.

18. Farrand, *Federal Convention*, vol. 3, p. 56.

19. McDonald, *E Pluribus Unum*, p. 304.

20. Mason, *States Rights Debate*, pp. 50, 55.

21. Farrand, *Federal Convention*, vol. 2, p. 415.

22. Ibid., vol. 3, p. 77.

23. Ibid., vol. 2, pp. 645–646. Washington, however, wrote Lafayette that it was little short of a miracle that the delegates had united to form a system "so little liable to well founded objections." Ibid., vol. 3, p. 270.

24. Ibid., vol. 2, p. 646.

25. Quoted in Warren, *The Making of the Constitution*, p. 752.

26. For these figures and most of the facts that follow, I depend upon McDonald, *E Pluribus Unum*, and Robert Allen Rutland, *The Ordeal of the Constitution* (Norman: University of Oklahoma Press, 1965).

27. McDonald, *E Pluribus Unum*, p. 336.

28. Ibid., p. 338.

29. "Considering its immediate background," Leonard W. Levy has written, "our precious Bill of Rights was in the main the chance result of certain Federalists' having been reluctantly forced to capitalize for their own cause the propaganda that had been originated in vain by the Anti-Federalists for ulterior purposes. Thus the party that had first opposed a Bill of Rights inadvertently wound up with the responsibility for its framing and ratification, while the party that had at first professedly wanted it discovered too late that its framing and ratification were not only embarrassing but inexpedient." *Legacy of Suppression* (Cambridge, Mass.: Harvard University Press, 1960), p. 233.

30. Ibid., p. 346.

31. Rutland, *Ordeal of the Constitution*, p. 154.

32. McDonald, *E Pluribus Unum*, p. 357.

33. The first thirty-six papers were published in book form on March 22, 1788. The complete papers did not appear in book form until May 28 of that year. By this time eight states had ratified. Warren, *The Making of the Constitution*, p. 767. See also Marvin Meyers, *The Mind of the Founder* (Indianapolis: Bobbs-Merrill, 1973), p. 121.

34. Rutland, *Ordeal of the Constitution*, pp. 306–307.

35. The distinction is between ideal types: neither type existed in "pure" form. The Connecticut Compromise and the provision for continued importation of slaves resulted from the pressures of politicians, but I do not mean to imply that *all* nationalists were statesmen and *all* their opponents politicians.

36. Harry V. Jaffa, *How to Think About the American Revolution* (Durham, N.C.: Carolina Academic Press, 1978), p. 82.

Index

Index